Church Union: Rome and Byzantium
(1204-1453)

Professor Joseph Gill, S.J.

Joseph Gill

Church Union: Rome and Byzantium (1204–1453)

VARIORUM REPRINTS
London 1979

British Library CIP data

Gill, Joseph
  Church union. — (Collected studies series; CS91)
  1. Orthodox Eastern Church — Relations —
  Roman Catholic Church — History   2. Church
  history — Middle Ages, 600-1500
  I. Title   II. Series
  281.9   BX324.3

  ISBN 0-86078-035-X

Published in Great Britain by   Variorum Reprints
                                     21a Pembridge Mews London W11 3EQ

Printed in Great Britain by   Galliard (Printers) Ltd,
                                     Great Yarmouth, Norfolk

                                     VARIORUM REPRINT CS91

CONTENTS

This volume contains a total of 360 pages

PREFACE

The articles reproduced in this volume are with one exception concerned with relations between the Christian Churches of East and West. The Fourth Crusade had brought the two Churches into closer contact than ever before, closer but not necessarily more friendly. The crusaders took Constantinople and then proceeded to occupy as much as they could of the Empire. Consequently, the Greek Church lay largely within the area of western political jurisdiction. Innocent III, acting seemingly on the principle *Cuius regio, eius iurisdictio* (in this not an innovator, but in line with practice in Illyricum, Sicily and southern Italy) considered that the Greek Church was thereby united with the Latin. Had he contrived to bring it about? And, when it occurred, did he abuse the opportunity for Church union that the conquest offered? On these questions there are many variations of historical opinion, and I express mine in these articles.

From 1204 onwards till the fall of Constantinople in 1453 talk of Church union never ceased — *Eleven Emperors of Byzantium seek Union with the Church of Rome*. The chief occasions were the councils of Lyons and Florence, both of which were thought to have succeeded. But they were very different. The Council of Lyons met for only a few months and there was no public discussion. Greek delegates were present at it. Knowledge of their activities comes from Latin sources, but the reception accorded in Byzantium to the union is well documented in Greek sources, and official Greek documents show that the Holy Synod was involved both before and after, but with no enthusiasm and little conviction. Emperor Michael tried to enforce acceptance of the union and had recourse to subterfuge and violence. At his death only the few genuine unionists continued faithful to the union and they paid very dearly for their steadfastness. The Greek

Church, relieved of the union, remained for a long time split by the older controversy about Patriarch Arsenius, but it was soon revivified by the emergence of yet another controversy, Palamism. In Crete and Cyprus, however, Greek Christians were still under Latin government and they suffered the limitations that that situation imposed.

In Byzantium for most of the fourteenth century Emperors and their rivals were at each others' throats, while the Turks occupied first Asia Minor and then large areas of Thessaly, Macedonia and Thrace. Appeals to the West for help to stem the Turkish encroachment increased in a steady crescendo. John V Palaeologus wrote to popes, went in person to the King of Hungary, and even made his personal submission to the Church of Rome — in vain. His son Manuel made insincere overtures to Rome; his grandson agreed to go with ample representatives of the Oriental Church to Italy to discuss dogma with the Latins. They met in Ferrara and Florence, and on 6 July 1439 they freely accepted the decree of union.

Or did they? Within a few years of the end of the council the Greeks repudiated its conclusions, claiming that their signatures had been extorted by duresse. They agree that, in respect of membership, the council was the most ecumenical of all ecumenical councils, and that in fact all but two of the Greeks entitled to sign the decree actually signed. So, as they wanted to reject the union, they had to allege some persuasive reason. They found it in duresse. Were they justified? There still exist quite good sources for the history of the Council of Florence, the two most important being Greek. These, however, differ considerably from each other, one being anti-Latin and anti-union throughout, the other anti-Latin to begin with and then pro-union. The fundamental initial step for anyone writing seriously on the Council of Florence is to study these two sources in depth, check them as far as is possible by other sources, and decide which is the more trustworthy as history. Very few people have attempted this task. Most writers follow the general opinion and perpetuate what may be — and in my view is — bad and inaccurate history. The first articles I ever wrote about the Council of Florence (and in the course of years I have written quite a number about it) were concerned with the sources — *The Printed editions of the 'Practica' of the Council of*

Florence (not included in this collection), *The Sources of the 'Acta' of the Council of Florence* and *The 'Acta' and the Memoirs of Syropoulus as History* (both of which are included in this volume, even though they had appeared in my *Personalities of the Council of Florence*, which is now out of print). When after this meticulous examination of the sources I had satisfied myself of their respective values as trustworthy documents, I wrote *The Council of Florence*. Later I examined the question of duresse — what degree of duresse the Greeks suffered and whether, in fact, it did seriously influence their decision in Florence. In a similar way the two articles reproduced here about Bessarion are a questioning of oft-repeated general views, on the basis of the evidence gleaned from the sources. The last article recalls that the Holy See did not cease to support Christians in the east against the Turks, even when the Greek Empire was no more.

I must now, and most willingly, express my thanks and indebtedness to a number of journals and institutions for kindly granting permission to reproduce the articles in this volume. They include the Pontifical Oriental Institute (Rome), the Center for Byzantine Studies of the Faculty of Philosophy, University of Thessalonica, the University of Edinburgh, the University of Birmingham and the editors of *Studi Veneziani, Byzantion, Byzantinische Zeitschrift, Byzantinische Forschungen, Byzantino-slavica, The Journal of Theological Studies,* and the *Eastern Churches Review.*

JOSEPH GILL, S.J.

Campion Hall,
Oxford
August 1978

I

FRANKS, VENETIANS, AND POPE INNOCENT III
1201-1203

Though sources dealing with the preliminaries of the Fourth Crusade are not lacking, still it is not easy to construct a detailed picture of what took place, yet without that it is easy to make superficial and misleading judgements about the events and the individuals responsible for them. The main sources are the letters of Innocent III available in the *Innocentii III regesta sive epistolae*, which contain besides the letters he wrote also a few of those addressed to him. Founded on them is the short *Gesta Innocentii PP. III* written by a sympathetic contemporary. In addition, various participants in the crusade left accounts – Villehardouin, one of the leaders who " never to his knowledge put anything in it [i.e. his book] contrary to the truth " but who never questions the wisdom of the " higher command "; the anonymous *Devastatio Constantinopolitana*; and *La Conquête de Constantinople* written by Robert de Clari, these last two from the point of view of pilgrims of lesser rank. Bishop Conrad of Halberstadt took back to Germany many relics after the sack of Constantinople and his account is repeated in the *Gesta Episcoporum Halberstadensium* with every sign of being very trustworthy. The story of Abbot Martin, another actor in the events, has been preserved by one of his monks, Gunther, in an account that is rather less precise than the others but very useful for recording impressions. The capture of Constantinople and the setting up of a Latin kingdom there was so stupendous an event that it figures in many chronicles of very local interest. These may be useful as reflections of the general attitude of the West to that event and to the Christians of the East, but they are unreliable for exact information unless they preserve authentic documents. For example, the *Annales Colonienses Maximi* can most unhistorically recount that it was at the request of Prince Alexius that Innocent III absolved the pilgrims from excommunication at Zara, and also give the authentic text of a letter sent in 1203 by the Count of Saint-Pol to the Duke of Brabant.[1]

The first event in the preparation of the crusade was the arrival in Venice of the six French envoys to arrange transport to the East. They reached the city in the first week of Lent and before the end of Lent an agreement was made that the army should pay 85.000 marks for their passage to Outremer and be assembled in Venice by St John's day, i.e., 24 June 1202. " Immediately both parties concerned sent messengers to Pope Innocent in Rome, so that he might ratify this covenant. This he very willingly did ".[2]

Some time after, in the autumn of 1201,[3] Alexius, son of the blinded ex-Emperor Isaac of Constantinople, escaped from custody to Italy. According to Nicetas he had for some time been in communication with his sister in Germany, the wife of Philip of Swabia.[4] He arrived in Ancona, went to Swabia to procure help to restore his father to the throne, and later he visited the Pope to enlist his support for the same end. Innocent gave him (so he wrote later) " an answer We thought suitable " – clearly not a favourable one [5] – and Alexius returned to Swabia. He was in

---

1. The letters of Innocent III or *Regesta Innocentii III* divided into Books (or years) are in Migne, *Patres Latini* (= PL) vols. 214-216. They will be quoted as *Reg.* with the number of the Book and of the letter.

2. The other main sources are: Villehardouin, *The Conquest of Constantinople*, trans. M.R.B. Shaw, Penguin Classics L 124, 1963 (= V): *Devastatio Constantinopolitana*, ed. G.H. Pertz in *Monumenta Germaniae Historica* (= MGH) Script. XVI, Hanover 1859, pp 9-12 (= D): Robert de Clari, *La Conquête de Constantinople*, ed. P. Lauer, Paris 1924 (= Clari): Bishop Conrad in *Gesta Episcoporum Halberstadensium*, ed L. Weiland in MGH SS XXIII, Hanover 1874, pp. 73-129 (= C): Gunther in Historia Constantinopolitana sub Balduino circa annum 1203 & 1204, in *Thesaurus monumentorum ecciesiasticorum et historicorum sive Henrici Canisii lectiones antiquae*, ed: J. Basnage, IV, Amsterdam 1725, pp. v-xxii (= G).
The local chronicle quoted here is *Annales Colonienses Maximi*, ed. K. Pertz in MGH SS XVII, Hanover 1861, pp. 729-847.

2. V p. 35.

3. C. M. Brand, *Byzantium Confronts the West 1180-1204*, Camb. Mass. 1968, app. II, pp. 275-6.

4. Nicephoros Gregoras, *Byzantina historia*, ed. L. Schopen, Bonn 1829, p. 710.

5. *Reg.* V 122, 16 November 1202.

Verona probably in 1202 and from there got into touch with Boniface, the Marquis of Montferrat, the elected head of the crusade, and with other of its leaders, whose sympathies he won. They sent envoys with him to Philip of Swabia to discuss his proposal.[6] Villehardouin gives no dates for these events. The *Gesta* record that Montferrat visited Philip of Swabia and later also the Pope. With Philip he almost certainly treated of the case of Alexius.[7] To the Pope he hinted at the project but went no further when he saw Innocent's opposition.[8]

Precisely when these various events occurred cannot be decided with certainty, but at the latest by autumn 1202, for by then Alexius III, Emperor of Constantinople (and uncle of the young Prince Alexius), had heard of what was being proposed and had sent an embassy with a letter to the Pope asking him to prevent it. Innocent's reply, dated 16 November 1202, was reassuring. Among other things he informed his imperial correspondent that Philip had interceded with the crusaders on behalf of Prince Alexius; that the army had replied that without the Pope's command and authority they could not act; and that, in consequence, they had sent the papal legate to Rome to learn his will; but " We shall make such a decision as can of its nature satisfy you ". The rest of the letter tells Alexius III that he is getting better treatment than he deserves and that he should fulfil some of his reiterated promises.[9] Capuano had been sent by the barons " to seek the will of the Pope ", presumably so that they could obey it; so on 16 November Innocent must have thought that he had the situation well in hand and that he could safely assure Alexius III that there would be no political mission to Greece.

The pilgrims had begun assembling in Venice in early summer 1202. They were fewer in numbers than had been anticipated. A fleet from Flanders via Marseilles went straight to Syria despite

6. V pp. 44-5.
7. CLARI p. 16.
8. *Gesta* lxxxiii.
9. *Reg.* V 122.

promises. Many knights travelled to Apulia instead of Venice.[10] Others came and departed again for other causes that will shortly appear. This put the leaders in a difficult position because they could collect the price of the voyage only from those present. The result was that they had not enough money to pay the sum agreed upon even when many knights had contributed plate and precious objects to swell the funds.

The Venetians put all the crusaders, including the knights, on the island of St Nicholas. Villehardouin wrote: " The Venetians set up a market for them, as abundantly supplied as any one could desire with everything necessary for the use of horses and men ",[11] but the accounts of pilgrims are all agreed that the conditions there were poor. The *Devastatio Constantinopolitana* records that in Lombardy no more than one night's hospitality was permitted for crusaders and that it was forbidden to sell them provisions. In Venice they were lodged in tents on St. Nicholas' island from 1 June till 1 October, whence it was forbidden to move them and they were treated as captives. Nonetheless many returned home, many managed to get to Apulia, and among those remaining disease broke out " so that the living could scarce bury the dead ".[12] Conrad of Halberstadt reported that " the Venetians detain them on the island of St Nicholas and do not let them return till they have paid all the debt".[13] Gunther of Pairis, telling the story of his Abbot Martin, speaks of the poor returning home when they had exhausted their few resources and of the rich, when they heard of the pact to divert the crusade from the Levant, seeking permission to be dispensed from their pilgrim's vow.[14] Robert of Clari remembered that they pitched their tents on the island and lived as best they could.[15]

To meet this situation the Venetians proposed to the French

10. V pp. 40, 41.
11. V p. 42.
12. D p. 10.
13. H p. 117.
14. G p. viii.
15. Clari p. 9.

that the crusading army should force the city of Zara in Dalmatia into subjection to Venice though it was a possession of the King of Hungary, who had himself taken the Cross and whose property therefore was under the protection of the Church and the Pope. In return for this service the payment of the deficit could be deferred till the crusaders could find occasion to pay it in full. Even Villehardouin notes that there was strong opposition to this scheme. Nevertheless it had to be accepted. After this agreement the Doge took the Cross and the crusade became popular with the Venetians, many of whom followed his example. By this time it was well on into September 1202.[16]

Meantime, on 22 July the papal legate, Peter Capuano, had arrived. He sent away various non-combatants, preached to and encouraged those waiting on the island of St Nicholas, and later went back to Rome.[17] His departure was certainly not before 13 August, for on that day there arrived Conrad of Halberstadt, who when he heard of the resolution about Zara (and so, probably not till late August or early September, after the arrival of Montferrat) wanted to leave the army and go straight to Syria. He consulted Capuano who urged him not to leave, as the Pope certainly would not want the crusade to be dissolved.[18] Abbot Martin had a like aversion to the Zara-project and he too was bidden by Capuano not to leave but with other religious to remain with the crusaders and restrain them as much as possible from the shedding of blood.[19]

Was Capuano really reflecting Innocent's mind? In so far as he asserted that the Pope wanted the crusade not to be dissolved but to remain united to fulfil its purpose, he was right. In so far as he suggested co-operation, even unwilling co-operation, in the sacking of Zara, he was possibly wrong. Most probably at the time when he advised Bishop Conrad and Abbot Martin he

16. V pp. 43-4.
17. D p. 10.
18. H p. 117.
19. G p. ix.

had not yet returned to Rome. According to the *Gesta* the Venetians, for fear that he would oppose the Zara proposal, would accept him only as a preacher, not as a legate, for a legate would have a voice in the direction of the crusade. They state further that he returned to Rome and that then the Pope wrote forbidding the expedition to Zara under pain of excommunication: this was announced by the Abbot of Locedio, and Montferrat was informed personally.[20] These statements of the *Gesta* are probably true, for Innocent in a letter to Capuano notes the Venetian refusal to recognize his legatine office;[21] Montferrat, though he was the leader of the crusading army, did not go to Zara till two weeks after its capture;[22] and Innocent refers to his ban in letters connected with the excommunication incurred for the Zara action.[23]

What happened was probably this. Capuano remained in Venice till late September when in the name of the barons he went to Rome to put the project of helping Prince Alexius before the Pope. At the same time he informed Innocent that the crusaders were definitely going to attack Zara. Innocent was very much opposed to the project, whereupon Capuano by letter informed some of the crusaders (the leaders?) of the papal prohibition with its attached sanction and the Abbot of Vaux was commissioned to promulgate it publicly if it should be necessary. What was forbidden was hostile action against Christians. (It is noteworthy that Vaux denounced the contemplated attack only after negotiation failed.) That a public announcement of the papal prohibition was made when the army was at Zara is recorded by Villehardouin,[24] Clari [25] and Bishop Conrad,[26] all eye-witnesses. Capuano left the Curia before advent 1202,[27] presumably to return

---

20. *Gesta* p. lxxxv.
21. *Reg.* VI 48; IX 139 esp. PL, 215 957B.
22. V p. 50.
23. *Reg.* V 161, 162.
24. V p. 47-8.
25. CLARI, p. 14.
16. H p. 117.
27. *Reg.* 215 147C.

to the army to report to the barons on his mission. He left the army again before their departure from Zara, possibly in late January when the decision had been taken to go to Constantinople, because before the end of April he dealt with the case of the excommunicated Frenchmen not in person but by messenger.[28] Some time later, authorised by a letter of the Pope dated 21 April, he went to Cyprus and Syria.

The fleet did go to Zara. It sailed on 1 October, arrived at Zara on 10 November and started the siege on 11 November. On 12 November citizens parleyed with the Venetians but the negotiations were broken off when the party in the army opposed to the attack told them that the French would not co-operate in the siege. The Abbot of Vaux forbade the assault in the name of the Pope. The barons, however, decided to honour their pledge to the Doge. Some six or seven days later the city fell and was divided between Venetians and French. Such is the account of Villehardouin.[29] Bishop Conrad also records that the attack was made " though there had appeared there apostolic letters forbidding the attack under pain of excommunication " and adds that after the capture some of the abbots would no longer have any contact with the Venetians and that very many of the crusaders went off to Hungary, hoping thence to reach Syria.[30] Robert of Clari asserts that letters threatening excommunication were sent to the Doge and the pilgrims when at Zara. " When the messages reached the host, the letters were read before the Doge and before the pilgrims. When the letters had been read and the Doge had heard them, he said that he would not because of the apostolic excommunication desist from avenging himself on the men of the city ".[31] Gunther reports that the city was forced to surrender

28. PL, 215, 103D.
29. V pp. 46-7.
30. H p. 117.
31. Robert de Clari asserts that letters threatening excommunication were sent to the Doge and the pilgrims when at Zara: " When the messages reached the host, the letters were read before the Doge and before the pilgrims. When the letters had been read and the Doge had heard them, he said that he would not because of the

but " without slaughter or blooodshed ".[32] The author of the *Devastatio* records that the city was terribly despoiled and, as the best of the spoils was taken by the barons, the poorer crusaders were dissatisfied and many went off with or without leave.[33] On 15 March the Venetians began to destroy the city with its walls and buildings [34] and on 20 April the fleet started on its voyage to the east.[35]

Before this, however, the French wanted to be absolved from the excomunication they had incurred by their action at Zara. Villehardouin says no more than that the Pope was severely displeased with them. As envoys sent to Innocent he names two ecclesiastics, Névelon Bishop of Soissons and Jean de Noyes, and two knights, Jean de Friaize and Robert de Boves.[36] They probably set out on their journey before the end of 1202, for Gunther records that they learnt of the negotiations with the envoys of Philip of Swabia for the restoration of Alexius's father to the throne of Constantinople only when they were at the Curia. According to the *Devastatio* the German envoys arrived at Zara on 1 January 1203.[37] The messengers to the Pope, therefore, must have lingered over their business, for it was early in April when they set out on their return to the army. Abbot Martin, impressed by the rumours of the strength of Constantinople and of the certain disaster to the crusaders if they attacked it, pleaded with the Pope to be allowed to return home. Innocent insisted that he first fulfil his pilgrim's vow by going to the Holy Land. At Benevento, on his return journey, he fell in with Cardinal Peter, the apostolic legate, " desirous of crossing directly to Acre ". Thereupon he handed over to his companions the apostolic letters containing

---

apostolic excommunication desist from avenging himself on the men of the city " (p. 14).

32. G p. ix.
33. D p. 10.
34. H p. 118.
35. D p. 10.
36. V p. 53.
37. D p. 10.

the form of absolution for the army, said goodbye to them on 4 April and reached Syria on 25 April.[38]

Among the apostolic letters confided to Abbot Martin there were two now to be read as numbers 161 and 162 of the fifth book of the *Regesta Innocentii PP. III*.[39] They are addressed respectively " To the Army of the Crusaders " and " To the Counts, Barons and Other Crusaders ". Both of them recount in the same words the story of the attack on Zara and the refusal of the Venetians to let the Pope adjudicate as the citizens asked. The envoys had urged that " not under the impulse of their own wills but as it were forced by a certain necessity " they had proceeded to the assault on Zara – but that (wrote the Pope) was not a sufficient excuse. Their own bishops (Soissons and others) had no power to absolve. The legate had been authorized to do that in person

---

38. G p. x. These dates are not easy to reconcile with other dates known from the *Regesta*. Capuano left the Curia before Advent 1202 (VI 130, dated 10 August 1203); and wrote proposing queries to the Pope, who on 21 April 1203 answered bidding him go to Syria in certain eventualities. Gunther makes him go before this letter was even written. This is possible, but very strange.

39. These two letters are very similar but no. 161 " To the Army of the Crusaders ", though it starts without salutation and blessing, which Innocent " was forced to deny them ", and in the body of the letter refers to the excommunication threatened before the attack on Zara, ends apparently intimating excommunication only if *in the future* they should damage Zara any further or not restore the spoils to the King of Hungary. No. 162 " To the Counts, Barons and Other Crusaders " has no doubt that all those involved in the attack on Zara lie under the ban and warns them that the absolution already given, as it were conditionally, by the Bishop of Soissons was unauthorized and invalid. Dr Tillmann (*Papst Innocenz III.*, Bonn 1954, p. 225 n. 28) suggests that no. 161 was written before Innocent knew that the crusaders were self-accused excommunicates and when he was, as it were, turning a blind eye to the whole episode, so as not to endanger the unity of the crusade, but that it was never sent because, when he learnt that the crusaders themselves were conscious of the ban, he could no longer pretend that they were not. Thereupon he wrote and sent no. 162.

I think that this hypothesis is unnecessary. The *Gesta*, whose author was contemporary with the events and quotes freely from the papal registers, refers to no. 161 and not to no. 162. Further no. 161 only seemingly, but not really, refers to a future excommunication: (They should make restitution etc.) *Alioquin, vos excommunicationis sententiae subjacere noveritis et a promissa vobis venia remissionis immunes*, i.e., " Otherwise realise that you are (already) lying under the sentence of excommunication and (will be) inelegibile for the promised favour of forgiveness ". Further no. 161 is apt for the army at large, while no. 162 is, as directed, applicable to the barons who were to bind their heirs to the obligations they themselves undertook on oath etc.

or by procurator. The barons must bind themselves and their heirs by oath to make satisfaction. Such is the tenor of the letters. If 4 April is the correct date for the meeting of Abbot Martin and the apostolic legate in Benevento, those papal letters would not reach the army till it was on the point of moving. It is noteworthy that letter no. 162 repeats the prohibition against invading Christian territory with the same formula as in the warning given in the summer of 1202 concerning Zara.

The letters arrived before at least the leaders of the crusade had departed and they were answered. The barons, accepting the Pope's conditions contained in letters both from him and from Capuano, enclosed the formula of their oath, dated Zara April 1203, and pleaded for understanding of the action of Montferrat, the head of the crusade.[40] Boniface also sent a letter to explain his action, namely, that in spite of strict injunctions to the contrary he had held back a papal sentence of excommunication addressed to the Venetians, " expecting and indeed being quite certain that in that place and time your letter could in no way be shown without the army being immediately dissolved and the fleet broken up ":[41] if, however, Innocent insisted that it be delivered, delivered it would be.

The French crusaders were not the only ones to have recourse to the Pope. The Apostolic Legate Capuano had submitted to him three points for solution, known to us from the papal reply, dated 21 April 1203. He sought advice, being afraid " that the Venetians most stupidly would refuse to avail themselves of the benefit of absolution, that they would be unwilling to accept [him] as apostolic legate and that, as [he had] heard for certain, they would want to proceed to Greece with the son of the ex-Emperor of

40. *Reg.* VI 99.
41. *Reg.* VI 100. The quotation continues: " remembering too your advice that much dissimulation would have to be practised in places and times, if the Venetians should aim at the dissolution of the fleet ". These words are a reflection of Innocent's distrust of the Venetians in general, without reference to any project in particular. Montferrat is suggesting that that was one of the " places and times " when in his view the papal advice was eminently applicable.

Constantinople, whom they mean to take with them ". To this Innocent replied: " Unless they accept the absolution according to the form which We made known to you exactly by our other letter, and promise faithfully not to dare to take up arms against Christians, and agree to receive you as legate of the Apostolic See ", you should leave their army and go to Jerusalem: deal in a similar manner with the French.[42] Innocent, if one may believe Gunther, had very grave doubts whether Prince Alexius could be reinstated in Constantinople " without the taking up of arms against Christians ", indeed without serious bloodshed, and possibly the dissipation of the whole crusade.[43] The *Gesta* assert that the Venetians remained adamant;[44] Capuano certainly went to Syria;[45] and the Venetians petitioned him to absolve them from their excommunication only after the first capture of Constantinople, whereupon he sent the Treasurer of Nicosia to act in his name.[46]

The proposal to divert the crusade still again to an enterprise away from Jerusalem that so disturbed Pope Innocent and Abbot Martin was not less disturbing to the crusading army. The envoys of Philip of Swabia acting for Prince Alexius arrived in Zara on 1 January 1203 and delivered their message to the leaders of the crusade in the Doge's palace. The project was debated among the French, and their army was thoroughly divided about it. The upshot was that, while some of the abbots harangued the soldiers against it, others pleaded not to dissolve the crusade. Finally a few of the leaders accepted (" I must tell you here that only twelve persons in all took the oaths on behalf of the French, no more could be persuaded to come forward ").[47] Numerous knights with the men under their command left, many of them to join

---

42. *Reg.* VI 48.
43. G p. x.
44. *Gesta* p. lxxxvii.
45. *Reg.* VI 209, dated 23 January 1204.
46. *Gesta* p. xc.
47. V p. 51.

I

the King of Hungary.[48] The ships began to move away on 20 April.[49] Prince Alexius reached Zara on 25 April before the last of the leaders had departed. The fleet assembled in Corfu, setting off again on 24 May and arriving in sight of Constantinople on 23 June.[50] In Corfu a large group of knights with their followers wanted to go to Brindisi and thence to Syria, and yielded only when the others pleaded with them on their knees.[51] All the chief sources witness to the desire of the crusaders to fulfil their vow in the Holy Land and not to be diverted elsewhere.[52]

How much Innocent III knew of what was going on in Zara cannot be determined. Some time before 21 April 1203 he had learnt from Capuano " who had heard it for certain ", that the army would take Prince Alexius to Constantinople. Whether the crusaders informed him officially of their pact with the Prince is not known. It is not unlikely that they did and that Innocent's letter to them of 20 June 1203 was the answer to that intimation as well as an acknowledgement of the letters sent by the penitent French knights from Zara in April. The leaders of the French pilgrims could favour the expedition with a good conscience. After the capture of Zara the Doge had told them: " It's already winter and we can't stir from here till Easter ".[53] By Easter the half of the year for which they had hired the fleet would have gone. After leaving Zara they would be without provisions and without money

48. V pp. 50-4.
49. D p. 10.
50. H p. 118; V p. 54. According to Bishop Conrad the inhabitants of Corfu drove the crusaders from the harbour on hearing of the arrival of the Prince: " Exercitus, igitur, eius auctoritate insula penitus devastata recessit " (H. p: 118). Cf. V. p. 58.
51. " Indeed it is only true to say that more than half the men in the army were of the same mind " i.e., to go straight to Syria; V pp. 55-6. The Count of Saint-Pol in a letter to the Duke of Brabant narrates the same: " Super hoc autem erat inter nos maxima dissensio et ingens tumultus, omnes enim clamabant ire apud Accaron; pauci fuerunt plus quam 20 qui Constantinopolim collaudassent, quorum fuit unus Marchio, comes Flandrensis... (*Annales Colonienses Maximi*, p. 812).
52. Quod cum populus cognovisset, se videlicet in Greciam iturum, convenerunt et facta conspiratione juraverunt se numquam illuc ituros ' (D p. 10): Cf. H. p. 118.
53. V p. 48.

to buy them or to pay the sergeants, i.e., the technicians to make, mount and fire their " petrarii " and other engines, and they felt that they could not arrive in Palestine so poorly provided for that they would add to the burden of the already straightened fighters there. (These are the arguments that they themselves believed to be valid and that they used to persuade the recalcitrant).[54] What is more, they were convinced that they would run no risk of again incurring excommunication, because that was threatened for " taking up arms against Christians " and they firmly believed on the word of the Prince that it would need no more than his presence in front of Constantinople for the gates of the city to be thrown open to welcome him.[55] When on arrival the gates were not opened, they paraded him round the walls, but without result.

The two letters that Innocent sent to the army on 20 June were addressed, the one to the Marquis of Montferrat and the three knights who had written to him in April, the other " To the Crusaders ". Neither letter begins with the usual salutation of benediction. The one to the barons opens with a long expression of the Pope's distress (a third of the whole). He grieves for his own sake, for their sake, and for that of the people – for their sake, that, having believed that they had cleansed out the old leaven, a little leaven (and would that it were only a little) had again corrupted the whole lump: for the people's sake, because the Saracens rejoice and pilgrims in Palestine sceptical about their ever arriving were departing. He rejoices, though, at

---

54. Letter of Saint-Pol, p. 812; PL, 215, 238B.
55. The crusaders were " persuaded by plausible-sounding reports and reasons that the greater part of the imperial city and the bulk of the Empire were longing for the arrival of the said Alexius whom it had raised to the purple by popular vote and with due solemnity " (Letter of Baldwin to the Pope and the West, summer 1203, PL, 215, 231B). Saint-Pol wrote to the Duke of Brabant that, when the fleet was a league away from Constantinople, " There we were astounded and very surprised at this, that none of the friends, none of the relatives of the young Emperor who was with us, or any messenger of theirs came to him to inform him of the state of things in Constantinople. We had not long to wait. The Emperor who actually held Constantinople ... sent his messengers " to tell them to go away (Annales Colon. Max. p. 812).

their penitence for the crime of Zara. But let their penitence be sincere – whoso still does what he has repented of is not penitent but a fraud and like a dog that returns to its vomit. " Let no one, therefore, among you rashly persuade himself that he may occupy or despoil land of the Greeks on the grounds that these are little obedient to the Apostolic See and because ... the Emperor of Constantinople, having deposed and even blinded his brother, usurped the throne. Indeed, no matter what evil in this and other things the Emperor and those subject to his jurisdiction have committed, it is not for you to pass judgement on their crimes; you did not take on yourselves the symbol of the Cross to avenge this injury, but rather the shame done to the Crucified to whose honour you have dedicated yourselves in a special way ". We most solemnly enjoin on you " not to deceive yourselves or let others deceive you into doing on a pretext of filial piety what will redound to your spiritual harm, but setting aside all specious opportunities and seeming necessities cross the seas to the help of the Holy Land and avenge the injury done to the Cross, getting from enemies the spoils that, should you linger on in Greek territory, you might be forced to extort from brethren. Otherwise, because We neither can nor ought, We offer you no promise whatsoever of the favour of forgiveness. We want you to bear in mind and We warn you not even venially to contravene the sense of our prohibition by which We forbade you under pain of excommunication to attempt to invade or harm lands belonging to Christians, unless either they unjustly hinder your journey or some other just and necessary reason should perhaps supervene, by which, after taking counsel with our legate, you may act otherwise ". That the guilt of the Venetians may not recoil on you, give them the letters which we directed to them and which you still retain.[56]

The second letter, addressed " To the Crusaders ", explains at length why they may travel with a Venetian fleet and have

56. *Reg.* VI 101.

necessary intercourse with the Venetians, though these are excommunicated and so *vitandi*. In addition it contains a sentence, rather out of context, that refers to Constantinople: " That you may not lack for provisions, We shall write to our most dear son the Emperor of Constantinople so that, as he himself promised Us in letters to Us, he will have victuals provided for you. But if by chance he should refuse them ", you may avail yourselves, as he may, of the right of living on the country as far as may be necessary, with a just intention. " But take careful and prudent precautions, if the Venetians should try to find occasion to dissolve the army, to manage to dissimulate, and put up with a great deal as the circumstances may demand, until you have reached your destination, where, as opportunity offers, suppress their malice as suits you ".[57]

Certain conclusions can be drawn with a fair degree of assurance from this somewhat meticulous examination of the affairs of the crusaders between 1201 and 1203.

1. *The Project of Zara.* – The problem arose only when the crusaders could not produce the agreed price of transit. They accepted the expedition only because they had to, so as to get the crusading army moving. They really had no choice. They had paid all the money they possessed to the Venetians for the magnificent fleet prepared specially for them, which was just. They could have all gone home again or, to fulfil their pilgrim oath, without resources have made for Apulia hoping finally to reach Syria, or they could accept the Venetian offer. There is no serious reason for thinking that " in accepting the expedition to Zara [the crusaders] were wanting to gain time and to win the consent of the Pope " [for the adventure of Constantinople].[58] They alleged this plea of necessity to Innocent when they sought absolution from the censure, and he accepted it. Apparently he expected from

57. *Reg.* VI 102.
58. L. BREHIER, *Les Croisades*, Paris 1907², pp. 155, 156.

the Venetians some attempt to disrupt the crusade, since he warned Montferrat to be prepared to dissimulate when necessary.

All the eye-witness sources except Villehardouin give an unfavourable report on the situation, and speak of the harsh treatment of the pilgrims, in Venice.[59]

2. *The Project of Constantinople*. – Philip of Swabia favoured this from the start; the Marquis of Montferrat was soon won over to it;[60] Venice cannot have rejected something so suited to its purposes; the crusading barons were attracted to it before ever they left Venice.

Not just a " few dissidents ",[61] but the mass of the crusading army was against it – and that included most of the knights. They had taken oaths to go to Syria, and neither the Pope nor Capuano would easily dispense them from their obligation. In any case they wanted to go for the sake of their own devotion and for the spiritual benefits accruing. At Zara there were numerous desertions of knights and soldiers recorded by Villehardouin,[62] the *Devastatio*,[63] Bishop Conrad;[64] and Clari mentions discord.[65] At Corfu, a stage nearer to Constantinople, there was a most serious threat of defection, recounted in detail by Villehardouin and Saint-Pol. The dissidents were persuaded to remain only when promised galleys for the Holy Land within a fortnight of their demanding them[66], and because the difficulties besetting the army financially and in respect of provisions, to be met by the promised largesse of Prince Alexius, could be solved only in Constantinople.

59. Cf. supra p. 88.
60. *Gesta* p. lxxxiii; Clari p. 16, quoting a speech of Montferrat, " Before Christmas [1201] I was in Germany at the court of my Lord the Emperor. Thither came a youth who was brother of the wife of the Emperor of Germany ... One could well go to the land of Constantinople and get provisions and other things, for the youth is the legal lord there ".
61. S. Runciman, *A History of the Crusades*, vol. III, Cambridge 1954, p. 116.
62. Cf. supra p. 95 and n. 47.
63. D. p. 10.
64. H. p. 117.
65. Clari, p. 32.
66. Cf. supra p. 96.

4. *Pope Innocent was opposed to the Expedition to Zara.* – He did not merely excommunicate the attackers after the assault [67] but threatened excommunication beforehand, and afterwards did not lightly agree to the absolution of the French.[68] Besides penitence he demanded from the barons oaths binding both them and their heirs and he imposed restitution of pillaged property to the Hungarian crown. Convinced that the Venetians were primarily responsible, he notified them of their excommunication and, in spite of the worst fears of Montferrat and the barons, insisted on that notification with the conditions for absolution being presented to them.

5. *Pope Innocent III was opposed also to the Expedition to Constantinople.* – When Prince Alexius tried to interest him in the restoration of his blind father to the throne, he received " the reply that We thought was suitable" – so Innocent describes it in a letter to Emperor Alexius III. Apparently it was not an encouraging reply, but whether the reason was his " having little confidence in [Prince] Alexius's ability to bring the Greek Church over to Rome " [69] or not cannot be safely asserted for lack of any documentary evidence.

His reaction when for the second time he was faced with the proposal is recorded in the same letter addressed to Emperor Alexius. There Innocent does not just " mention the possibility of the diversion of the crusade " [70] but treats of it at length and discounts it. His correspondent, the Emperor, had sent an embassy to him to inform him of the plan and to ask him to " restrain the Christian army from such a project ". In reply Innocent describes first the visit to himself of Prince Alexius and then the mission of Cardinal Capuano on behalf of the pilgrim barons to learn his

---

67. D. M. NICOL, *The Fourth Crusade and the Greek and Latin Empires, 1204-61,* in *Cambridge Medieval History* (= CMH), IV, Part. I, Cambridge 1966, p. 279.
68. PL, 215, 262B.
69. CMH, p. 280.
70. CMH, p. 280.

views about the imperial restoration. The promises of money, of help for the crusade, and of zeal for Church union offered in return by Philip of Swabia and the Prince are noted in detail, and the Pope ends his description of the occasion saying that, in spite of the pressure brought to bear on him to favour the suggestion since " the Church of the Greeks shows little obedience and attachment to the Apostolic See", yet (he wrote) "We shall decide what can of its nature give you satisfaction ".[71] So Innocent knew of Alexius's " elaborate promises " before they were repeated at Zara and clearly was not " convinced that an unparalleled opportunity presented itself for securing unity of the Churches and the active co-operation of the Greeks in the Holy War ".[72]

That the decision to proceed to Constantinople was taken at Zara before the barons sought absolution from their excommunication is open to doubt: it is on the face of it unlikely. It is true that Villehardouin, a primary source, records the arrival of Philip's envoys as occurring roughly a month after the capture of Zara (i.e., towards the end of December) and mentions the rendezvous with Prince Alexius in Corfu as fixed " in the following year ", i.e., 1203:[73] only later does he refer to the excommunication question which is introduced with an indefinite phrase, " In the course of the winter ". The other primary sources speak of the excommunication deputation first and then of the decision concerning Constantinople. The *Devastatio*, which does not mention the excommunication, states that Philip's messengers reached Zara on the feast of the Circumcision, i.e., 1 January.[74] According to Gunther the deputation (with his hero, Abbot Martin, a member of it) was in Rome when the first rumours of the new diversion proposal reached them.[75]

That Innocent persisted in his opposition to the project is

---

71. *Reg.* V 122, esp. PL, 214, 1124DC.
72. CMH, p. 280.
73. V p. 52.
74. D p. 10; H p. 118.
75. G p. ix.

confirmed by Capuano's queries of early 1203. Had the Pope been in favour, there would have been no sense in the legate's asking what to do when " he had heard it for certain that they meant to go to Constantinople taking the young prince with them " – he would have known the answer without asking: it would have been: " Go with them ". Instead he was told that the Venetians must promise not to take up arms against Christians, otherwise he should go to Syria leaving the crusade to its fate. That is far from suggesting that " the Fourth Crusade set out for Constantinople with the connivance if not with the blessing of Innocent III ".[76]

Nonetheless Montferrat, writing to the Pope in 1205, alleged the advice of Cardinal Capuano as an excuse for his being in Greece (he was already in possession of his fief of Thessalonica) in a letter re-asserting all his good intentions and his readiness still to go to the Holy Land: " But your undertaking to conduct that youth who kept declaring that the Empire of Constantinople was his by right was the advice of our dear son Peter ... legate of the Apostolic See [we have only the Pope's answer of late August 1205 which with the necessary change of pronouns repeats Montferrat's letter] and it was not so much human counsel as driving necessity that after the overthrow of Zara made the army diverge to get provisions in Greece". Later in the letter, where he is giving his answers to Boniface, the Pope returns to this point: " But you against justice and with unrighteousness, nay rather with usurped power,[77] alleged the

---

76. CMH. p. 280. A similar judgement is suggested by E. H. McNeal and R. L. Wolff, *The Fourth Crusade*, in *A History of the Crusades*, II, ed. R. L. Wolff and H. W. Hazard, Philadelphia 1962, p. 176: " How far does the curious papal failure to condemn the diversion in time argue Innocent's complicity in a plot? Some modern historians believe that the pope was protesting " for the record ", and had secretly endorsed the attack on Constantinople. The Greeks, from that day to this, have regarded Innocent as the ringleader of the plot. It seems more likely that Innocent rather allowed the diversion to happen. Perhaps he felt he could not prevent it. Moreover, it promised to achieve — though by methods he could not publicly endorse — one of the chief aims of his foreign policy, the union of the churches, and simultaneously further a second aim, the crusade ".
77. PL, 215, 712A

advice of the apostolic legate as if by that you could lawfully go with the aforesaid youth to give back to him the Empire of Constantinople ". The Pope, however, concludes the letter by allowing that good may result from evil and that, now in possession of his territory, Montferrat should hold on to it and rule it justly, but should still retain his intention of fulfilling his crusader's vow.[78]

It is unlikely that Capuano counselled Montferrat to take the prince back to Constantinople, for the answer he had to return to him and the other French barons after his mission to the Curia was the papal negative, and not long afterwards his query to Innocent on the same point implied the same negation. One may suspect that at Zara Montferrat informed the legate that the expedition to Constantinople would certainly take place (" you have it for certain that ...") and that later he touched up his picture of the occasion – a picture meant to soothe the Pope [79] – heightening a non-committal answer into a counsel. Earlier in the same year 1205, Dandolo had sent with two messengers a very clever letter to the Pope explaining why the Venetians were right and Innocent wrong as regards both Zara and Constantinople, but even he does not allege any quasi-papal consent via Capuano for the journey to Greece. For him it was " a divine inspiration rather than a human counsel ".[80]

The Fourth Crusade set out for Constantinople without the blessing certainly and without the connivance of Pope Innocent. He could not stop it, for the Doge and the barons took the direction of the army into their own hands. From the first, seemingly, the Venetians, refusing to recognize Capuano as legate, meant to exclude any control of the crusade by the Church. When Innocent learnt of the decision to go to Constantinople in opposition to his

78. *Reg.* VIII 133.
79. Montferrat in winter 1203-4 wrote: " Cumque vos ad navigandum in Syriam totis viribus pararetis ", reported in Innocent's letter PL, 215 711B. Villehardouin records that already in summer 1203 the crusaders had agreed to stay on till March 1204 (p. 78).
80. *Reg.* VII 202, esp. PL, 215 511D.

" will " made known by Capuano at the end of 1202, he reiterated in the most positive terms the prohibition with its sanction against damaging Christian territories and applied that in particular to the Empire of Constantinople,[81] brushing aside as worthless any specious excuses about upholding the Church or defending others' rights. The half of his letter of 20 June 1203 to the leaders is devoted to that and to insisting that they remember and pursue the true end of the crusade. In his letter " To the Crusaders ", the only destination mentioned is the " land of the Saracens " or " the Province of Jerusalem "; he would write " to his most dear son in Christ ", the Emperor, urging him to provide provisions in accordance with his promise.

" Do not be like dogs returning to their vomit "; " Let no one deceive himself into thinking he may occupy territory of the Greeks "; " It is not for you to judge the Emperor but to defend the Cross "; " Put aside all specious excuses and go to Palestine "; " Under pain of excommunication We forbid you to invade or damage Christian lands ". To label these adjurations as " a half-hearted condemnation, to the Greeks a seeming proof that Innocent was the power behind the whole intrigue of the expedition to Constantinople",[82] is an injustice to the reputation of Innocent III.

---

81. " Territories of the Greeks " included mainland Greece, the Morea, the Ionian Islands and the islands in the Aegean, Crete, and Asia Minor, as well as Constantinople. The fleet, whatever route it took eastwards, was often bound to be in the vicinity of " territories of the Greeks ".

82. RUNCIMAN, *Op. cit.* p. 117. A. FROLOW, *La déviation de la IVe croisade vers Constantinople*, Paris 1955, pp. 42-4, is definite that Pope Innocent was opposed to the expedition to Constantinople. He seems, however, to attribute his attitude solely to political acumen, not to favour what might further the designs of Philip of Swabia, the Pope's motive appearing clearly from the fact that when he learnt that Baldwin was Emperor of Constantinople and not Philip's relative and ally, Montferrat, his tone of reproach changed to one of triumph (p. 45).

But Innocent was more than a politician. Opposition to Philip of Swabia was certainly one of his reasons for not wanting to put Philip's brother-in-law, Alexius, in power in Constantinople, but a more impelling motive was his desire to see the crusade be true to its purpose and the crusaders fulfil their vow of freeing the Holy Land. He was also afraid that the Venetians would contrive by devices like Zara and Constantinople to disrupt the crusade.

That the longing to see (and acquire) some of the fantastic relics that abounded in Constantinople drew the soldiery there may be true, but the major sources give no indication that it was. They make it plain that many in Venice, many more at Zara, and " more than half " in Corfu wanted to go the quickest way to Outremer and that no appeal to the veneration of relics was included among the reasons advanced by the leaders to overcome their reluctance to going to Constantinople.

II

Innocent III and the Greeks : Aggressor or Apostle?

Walter Norden, author of the deservedly well-known book, *Das Papsttum und Byzanz*, freely admits that Pope Innocent after the conquest of Constantinople in 1204 did not try to impose upon the Greeks conformity with the Latins in faith and rite. He then asks why and answers in these words.

> The Curia employed this restraint simply and solely for political ends. It appears here obviously that the papacy, as a purely ecclesiastical power and also in spheres where she entered not as a directly political power whether in Italy or in the world at large, aimed in the main at a political goal, in so far, that is, as for her it all came to this – to govern and to wield influence. Since Innocent III in respect of the Greek Church let the spiritual drive fall back into the second place and declared himself satisfied with obedience from the Greek clergy in respect of Rome, he disclosed the basic characteristic of the Roman Church as being one of spiritual politics; he revealed it as the continuation, admittedly rooted in the consciousness of a religious mission, of the *Imperium Romanum*. The transformation of Greek priests, who hitherto had stood outside the Roman organism, into pliant tools of Roman domination, as if in government offices, was the chief objective of the Curia in latinised Byzantium; on the other hand, she considered the conversion of the Greeks to the Roman faith – which [conversion], by the way, as we saw, she by no means lost sight of and which she regarded, owing to the predominantly Latin character of Romania [i.e. the Empire], merely as a question of time – as an affair of a less pressing nature, as one of second-rate importance. She left, however, the Greek rite definitely free.[1]

Norden's judgement of Pope Innocent's actions is shared by many other historians.[2] The papal letters, especially those directed to countries and Churches outside the Latin Church – but not only those – seem *prima facie* to endorse that judgement fully. They abound in assertions of the primacy of the see of Rome, of the exalted position of its bishop as successor of St Peter and vicar of Christ and of his consequent universal jurisdiction. In his first letters to the Greek emperor Alexius III and the patriarch John Camaterus (August 1198) Innocent reminds them both that the Greek Church should return as daughter to the Church which is mother and mistress of all the faithful.[3] A year later, replying at length to the patriarch's rebuttal of his claims, he gives argument after argument in their favour, that 'the Roman Church, not by the decision of some council, but by divine ordinance is head and mother of all the Churches'.[4] When an occasion offered for these convictions to be given practical effect he did not let it slip. After the first capture of Constantinople in 1203 by Alexius IV and the crusaders, Innocent wrote to them all urging that a proof of the sincerity of their promises and excuses would be if they prevailed on the patriarch 'to recognise the primacy and the supreme teaching office of the Roman Church, to promise reverence and obedience to Us, and to request from the Apostolic See the pallium taken from the body of St Peter, without which he cannot validly [*rite*] exercise the patriarchal office'.[5]

What the pallium signified is described in the formula used at its bestowal on the Bulgarian archbishop of Tirnovo. It was 'the mark of the fulness of the pontifical office', and was to be worn by metropolitans only in churches subject to them and on certain feastdays and occasions. There was this limitation because 'only the Roman Pontiff uses the pallium in the Mass always and everywhere, since he has been invested with the fulness of ecclesiastical power, which is symbolised by the pallium. Others should wear it neither always nor everywhere but on certain days and in their own Church in which they have received ecclesiastical jurisdiction, for they are called to a part of the solicitude [of the Churches] not to the plenitude of power'.[6]

Let these few quotations suffice to illustrate the way Innocent insisted on the claims of the see of Rome and of its occupant. They could be supplemented by dozens and dozens of others from his sermons and letters to Bulgaria, Armenia and other countries, to Greeks and Latins in the Eastern Empire, to prelates and kings in the West. They witness to his absolute conviction and belief that as pope he was head of all Christians, vicar of Christ, successor of St Peter, heir to the universal jurisdiction accorded by Christ to the prince of the Apostles, and holder of a teaching office that others should honour. If his endless repetition of statements to this effect strikes us as utterly extravagant and almost nauseating, yet we should not forget that the substance of them was, and is, the belief of the Roman Church, usually expressed, may be, in more sober terms but not less firmly.

In 1439 the Council of Florence with the approval of the numerous Greek members present, in words almost reminiscent of Innocent III, defined:

> Also in the same way we define that the holy, apostolic See and the Roman Pontiff hold the primacy over the whole

world and that the Roman Pontiff himself is the successor of St Peter, prince of the Apostles, and that he is the true vicar of Christ, head of the whole Church and father and teacher of all Christians, and that to the same in St Peter was given plenary power of feeding, ruling and governing the whole Church, as is contained also in the Acts of the ecumenical councils and the sacred canons.[7]

The first Vatican Council in 1870 repeated verbatim the definition of Florence and continued:

> In consequence we teach and declare that the] Roman Church possesses by dominical ordinance a primacy of ordinary power and that this power of jurisdiction of the Roman pontiff is truly episcopal and immediate. Pastors of all ranks and rites and the faithful, each one separately and all together, are held to the duty of hierarchical subordination and of true obedience, not only in questions of faith and morals but also in those that pertain to the discipline and the government of the Church spread over all the world.[8]

The second Vatican Council in various places in chapter III of the dogmatic constitution *Lumen gentium* repeated the teaching of Vatican I. 'This holy council, following in the footsteps of Vatican I', teaches that Christ founded a Church with bishops. 'In order that the episcopate should be one and undivided, He set St Peter over the other Apostles and in him established a perpetual and visible principle and foundation of unity of faith and communion.[9] This doctrine about the institution, permanence, validity and reason of the sacred primacy of the Roman pontiff and of his infallible authority and office, the Holy Synod again proposes to be firmly believed by all the faithful.' 'In virtue of his office, that is, as Vicar of Christ and Pastor of the whole Church, the Roman Pontiff has full, supreme and universal power over the Church, which he may always exercise freely'.[10]

This fact that the universality of the jurisdiction of the bishop of Rome was for Innocent and the western Church a doctrine, and not merely an aim, has been forgotten by many. In consequence they can affirm or imply that Innocent's insistence on the oath of obedience in, for example, his dealings with the Greeks was to put faith in the second place or in no place at all, and to pursue a policy of purely political domination. That is not so. The oath of obedience was the external sign of acceptance of the Roman teaching on the primacy and, while it may also have tended towards – and, if you like, have been meant by Innocent to tend towards – political domination, its primary purpose was to insist on the point of doctrine that it asserted.

Innocent, however, is blamed for harping on this one point

and ignoring whatever other dogmatic questions divided the Churches. In his letters he often stated that the Greek Church had left the universal Church by embracing error. He specified only two forms of that error; the one, their denial of the primacy of Rome; the other, their rejection of the *Filioque* doctrine. He never, it is true, personally [11] exhorted the Greeks to recant their trinitarian aberration, whereas he never ceased to insist on their acceptance of obedience. But the reason is not far to seek. The one included the other. The full idea of Roman supremacy implied also a superior teaching authority. Whoever sincerely accepted that Peter and his successors were the rock on which the Church was founded and the principal receivers of the keys accepted a papal primacy of teaching as well as of jurisdiction, for the rock meant inerrancy in faith and the keys a supremacy of jurisdiction. Innocent wrote to the patriarch of Constantinople and the emperor in identical terms on this point.

> Seeing then ... that the Roman Church is the head and mother of all Churches not by the decision of some council but by divine ordinance, so, because of difference neither of rite nor of dogma, should you hesitate to obey Us as your head generously and devotedly in accordance with ancient custom and the canons, since what is certain is not to be abandoned in favour of what is doubtful. [12]

For Innocent what was certain was the primacy of faith and jurisdiction of the successor of St Peter. What in another Church did not harmonise with that was at the least doubtful.

An example, typical in many ways, of Innocent's expression of this conviction is contained in the long letter that he wrote on 13 November 1204 'To the Bishops, Abbots, and other Clerics with the Army of the Crusaders in Constantinople'. It consists of an intricate exegesis of the visits of Mary Magdalen and the apostles Peter and John to the tomb of the risen Lord. St Peter and the Latin Church are the New Testament; St John and the Greek Church, the Old Testament. [13] St Peter entered the tomb; St John remained outside. So the Latins had the fulness of the teaching of the New Testament; the Greeks enmeshed in the Old Testament fell short of that, being in error in their trinitarian doctrine.

> If this mystery had been understood by the Greeks, they would already have entered with the Latins into the sepulchre, knowing that God is not a God of dissension but of peace. But, because John did not yet know the scriptures, namely, that Christ must rise again from the dead, it is nothing to be surprised at if the Greeks still do not know that, where the Spirit of Christ lives, the letter is dead. But they will soon know; such is Our belief and hope. They will know; yes, they

will know; and the rest of them will be converted with all their hearts . . . For [John] will see what Peter had seen and will believe what the Church of the Latins believes, so that henceforward they will walk in the house of the Lord in harmony.[14]

Though he never doubted about the supremacy of the Church of which he was the head, Innocent did not employ or permit repressive measures to impose the Latin Church on the Greeks. He recognised as valid the orders of bishops, priests and deacons of the oriental Church. It is true that he thought the ordination rites defective because they contained no anointings. In the more pliant Bulgarian Church he ordered that the missing unctions should be supplied to those already consecrated and ordained, but in the Greek Church he allowed bishops and abbots already in office to remain unmolested, even though new bishops and abbots were to have the anointings. When the Latin archbishop of Athens deposed Theodore of Negroponte because he would not submit to supplementary anointings, Innocent on the appeal of the victim appointed a commission to reinstate him; and this was done. Otherwise he changed nothing of the Greek rite, though there were many differences of detail between it and the Roman rite. He encouraged monks to abide in their monasteries, for which he cherished an admiration : 'But, because to the Greek people was given St John, who was the source of the religious life of perfect monks, the Greek Church well portrays the character of the Spirit, who seeks and loves spiritual men'.[15] The monasteries of Mount Athos and others he took under his protection. He sent legates to meet the Greeks in theological conversations to draw them to unity. Benedict, cardinal of S. Susanna, was well known for his gentleness of manner and geniality of character. Pelagius, bishop of Albano, has a reputation for being harsh and brusque, but Nicholas Mesarites in his account of the discussions held with him in 1214 portrays him (not quite fairly) as proud, but not as overbearing.

But, of course, Innocent did insist on all prelates taking an oath of obedience to himself and to the Latin patriarch. Yet even this insistence was to be tempered as much as possible with moderation. The reluctant were to be given three canonical warnings before excommunication. If they persisted in their contumacy the cardinal legate (but not Morosini) should remove them from the administration of their bishoprics and replace them, but not even he should promulgate the sentence of degradation, so as to leave the door open to a possible change of heart.[16] Few Greek bishops did, however, take the oath and among them no one of high importance. They preferred to leave their sees for Nicaea or Epirus and the hope of a final Greek triumph. The oath of obedience was, in fact, a form of pressure from which many suffered.

What might have been the alternative? To leave the Greek patriarch and hierarchy in their sees and the whole Greek Church in the same schismatical relationship with the Latin as before, though by then the Latins were the kings and princes of the country and established in every part? The mentality of today would approve of this solution. But I wonder if it was possible for the men of yesterday. Innocent would not tolerate two bishops in any one diocese. Such would have been a monster, a body with two heads.[17] Would it have been conceivable in the thirteenth century that Latins of pure faith (as they believed) and unassailable rite should be under Greeks whose faith was defective and whose rite and customs strange and in part distressing?

For Innocent there was no problem seeking a solution. The new situation had simplified the issue. In his eyes the military conquest of the Greek Empire involved automatically the union of the eastern and the western Churches. He declared this time and again in his letters after the capture, and offered no explanation. He only drew practical conclusions that he hoped would follow. In his letter to the ecclesiastics of Constantinople of 13 November 1204 he wrote : God 'transferred the Empire of Constantinople from the proud to the humble, from the disobedient to the devoted, from schismatics to Catholics, that is, from the Greeks to the Latins . . . the right hand of the Lord has done acts of valour to exalt the holy Roman Church, as it brings back the daughter to the mother, the part to the whole, and the member to the head'.[18] In his next letter to them he comes back to the idea more than once. Commenting on the incident of Our Lord preaching from Peter's boat and of the miraculous draught of fishes, he wrote :

> The other ship was the Greek Church . . . [which] We summoned to come to help Us, that is, that returning they should take up again part of Our solicitude as helpers in the providential task allotted to Us. But by God's grace they came because, after the Empire of Constantinople was transferred in these days to the Latins, the Church also of Constantinople came back to obedience to the Apostolic See as a daughter to her mother and a member to the head, so that for the future there might reign between Us and them an undivided partnership. Truly We proclaim them brethren, partners, and friends, because, though We have over them the office of government, it is a government that leads not to domination but to service . . . See, then, our partners come to help us, because the Church of the Greeks returns to obedience of the Apostolic see.[19]

These quotations express Innocent's conviction clearly, a conviction he did not change. He reiterated it time and again as the years passed. It figured even in the Acts of the Council of the Lateran, which preceded his death by only a little over a year. The fourth *capitulum* of that council, entitled 'On the Pride of the Greeks against the Latins', opens with the words : 'Whereas we wish to cherish and honour the Greeks, who in our day return to obedience to the Holy See, by maintaining as far as we can in the Lord their customs and rites, nevertheless...'[20]

This equating of political conquest with ecclesiastical union as being almost axiomatic is strange. The explanation may lie in historical precedent. Allegiance to Constantinople or Rome of the Greek churches and monasteries of Sicily and South Italy tended to come and go according as Greek or Norman held the reins of government. On the whole the popes had defended the Greek rite and been not a little responsible for its survival despite the determination of Normans like Roger of Sicily to latinize everything. It showed that the Greek rite could flourish under Roman jurisdiction, and, in point of fact, it was flourishing in Innocent's day and with his support. The interpreter of both Cardinal Benedict and Cardinal Pelagius was the Greek abbot of Otranto, Nicholas. Then, too, the will of monarchs, particularly of oriental monarchs, counted for much. Leo the Isaurian, as a retaliation for opposition to his iconoclastic policy, had punished Rome by transferring Illyricum and Sicily to the jurisdiction of Constantinople. Innocent believed that the Greek emperors of his day could command obedience from the patriarch and the Church. He told Alexius III : 'Strive – nay! seeing that you can do it, bring it about – that the Church of the Greeks return to the unity of the Apostolic See and that the daughter come back to the mother'.[21] Alexius IV, too, was expected to direct both patriarch and Church towards Rome.[22] The princes, not the Churches, of Serbia, Bulgaria and Armenia had all solicited his protection, and the Churches had enthusiastically concurred. In Jerusalem, Antioch and Alexandria Latin patriarchs had been appointed. In Jerusalem the see was vacant when the Latins arrived; in the other two cities it was a question of Latin or Greek influence and in Antioch an irate prince manipulated the patriarchate to further his own interests. In Cyprus also, with the political domination of western power, the main sees of the local Church were put into Latin hands and the indigenous Greek Church was made subordinate. In other words, it had been the custom and it was the custom. Innocent did no more than follow the custom in the conviction that he was conferring the benefit of the truth on the misguided.

For, after all, the victory of the pilgrim army was an act of God.

Emperor Baldwin in his letter announcing the capture of the eastern capital had no doubt of it: 'God's wonders follow ever one on another in our regard, so that even the infidel should not doubt that the hand of God is bringing all this to pass, since nothing of what we had previously hoped for and forecast succeeded and then in the end the Lord provided new aids when nothing of human counsel remained'.[23] Pope Innocent was equally convinced. He opened his letter to the Latin ecclesiastics of Constantinople with these words:

> We read in the prophet Daniel that it is God in heaven who reveals mysteries; He changes times and transfers kingdoms. This we see fulfilled in our day in the kingdom of the Greeks and we rejoice, since He who holds power in the kingdom of men and who will give it to whomso He wills, has transferred the Empire of Constantinople from the proud to the humble, from the disobedient to the devoted, from schismatics to Catholics, that is, from the Greeks to the Latins. Indeed, that was done by the Lord and it is marvellous in our sight. This is verily the change of the right hand of the Most High in which the right hand of the Lord performs acts of valour'.[24]

Not only was the victory the act of the right hand of the Lord to favour the Latins and their faith. It was at the same time a punishment of the Greeks for their sin of schism. The emperor Baldwin in the same letter recorded his belief. 'These and other ravings [i.e. the Greek errors and their treatment of Latins] which the limits of a letter cannot narrate at length, when the cup of their iniquities had been filled full (iniquities which moved even God to nausea), divine Justice by our means visited with a worthy vengeance and, driving out men who hate God and love only themselves, has given to us a land flowing with abundance of every good'.[25] This is a theme that Innocent only touched on in his communications to the crusaders, but he agreed with it and in a letter to Theodore Lascaris himself he propounded his belief though with moderation. Lascaris had written to the pope accusing the Latins of apostasy for turning Christian arms against Christians, of sacrilege for sacking holy places in Constantinople, of perjury for breaking treaties. Innocent replied: 'We do not excuse the Latins whom often We have reproved for their excesses, but We have thought good to put before you in this letter the excuses they make for themselves', whereupon he repeats almost verbatim the explanation offered him in August 1205 by Montferrat.[26] He continued:

> But allowing that they are not altogether without blame, still We believe that through them the Greeks were punished by a just judgement of God, because they acted to rend the seam-

less garment of Jesus Christ. For since God's judgements are so hidden that they are called a vast abyss by the prophet, it often occurs that by His hidden, but ever most just judgement, the evil are punished by the agency of the evil.

He ended by counselling Theodore to accept that judgement and to submit to the Latin emperor Henry, to whom divine power had given the empire.[27]

When Constantinople was taken by the crusade that Innocent had set in motion and promoted, he could and, I think, did expect that the conquered territories would become a fief of sorts of the Holy See, even though he had never approved of the diversion of the army to the Bosphorus. His letter answering Baldwin's announcement of the victory suggests such a hope and it was in harmony with the trend in the West. Whether this supposition is true or not, once he had received the terms of the pact entered into by French and Venetians before the final assault on the city, he could no longer harbour any such hopes. The pact eliminated as far as it could papal interference in the new empire. The victors allotted territories and within them ecclesiastical administration. They set up canons of the cathedral of S. Sophia and elected a new patriarch. They appropriated all church property, allowing to the ecclesiastics – diocesan clergy and monasteries – what they judged should suffice for their needs. Innocent, of course, did not accept these conditions, but there was little he could do about it immediately and in fact the problem of church property was not satisfactorily settled within his lifetime.

A consequence was that, as he had no rights as a sovereign and since the Church, whether Latin or Greek, in the empire was on the whole without estates and poor (some dioceses could support not more than two canons), he could exercise little influence on the progress of political events. Further, most of the magnates of the empire from the emperor downwards were at loggerheads with the Holy See because of their depredations of ecclesiastical property, their refusal to pay tenths, and their forbidding of legacies for pious purposes. Moreover, they alternately supported the Greek clergy against their Latin superiors and exploited the same Greeks contrary to the protective measures taken by their Latin superiors. The princes of Athens and Achaia were frequent offenders and the utmost sanction of the Church, interdict, had to be threatened and applied in order to force amendment. The means used to achieve order in the Latin Church and obedience from the Greek Church were canonical, the application of the canons, and that, as has been noted, not harshly but with a certain moderation.

Innocent III was a canonist who had studied at Bologna under the famous Uguccio, whose teaching he followed closely.[28] One thinks that he had the canonist's mind, that is, a tendency to adhere somewhat narrowly to the law; that having established the legal principle he applied it exactly. That is what he seems to have done in his relations with the Greeks. In theory the conquest of their empire brought with it the subjection of their Church. Hence, after 1204, it was reunited with the Latin Church and under the authority of the pope. That was to be acknowledged by individuals through the oath of obedience. Once a man had taken the oath he was legally the equal of the Latins, and submissive Greek bishops 'should enjoy in their dioceses the same liberty as the Latins enjoy in theirs'.[29] Conversely, till they took the oath, they were schismatics and out of the Church of God. Hence, when the Lateran Council was convoked, Innocent summoned to it all the western bishops and many other western clerics whose reform or help was to be gained by the council. From the East he invited those who were canonically members of the Church, those who had taken the oath of obedience. Such action was canonical; it was logical; and so it was done.[30]

When in that Lateran Council of 1215 Innocent approved the fourth *capitulum* with its introductory phrase, 'The Greeks return to obedience to the Holy See,'[31] it was obvious to everybody that in fact they did not. No Greek metropolitan or archbishop had made his submission. There was a Greek patriarch in Nicaea on whom the Greeks centred their Church loyalties. Most bishops and many monks had gone either to Nicaea or to Epirus to escape from the oath. On the other hand a fair number of suffragan bishops, the great bulk of the parochial clergy and a generous proportion of monks remained within the old diocesan organisation of Greece, where now, however, all the larger dioceses had Latin incumbents. But even so, it cannot be said that the Greek clergy who remained within the empire had in their hearts abandoned their allegiance to the Greek patriarch no matter where he resided.

In view of this should Innocent have dropped the pretence that there was a union and have changed his tactics in respect of the Greeks? Perhaps one should rather ask, not 'Should Innocent have changed his tactics?', but 'Could he?'. Having once begun insisting on the oath of obedience, which for him and for the Greeks implied a point of doctrine, he could hardly have openly ceased to demand it without seeming himself to call that doctrine in question. That would have been true of any pope. It was doubly impossible for Innocent with his legal mind and legal methods. And it would not have helped. At that time just after the capture of Constantinople and the pillaging, in the knowledge of what had happened in the patriarchates of Jerusalem, Antioch and Alexandria and in Cyprus, where the Latins had latinised the Greek

Church as far as they could, and aware of the Latin encroachment on the Churches of Serbia and Bulgaria, the Greeks would not have combined with the Latins on any terms. The usurper Murtzuphlus, who deposed Isaac II and Alexius IV, opened sincere or feigned negotiations with the crusaders, which the emperor Baldwin reported to the pope. On one point he was adamant. 'But he so firmly refused the obedience to the Roman Church and the aid for the Holy Land that Alexius had guaranteed by oath and an imperial rescript, that he would prefer to lose life itself and that Greece should be ruined rather than that the Oriental Church should be made subordinate to Latin prelates'.[32] Murtzuphlus's words most probably reflected the sentiments also of the leading Greeks.

Nevertheless, fifty years later, in 1254, an emperor of Nicaea with the backing of the patriarch of Nicaea offered to Innocent III's third successor union of the Churches on conditions almost identical with those that Innocent had stipulated. The Greek Church and clergy would commemorate the pope in the liturgy, show him canonical obedience, accept him as a court of appeal, obey his decision if not against the canons, acknowledge his right to preside at general councils and accept his judgements there if not against scripture or the canons, and they would approve his verdicts in all other ecclesiastical business if not against the canons. The *Filioque* dispute, it is true, should be settled by free discussion in a general council, but at that time there was a fair prospect of agreement even on that thorny question: Nicephorus Blemmydes, whose reputation for learning brought him great respect and influence – he was selected as patriarch to succeed Manuel II in 1255 but refused the office on grounds of ill health – was then multiplying treatises to disprove 'from the Father only' in favour of 'from the Father through the Son'. There was a price, of course, set for this acquiescence: the restoration to their respective thrones in Constantinople of Emperor Vatatzes and Patriarch Manuel, with the ejection of their Latin rivals.[33] What would have been the result if these proposals had been implemented there is no knowing – whether or not the Greek Church at large would have followed the lead given by their emperor and their patriarch. What actually happened was that all the three protagonists, pope, emperor and patriarch, died in 1254. The new emperor of Nicaea, Theodore II Lascaris, finding the political situation easier, was less interested, and the negotiations though renewed came to nothing. The whole incident, however, suggests that Innocent III was less extravagant in his expectations and demands than is sometimes supposed.

The personages of the past were men as we are, with the same basic qualities, virtues and vices. They, like us, could rise to

II

heights of heroism. They, as we, could be victims to the lust for power, for riches, for pleasures of all kinds. Innocent III was a man, and a man in a position where he wielded power and could have striven, consciously or unconsciously, continually for more. Exalting the Holy See and ruling the Church, he could have been seeking his own satisfaction in the name of religion.

But the people of earlier centuries, though basically like us, were conditioned very differently. They thought largely in other categories; their scale of values was different; their outlook was simpler, more direct. Religion made a greater impact on them than it normally does on men of today. It entered into the very fabric of their lives. The Church was world-wide, supranational, divine. Faith was God-given; heresy the greatest of evils. The Holy Land and Jerusalem were worth fighting for. Religion added its sanction to the daily relations of man with his fellowmen; of villeins with their lords; of lords with their feudal masters. Oaths and excommunications might for a time be lightly regarded, but in the end they usually prevailed. The one essential for every man was to ensure his eternal salvation.

Innocent was also subject to these religious influences and that to an unusually high degree because of his upbringing and training. For him the Church was indeed divine, founded by Christ, constructed hierarchically, endowed with supreme authority. That authority, though it was by no means confined to him, was conferred in its fulness on St Peter and then on his successors in the see of Rome. Innocent was such a successor. He did not have to seek authority. He possessed it. His task was to apply it to the highest good of man and the benefit of the Church as the ark of salvation. Was that his ultimate purpose and intention in his dealings with the Greeks? To judge him one must force oneself back to his day and clothe oneself with its mentality. A difficult task.

Notes

1   W. Norden, *Papsttum und Byzanz* (Berlin 1903) pp. 195–6.
2   For example A. Luchaire, *Innocent III. La question de l'Orient* (Paris 1907) pp. 235–6; H. Tillmann, *Papst Innocenz III* (Bonn 1954) p. 219, blames him for subordinating Church union to politics.
3   *PL*, CCXIV, cols 326C, 328C.
4   12 Nov. 1199, *PL*, CCXIV, col. 764C.
5   7 Feb. 1204, *PL*, CCXV, cols 260D, 262A.
6   *PL*, CCXV, cols 294CD.
7   *Acta graeca Concilii Florentini*, ed. J. Gill (Rome 1953) p. 464.
8   *Conciliorum oecumenicorum decreta*, edd. J. Alberigo, P.-P. Ioannou, C. Leonardi, P. Prodi (Freiburg im B., 2 ed. 1962) pp. 789–90.

9   Cf. Innocent III, 'Christ entrusted the Church to Peter for
    ruling, that unity might exclude division', *PL*, ccxv, col.
    512D.
10 *Constitutiones, Decreta, Declarationes* (Vatican City State 1966)
    para. 18, pp. 124–5, para. 22, p. 132.
11 He commissioned his legates to persuade the Greeks on the
    Filioque and other questions.
12 *PL*, ccxiv, cols 764C, 771B.
13 Innocent considered Constantinople Joannine because St
    John lived at Ephesus.
14 *Reg [esta Innocentii III]*, vii.154, esp. *PL*, ccxv, cols 459CD.
15 *PL*, ccxv, cols 458D.
16 Letter to Morosini of 2 Aug. 1206, *Reg*. ix.140, esp. *PL*,
    ccxv, col. 963.
17 Lateran Council, *capitulum* 9, Mansi, xxii, col. 998.
18 13 Nov. 1204, *Reg*. vii, 154.
19 20 Jan. 1205, *Reg*. vii.203 esp. *PL*, ccxv, cols 513D,
    514AD.
20 Mansi xxii, col. 989.
21 *PL*, ccxiv, col. 327A
22 *Reg*. v.229.
23 *Reg*. vii.152, *PL*, ccxv, col. 447B.
24 *Reg*. vii.154, *PL*, ccxv, cols 456A.
25 *Reg*. vii.152, *PL*, ccxv, col. 452C.
26 *Reg*. viii.133.
27 *Reg*. xi.47. A similar thought was expressed by a group of
    'Bishops, priests, deacons and other clergy and faithful of
    Constantinople', admittedly in a letter to the pope seeking
    leave to elect a patriarch for themselves (1206) : 'For our sins
    we have been given over to this Christian people by a judge-
    ment of God more kindly than just' – their misfortunes con-
    tinued without ceasing because they had not yet sincerely
    repented. A. Heisenberg, *Neue Quellen zur Geschichte des
    lateinischen Kaisertums und der Kirchenunion*. I : *Der Epitaphios
    des Nikolaos Mesarites auf seinen Bruder Johannes* (Munich
    1922) p. 63.
        Two and a half centuries later, when Mahomet the Con-
    queror reigned in the Byzantine capital, Patriarch Gen-
    nadius would believe that it was a punishment for sin. *On
    the Fall of Constantinople*, in Petit, Sidéridès, Jugie, *Œuvres
    complètes de Gennadios-Scholarios*, iv (Paris 1931) pp. 215–23.
28 Cf. M. Maccarrone, *Chiesa e Stato nella dottrina di papa Inno-
    cenzo III, Lateranum*, nova serie., an. vi.3–4 (Rome 1940).
29 *Reg*. xv.134.
30 Innocent did not propose as matter for the council the
    doctrines of the primacy and the *Filioque* : it was a practical
    council for reform and the crusade. But even if he had, it is
    most unlikely that he would have altered his mode of action
    to invite 'schismatics'.
        At Lyons in 1274, agreement (of a sort) on the Trinitarian
    doctrine was a preliminary condition for the presence of the
    Greeks. It needed the Great Schism of the West to open the
    way for a Council of Florence where there was no previous
    agreement, genuine debate and (I personally am convinced)
    a real, though short-lived, union.

31   Mansi xxii, col. 989.
32   *PL*, ccxv, col. 450A.
33   *Acta Alexandri P.P. IV (1254–1261)*, edd. T.T. Haluscynskyj and M.M. Wojnar, Pontificia commissio . . . iuris canonici orientalis, Fontes, 3 ser., iv, 11 (Città del Vaticano 1966)
no. 28, pp. 39–44.

Vatatzes had already put out a feeler in this direction when
he asked the Roman envoys to Nicaea in 1233 whether, if
the patriarch agreed to obey him, the pope would give him
back his right [to the patriarchal throne in Constantinople] –
restituet ei Dominus Papa ius suum? P.G. Golubovich, 'Disputatio Latinorum et Graecorum', in *Archivum Franciscanum
Historicum*, xii (1919) p. 445. This suggests that patriarch
Germanus, like his successor Manuel, would not have
repudiated the proposal.

W. Norden, *Das Papsttum und Byzanz* (Berlin 1903) p. 372
n. 3 and App. XII, attributes to patriarch Manuel ii a
treatise on the Holy Spirit found in Bibl. Bodl. Oxford. cod.
Barocc. 131, fols 361^v–3^v. But the *incipit* and *desinit* show that
it is identical with Blemmydes's *Oratio II ad Theodorum
Lascarin*, *PG*, cxlii, cols 565–84.

III

AN UNPUBLISHED LETTER OF GERMANUS. PATRIARCH OF CONSTANTINOPLE (1222-1240)

INTRODUCTION

In 1222 Germanus was elected in Nicaea to be Patriarch of Constantinople. He held office till 1240. He was a man vigorous in
action, learned, apostolic and a writer of merit. The rulers of Epirus
with the co-operation of the local synod had been appointing bishops
to vacant Sees of the area without reference to the Patriarch in
Nicaea. Germanus insisted that they were infringing his rights.
His demands were resisted as long as the fortunes of Epirus were
in the ascendant and there was a real breach between the Nicene
and the Epirote Churches for some time. Afterwards opposition
faded and the Patriarch sent an *apocrisiarios* who brought the
western dioceses back into obedience.

At about the same time the Greek hierarchy of Cyprus, subjected
to restrictive regulations by the Latin Church of the island, appealed
to Germanus for counsel whether to conform with them, at least
outwardly, and so to be able to live on the island and perform
their pastoral duties for their flocks, or to refuse compliance and
be exiled, leaving their faithful without the ministries of the Church.
The Patriarch allowed by 'economy' some conformity with the
impositions of the Latins, but not acceptance of obedience to the
Roman See by the ceremony of *hominium*. Six years later, moved
by complaints that reached him from Cyprus, he wrote another
letter to the island, strongly attacking the Roman Church, and
bidding the Cypriot faithful to refuse all contact with any of their
clergy who submitted to the Latins, though, as he well knew, these
were in fact the archbishop and other bishops of the island with
many of the leading ecclesiastics.

Three years later (1232), doubtless at the instigation of Emperor
Vatatzes, he wrote conciliatory letters to the Pope and the cardinals
suggesting contacts for union of the Churches. In consequence,

in 1234 there were discussions in Nicaea and Nymphaeum, when four Friars represented the Western Church. These meetings, however, did nothing to improve relations between the Churches. Shortly afterwards Germanus sent a letter to the Latin Patriarch of Constantinople, Nicholas di S. Arquato (1234-1251), on behalf of Greek priests held in confinement in Constantinople for ecclesiastical reasons. He wrote also many sermons, some tractates and poems, and the letter to the monastery of St John the Baptist in Petra, that is published here.

The monastery of St John the Baptist, the Precursor, in Petra had a long history. It was said to have been founded under the Emperor Zeno, and it survived the fall of Constantinople till c. 1578, at which time it was deserted and in ruins. R. Janin affirms that it was certainly occupied by Latins after 1204, on the strength of the statement of Bryennius (†c. 1436) that all the miracle-working sanctuaries of the capital ceased to produce miracles during the Latin occupation except for a few, among which he specifically mentions St John, the Precursor, in Petra (¹). The letter here published, however, though it records the resistance of the monks to Latin 'heresy' and speaks of their endurance of suffering, suggests rather that they were still in possession of their monastery when it was written, for its list of "Maltreatment, distress, penalty, confiscation of goods, expropriation of possessions, persecution, exile, dangers, death" reads more like rhetoric than history. Had the monks really been evicted and in exile, Germanus would have dilated on that fact in more specific and emphatic terms. Also, no reference to St John in Petra is found in papal documents of the period, though they mention various other monasteries, either because they had appealed to the Holy See for protection or because the Greek monks were being expelled in favour of Latin monks, when they persistently refused obedience to the Latin ecclesiastical authorities.

The letter itself is not dated nor does it contain any indications that might help the enquirer deduce a date for it. It is found in two manuscripts, the one in Berlin (hereafter = B), the other in

---

(1) R. JANIN, La géographie ecclés. de l'empire byz. I. Le siège de Constantinople et le patriarcat oecuménique, vol. 3. Les églises et les monastères (Paris, 1953), pp. 435-443, esp. p. 436.

Moscow (hereafter = M). M carries a title of several lines in length : "Of Germanus, patriarch etc.". B once had a title several lines in length, but it no longer has. The title has been not merely erased with a knife but obliterated by some chemical so that now the empty space of paper is discoloured brown and even with the aid of ultra-violet light hardly a letter can be faintly discerned([1]).

The item in B before our letter and the one after it are both works of Mark Eugenicus, metropolitan of Ephesus and bitter opponent of the union of Florence († 1445). So it has been presumed that this letter with no title was also from the hand of Mark, an assumption apparently confirmed by the fact that a long quotation from Mark's *Confessio fidei in Concilio Florentino conscripta* occurs in the middle of it. However, this quotation could be a deliberate interpolation designed to suggest attribution of the letter to Mark or, since the quotation covers one folio exactly — 96v and 96r — of B, it could be the result of a mistake either by the copyist of B or more likely of a prototype of B, especially as the previous item in B is precisely the *Confessio fidei* from which the quotation is taken ([2]). It is certain, however, that the handwriting of the interpolation is the same as that of the rest of the letter.

The general anti-Latin tone of the quotation harmonises with the anti-Latin character of the letter, but both at the beginning of it and at the end it is clumsily connected to its grammatical context. That suggests that it is an interpolation and not a mere quotation, a conclusion strengthened by other considerations. Interpolation in B is more likely than excision in M. Resistance to Latin heresy and strong language about persecution, exile and various other hardships threatened or experienced are more consonant with the situation in Constantinople in the third and fourth decades of the thirteenth century than they are with the fifth decade of the fifteenth. Also the fact that the quotation is precisely the length of one folio is significant. Then, the letter is positively attributed to Germanus in M, whereas in B there is a suspicious erasure, a blank and no author's name. So it seems more reasonable

(1) I owe this information to the courtesy of Dr Hans-Erich Teitge, curator of manuscripts of the *Staatsbibliothek* of Berlin, who at my request examined the page. I gladly take this opportunity to express to him my sincere thanks.
(2) Is there a corresponding lacuna in B in the text of the *Confessio*?

to conclude that the letter is from the pen of Germanus, and as such it is published here, without the quotation from Eugenicus. The manuscripts are :

Phill., 1483 in the *Deutsche Bibliothek of Berlin* ; paper ; xv, xvi centuries ; ff. 75v-79v ; written by two hands. The script of the letter is elegant ; there are few itacisms ; correct accents and breathings ; no iota subscripts. An initial letter 'rho' has a breathing only when found in the word ῥωμαῖοι in its various cases.

Moscow Library, no. 250 (according to the catalogue of Archimandrite Vladimir, I, Moscow, 1894) ; paper ; xvi century ; ff. 542r-544r. It is beautifully written with some capitals in red ; correct accents and breathings ; no iota subscripts.

1. These two MSS are interconnected for both have some strange errors in common ; e.g., συνιασμόν (for συνιδιασμόν l. 20) ; αὐληρημάτων (perhaps for αὐ<τοῦ> ληρημάτων l. 74) ; l. 108 ὑπὸ τῶν ζώων (certainly a mistake) ; ἀνειμμένως (for ἀνειμένως) l. 68 ; δυσεβῶν (for δυσσεβῶν) l. 38

2. Neither is a copy of the other.

a) B is not from M ; e.g., l. 13 M omits τιμίου ; l. 62 ἐκπορευόμενον M, ἐκπορεῦον B which is correct ; l. 74, ὠριγένους M, ὠριγένην B which is correct ; l. 114, λέγεις M, λέγω B which is correct ; l. 155, γένοιτο M, γένοιο B which is correct ; l. 155, ἐξ omits M.

b) M is not from B ; e.g., it omits the quotation from Mark Eugenicus ; l. 128 βρενοθυόντων B, βρενθυόντων M which is correct ; αὐτῶν l. 127 (written above the line to correct an omission) αυ θῶν with the ' α ' corrected to ' ε ' B, αὐτῶν ἐθνῶν M.

3. Therefore as a text B is to be preferred to M ; cf. 2 a) above.

So the text printed here is that of B without the quotation-interpolation, with the variant readings of M in an apparatus. Division into paragraphs and to a great extent the punctuation (and the iota subscripts) are mine.

Campion Hall.
Oxford.

Ὁμολογία τῆς αὐτῆς ἀληθοῦς πίστεως

Γερμάνου τοῦ ἁγιωτάτου πατριάρχου πρὸς τοὺς μοναχοὺς τοὺς
ἐν τῇ μονῇ τοῦ μεγάλου ἐνδοξοτάτου προφήτου καὶ Βαπτιστοῦ
Ἰωάννου τῆς ἐπιλεγομένης Πέτρας ὅτε οὐκ ἐπείθετο τοῖς δόγμασι
5 τῶν Λατίνων.

75v   Πατέρες μου ἅγιοι καὶ κατὰ Κύριον τέκνα καὶ ἀδελφοί, εἴη ἡ
ἁγιωσύνη ὑμῶν φυλαττομένη πάσης βλάβης, πάσης κακώσεως,
πάσης ἐπειρίας ὑψηλοτέρα, τοῦ παντοδυνάμου Θεοῦ συνέχοντος
ταύτην καὶ διακυβερνῶντος καὶ διεξάγοντος προστασίαις τοῦ
10   τιμίου Προδρόμου καὶ Βαπτιστοῦ.
Μαθόντες ἡμεῖς οἷαν ἔνστασιν κατὰ τῶν ἀθέων Λατίνων καὶ
76r || πεποιήκατε καὶ ποιεῖτε εἰς δόξαν ἀφορῶσαν Θεοῦ καὶ εἰς
μεγαλεῖον καὶ ὕψωσιν τῆς ὑπερυψήλου μονῆς τοῦ τιμίου Προδρόμου, καὶ εἰς καύχημα καὶ σεμνολόγημα τῆς ὀρθοδόξου πίστεως
15   καὶ παντὸς τοῦ τῶν μοναζόντων εὐσεβοῦς συντάγματος, εἰς δο-
ξολογίαν ἐκινήθημεν τοῦ Θεοῦ, τοῦ τοὺς τοιούτους φωστῆρας ἐν
τῷ νῦν καιρῷ ὑμᾶς ἀναδείξαντος ζηλωτὰς τῆς εὐσεβείας, τῆς
ὀρθοδοξίας προμάχους, τοῦ ψεύδους στηλιτευτάς, πάντα προελο-
μένους παθεῖν κάκωσιν, θλίψιν, ζημίαν, τῶν προσόντων ἀφαί-
20   ρεσιν, τῶν οἰκείων συνιδιασμόν, διωγμόν, ἐξορίας, κινδύνους,
θάνατον, ἤ τι καθυφεῖναι τῆς ἀληθείας ἢ ὅλως χρανθῆναι τῇ μυ-
σαρᾷ τῆς αἱρέσεως κοινωνίᾳ.
Μὴ γὰρ δὴ ἀπατάτω τις καὶ ὑμᾶς, ὦ ἱερώτατοι, ὡς μικρά τίς
ἐστιν ἡ τῶν ἀθέων Λατίνων αἵρεσις ἢ ἑνὶ ἢ δυσὶν ἢ τρισὶ σφάλ-
25   μασι τὰ τῆς αἱρέσεως αὐτῶν περιορίζεται. Οὐ μὰ τὴν σωτηρίαν
ἡμῶν, ἀδελφοί, οὐχ οὕτως ἔχει. Μή τις ὅλως ἀπατηθείς · ἀλλὰ
σχεδὸν ἡ τῶν Ἰταλῶν αἵρεσις ἀνακεφαλαίωσίς ἐστι πασῶν τῶν
αἱρέσεων τῶν μετὰ τὴν ἔνσαρκον ἐπιδημίαν τοῦ Κυρίου ἡμῶν
Ἰησοῦ Χριστοῦ κατὰ διαφόρους καιροὺς παρὰ τοῦ ἀρχηγοῦ τῆς
30   κακίας τῇ ἁγίᾳ τοῦ Θεοῦ καὶ ἀποστολικῇ ἐκκλησίᾳ ἐμβληθεισῶν,

2-5 Title obliterated in B.   4. ἐπιλεγομένης] εὐλογημένης M, an easy
misreading by a scribe. There is extant a will referring to this monastery,
of the beginning of the 14th century, headed ʽΗ διαθήκη <τοῦ> κτήτορος τῆς
ὁσίας μονῆς τοῦ τιμίου προδρόμου τῆς ἐπιλεγομένης Πέτρας (quoted by R.
Janin, op. cit., p. 436).   10 τιμίου] omit M   15 τοῦ] omit M
20 συνιδιασμόν] συνιασμόν BM   23 καί] omit B

PROFESSION OF THE SAME TRUE FAITH

Letter of Germanus, the most holy Patriarch to the monks in the monastery of the great and most renowned prophet, John the Baptist, of the place called Petra, when it was not yielding to the dogmas of the Latins.

My holy fathers and children in the Lord and brothers, may your holiness be preserved from all harm, all ill-treatment and be beyond all incident, with the support, the guidance and the execution of God Almighty at the intercession of the venerable Precursor and Baptist.

We have learnt what resistance against the godless Latins you have opposed and do oppose, a resistance that redounds to the glory of God, to the greatness and exaltation of the eminent monastery of the venerable Precursor, to the boast and pride of orthodox faith and of the whole of the religious order of monks. We were moved to offer praise to God who has manifested in our day such beacons of light as you are, zealots for right religion, champions of orthodoxy, denouncers of lies, who have deliberately elected to endure all things — maltreatment, distress, penalty, confiscation of goods, expropriation of private possessions, persecution, exile, dangers, death, rather than yield any point of the truth or be defiled by any loathsome contact with heresy.

For let no one deceive even you, most holy brethren, into thinking that the heresy of the godless Latins is of small moment or that the subjects of their heresy are confined to one or two or three errors. No, in the name of our salvation, brothers, it is not so. Let no one be deceived. The heresy of the Latins is almost the recapitulation of all the heresies that after the incarnate life on earth of Our Lord Jesus Christ have in the course of time been injected by the prince of evil into the holy and apostolic Church of God. These,

144

ἃς δὴ καὶ πολλοῖς μόχθοις καὶ κόποις οἱ ἐν διαφόροις καιροῖς
διαλάμψαντες ἁγιώτατοι πατέρες ἡμῶν καὶ διδάσκαλοι καὶ τῆς
ὀρθοδοξίας φύλακες μακρὰν ἀπ' αὐτῶν ἀπήλασαν, συνεργείᾳ τῶν
εὐσεβῶν καὶ ὀρθοδόξων βασιλέων.

35 Ἐφ' ᾧ καὶ διαπονηθεὶς ὁ τοῦ ἡμετέρου γένους πολέμιος, καιροῦ
δραξάμενος ἐπιτηδείου, πάσας αὐτὰς ἀθρόον διὰ τῶν ἀθλίων
76v Λατίνων εἰς τὴν ‖ καθ' ἡμᾶς οἰκουμένην εἰσήλασεν. Ἡ γὰρ τῶν
ἀξύμων προσαγωγὴ Ἀπολιναρίου καὶ Ἀρείου τῶν δυσσεβῶν καὶ
ἐχθρῶν τοῦ Χριστοῦ παρεισφθείρει τὴν αἵρεσιν· ἄνουν γὰρ ὁ
40 μέν, ὁ δὲ καὶ ἄψυχον ὁ Ἄρειος τὴν δεσποτικὴν ἐδόξαζε σάρκα,
τὸ πάθος τῇ θεότητι τοῦ Μονογενοῦς προσάπτων καὶ οὕτως
ἑτεροούσιον ἀποδεικνὺς τὸν ὁμοούσιον Λόγον τοῦ Πατρός, κἀν-
τεῦθεν εἰς τὴν τῶν θεοπασχιτῶν αἵρεσιν περιπίπτει, καὶ σύγχυσιν
παρεισάγει τούτῳ τὴν Εὐτυχοῦς, καὶ τὰ δύο θελήματα ἀναιρεῖ
45 καὶ τὰς δύο φυσικὰς ἐνεργείας· τὸ γὰρ ἄψυχον οὔτε θέλημα ἔχει
λογικὸν οὔτε ἐνέργειαν λογικὴν ἀλλὰ μᾶλλον κτηνώδη· τοιαύτην γοῦν οἷς αὐτοὶ πρὸς θυσίαν προφέρουσι τὴν κυριακὴν παρι-
στάνουσι σάρκα. Τὴν γὰρ προζύμην καὶ τὸ ἅλας ἀντὶ ψυχῆς καὶ
νοὸς οἱ ἅγιοι πατέρες ἡμῶν καὶ διδάσκαλοι τῆς ὀρθοδοξίας καὶ
50 τῆς ἁγίας ἐκκλησίας τοῦ Θεοῦ προστάται ἐξελάβοντο· ὧνπερ
στερουμένη ἡ ἄζυμος θυσία τῶν ἰουδαιοφρόνων Λατίνων μετὰ
τοῦ ἰουδαΐζειν καὶ ταῖς προειρημέναις αἱρέσεσι παρασκευάζει
περιπίπτειν αὐτούς.

Ποῖος δ' ἄν τις λόγος ἐπεξέλθοι; Ὅσαις πάλιν αἱρέσεσιν οἱ
55 κατάρατοι περιπίπτουσι, δογματίζοντες καὶ ἐκ τοῦ Υἱοῦ τὴν
οὐσιώδη ὕπαρξιν ἔχειν τὸ Πνεῦμα τὸ ἅγιον; Τοῦτο γὰρ δύναται
ἡ ἐκπόρευσις. Δύο γὰρ αἴτια διατοῦτο παρεισάγουσιν οἱ βδε-
λυροὶ καὶ ἀποτρόπαιοι, καὶ τὴν πρὸ τοσούτων ἀφανισθεῖσαν αἵρεσιν Μάνεντος καὶ Μαρκίωνος καὶ Σίμωνος ἀναζητεῖν καὶ παρρη-
60 σιάζεσθαι παρασκευάζουσι, καὶ τὴν Μακεδονίου δὲ πνευματο-
77v-78r μαχίαν προσαγορεύουσιν, ἔλαττον ἀποδεικνύντες τὸ Πνεῦμα ἅτε
δὴ μὴ καὶ αὐτὸ ἐκπορεῦον, ἐκπορευόμενον δὲ μόνον ‖ ‖ ἐκ τοῦ Πατρὸς καὶ τοῦ Υἱοῦ.

---

38 δυσσεβῶν] δυσεβῶν BM   40 καί] in B 3 faint letters which may be
καί : M omit   61. ἔλαττον] ἐλάττονα BM   62 ἐκπορεῦον] B ;
ἐκπορευόμενον M After μόνον B includes a long quotation from the Confessio fidei, which Mark Eugenicus, metropolitan of Ephesus, composed during the Council of Florence in 1439, edited by L. Petit in Patrologia Orientalis,
XVII (Paris, 1923), p. 436 (end) to p. 439 (beginning).

indeed, our most holy fathers, doctors and custodians of orthodoxy, who at different times have been outstanding, drove far from themselves with the co-operation of truly religious and orthodox emperors.

Whereupon the enemy of our race laboured hard and, grasping the appropriate occasion, drove them all pell-mell into our world by the agency of the miserable Latins. For the introduction of unleavened bread [in the Eucharist] infiltrates the heresy of those two impious enemies of Christ, Apollinaris and Arius. The one believed that the Lord's flesh was without a mind ; the other, Arius, that it was even without a soul for he attributed suffering to the divinity of the Only-begotten and so portrayed the consubstantial Word of the Father as of another substance, thereby falling into the heresy of the Theopaschites, introducing into him the confusion taught by Eutyches and denying the two wills and the two energies of the natures, for what has no soul has neither a rational will nor a rational energy, but an animal one. And of such sort they present the Lord's flesh in what they offer for their sacrifice. For our holy fathers and doctors of orthodoxy and protectors of the holy Church of God took the ferment and the salt as symbols of soul and mind. The unfermented sacrifice of Jewish-minded Latins, being deprived of these, makes them prone to lapse into the above-mentioned heresies together with their Judaizing.

What kind of argument would escape this conclusion? Into how many heresies do not these abominable people still fall, when they affirm that the Holy Spirit has his substantial existence also from the Son? For that is what Procession means. Shameless and ill-omened, in this way they infiltrate two causes and prepare the way to reopen in free debate the heresy of Mani, Marcion and Simon that had disappeared many long years ago, and they proclaim the Pneumatomachian error of Macedonius, for they portray the Spirit to be inferior in so far as he does not actively make to proceed but only proceeds from the Father and the Son.

Καὶ οἷς ἕπεται ἀπὸ τῆς αἱρέσεως αὐτῶν συναίρεσις τῶν δύο
65 ὑποστάσεων ἀναφαίνεται καὶ ἡμισαβέλλιος παρρησιάζεται αἵρεσις τοῦ Υἱοῦ καὶ τοῦ Πατρὸς ἀναχεομένων εἰς μίαν ὑπόστασιν,
ἵνα δῆθεν ὡς ἐξ ἑνὸς αἰτίου τὸ Πνεῦμα ἐκπορευθῇ τὸ ἅγιον. Οἷς
δὲ διιστῶσιν ἀλλήλων τὰς ὑποστάσεις καὶ ἀνειμένως πάλιν ἐνί-
στανται τὴν ἐκπόρευσιν ἐκ τοῦ Πατρὸς καὶ ἐκ τοῦ Υἱοῦ γίνεσθαι
70 τὴν τοῦ ἁγίου Πνεύματος, τὸ πρῶτον παρεισάγουσι καὶ τὸ ὕστερον καὶ τὸ μᾶλλον καὶ τὸ ἧττον · ὅπου δὲ ταῦτα, καὶ ἑτεροουσιότης
μεσολαβεῖ καὶ ἀνισότης τῆς φύσεως καὶ κατατομή.

Τὸ δὲ πουργατόριον πῦρ, ὃ αὐτοὺς καὶ μόνους διαδέξεται, οὐχὶ
τὸν Ὠριγένην εἰσάγει μετὰ τῶν αὐ<τοῦ> ληρημάτων, ὃς σὺν
75 αὐτοῖς διὰ παντὸς παρὰ πάντων τῶν εὐσεβῶν ἀναθεματίζεται ;
Τὸ δὲ κοινωνεῖν αὐτοὺς τοῖς βδελυροῖς καὶ βεβήλοις Ἀρμενίοις,
οὐχὶ καὶ μονοφυσίτας καὶ θεοπασχίτας καὶ πάσης αἱρέσεως καὶ
παντὸς ἀναθέματος κοινωνοὺς ἀπελέγχει ; Πῶς ἂν τὰ καθέκαστον
αὐτῶν ἀπαριθμήσαιμι ; Ῥάδιον ἄν τις τὴν τῆς πόλεως ἐκκαθάρῃ
80 κοπρίαν ἢ τὸ πολυμιγὲς καὶ πολυσύνθετον τῆς λατινικῆς αἱρέσεως · ὧν τὴν κακίαν ἀποστυγήσασα ἡ ἁγιωσύνη σου ἀξίως τοῦ
ἐν αὐτῇ Πνεύματος διεπράξατο.

Φησὶ γὰρ ὁ μακάριος ἀπόστολος Ἰωάννης ὁ Θεολόγος ἐν τῇ
καθολικῇ αὐτοῦ ἐπιστολῇ · « Ὅστις ἔρχεται πρὸς ὑμᾶς καὶ ταύ-
85 την οὐ φέρει τὴν διδαχὴν » τοῦ Κυρίου ἡμῶν Ἰησοῦ Χριστοῦ,
« εἰς οἰκίαν μὴ παραδέχεσθε, καὶ χαίρειν αὐτῷ μὴ εἴπητε ». Ἆρά
σοι οὐ δοκεῖ μὴ φέρειν τοὺς Λατίνους τὴν τοῦ Κυρίου ἡμῶν Ἰησοῦ
Χριστοῦ διδαχὴν ἀλλά τινος ἑτέρου ; Ἀντιχρίστου ἴσως ; Καὶ
ὅπως ἄκουε. Τοῦ Κυρίου ἡμῶν Ἰησοῦ Χριστοῦ ἀριδήλως ‖
90 τὴν ἐκπόρευσιν τοῦ ἁγίου Πνεύματος ἐκ τοῦ Πατρὸς θεολογή-
σαντος τῷ εἰπεῖν · « Ὅταν δὲ ἔλθῃ ὁ Παράκλητος τὸ Πνεῦμα τῆς ἀληθείας ὃ παρὰ τοῦ Πατρὸς ἐκπορεύεται », οἱ Λατῖνοι ἀντιφερόμενοι τῷ
Χριστῷ καὶ μὴ ἀληθεύοντα ὥσπερ ἀποδεικνύντες φασὶ <ὅτι>
τὸ Πνεῦμα τὸ ἅγιον ἐκ τοῦ Πατρὸς καὶ ἐκ τοῦ Υἱοῦ ἐκπορεύεται,
95 καὶ μᾶλλον τὴν αὐτῶν αἵρεσιν ἐπιτετευγμένην θεολογίαν εἶναι
βιάζονται ἢ τὴν τῆς ἀληθείας ἐκφαντορίαν τὴν περὶ τοῦ ἁγίου
Πνεύματος. Οὕτως εἰσὶ προδήλως μαχόμενοι τῷ Θεῷ.

Τίς ἂν οὖν κύριος ὢν λογισμοῦ, καὶ Θεῷ ζῶντι πιστεύων καὶ

68 ἀνειμένως] ἀνειμμένως ΒΜ   74 Ὠριγένην] Β ; Ὠριγένους Μ
αὐ<τοῦ> ληρημάτων] αὐληρημάτων ΒΜ   93 <ὅτι>] omit ΒΜ ;
added

Following on this, from this one heresy of theirs a companion heresy of two hypostases rears its head and the semi-Sabellian heresy is freely affirmed with the Son and the Father being fused together into one hypostasis, so that the Holy Spirit may be said to proceed from one cause. Those who separate the hypostases from each other and lightly again affirm that the Procession of the Holy Spirit is from the Father and the Son introduce first and later, and more and less. Where this is so, there intervene differences of substance, inequality of nature and excision.

Does not the fire of Purgatory, which receives them and them only, introduce Origen and his ravings, who with them is thoroughly condemned by all the faithful? Does not the fact that they are in communion with the abominable and unhallowed Armenians convict them of being Monophysites and Theopaschites and partners in every heresy and every anathema? How should I enumerate all their follies in detail? It would be easier to clear away the ordure from the city than the confusion and the complications of the Latin heresy. Your Holiness has abhorred their wickedness and done away with it in a manner worthy of the Spirit within you.

The blessed apostle John, the Theologian, says in his Catholic Epistle : "If anyone comes to you and does not bring this doctrine" of Our Lord Jesus Christ, "do not receive him into the house or give him any greeting" (1). Do you not think that the Latins do not bring the doctrine of Our Lord Jesus Christ but of someone else? Perhaps of Antichrist? Hearken to this. Though Our Lord Jesus Christ plainly taught the doctrine about the Procession of the Holy Spirit from the Father with the words : "When the Counsellor comes, the Spirit of Truth, who proceeds from the Father" (2), the Latins, opposing themselves to Christ and, as it were, exhibiting him as one who does not speak the truth, say that the Holy Spirit proceeds from the Father and the Son and are more earnest to show that their heresy is a satisfactory doctrine than that it is a revelation of the truth about the Holy Spirit. Patently, then, they are at war with God.

Who at all who is in possession of his mind, who believes in the

(1) 2 *John* I, 10.
(2) *John* XV, 26.

148

ἀληθινῷ, καὶ ἀνάστασιν νεκρῶν ἐκδεχόμενος, καὶ κρίσιν ἐλπίζων
100 καὶ ἀνταπόδοσιν, ἀνάσχοιτο ὅλως ἔχειν τι μετὰ τῶν Λατίνων; Οὕτως οἶδε Θεὸς κατὰ διαφόρους γενεὰς καὶ γενεὰς ἀνιστᾶν τοὺς ἀγα-
πῶντας αὐτὸν καὶ τῇ ἀκριβεῖ φυλακῇ τῆς εἰς αὐτὸν ὁμολογίας ἐν τῇ
τηρήσει τῶν αὐτοῦ ἐντολῶν δοξάζοντας τὸν Παντοκράτορα Κύριον, καὶ αὖθις ἀντιδοξαζομένους παρ' αὐτοῦ, καθὼς αὐτὸς ἔφησε ·
105 «Τοὺς δοξάζοντάς με δοξάσω · οἱ δὲ ἐξουθενοῦντές με ἀτιμασθή-
σονται».

Οὕτως ἀνέστησε τὸν Νῶε καθ' οὓς καιροὺς πᾶν τὸ
τῶν ἀθρώπων γένος εἰς πᾶσαν ἐξώκειλεν ἁμαρτίαν ἵνα δι' αὐτοῦ
σώσῃ <αὐτὸν μετὰ> πάντων τῶν ὑπὸ τῶν ζώων εἰδῶν καὶ
κατακρίνῃ δι' αὐτοῦ τοὺς ἐν τοῖς καιροῖς ἐκείνοις ἀποστάντας
110 Θεοῦ · οὕτως ἐν Σοδόμοις τὸν Λώτ · οὕτως ἐν Χαναναίοις τὸν
Ἀβραὰμ καὶ τὸν Ἰσαὰκ καὶ τὸν Ἰακώβ · οὕτως ἐν Αἰγυπτίοις
τὸν Μωισῆν · οὕτω τοὺς προφήτας ἐν Ἰουδαίοις · οὕτω τὸν Ἡλίαν
ἐν Ἰσραήλ · οὕτω τοὺς Μακαβαίους κατὰ τοῦ Ἀντιόχου · οὕτω
τὸν Δανιὴλ καὶ τοὺς τρεῖς παῖδας ἐν Βαβυλῶνι — τί μὴ λέγω
79r 115 τοὺς ἐγγὺς καὶ γνωρίμους ‖ ἡμῖν — οὕτω τοὺς προπάτορας ἡμῶν
τοὺς μακαρίους ἐκείνους ἄνδρας, τοὺς τῆς ἄνω μητροπόλεως
οἰκήτορας, τοὺς δεξιοὺς παραστάτας Θεοῦ · οὕτω καὶ ὑμᾶς τοὺς
Πετρηνοὺς μοναχούς, τοὺς ζηλωτὰς καὶ καθηγεμόνας ἡμῶν οἳ
διὰ πίστεως καὶ τοῦ μὴ ὑποκύψαι ὅλως τοῖς αἱρετικοῖς Ἰταλοῖς
120 κατηγωνίσαντο ταύτας τὰς βασιλικὰς βασιλείας. «Ἐπέτυχον
ἐπαγγελιῶν ὧν ἐπηγγείλατο ὁ Θεὸς τοῖς ἀγαπῶσιν αὐτόν» ·
«ἔφραξαν στόματα λεόντων», τῶν ἀθέσμων ἐκείνων καὶ παρανόμων
φατριαρχῶν καὶ καρδηναλίων · «ἔσβεσαν δύναμιν πυρός», τὴν
ἀκάθεκτον ὀργὴν τῆς λατινικῆς μανίας · «ἔφυγον στόματα μα-
125 χαίρας», οὐδὲ γὰρ παρεχώρησεν ὁ ἀγαθὸς Θεὸς οὐδένα ἐξ αὐτῶν
ἀδικηθῆναι · «ἐνεδυναμώθησαν ἀπὸ ἀσθενείας», εὐτελεῖς γὰρ ὄντες
τὸ φαινόμενον καὶ ἀνίσχυροι καὶ ἀδύνατοι περιεγένοντο τῶν
γιγαντιαίων ἐκείνων, τῶν κατοφρυόντων, τῶν βρενθυόντων, τῶν
τὰ μεγάλα φυσώντων · εἶχον γὰρ τὸν ἐνδυναμοῦντα αὐτούς, τὸν
130 ἐνισχύοντα, τὸν ἀντιλαμβανόμενον, τὸν τρέποντα τοὺς ἀλλοφύ-

---

108 <αὐτὸν μετὰ> or something similar seems to be needed : τῶν ὑπὸ τῶν
ζώων εἰδῶν] seems to need amendment — perhaps ὑπάτων and εἴδη.
114 λέγω] B ; λέγεις M   123 καρδηναλίων] καδηναλίων BM.   128 βρεν-
θυόντων] M ; βρενοθυόντων B

living and true God, who is awaiting the resurrection of the dead and sets his hope in judgement and retribution, would bear to have anything to do with the Latins? Thus God knows how to raise up from generation to generation those who love him and who glorify the Almighty Lord by the perfect custody of their confession in him in the observance of his commandments and who are being glorified in their turn by him, just as he said : "Those who honour me I will honour, and those who despise me shall be lightly esteemed" (1). So, in the days when the whole race of men had suffered shipwreck on all kinds of sins he raised up Noe so that he might save him with all the kinds of animals and through him condemn such as at that time had withdrawn themselves from God. So he dealt with Lot among the Sodomites. So, with Abraham, Isaac and Jacob among the Canaanites. So, with Moses amidst the Egyptians. So, with the prophets among the Jews. So, with Elias in Israel. So, with the Maccabees against Antiochus. So, with Daniel and the three youths in Babylon. But why should I not mention those near and known to us? So he dealt with our forefathers, those blessed men, dwellers in the heavenly city, who stand at the right hand of God ; so with you too, monks of the Petrine monastery, zealots and guides for us, who by faith and unyielding opposition to the heretical Italians have conquered these royal realms. "They received the promises which God had promised to those who love him" (2) ; "they stopped the mouths of lions" (3), of those lawless and licentious leaders of factions (4) and cardinals ; "they quenched raging fire" (5), the unrestrained anger of Latin madness ; "they escaped the edge of the sword"(6), for the good God let no one of them suffer injustice ; "they won strength out of weakness"(7), for though seemingly without position and strength and power, they overcame those men of might, supercilious, swaggerers, boasters, for they had a helper who gave them power and strength and assistance, who defeated those aliens and

---

(1) 1 *Sam.*, X, 30.

(2) *Jas.*, I, 12.

(3) *Heb.*, XI, 33.

(4) Writing φατριαρχῶν (which has an alternative spelling φρατριαρχῶν) was Germanus alluding to the Frati, Franciscans and Dominicans, who at that time were beginning their missionary activity in the East?

(5) *Heb.*, XI, 34.

(6) *Ibid.*

(7) *Ibid.*

λους, τὸν συμποδίζοντα, τὸν τὰς βουλὰς αὐτῶν ἀποδεικνύντα
κενάς · «παρεμβολὰς ἔκλιναν ἀλλοτρίων» κατὰ τῶν Λατίνων
διαφόρως προσβάλλοντες αὐτοῖς πολλοῖς καὶ ποικίλοις συστή-
μασι. Τοῦτο δὴ τῶν ἀρίστων στρατηγῶν, τῶν περιωνύμων τα-
135 ξιαρχῶν, τῶν ἀκαταμαχήτων πολεμιστῶν.
Ἔνθεν τοι καὶ ὑμεῖς τὴν αὐτὴν ἐκείνοις οἰκοῦντες καταμονήν,
τὸν αὐτὸν ἐκείνοις εὐτυχοῦντες προστάτην κατὰ τῶν αὐτῶν ἐθνῶν καὶ ὑπὲρ τῶν αὐτῶν δογμάτων, καὶ νῦν ὑμῖν ὁ ἀγών. Διὸ
79v   καὶ ἀξίως πάντως ‖ καὶ τοῦ Θεοῦ καὶ τοῦ τιμίου Προδρόμου
140 καὶ τῶν ἁγίων ἐκείνων καὶ ἠγωνίσασθε καὶ ἀγωνίζεσθε καὶ
ἔτι ἀγωνιεῖσθε τελεώτερόν τε καὶ ὑψηλότερον ὡς ἂν καὶ τῆς
αὐτῆς ἐκείνοις δόξης καὶ τῶν ἀκηράτων ἀξιωθῆτε στεφάνων
καὶ σὺν τοῖς ἀπ᾽ αἰῶνος ἁγίοις κληρονόμοι γένησθε τῶν αἰώνων ἀγαθῶν, « ὧν ἡτοίμασεν ὁ Θεὸς τοῖς ἀγαπῶσιν αὐτὸν » καὶ
145 ὑμῖν τοῖς ὑπὲρ αὐτοῦ καὶ δι᾽ αὐτὸν προθυμουμένοις ἀποθα-
νεῖν · ὧν αἱ θεῖαι καὶ ἱεραὶ εὐχαὶ γένοιντο καὶ ἡμῖν τοῖς εὐτε-
λέσι καὶ ἐλαχίστοις εἰς ἀντίληψιν καὶ βοήθειαν καὶ παντὸς κακοῦ
ἀποβίωσιν.
Διό, θεσπέσιε πάτερ καὶ τῆς ἱερᾶς κιβωτοῦ τῆς θεοδμήτου
150 τοῦ Προδρόμου μονῆς ἄναξ, μετὰ τοῦ τοιούτου κατορθώματος
ἀσφαλίζου καὶ τοὺς ἐνοικοῦντας αὐτοῦ ταῖς ἱεραῖς σου διδασκαλίαις καί, τοῦ Θεοῦ συνεργοῦντος καὶ τοῦ τιμίου Προδρόμου
συναντιλαμβανομένου, δυνηθείης ἂν καὶ τοὺς θηριώδεις καὶ κτη-
νώδεις τῷ χρόνῳ μεταβαλεῖν καὶ εἰς ἀνθρωπίνην γνώμην ἐνα-
155 γαγεῖν, καὶ οὕτω γένοιο στόμα Θεοῦ ὡς ἐξ ἀναξίων τοὺς ἀξίους
ἐξαγαγὼν « καλύψεις πλῆθος ἁμαρτιῶν » ὡς τοὺς τὴν « πρὸς θάνατον ἁμαρτάνοντας ἁμαρτίαν » ταῖς ἱεραῖς ἀποθήκαις ἐκεῖθεν
ἐφελκυσάμενος καὶ πρὸς πόας ζωοπαρόχους μεταγαγὼν καὶ πρὸς
160 ὕδωρ ἐπάγων τῶν τοῦ σωτηρίου πηγῶν, οὗ γένοιτο πάντας ἐμ-
φορηθῆναι ταῖς πρεσβείαις τῆς πανυπεραγίου Θεομήτορος, τοῦ
τιμίου ἐνδόξου προφήτου Προδρόμου καὶ Βαπτιστοῦ Ἰωάννου
καὶ πάντων τῶν ἁγίων. Ἀμήν.

133 προσβάλλοντες] προσβάλλοντα BM   137-138 ἐθνῶν] M ; αὐτῶν (inserted above line as correction of an omission) αὐ θῶν with ‛α᾽ corrected to
‛ε᾽ in B.   153 δυνηθείης] δυνηθείς BM   155 γένοιο] B ; γένοιτο M
ἐξ] om. M.

bound them hand and foot and showed up the emptiness of their plans ; "they put foreign armies to flight" (¹) against the Latins in diverse ways assailing them with many and varied schemes. This, indeed, is the art of the best generals, of famous commanders, of invincible warriors.

You also, then, who dwell in the same habitation as they, who rejoice in the same protector as they against the same nations and for the same doctrines — yours now is the contest. So, in a manner fully worthy of God, of the venerable Precursor and of those saints, you have contended, you do contend and you will still contend more thoroughly and proudly that you may merit the same glory as they and their unsullied crowns, and with the saints of yore be heirs of the eternal benefits "which God has prepared for them that love him"(²)and for you also who are ready to die for him and on his account. May their divine and holy prayers be for you, men held in no account and in least esteem, a support, a help and an end of all evil.

Therefore, Father, oracle of God and lord of the holy cell of the God-founded monastery of the Precursor, with the encouragement of so great a success strengthen by your holy counsels those who dwell therein, and, if God should co-operate and the venerable Precursor lend his aid, you would be able to change with time those savage and animal-like men and bring them to a human disposition and you would thus become the mouth of God and, as having brought forth worthy men from unworthy, you "will cover a multitude of sins" (³), in so far as you will have drawn those "who are sinning a sin unto death" (⁴) thence to holy abodes and have conducted them to life-giving pastures and be leading them to the water of the springs of salvation, where may it be possible for them to take their fill by the intercession of the all-holy Mother of God, of the venerable glorious prophet and Precursor, John the Baptist, and all the saints. Amen.

(1) *Ibid.*
(2) 1 *Cor.*, II, 9.
(3) 1 *Pet.*, IV, 8.
(4) 1 *John*, V, 16.

IV

THE TRIBULATIONS OF THE GREEK CHURCH IN CYPRUS
1196 - c. 1280[1]

In 1191 Richard Lionheart on his way to the Holy Land took the island of Cyprus. He sold it first to the Templars and then to Guy de Lusignan (1192). Guy died in 1194 and was succeeded by Aimery, who asked for and in 1197 was given a crown by Henry VI. Having founded a Latin kingdom in Cyprus, he next wished to give an organisation to its Latin Church. Christianity on the island traced its origins to St Barnabas, the companion of St Paul, and from time immemorial had formed an autocephalous Church of oriental rite. At the end of the twelfth century it had thirteen suffragan dioceses under the metropolitan See of Famagusta. The population of the island was very mixed but predominantly Greek with, already before the conquest of the English king, a fair sprinkling of Latin faithful and institutions, the fringes of the western crusaders. When Guy acquired the island, he gave the land generously as fiefs to Frankish knights who, loyal to him, would secure it against his enemies. It was for this growing Latin element in the island that Aimery was intent on establishing an ordered Church. In answer to his request Pope Celestine III in 1196 made Nicosia a metropolitan church with suffragan dioceses at Limassol, Paphos and Famagusta. These the king offered to maintain with a monthly grant, but Celestine insisted

[1] Cf. M.L. de Mas Latrie, *Histoire de l'île de Chypre sous le règne des princes de la maison de Lusignan,* 3 vols. (Paris, 1855-91), Vol. I = narrative; vols. II and III = documents. J. Hackett, *A History of the Orthodox Church of Cyprus* (London, 1901). G. Hill, *A History of Cyprus* vol. II and chap. XVI of vol. III (Cambridge, 1948), greatly dependent on Hackett for its Church history. E.C. Furber, 'The kingdom of Cyprus 1191-1291', in *A History of the Crusades[2],* vol. II, edd. R.L. Wolff and H.W. Hazard (Madison, 1969). H.J. Magoulias, 'A Study in Roman Catholic and Greek Orthodox Relations on the Island of Cyprus between the Years A.D. 1196 and 1360' in *Greek Orthodox Theological Review,* 10 (1964), pp. 75-106.

on their having from the start independent provision. In the words of the chronicler Makhairas, he replied: "My fair son, those who receive a monthly wage are at the will of those who pay them their wage, and when he wishes to dismiss them, their bread is in his hand, and the servant will be in a stress and will come off ill"[2]. So the king and the pope gave villages of various values to establish the benefices for the dioceses and their officials[3].

Meanwhile the Greek bishops were not dispossessed but remained in their Sees. The Greek archbishop at the time of the establishment of the Latin hierarchy was Sophronius, who died c. 1203. When no successor was appointed by the Emperor of Constantinople — it needs very little imagination to understand why[4] — and time was passing, the Greek bishops sought the approval of King Aimery († 1 April 1205) and proceeded to elect as archbishop Isaias, archbishop of Lydda, then in Cyprus, a refugee from his See at that time in the hands of the Saracens. He carried on the administration of the Church and consecrated bishops for vacant dioceses. But, afraid perhaps that his position was uncanonical, he submitted his case to the Patriarch of Constantinople (in Nicaea), who with his synod, on 4 June 1209 declared his election and his subsequent acts valid[5]. Information about the Greek Church in Cyprus for the next decade is lacking, which argues that nothing especially untoward disturbed its regular administration.

In the Latin Church of the island things were less stable. More and more churches and chapels were built for the convenience of the Latin faithful whose numbers grew, whereas many Greeks, especially landowners, had left the island since its conquest by the Westerners. Carmelites, Premonstratensians, Benedictines and other Orders founded monasteries. The archidiocese of Nicosia was

---

[2] Leontios Makhairas, *Recital concerning the Sweet Land of Cyprus entitled "Chronicle"*, ed. and trans. R.M. Dawkins (Oxford, 1932), p. 27.

[3] J.L. La Monte, 'A Register of the Cartulary of the Cathedral of Santa Sophia of Nicosia', in *Byzantion*, 5 (1929-30), pp. 441-522, under date 13 December 1196.

[4] The attention of the Emperors of Constantinople was completely engaged with the Latins in 1203 and later.

[5] K. Hadjipsaltis, 'The Relations of Cyprus with the Byzantine Kingdom of Nicaea' (in Greek), in *Kypriakai Spoudai*, 28 (1964), pp. 135-68, esp. pp. 135-44.

given a new cathedral begun in 1209 and finished in 1228. There was friction between the Church and the king over the election of a new archbishop in 1210, and the Latin clergy were claiming as theirs all the properties that had once belonged to the Greek Church. King Aimery's heir, Hugh, while participating in the Fifth Crusade died young (10 January 1218) and left his throne to a five-month-old boy, Henry. The young prince's mother became regent and associated with herself in office a leading baron, Philip d'Ibelin. These took the occasion of the presence on the island of the papal legate to the crusade, Cardinal Pelagius, to settle the questions outstanding between Church and State. The Bishop of Famagusta took the resulting agreement to Rome for papal approval, which was given in a document dated 17 December 1221[6].

The convention was designed to meet the demands of the Church, the barons and to some extent of the Greeks on the lines of the arrangements obtaining in the Kingdom of Jerusalem. The lay powers were to pay tithes on all revenues to the Latin hierarchy. The crown remitted certain taxes to the *rustici* of the archbishop and bishops of Cyprus. Greek priests and deacons were to be free from poll-tax and forced labour, but should give canonical obedience to the Latin bishop of their area. As the number of Greek priests and deacons in the island was very large, the barons' rights were safeguarded by insisting that they remain in their own villages, that candidates for ordination needed permission from their lay lord and that anyone ordained surreptitiously should not enjoy clerical immunities. Greek priests and deacons ordained with their lord's permission could be moved from place to place by the bishop, but without their sons and daughters, and they should be replaced by a 'good countryman'. At the election of abbots in monasteries the lay lord should have right of canonical assent and the election should be confirmed by the local Latin Ordinary. Abbots were in all things to be obedient to their Latin bishops and should not be moved without his consent. The churches and abbeys of the Greeks should be left in

---

[6] To Queen Alice, *Acta Honorii III (1216-1227) et Gregorii IX (1227-1241)* (= Pontificia Commissio ad Redigendum Codicem Iuris Canonici Orientalis, Fontes, Series III, vol. III), ed. A.L. Tautu (Città del Vaticano, 1950), n. 85. A similar letter was sent to the Latin hierarchy, (P. Pressutti, *Regesta Honorii papae III*, 2 vols. (Rome, 1888-95) n. 3628).

undisturbed possession of whatever properties they had acquired by permission or gift of the Latin lords after the Latin domination.[7]

The Bishop of Famagusta had, it seems, been commissioned by Queen Alice to induce the Pope to leave within the Latin dioceses (which, of course, territorially covered the whole of Cyprus) the Greek bishops, functioning as bishops, though they would not yield obedience to the Latin Church. Honorius, despite his desire "to cherish and honour Greeks who return to the obedience of the Apostolic See by upholding as far as, with God, We can, the customs and rites of those Greeks", could not fall in with her request as being also against a canon of the late Lateran Council, forbidding two independent bishops in any one See — a monster with two heads. Indeed he commissioned the Patriarch of Jerusalem to go with two archbishops to Cyprus and examine the situation. He told them that he had been informed that a Greek archbishop and some Greek bishops without any apostolic warrant, or consent of the local Latin hierarchy, had been established there; they paid obedience neither to the Roman Church nor to the prelates there and, "what was worse, continued the former errors of the Greeks, granting permission to people separated on account of fornication to contract new marriages and secretly, since they dared not do it openly, repeating sacraments conferred by Latin priests and bishops". In virtue of the canon of the council and because their action could lead to the loss of Cyprus to the Roman Church and even to the Latin power, the commissioners were to eject the Greek bishops as intruders and not to allow them for the future to remain with any function of authority *(velut praesides ullatenus commorari)*. Greek abbots and other clerics should render canonical obedience to the Latin prelates. The recalcitrant should be constrained to obey by ecclesiastical censures.[8] A few weeks later the same commissaries were bidden to bring certain dissident Syrians, Jacobites and Nestorians into obedience.[9]

The agreement about tithes and the rest did not put an end to the tensions even between the Latin Church in Cyprus and the Latin

[7] J.L. La Monte, *Art. cit.*, under date, October 1222; J. Hackett, *Op. cit.*, p. 81.

[8] 3 January 1222, Tautu, *Honorius*, n. 87.

[9] January 1222, Tautu, *Honorius*, n. 88.

barons. Owing probably to representations from the Latin hierarchy of the island, on 8 March 1222 the Pope wrote to the Queen and the barons insisting that all properties that had previously belonged to the Greek Church pertained by right to the Latin clergy.[10] In consequence, when Pelagius was in Cyprus on his return from Egypt, a meeting of the political and ecclesiastical authorities was held in Famagusta in the late summer of 1222 with him, a Knight Templar and a Knight Hospitaller as assessors. They issued a new form of agreement acceptable to both sides. It was very little different from the old convention of two years before. It stressed a little more the position of the Latin hierarchy — a Greek candidate for ordination needed previous permission from his Latin Ordinary, and a Greek bishop ordaining in Cyprus without leave of the local Latin bishop and of the lay lord should be suspended from ordaining. It also added two important new clauses. Presumably because the monasteries were becoming a refuge of many who wanted to avoid labour-service to their lords, it was decreed that a delegate of the Latin bishops together with a baillie appointed by the crown should assess how many monks each monastery should reasonably have and this number should not be exceeded. Finally, the number of Greek bishops was reduced to four (that is, equal to the number of the Latin); they should be obedient to the Latin bishops "according to the custom of the Kingdom of Jerusalem" and should reside in specified small towns on the periphery of the Latin Sees.[11]

Even this new agreement did not produce harmony, for the barons, in opposition to the Queen, were averse to paying tithes to the Church. To encourage her, Queen Alice was the recipient of two letters from the Pope exhorting her to observe the pact and not to be put off by difficulties.[12] In fact the payment of tithes had caused a serious rift between the two regents, Philip d'Ibelin refusing flatly to

[10] La Monte, *Art. cit.*, under date 8 March 1222.

[11] The document is dated 14 September 1222. If Honorius had by his action of 3 January 1222 intended to banish all Greek bishops from Cyprus, this agreement was a compromise solution. At any rate, he confirmed it on 21 January 1223 in letters to Queen Alice and the Latin hierarchy (Tautu, *Honorius*, n. 108; La Monte, *Art. cit.*, under date 14 September 1222; Pressutti, *Op. cit.*, n. 4212).

[12] 10 May 1224, 5 March 1225, Pressutti, *Op. cit.*, nn. 4998, 5361.

pay them.[13] Alice fled to Syria and married Bohemond of Tripoli in 1225.

The reduction of the number of Greek dioceses was effected and the Latin bishops insisted on obedience from the Greek clergy. Archbishop Neophytus refused to ask for confirmation of his election and was banished from the kingdom. Thereupon the Bishop of Soli and the Abbot of Apsinthi (both named Leontius) in the name of the Cypriot Church went to ask the Patriarch of Nicaea how they should act. The Latin archbishop, they said, demanded obedience as a prerequisite for ministering to the flock. That would imply promising obedience in the archbishop's hands, that Greek bishops and abbots must give notice to the Latin Ordinary before entering into office, and that there would be right of appeal for Greeks to the Latin archbishop from the judgements of Greek ecclesiastical courts. If they obeyed the Latin injunctions, they would seem to be unfaithful to their own Church; if they did not, their flocks would soon be without pastors. The first decision of the Patriarch with his synod was that none of these demands was against the faith and that all could by 'economy' or rather 'pretence' be complied with without blame. A turbulent crowd of exiles from Constantinople then intervened shouting that such action would play into Latin hands. Whereupon the synod modified its first decision. Approval was not given for the act of *hominium,* but the notice of election and the right of appeal were assessed as morally 'indifferent' and in the circumstances excusable.[14]

Archbishop Neophytus in the course of the journeys of his exile went also to Nicaea. There he received from Emperor Vatatzes official nomination as head of the Church of Cyprus. He then

---

[13] While the tithes still belonged to the Greeks, Philip d'Ibelin had commuted those due from his estates for a lump sum. The change over to the Latins made him liable again; Cf. Hackett, *Op. cit.,* p. 86.

[14] 'Indeed where there is implicated no abandonment of the canons, tradition, rites, the very faith, if adroitly and with no offence to the Church of Christ the Cypriot bishops can carry on and, by seeming to submit, to uphold the churches which in truth are collapsing and save them from the soul-destroying pressure that hangs over them, I think that such economy, or rather such pretence, can be pardoned and, with St Paul on their side, they should be deemed blameless' (*MPG,* 140 601-613, esp. 608D-609A).

returned to his archdiocese and, presumably with the Emperor's approval (and, as he mistakenly thought, with that also of the Patriarch and the synod), there he and his bishops did all that was necessary to comply, at least externally, with Latin regulations in their regard. Letters of complaint from some of their faithful reached the Patriarch in Nicaea.[15] Incensed, in 1229 he directed an encyclical letter to the Cypriots censuring, though without mentioning specific names, Neophytus and the clergy that had conformed.

The greater part of this forceful letter was an attack on Rome and its pretensions — Rome wanted to make the five patriarchates into one: its greatest act of effrontery had been to add to the Creed: modern popes, therefore, had broken continuity with the popes of the seven councils, innovating new dogmas and canons: it was, therefore, an enormity to obey the Roman See of the day. He enjoined on all the laity of Cyprus to boycott priests who had accepted obedience to Rome; they should not frequent their churches or accept their blessing — indeed it was far better to pray at home than in their churches. If any priest had yielded, before he was let into their church, he should declare before the Latin archbishop and bishops: "It shall not be so; but let the synodal excommunication be enforced", and he should have recourse to the synod and Patriarch in Nicaea. Clergy who wish to abide in the Church must not yield obedience to bishops who have submitted to Rome. These are a scandal to the Church. There is nothing the faithful should not endure to preserve their faith.[16]

Not content with one letter, Patriarch Germanus kept sending orders and advice to people in the island. Finally Neophytus appealed to Vatatzes to intervene. He complained that, though Cyprus was autocephalous and outside patriarchal jurisdiction, yet Germanus was leaving no one in peace. He claimed that Patriarch and synod had consented to his gesture of corporal submission, done so as to keep together the Church and the numerous inhabitants of Cyprus. He had been accused, he wrote, of responsibility for the deaths of the thirteen martyrs condemned for their faith to be burnt,

[15] K. Hadjipsaltis, 'The Church of Cyprus and the Oecumenical Patriarchate in Nicaea' (in Greek), in *Kypriakai Spoudai,* 15 (1951) pp. 63-82, esp. 75-77.

[16] MPG, 140 613-21.

a charge he rebutted, for they had brought the death penalty on themselves for their insulting language about Latin doctrines in the course of their trial. He ended by asking Vatatzes whether he should leave the island or stay.[17] Actually, he stayed for nearly twenty years more.

The thirteen martyrs mentioned by Neophytus were referred to also by Patriarch Germanus in the letter he sent to Pope Gregory in 1232. This letter was very different from his missive to Cyprus of a few years previously, for it was an invitation to the Latin Church to conversations for unity. But in it he told the Pope that one thing had so far been lacking to the obstacles set by the Latins to the worship of God by the Greeks — martyrdom — and that had come in the island of Cyprus. Thirteen monks had endured imprisonment, maltreatment and finally the stake, and so entered into their heavenly repose.[18]

The Roman Church was particularly sensitive ᴐ the Greek condemnation of the Eucharist in unleavened bread, especially as it did not reject the eastern practice of using leavened bread. The insulting language that, according to Neophytus, was the cause of the condemnation of the Cypriot martyrs was, in the *Relation* published by Sathas,[19] in reference to the Latin Mass. In Nymphaeum, where as a result of the initiative of Patriarch Germanus theological conversations were held in 1233, the Greek synod formally denied

---

[17] Hadjipsaltis, The Church of Cyprus', pp. 75-82.

[18] Tautu, *Honorius*, n. 179a, esp. p. 246

[19] 'An Account of the Thirteen Holy Fathers executed at the Stake by the Latins on the Island of Cyprus in the Year 6739' (=1231) (in Greek), ed. K. Sathas in *Mesaionike Bibliotheke* II (Venice, 1873), pp. 20-39. This account was written long after the event and is inaccurate. A letter of Pope Gregory IX to the Archbishop of Nicosia, dated 5 March 1231: (After treating of a marriage scandal) 'Adjecisti preterea de quibusdam monachis grecis, qui, male de fide catholica sentientes, publice protestantur non esse in altari nostro Eucharistie sacramentum, nec de azimo sed de fermentato potius debere confici corpus Christi, alia plura enormia que errorem sapiunt manifestum publice proponendo; propter quod illos usque ad beneplacitum nostrum carceri deputasti, et diligenter a te moniti nolunt ab errore hujusmodi resilire absque sui consilio patriarche... contra predictos monachos sicut contra hereticos processurus, nullis litteris veritati et justicie prejudicantibus a sede apostolica perpetratis' (Mas Latrie, III, p. 629).

validity to the Latin Eucharist. There must have been, too, other occasions of friction about it in subsequent years, for in 1238 Pope Gregory IX directed the (Latin) Patriarchs of Antioch and Jerusalem and the Archbishop of Nicosia not to allow any Greek priest in the dioceses subject to them "to celebrate at all unless first he had sworn in the presence of his subjects obedience to the Roman Church and had abjured every heresy and especially that by which they falsely say that Latins by reason of celebrating with unleavened bread are heretics".[20]

The sequence in Cyprus is recorded in another papal letter addressed two years later to the Archbishop of Nicosia, repeating information received from him. Archbishop Eustorgius had called the Greek archbishop and bishops together and had informed them of the instructions he had received. These raised various objections to complying with the papal directive and, when they failed to move the Latin archbishop, they persuaded him to give them a few days' grace to consider their action. Before, however, the time was up, "with the abbots, monks and the more important priests, they stripped the monasteries and churches where they lived of all their goods and secretly left the province and have gone, it is said, to Armenia, threatening with a sentence of excommunication the rest of the abbots, monks and Greek priests who are left in the province, if they should obey the apostolic order". Gregory tells Eustorgius to expel any who refuse compliance and to fill the derelict churches with Latin priests or other suitable persons, and to make his excommunication of the recalcitrant Greeks and their abettors effective, if necessary, with the aid of the secular arm.[21]

A letter of King Henry of Cyprus to Emperor Vatatzes discloses that Neophytus with his bishops had again gone to the imperial court in Nicaea, where they were benevolently received. Vatatzes had written to the Cypriot King on their behalf and Neophytus also sent a

---

[20] 19 March 1238, Tautu, *Honorius*, n. 230. La Monte, *Cartulary*, nn. 28 (LXIX) and 48 (LXXI) wrongly interprets the documents to make the Latins try to force the Greeks to use unleavened bread in the Liturgy. The Latins always allowed the use of leavened bread: they resented the rejection of the use of unleavened bread by the Greeks.

[21] 13 April 1240, Tautu, *Honorius*, n. 262.

82

letter by a priest Constantine, who viva voce gave an account of the situation of the Greek exiles and of the Emperor's kindness.[22] But the departure of Neophytus and other prelates from the island did not mean that all was then tranquil in the Greek Church of Cyprus. It is true that Innocent IV, as almost the first act of his reign, on 14 July 1243 took under papal protection a Cypriot monastery that asked for that privilege and declared it exempt from the dime on what it had possessed before the Lateran Council of 1215.[23] But a few years afterwards (23 July 1246) he had to strengthen the hand of the Archbishop of Nicosia to deal firmly with turbulent monasteries that would neither themselves obey nor let others obey the established regulations.[24] That was Innocent, the canon-lawyer, in action. But he was not always the rigorous canon-lawyer. A mellowing, indeed almost a reversal of legalist policy, was discernible in Innocent's relations with Christians of oriental rite in the East, especially those of Cyprus. On 7 July 1246 he appointed Fra Lawrence, a Franciscan, "Our penitentiary", to be his legate and an "angel of peace" in Armenia, Iconium, Turkey, Greece and the kingdom of Babylon, and over all Greeks, as well as Jacobites, Maronites and Nestorians, in Asia Minor, in the patriarchates of Antioch and Jerusalem, and in the kingdom of Cyprus. He was to protect the "Greeks of those parts by whatsoever name they go", not to allow them to be harassed, to redress injuries inflicted by Latins, to impose on those same Latins amendment, if necessary by the use of ecclesiastical censures.[25] He advised the Greek Patriarch of Antioch, the Catholicos of the Armenians and the Patriarch of the Maronites with their suffragans of the appointment and invited their co-operation with his legate. Lawrence interpreted his commission too widely. He forbade the (Latin) Patriarch of Jerusalem to have any dealings at all with his Greek subjects and led these to believe that they were exempt from

---

[22] Hadjipsaltis, 'The Relations of Cyprus', pp. 65-72.

[23] *Acta Innocentii PP. IV (1243-1254)* (=Fontes, III, IV, I), edd. T.T. Haluscynskyj and M.M. Wojnar (Rome, 1962) (hereafter Wojnar, *Innocent)* 14 July 1243, n.1.

[24] Ibid., n. 30

[25] Ibid., n. 31

his patriarchal jurisdiction. Consequently he received a mild correction from the Pope[26] but not a cancellation of his faculties, for two months later a letter addressed to patriarchs, archbishops and bishops "in eastern parts" insisted that all censures imposed by the legate on both Latins and Greeks — except on prelates — were to be strictly observed and upheld.[27] A few days later Innocent fanned the flame of Fra Lawrence's zeal. He was to be particularly earnest in trying to win to devotion to the Holy See the Greek Patriarch of Antioch and his suffragans.[28] The Friar was also told to correct on the spot cases of minor and obvious injustice suffered by orientals at the hands of Latins, but to refer to the Pope issues of major importance.[29]

No more letters addressed to Brother Lawrence as legate are to be found in the papal registers. It seems, then, that his commission lapsed after 1247. But the Pope had not let the idea drop or changed his policy. On 22 June of the next year he appointed the Cardinal Bishop of Tusculum, Eudes de Chateauroux, as legate for the East. He informed all the relevant authorities, both ecclesiastical and secular, of the appointment as well as King Louis of France then in the East, and gave the legate ample faculties.[30] The spirit with which Chateauroux was to perform his office is decribed in the opening paragraph of a papal letter dealing with Cyprus, addressed to him. He should show to the orientals "inner bowels of paternal charity" and "a flowing breast of motherly sweetness" to win them from "the hateful schism of oriental separation". Lawrence, the letter continues, had recalled from exile the Greek archbishop of Cyprus, who with his suffragans presented himself before Eudes and made a manual profession of obedience to the Roman Church. Thereafter the Greek hierarchy of the island had sent a list of petitions directly to the Holy See, which amounted to a restitution of the situation as it had been before the making of the agreements under Cardinal

[26] 4 June 1247, Wojnar, *Innocent*, n. 35.

[27] 3 August 1247, Wojnar, *Innocent*, n. 37.

[28] 7 August 1247, Ibid., n. 39.

[29] 7 August 1247, Ibid., n. 40.

[30] Wojnar, *Innocent*, nn. 60-3.

Pelagius. They asked to have their former fourteen episcopal Sees and that these should not be subordinate to the local Latin hierarchy but directly dependent on Rome; free jurisdiction over their faithful with application of their own canon law; the payment to them of the dime on monastic revenues and on free Greeks and Syrians; traditional power over the Greek laity with right of appeal, not to Nicosia, but to the Pope or his local legate, who also as delegate should receive their profession of obedience to the Holy see; finally, that the penalties enacted by Cardinal Pelagius for disobedience to his regulations should be abolished. This proposed reversal of previous papal policy, radical though it was, Innocent did not rule out of court. He recommended it "and their other just requirements" to the earnest consideration of the legate, as the man on the spot, who should consult unbiased advisers and enact with papal authority "what you think is most to their purpose for the salvation of souls, the lasting peace of the Church and the wholesome increase of Catholic obedience".[31]

It was perhaps too much to expect that the Latin hierarchy of Cyprus would take happily to the new policy. There is extant the list of excommunications that the Latin archbishop, Hugh da Fagiano, read out publicly in "the great cemetery of the church of Nicosia on Palm Sunday of 1251" — the promulgation of excommunications commonly made each year in the West and indeed also in the East. Among other proscriptions all Greeks who had received the sacraments of confirmation and matrimony in the Roman rite were to follow the Roman law of church-going, annual confession etc., and to adhere to the Roman rite only, under pain of bann. "Those are excommunicated who say that the Roman Church is not the head of all Churches and do not obey her". Under a similar penalty were all Greek priests and deacons "who have not made and will not make the act of obedience to the Roman Church and the church of Nicosia"; also those who do not pay their dime honestly to the church of Nicosia. This fairly long list of punishable crimes sounds more hostile to the Greeks than in fact it is. It was no more than the

---

[31] 21 July 1250, Wojnar, *Innocent*, n. 74. The Archbishop who was recalled by Brother Lawrence was Neophytus.

repetition or application of the regulations enacted in 1220 and 1222.[32]

The Greek archbishop of Cyprus, Neophytus, died in 1251 and the other Greek bishops petitioned Rome for leave to elect a successor, which was granted even though the canonical interval for filling the See was past.[33] Cardinal Eudes was instructed to deal with any opposition.[34] Opposition there was from the Latin hierarchy, and Innocent bade his legate restrain the local Latin archbishop and his suffragans from harassing the Greek bishops. These elected a certain Germanus and themselves went to Rome to the Pope for confirmation of their candidate in office. But the election was judged invalid and was quashed. Innocent, however, gave them leave to re-elect either the same person or another, but this time canonically, and wrote to his legate telling him to confirm the election without more ado if it should be rightly done. To avoid unnecessary complications, he empowered the Dominican and Franciscan superiors of the area to act, in case the cardinal was absent. The Pope, canonist though he was, was riding rough-shod over canon law to satisfy and please the Greeks, as the end of his letter showed: "Notwithstanding the aforesaid election which was null, or the constitution of the council [the Fourth Lateran, forbidding two bishops in one diocese], or any contrary enactment issued, it is said, by Pelagius, Bishop of Albano of happy memory, then legate of the Apostolic See in those parts, even though they were later confirmed by the same See".[35]

Greeks and Latins facing each other in Cyprus on equal terms brought all the doubts and difficulties that Latins harboured about the Greek rite into open expression. The Latin hierarchy, it seems, had formulated their reserves, the Greeks had answered and the legate, seeking advice, had forwarded both queries and answers to

[32] Wojnar, *Innocent*, n. 78. This would be a yearly event. The Pope did the same each Maundy Thursday (e.g. Tautu, *Honorius*, n. 236); the Greeks on the Sunday of Orthodoxy.

[33] 20 December 1251, Wojnar, *Innocent*, n. 79.

[34] Same date, Ibid., n. 80.

[35] 25 February 1254, Wojnar, *Innocent*, nn. 103, 103a. The papal document gives the name of the elect as 'George'; it is probably a mistake for 'Germanus'.

the Holy See. Innocent based his decisions on a broad principle: "Indeed, many of the Greeks have been returning to devotion to the Apostolic See and pay it reverence and attentive obedience. It is, then, lawful and fitting that by allowing their customs and rite as far as with God We can, We should retain them in the obedience of the Roman Church, though We neither can nor wish to defer to them in what might occasion danger for souls or tarnish the Church's good name". On this principle he decided that at baptism unctions as used in the Roman rite should be performed, though the Greek custom of anointing most of the body (which, though apparently he did not realise it, for the Greeks constitutes the sacrament of confirmation) may be permitted as having little reference to the sacrament [of baptism]. Confirmation should be reserved to a bishop, who can consecrate his own chrism or, if he prefers, obtain it from his patriarch or metropolitan. Anointing with oil should be employed only for the sick and not used as a satisfaction for sins in the sacrament of penance. In the Eucharist the custom of putting hot water in the chalice is in order, but the sacrament for the sick should not be reserved for more than fifteen days lest the species of bread deteriorate. In the celebration of Mass, provided the form of words used by Our Lord is retained, they many follow their own custom, but not after three o'clock in the afternoon. Candidates for the priesthood should be sufficiently instructed. Altars, chalices and vestments should be suitable and clean. The Greek customs of Lenten fasting and of married priests acting as confessors should not be made into a source of difficulty. No doubt should be left that fornication between the unmarried is a grave sin. The Pope "wishes and expressly orders" that Greek bishops should confer the seven orders as in the Roman rite when they ordain, "but those who are already ordained by them in their way, owing to their very great number, may be left in their orders". Greeks do not condemn but rather approve of second and third marriages; a second marriage, however, should not be [solemnly] blessed. Marriage between parties in the Greek eighth, Latin fourth, degree of consanguinity or affinity is illicit, but such marriages already performed may be considered dispensed and valid. The Pope had been led to believe that Greek doctrine about the hereafter coincided with the Latin, but that the orientals did not employ the name 'Purgatory' for the place of temporal punishment; thinking it a patristic name, he wished them to use it.[36]

In these decisions Innocent was making no innovations. His decretal, however, is more detailed than any previous papal assessment of Greek customs and, in spite of restrictions in favour of Latin usage in points that later would not be thought fundamental, it has a tone of sympathy with the Greeks and judges many more customs as unessential and indifferent, and so permissible, than did, say, the Latin hierarchy of Cyprus. The document was to be explained to the Greek bishops of the island and they were to observe it. The Latin bishops too were to observe it in the sense that they were forbidden to bring pressure to bear on the Greeks in violation of its regulations. The Apostolic Legate had already been warned "not to allow the Greek bishops to be harried by the [Latin] archbishop and his suffragans"[37] and the admonition was repeated at the end of the decretal itself.

A few weeks before addressing to his legate this long document about Greek customs, Pope Innocent had informed him that other questions at issue between the Churches would be left temporally in abeyance pending further consideration. There is no indication what those questions were or what answers were given to them. They probably concerned the independence of the Greek Church in Cyprus from the Latin archbishop of Nicosia and its subjection directly to the Holy See, and the answers were probably favourable to the Greeks. At any rate, it seems quite certain that Germanus, after promising canonical obedience through Chateauroux, was made independent of the Latin archbishop of Nicosia; that the Latin archbishop lost jurisdiction over the Greek faithful who were subject to Germanus and so had no right to impose ecclesiastical penalties on Germanus's Greek subjects or to cancel penalties that had been imposed by him, to eject the vicar appointed by Germanus when he went to Rome to the Pope or to excommunicate the Greek archbishop himself. This appears from the complaints that Germanus made to the Holy See and the fact that the answer of

[36] 6 March 1254, Wojnar, *Innocent*, n. 105.

[37] 17 February 1254, Ibid., n. 102.

Archbishop Hugh's procurators was not to deny that the Greek had been exercising those rights but that he had been doing so invalidly and, by implication, that Pope Innocent IV had acted uncanonically in granting them.[38]

While these negotiations about Cyprus were going on Innocent IV was entering into promising relations on a larger scale with Emperor Vatatzes of Nicaea and Patriarch Manuel. It would, however, be a mistake to conclude that his benevolent attitude to Cyprus and other eastern countries was subordinated in any way to his wider aspirations. It was in 1246, that is, as soon as he had concluded the Council of Lyons and effectively checked Frederick II's challenge to the Church, that he sent Fra Lawrence to the East as his 'angel of peace'. He continued the policy of conciliation through his legate Chateauroux in 1248 and only in 1250 did his relations with Vatatzes begin, in which he showed the same spirit of accomodation as he did in the Levant. Judged by the standards of the day he was 'ecumenical' and open-minded far in advance of his contemporaries.

Unfortunately Innocent IV died on 7 December 1254, a few months after the issue of his decretal about Cyprus and before the situation there had had time to settle. His successor, Alexander IV, was perhaps not as broad-minded as he and certainly not as strong a character. When controversy over the Greek Church of the island erupted once again, he ordered a thorough enquiry, but the result was the reintroduction of the old Latin domination. The insistence of the Latin hierarchy on their status prevailed. The vision of Innocent IV was lost. It will be recalled that in the last years of his reign Innocent IV, notwithstanding the ninth canon of the Fourth Council of the Lateran (1215) and other regulations, had allowed the Greek bishops of Cyprus to re-elect as their archbishop and metropolitan Germanus, after his first election had been quashed as uncanonical, and had made him exempt from the local Latin hierarchy, subject only to the Holy See. The Latin archbishop of Nicosia, Hugh,

---

[38] *Acta Alexandri P.P. IV (1254-1261)* (= Fontes, III, IV, II) edd. T.T. Haluscynskyj and M.M. Wojnar (Rome, 1966) (hereafter Wojnar, *Alexander*), n. 46, 3 July 1260. It appears also from the fact that Pope Alexander in his crimping solution left Germanus still independent of the Archbishop of Nicosia, as will be narrated shortly.

nevertheless summoned him to appear before him to answer various charges. The Greek claimed his papal protection and did not obey. In consequence, he was excommunicated by Hugh, who subjected both him and many of his faithful to other oppressions. Germanus with his bishops went to Anagni to complain to the Pope, who certainly meant to give him a fair hearing, for he appointed the same Eudes de Chateauroux, who had been apostolic legate in Cyprus, to hear the case between the Greek archbishop and some procurators of the archbishop of Nicosia then by chance at the Curia.

The Latin plea was that Germanus's election was invalid since the bishops who elected him, being excommunicated, had no right to do so, that Pope Celestine had removed the Greek bishops from their Sees and had established a Latin archbishop with three suffragans as the official hierarchy for the whole of the island with rights to tenths etc. formerly of the Greek Church, and that the legate Pelagius had limited the number of Greek bishops to four and made them subject to the Latin bishops, an arrangement subsequently confirmed by Rome. The legal process dragged on in interminable argument, till Germanus, pleading poverty, begged the Pope to impose a settlement, "so that under obedience to the Roman Church the Greeks might live at peace with the Latins".

This, in brief, is what Alexander decreed. 1. For the future there should be only four Greek bishops and they should reside in the towns allotted to them by the legate Pelagius. 2. When a See was vacant, a successor should be elected and the Latin bishop of the area should approve the election, summon the other Greek bishops to perform the consecration, and give jurisdiction to the newly consecrated prelate when he had received from him an oath of obedience to the Holy See and to the Archbishop of Nicosia. (The formula of the oath is added.) 3. Only the Pope shall condemn, depose or translate Greek bishops. 4. The Greek bishops should have jurisdiction over their Greek institutions and faithful, and in legal actions between Greeks; but if a Latin were involved it should be decided by the Latin bishop of the region; there should be right of appeal from the Greek court to the local Latin bishop and, if necessary, thence to the Archbishop of Nicosia. 5. In any diocese there should be only one consistorium of ordinary jurisdiction for the Greeks. 6. Greek bishops and abbots with their priests should once a year attend the diocesan synod (but not the provincial one) summoned by the Latin bishop and obey its regulations, unless these clashed with their rite. The Latin bishop could make a visitation of the Greeks with rights similar to those of a metropolitan, but only 5, 4 or 3 times each year (according to diocese), and they should be entitled to a fixed stipend of 300 solidi from the Greeks. 7. If the needs of the Greeks necessitated other visitations, these should be done gratis, since the goods of the Church are given to bishops for the expenses of their pastoral office. 8. The right to tenths in the island belonged to the churches of the Latins, and all men should pay them. Though the Church of the Greeks would not in future possess a metropolitan, the existing archbishop was to retain that dignity for his lifetime, to be independent of the Latin archbishop, and to have his abode in Soli, whose present bishop would be transferred to Arsinoê. 9. Germanus should retain metropolitan rights over the Greek bishops of consecrating and making visitations, but on his death there should be no other Greek archbishop. 10. As bishop of Soli, he should take the oath of obedience to the Latin archbishop, but in practice remain exempt from his jurisdiction; over all other Greeks the Latin hierarchy has jurisdiction. 11. Appeal from the Greek archbishop shall be to the Latin archbishop. After the Greek archbishop's relinquishing of office, the Latin metropolitan making his visitation of any city or diocese shall receive once annually 60 solidi from the Greek community. The Syrians of the island are under the same obligations as the Greeks.[39]

Such was the settlement that Pope Alexander IV gave to the ecclesiastical situation in Cyprus. Apart from the exceptions made for Archbishop Germanus for as long as he retained office, it was a complete return to the regulations obtaining before Innocent IV introduced his new ideas of toleration. Innocent, it is true, was in that respect out of step with current thought in both the Latin and the Greek Churches, for in both the broader views that unexpectedly made their appearance in the negotiations of 1252-4 between Rome and Nicaea faded out with the deaths of their chief promoters. They had been very short-lived in Cyprus. Alexander's Bull sounded their knell, especially as a new piece of legislation, fruit of a local synod

[39] Ibid.

held under Raphael, archbishop of Nicosia, still further extended Latin influence over the Cypriot Church. The regulations and instructions of this 'Constitution', as it was called, are based on the legislation of Pope Celestine, the Fourth Lateran Council, the decretal that Pope Innocent had issued on 6 March 1254, and on the settlement authorised in 1260 by Alexander IV.[40]

After a preamble about the unity of the Church and variety of rite ("as the canons testify, diversity of custom within the unity of the same faith raises no difficulty"), the Constitution treats of a number of matters in twenty-seven paragraphs. These for the most part do no more than repeat the enactments found in the sources. The four Greek bishops subject to the Latin hierarchy are to teach by word and example their Greek faithful. In respect of the sacraments, the use of unctions at baptism, confirmation only by a bishop, liberty to use either leavened or unleavened bread in the Eucharist, the prohibition of reservation for the sick beyond 25 days (15 days in Innocent's regulations), a penalty against those who deny the validity of the sacrament consecrated in unleavened bread, the conferring of the three minor orders, prohibition of marriage between parties in the fourth Latin (eighth Greek) degree of relationship, Pope Innocent's remarks on Purgatory — the regulations on these are all repetitions. There is, however, introduced an added tendency to Latinisation when the Constitution treats of the preparation of the holy oils by bishops, the application of the Lateran canon imposing yearly confession, the prohibition of giving Holy Communion to sick persons who have not confessed, and the imposition of a sacramental penance in confession proportioned to the guilt of the penitent. Banns are to be called for marriage. Monks are to observe the rule of St Basil exactly, sleeping

---

[40] Wojnar, *Alexander*, n. 46a. There is no certainty when this Raphael held his synod of Nicosia, nor, apart from this document, is there evidence that he existed. Some authorities place him shortly after 1260, others between 1270 and 1280, E.C. Furber (in *Crusades* II edd. Wolff and Hazard, p. 628) as from 1278 to 1286; others later still. It is likely, however, that the Constitution was composed shortly after the last of its sources saw the light, viz. 1260. There is no mention in it of a Greek archbishop-metropolitan, and so probably Germanus had already ceased to hold office; but there is no information as to when that was.

in a common dormitory and refraining from various works. The penalty of excommunication is imposed on any who hinder the baptism of Saracens or other pagans who desire it. There is, too, a list of excommunications to be published frequently by proclamation (very like the one, recorded as having been made "in the great cemetery of the church of Nicosia" in 1251). This Constitution is to be drawn to the attention of the faithful and explained by the Greek bishops four times a year. At the end of the document there is found a paragraph that deals with the burial of Religious and bears the name of Pope Boniface VIII (1294-1303). If it is really a part of the original, the date for the whole must be brought back at least till the end of the thirteenth century. It is more likely, however, that it is a later interpolation, particularly as it seems to have no reference to Cyprus or Greeks.

It can be taken for granted that the Latin bishops did not fail to ensure that the Greek clergy and laity were regularly informed of the new ecclesiastical settlement. Poor Germanus, when he asked Pope Alexander to intervene, had hoped that "the Greeks might live at peace with the Latins under obedience to the Roman Church". What the settlement effected was a renewal of the old division between Greeks who acknowledged dependence on the Archbishop of Nicosia and those who did not. Alexander's successor, Urban IV, was constrained to reprimand the Regent of Cyprus for not supporting the Church against "Greeks and Syrians, laymen of the kingdom of Cyprus", who rendered life impossible for Greek priests and clerics who accepted Roman authority, dubbing them heretics, refusing them the accustomed contributions for their maintenance, even wrecking their houses and ravaging their vineyards, and reducing them to such a pitch of destitution that the Archbishop of Nicosia for pity's sake felt forced to take them into his own house and feed them. The Regent (who obviously sympathised rather with the recalcitrant Greeks) was admonished, under pain of penalty, to assist the Latin archbishop to make the regulations of Pope Alexander's settlement prevail.[41] The papal reproof cannot have been very

---

[41] *Acta Urbani IV, Clementis IV, Gregorii X (1261-1276)* (=Fontes, III, V, I), ed. A.L. Tautu (Città del Vaticano, 1963), n. 4, 23 January 1263.

effective for it was repeated less than a year later[42] and still again shortly before Urban's death on October 1264.[43]

[42] 13 April 1264, Raynaldus, *Annales ecclesiastici*, 1264, n. 66.

[43] Tautu, *Urban IV*, n. 14.

V

The Church union of the Council of Lyons (1274) portrayed in Greek documents

INTRODUCTION

The Manuscripts

Codex Chisianus gr. 54 in the Vatican Library and *Codex Alexandrinus gr.* 182 of the Patriarchal Library of Alexandria (¹) contain the texts of several imperial and synodical documents concerning the Second Council of Lyons, whose seventh centenary occurs in this year 1974. These documents are not unknown, for inter alia Fr V. Laurent has given lengthy résumés of them in his *Regestes* of the Patriarchate of Constantinople and has published a French translation of one of them (²). The Greek texts, however, are not yet published, yet they deserve to be because they have considerable historical importance. To honour the memory of the Council of Lyons in this centenary year they are edited here.

The two manuscripts that contain the texts are of different dates. The Vatican one is attributed by the editor of the catalogue of the Chisiani codices to the fourteenth century. Unfortunately water and other destructive elements have so damaged it that it is illegible. The titles in red have survived just a little better than the black lettering and can still be deciphered. They are enough to show that the Alexandrine manuscript, written in 1520, is connected with it, probably directly dependent on it. It has verbatim the same titles, which are not parts of the original docu-

(¹) T. D. MOSCONAS, *Κατάλογοι τῆς Πατριαρχικῆς Βιβλιοθήκης, Α'* in *Studies and Documents*, Univ. of Utah Press, 1965 = G. CHARITAKIS, *Κατάλογος τῶν χρονολογημένων κωδίκων τῆς Πατριαρχικῆς Βιβλιοθήκης Καΐρου,* in *'Επετηρὶς τῆς 'Εταιρείας τῶν Βυζαντινῶν Σπουδῶν,* 4 (1927) no. 27 (285) pp. 134-7.

(²) *Lettre inédite de Jean XI Beccos, patriarche de Constantinople (1275-1282), au Pape Grégoire X (1271-1276),* in *L'Unité de l'Eglise,* XII (1934), pp. 266-70.

ments but descriptive headings added either by the first compiler or by some copyist. The Alexandrine manuscript was finished on 7 April 1520 by the monk Jacob from Thessalonica in the town of Ostrovia within Sarmatia.

Owing, then, to the illegible state of the Vatican manuscript I have had to rely on the codex in Alexandria, photographs of which were sent to me by my kind friend, the late librarian of the Patriarchal Library, Dr Theodore Moschonas. To him I express my deepest thanks. This manuscript is in excellent condition. The letters are well formed; the words are accurately accented; the usual abbreviations are employed consistently; there are few instances of itacisms — all of which denotes that Jacob was a good copier, for his short note at the end about himself has enough mistakes in it to suggest that he was not a good grammarian.

The Documents contained in the MSS

Both manuscripts begin with tractates of George Moschabar about the Holy Spirit and a 'synodical excerpt' for the second day of Pentecost. There follow nine items on the Council of Lyons. The first purports to be the text of the oath taken by the Greek delegates to Lyons, that was sent by the *perdekatourioi* in 1275 to Syria and all Roman and Italian countries. This has been printed out in full by Charitakis in his catalogue (¹). The remaining eight in the order in which they are found in both manuscripts are:

1. A theological definition of the Filioque doctrine;
2. A letter of Beccus to the Pope;
3. A Statement in Writing (*Tomographia*) of the synod excommunicating the opponents of union;
4. A Declaration of loyalty to the Emperor by the *archontes* of the imperial palace;
5. A Declaration of acceptance of the union by the officials of the Great Church, with 41 signatures;
6. The *pittakion* of Patriarch Joseph I on the conditions of his abdication (appended to no. 5 without any special title);
7. The imperial Chrysobull about union;
8. A Statement of the hierarchy accepting the Chrysobull.

(¹) Pp. 135-6.

The Dates of the Documents

1. *Documents 2, 3, 5:*

The first problem is to establish as nearly as possible the dates of the above documents, for their order in the codex is not the true chronological order. **Doc. 3,** the *tomographia*, was composed and signed by the bishops of the synod on 19 February of the fifth indiction, i.e., 19 February 1277 — this is stated in the Document itself. **Doc. 2** is a letter accompanying a copy of the *tomographia* that was being sent to the Pope; it therefore dates from shortly after 19 February 1277. **Doc. 5** is an acceptance by the signatories of the *tomographia* and likewise dates from shortly after 19 February 1277. All these documents, then, belong to the first half of 1277.

2. *Documents 7 and 8:*

Doc. 7, the chrysobull, is another nodal document. The date of its promulgation can be decided, at least approximately, from information given by the historian Pachymeres. He relates the story of Holobolus, an early ally of the Emperor's in his project of union, who in a fit of pique at not being invited to sit at a meeting of all clerics with the Emperor, went back on his previous support of Michael's policy and, in an altercation that followed, angered Palaeologus by displaying loyalty to the son and heir of the late Emperor, the boy John, who had been blinded by Palaeologus to render him unfit to rule. For his audacity Holobolus was exiled to Nicaea. 'Within a year' he was brought back and treated ignominiously by being paraded round the streets of Constantinople in chains and with the intestines of a newly-slaughtered sheep hanging round his neck. That was on 6 October, six days after the death of the ex-Patriarch Arsenius, which occurred on 30 September. Pachymeres records the day and the month but does not specify the year. He goes on to recount the panic of the clerics who had witnessed the treatment of Holobolus, for they knew that this was meant to indicate what would happen to them unless they ceased opposing the imperial plans. They begged the Emperor to hold his hand "till the envoys should return from Rome. But though they petitioned earnestly, they did not persuade the monarch; on the contrary, they would be condemned for disloyalty to the Emperor if they did not comply in the business of their signatures. But, as some were taking refuge in flight for fear that they might be forced to further steps, the Emperor quickly had a chrysobull issued full of the most frightful curses and of the most bloodthirsty oaths that there should be no more violence, duresse or false accusations, and no suggestion of changing the Creed by one jot or tittle, or anything else except the three points of primacy, appeal and commemoration and these he asked for as bare formalities by economy; but otherwise he threatened utter destruction" (¹). It is clear, then, that the chrysobull came shortly after, and in consequence of, the punishment of Holobolus on 6 October. Pachymeres goes on to say that it had its effect. People were reassured and signed. Some who had fled returned and "are united to the Church, none of the clerics being excepted" (²).

The year in which all this happened can be deduced from the letter that the Greek envoys carried to the Council of Lyons on the part of the Church. They embarked on *Laetare* Sunday 1274, i.e., 11 March (³). The letter from the Church begins with a salutation to the Pope from 13 metropolitans with their synods, 13 metropolitans without mention of synods and 9 archbishops. It recounts at length the Emperor's efforts to bring the Greek Church to union. "Some of us agreed immediately and embraced the proposals of peace. Others were more obstinate, pondering the question over for a long time in their minds and making conditions, but the persistence of the God-crowned Emperor prevailed in the end and by now he has all in agreement to this union, by which we consent to accord to the Apostolic See of ancient Rome the primacies ascribed to it of old" (⁴). It follows, then, that the prelates "came to the same conclusion as the Emperor" (to use a phrase from doc. 8) before 11 March 1274; indeed before the end of February 1274, the date of the synodical letter to the Pope.

The date of the chrysobull can be determined even further.

(¹) G. PACHYMERES, *De Michaele Palaeologo*, ed. I. Bekker (Bonn, 1835), p. 395.

(²) *Ibid.*, pp. 395-6.

(³) B. ROBERG, *Die Union zwischen der griechischen und der lateinischen Kirche auf dem II. Konzil. von Lyon (1274)* (= Bonner Historische Forschungen 24) (Bonn, 1964) p. 229.

(⁴) *Acta Urbani IV, Clementis IV, Gregorii X (1296-1276)* (= Pontificia Commissio ad Redigendum Codicem Iuris Canonici Orientalis, Fontes, series III, vol. V, tom. 1) ed. A. L. TAUTU (Città del Vaticano, 1953), no. 42, p. 125, par. 266.

The *tomographia*, composed and signed on 17 February 1277, states: "Our Emperors lavished zeal and unremitting labour on this and we ourselves followed up and furthered their intent and, as was right, added our endeavours to theirs, for we knew that it was just and profitable especially for us to attribute to the Apostolic See the prerogatives and privileges that of old had been attached to it. For this cause, then, with God's help we brought this great and God-loved task to a successful conclusion on 24 December of the second indiction [1273], on the very eve of the devout celebrations of the Lord's birth" (1).

The bishops, then, as a body formally accepted the Emperor's unionistic policy on 24 December 1273. The occasion when they did that might have been the synod held before the issue of the chrysobull, when they had accepted union but determined to ask for a chrysobull to define its conditions and to give guarantees. In that case, **Doc. 7**, the chrysobull, must date from shortly after 24 December 1273 and **Doc. 8**, the synodal acceptance, from very soon after that. Or 24 December might have been the date of **Doc. 8** itself, in which case the chrysobull would date from a short time previously. All the sources make it quite clear that the bishops had assured the Emperor of their acceptance of papal "prerogatives and privileges" before the synodical letter addressed to Pope Gregory was composed and signed.

The phrase, however, in the long excerpt from Pachymeres quoted above, "till the envoys should return", might be said to imply that they were already in Lyons and that the events being narrated date from the autumn of 1274 and not from that of 1273. The implication could perhaps be accepted if there were not too many arguments against it. The rest of the narrative fits 1273, and this dating is supported by the fact that the bishops certainly gave their assent to union to the Emperor before they signed their letter to the Pope in February 1274; **Doc. 3** gives the precise date 24 December 1273; the *pittakion* of Patriarch Joseph, though it

---

(1) Doc. V (3). The signatories of the document of 24 December will have been the same 26 metropolitans and 9 archbishops as signed the synodical profession of faith for the Pope about two months later. Their Sees are recorded in the salutation at the beginning of that profession of faith but not their names, and the titles (but not the names) of the curial officials who signed are also in the salutation. These correspond with the titles (followed by the signatures) appended to the Statement in Writing proposed to and accepted by the officials of St Sophia in 1277.

was written before the departure of the envoys on 11 March 1274 (Joseph retired to a monastery on 11 January 1274), nevertheless contains a condition about the return of the envoys for his abdication. So one must conclude that **Docs. 7** and **8** date from late 1273 or early 1274.

3. *Documents 1, 4, 6:*

There remain three short documents without any internal indication of date. The incident of the abdication of Patriarch Joseph I (**Doc. 6**) is mentioned by Pachymeres (p. 385) after he records the departure for Lyons of the Greek legates, which took place on 11 March 1274, but without any indication of a specific date. It must, however, antedate the end of February 1274 because the 'profession of faith' drawn up by the synod and carried to Lyons by the legates refers to the Patriarch's bargain (¹). Also it almost certainly antedates **Doc. 2**, composed on about 24 December 1273, for had Joseph been present at the synod and with the other bishops accepted union, mention of that fact would certainly have been made. Had he been present and dissented, that also would certainly have been recorded for it would have created a tense situation.

The Declaration of Loyalty to the Emperor by the palace officials (**Doc. 4**) makes no mention of pope, primacy or Holy Spirit. But it does say that it was occasioned by the discord that had arisen over the union. Officials were at loggerheads over it and calling one another schismatics. The situation of 1277, as it is portrayed by the synodal **Document 3**, fits the disturbance among the *archontes* and perhaps this **Doc. 4** should be dated mid-1277.

The Theological Definition (**Doc. 1**) is no more and no less than an accurate translation of the dogmatic decree promulgated in the sixth session of the Council of Lyons on 17 July 1274 (²). There are two versions of that Latin decree, the one beginning *Cum sacrosancta*, which was the one read out on 17 July in the council itself in the presence of the Greeks, the other, which is

---

(¹) *Acta Urbani*, ed. TAUTU, p. 126, par. 268.

(²) A. FRANCHI, *Il Concilio II di Lione* (= Studi e Testi Francescani 33) (Roma, 1965) p. 98. For the text of the decree cf. ROBERG, *Op. cit.*' p. 247

Cum sacrosancta with a new *incipit* and opening phrase, is the text *Fideli ac devota* as, with all the other decrees and canons of the council, it was officially promulgated on 1 November 1274 (¹). Our Greek text is a translation of the decree in its original form, *Cum sacrosancta*, which suggests that the legates brought it back with them either in Latin to be translated into Greek in Constantinople or already turned into Greek in Lyons. The title given to this decree in both the Greek manuscripts states that it was accepted by all the bishops of that time in Constantinople.

The Titles of the Documents

The titles, however, are not part of the original documents. They are the work of either the first compiler or of the scribe of Codex Chisianus gr. 54, or of an earlier scribe. One title at least is manifestly wrong. **Doc.** 1 is said to have been composed by Cyprius for the late Palaeologus after the death of the late Charles (presumably of Anjou). It was obviously written during the lifetime of Palaeologus, as it was his chrysobull, and Charles outlived the Greek Emperor by more than two years. Whether it was George Cyprius who wrote **Docs.** 7 and 4 or not, is not certain, but the assertions in the titles of these documents could well be true, for Cyprius was an active supporter of Michael's unionist efforts, as Pachymeres in several places attests. If it is so, it could be a reason for dating **Doc.** 4 closer to **Doc.** 7, i.e., the end of 1273. **Docs.** 6 and 8 have no titles in the manuscripts. They are separated from the texts in front of them only by a wide empty space.

The Edition

The documents are printed here, not in the order in which they are found in the manuscripts, but in their chronological order numbered in Roman numerals, with the manuscript order in Arabic numerals set in brackets. With the Theological Statement there is printed the Latin text of *Cum sacrosancta*. All the other documents have an English translation. Division into paragraphs, punctuation, correction of a few itacisms and the translations into English are the work of the present writer.

(¹) S. KUTTNER, 'Conciliar Law in the Making', in *Miscellanea Pio Paschini* II (= Lateranum N.S. 15) pp. 39-81.

TEXT

I (7)

Ὑπόσχεσις καὶ συμφωνία καὶ χρυσοβούλλιος λόγος περὶ τῆς τῶν λατίνων
ὑποθέσεως ἀπὸ τοῦ Παλαιολόγου ἐκείνου μετὰ θάνατον τοῦ Καρούλου
ἐκείνου συγγραφεὶς παρὰ τοῦ Κυπρίου

Βασιλεῖ δὲ ὅμως οὐδὲν ἂν εἴη οὕτως ὀφειλόμενον ἕτερον ὡς ἐπιμε-
5 λεῖσθαι μὲν ἐκείνων ἃ πρὸς δόξαν ἥγηται συμβάλλειν Θεοῦ, ἐπιμελεῖσθαι
δὲ αὐτίκα καὶ ὧν ἐνεργουμένων τὸ λυσιτελὲς τοῖς ὑπηκόοις ἐγγίνεται ·
ὅπου δὲ κατὰ ταὐτὸν δοκεῖ συμβαίνειν ἀμφότερα, τοσοῦτον μᾶλλον
ἀναγκαῖον τὴν σπουδὴν ἐπιδείκνυσθαι, ἵν' εἴη καὶ τὸ κέρδος ἑκατέρωθεν
ἧκον καὶ τὸ μὲν πρεσβεύει Θεόν, τὸ δὲ τοὺς ὑπ' αὐτὸν ὠφελεῖ · καὶ
10 Θεοῦ μὲν εὐεργεσίαν ἀμείβεται, ἀντιδιδῶ δὲ καὶ τῇ τῶν ὑποτεταγμένων
εὐνοίᾳ, τὴν παρ' ἑαυτοῦ ῥοπὴν ἀξιόχρεων. Οὕτω γὰρ ἂν οὐδ' ὥσπερ
δωρεὰν τρυφῆς παρὰ τῷ βίῳ τὴν ἀρχὴν ἡγήσαιτο πάντη, ἀλλ' οἱονεὶ
Θεοῦ διακονίαν πιστευθεῖσαν αὐτῷ δι' ἧς ὑπηρετήσας τῇ χρείᾳ τῶν
ἁπάντων καθηκόντων ἐφ' ἕκαστον, ἐντεῦθεν δυνηθείη καὶ αὐτὸς τὴν
15 σωτηρίαν ἑαυτῷ πραγματεύσασθαι.

Ἀλλ' ἐγὼ μὲν ἀχρεῖον ἐμαυτὸν ἥγημαι δοῦλον καὶ οὐδὲ πεποιηκότα
ὅσον ὀφείλω καὶ καθυστεροῦντα δὲ ὅμως ἐφ' ἅπασιν · εἰ γὰρ ἂν ἐκείνως
ἔχων, καλῶς ἐδόκουν μοι συμβαίνειν τὸ τοῦ εὐαγγελικοῦ παραγγέλ-
ματος · νῦν δὲ τοῦτο δὴ νομίζω ἐμαυτῷ τε πρὸς τὸ ὁμογενὲς ἀρκοῦσαν
20 οἷον χρέους ἀπόδοσιν · καὶ πρὸς τὸν Θεόν μου δικαιώσεως τρόπον · ὅτι
τὸ διερρωγὸς τῆς ἐκκλησίας σῶμα ἅπασαν ἐθέμην σπουδὴν πῶς ἂν εἰς
μίαν συναρμολογηθὲν καὶ αὖθις συνάφειαν αὐτῷ Θεῷ ἀποδοθείη κεφαλῇ
μιᾶς ὁλομελείας ὡς τῷ ἀποστόλῳ δοκεῖ.

Ἀλλ' ἐπειδή, Θεοῦ προνοίᾳ τοῦ καλῶς τὰ πάντα διϊθύνοντος τὰ ἡμέ-
25 τερα, τὴν τῶν ἁγίων ἐκκλησιῶν εἰρήνην εἰς χρηστὸν περιηγάγομεν τέλος,
δεῖ δὲ εἰδέναι καὶ ἐφ' οἷς εἰς ταύτην συνήλθομεν. Ἠτήσατο δὲ τοῦτ' αὐτὸ
καὶ πᾶσα ἡ τῶν ἀρχιερέων ὁμήγυρις, ἡ τὴν καθ' ἡμᾶς ἁγίαν σύνοδον
συγκροτεῖ, ἐπωφειλημένον καὶ αὐτοῖς ὂν κήδεσθαι τῶν πατρικῶν ‖ παραδόσεων. Ἡ βασιλεία μου διπλῆν ὑπὲρ τούτου ἀναλαβοῦσα τὴν προθυμίαν

---

10. ἀντιδιδῶ: MS. Should it be changed to ἀντιδίδοται?

TRANSLATION

I (7)

Promise and Agreement and Chrysobull-Statement about the Business of the Latins from the Late Palaeologus after the Death of the Late Charles Drawn up by the Cypriot.

There is nothing so necessary in an emperor as to be solicitous about what he deems will redound to the glory of God, and also to be solicitous about what, if it is effected, brings profit to his subjects. Where, however, it seems to be advantageous to both at once, there much more must he show zeal, in order that gain may come from both sides; the one honours God, the other aids those under him; in exchange he gets the beneficence of God, on the other hand he receives in return from the goodwill of his subjects influence for himself which is by no means small. So in life he would in no way regard his rule as a gift for his pleasure, but as a service of God entrusted to him, through which he might meet the demands of all his duties in every situation and thus himself be able to work out his salvation.

But I deem myself an unprofitable servant and not as having performed as much as I ought, on the contrary, as having fallen short in everything; for if I were such, the words of the message of the gospels would seem to fit me. But now I think that this for me is a return to my fellow-men commensurate with my debt, and a way of making amends to my God, that I set myself with all earnestness to see how the broken body of the Church may be fitted together to become one and be given back again its union with God himself, who is the head of a single body with all its members, as the Apostle conceives it.

Since, then, by the providence of God who directs all our affairs well, we brought the peace of the Churches to a beneficial conclusion, the conditions on which we combined to arrive at this peace should be known too. The whole bench of bishops which constitutes our holy synod asked precisely for this, for it was incumbent on them to be concerned about the traditions of the

τὸν παρόντα χρυσοβούλλιον αὐτῆς λόγον ποιεῖται καὶ δι' αὐτοῦ ταῦτα
διατρανοῦσα βεβαιοῖ καὶ ἐπασφαλίζεται ὡς τὰ τῆς εἰρήνης τῶν ἐκκλησιῶν τῆς τε ῥωμαϊκῆς καὶ τῆς ἡμετέρας ἐπὶ τρισὶ τούτοις προβέβηκε·
τῷ τε τὸν ἁγιώτατον πρόεδρον Ῥώμης ὡς οἰκουμενικὸν πάπαν καὶ
5 τοῦ ἀποστολικοῦ θρόνου διάδοχον ἄκρον ἔχειν καὶ πρῶτον ἀρχιερέα·
τῷ τε πρὸς αὐτὸν ὡς ὑπερέχοντα τὴν ἐκκλησιαστικὴν ἐνάγεσθαι κρίσιν
ἣν ἀποφανθεῖσαν ἐνταῦθα στέργειν ὁ καταδεδικασμένος οὐ βούλεται,
ἀδικεῖσθαι οἰόμενος· καὶ ἐπὶ τρίτῳ, τῷ τοῦ ὀνόματος αὐτοῦ ἐν τοῖς
ἱεροῖς διπτύχοις ποιεῖσθαι ἀναφοράν.

10 Ὃν τρόπον διαφέρειν τὰ τοιαῦτα τούτῳ διέγνωμεν, ἄνωθεν μὲν ἐξ
αὐτοῦ τοῦ πρώτως ἐν χριστιανοῖς βασιλεύσαντος, τοῦ μεγάλου δηλαδὴ
Κωνσταντίνου, ὃς καὶ τῷ τῆς εὐσεβείας ζήλῳ ἐπισεμνύνεσθαι τῇ κλήσει
τῶν θείων ἀποστόλων ἔδοξε καὶ βασιλέων ὀρθοδόξων ὀνομάσθαι πατήρ·
εἶτα καὶ ἀκολούθως κἀκ τῶν πατρικῶν καὶ ἱερῶν θεσμῶν καὶ κανόνων.

15 Ἐπὶ τούτοις τοίνυν συνήλθομεν· ἐπὶ τούτοις καὶ τὴν ἕνωσιν τελε-
σθῆναι ᾑρετισάμεθα· ἵνα δηλονότι ἡ μὲν καθ' ἡμᾶς ἁγία ἐκκλησία
ἀμετακινήτως ἐμμένῃ ἐν πᾶσι τοῖς ἄνωθεν παραδεδομένοις αὐτῇ δόγμασί
τε καὶ ἔθεσι, μηδέν τι παριδοῦσα μηδὲ μεταλλάξασα τούτων, ἀλλὰ
κρατυνομένη εἰς αἰῶνα τὰ σύμπαντα ἐφ' οἷσπερ ἔχει μέχρι τοῦ παρόντος
20 εἰωθυῖά τε καὶ πρεσβεύουσα· τὰ δὲ ἀπαριθμημένα ταῦτα πρεσβεῖα
ἀπονέμῃ συντηροῦσα τῷ ἀποστολικῷ θρόνῳ κατὰ τὴν ἀρχῆθεν δικαιο-
δοσίαν, ἣν καὶ βασιλέων εὐσέβεια καὶ πατέρων θείων νόμοι καὶ κανόνες
ἐκύρωσαν καὶ ἄλλος ἄλλου μεταδεξάμενος συνδιέστερξαν εἰς τέλος,
ἄχρι καὶ αὐτοῦ τοῦ τῆς διαστάσεως χρόνου.

25 Ἔσται γὰρ οὕτως ἡ εἰρήνη ἐπωφελὴς κατὰ πάντα λόγον τοῖς χριστιανῶν πράγμασιν, ἀκίνδυνος δὲ ἄλλως καὶ μηδεμίαν εἰς ψυχὴν φέρουσα
τὴν ζημίαν· ᾗ δὴ καὶ ἐμμένειν ἅπαντας δίκαιον παντάπασι φαίνεται. Τὸ
γὰρ ⟨ἡμᾶς⟩ μέχρι τοσούτου συμβαίνειν τοῖς ἀπὸ τῆς ῥωμαϊκῆς ἐκκλησίας,
μηδὲν ἢ μικρὸν ἢ μεῖζον τῶν οἰκείων παριδόντας ἢ μεταποιήσαντας,
30 οὔτε τῷ ὀρθῷ καὶ εὐσεβεῖ ἀνθίσταται λόγῳ ὡς καὶ πάντες καλῶς ἂν
εἰδεῖεν οἱ τοῖς θείοις λόγοις ἐντεθραμμένοι, οὔτε μὴν ταῖς πατρικαῖς
παραδόσεσι διαμάχεται. Ἡ μὲν οὖν εἰρήνη τοιαύτη τις ἐπὶ τοιούτοις
ἐγένετο, Θεῷ μὲν ὡς ἡ βασιλεία μου πεπληροφόρηται φίλη, καὶ ἀνθρώ-
155ʳ ποις δὲ τοῖς ‖ μὴ πάντη ἀγνώμοσι σφόδρα ἐπαινετή.

---

19 τὰ: MS. τὸν; corr.   28 ἡμᾶς: addidi

Fathers. My Majesty, having assumed a double initiative in this regard, produces this present chrysobull and by this means, clarifying the situation, asserts and guarantees that this business of peace of the Churches, the Roman and ours, went through on these three conditions: that the most holy bishop of Rome as oecumenical Pope and successor on the apostolic throne is the supreme and first bishop; that to him as being superior belongs ecclesiastical decision on a judgement given here which a condemned man, considering himself unjustly treated, will not accept; and thirdly, that his name be commemorated in the holy diptychs.

The excellence of these prerogatives we discern in this way: first from of old by the very first Emperor of Christians, namely, Constantine the Great, who for his zeal for orthodoxy was thought fit be honoured with the title of the divine apostles; secondly and in consequence, by reason of the holy decrees and canons of the Fathers.

On these conditions, then, we agreed; on these we decided that union should be concluded, so that, in other words, our holy Church should remain without change in all the dogmas and customs transmitted to it from of old, neither neglecting nor altering any point of them but standing firm for all time on what it has till this present day practised and honoured. On the other hand, it will conserve and accord to the apostolic throne those innumerable prerogatives in accordance with the jurisdiction observed from the beginning, which the piety of emperors and the laws and canons of the divine Fathers sanctioned and, one receiving them from the hands of another, held them with common approval to the end, right up to the time of the division.

For in this way the peace will be from every point of view profitable to the Christian world, importing no danger at all and no harm whatever for souls; it is clearly right for all to abide by it in every detail. For the fact that we agree with members of the Roman Church when we have neglected and changed nothing either small or great of our own is neither opposed to right and pious reason, as all reared on the word of God would know full well, nor does it offend the traditions of the Fathers. So this peace, completed on such conditions, is pleasing to God as My Majesty has been fully assured, and exceedingly praiseworthy in the eyes of such men as are not completely senseless.

Ὅμως δ' οὖν δι' ἀσφαλείας περιουσίαν ἐκτίθησιν ἤδη καὶ τὸν
παρόντα χρυσοβούλλιον λόγον αὐτῆς καὶ παρεγγυᾶται διὰ τούτου καὶ
βασιλικῶς παρακελεύεται ἅπασι μετὰ τὸ ἀποδοῦναι τὴν εἰρημένην τιμὴν
καὶ τὰ προμνημονευθέντα ταῦτα πρεσβεῖα πνευματικῶς τε καὶ ἐγκανο-
5 νικῶς τῷ ἁγιωτάτῳ καὶ μακαριωτάτῳ πάπᾳ καὶ τῇ ἀποστολικῇ ῥω-
μαϊκῇ ἐκκλησίᾳ ἀμεταθέτως ἐν τοῖς ἄλλοις ἅπασιν ἔχειν τοῖς ἡμετέροις
δόγμασί τε καὶ ἔθεσι· τὰ μὲν ὡς Θεοῦ φωνάς, τὰ δὲ ὡς πατρῷον κλῆρον,
διὰ βίου τηροῦντας ἀπαραποίητα.

10 Ἐπειδὴ τὰ τοιαῦτα οὐ μόνον οἱ τῶν ἄλλων ἐκκλησιῶν φωστῆρες,
ἀλλὰ πρὸ αὐτῶν δὲ πάντως ὡς ὑπερκειμένης ὄντες τιμῆς καὶ οἱ κατὰ
καιροὺς ἁγιώτατοι πάπαι συγκατασκευάσαντες φαίνονται καὶ ἐπαινέ-
σαντες καὶ παραδεδωκότες αὐτοὶ τῇ καθ' ἡμᾶς ἁγίᾳ ἐκκλησίᾳ ὡς
κοινοὶ τῆς οἰκουμένης διδάσκαλοι. Αὐτίκα γὰρ ἅπερ ἡμῖν ἡ πρώτη
15 ἐθεσμοθέτησε σύνοδος, ταῦτα καὶ ὁ ἐν ἁγίοις Σίλβεστρος ἐπεκύρωσε·
ἃ δὲ ἡ δευτέρα ὁ ἁγιώτατος Δάμασος, οὗτος γὰρ κατ' ἐκείνην τῷ ἀποστολικῷ ἐνίδρυτο θρόνῳ· τὰ δὲ τῆς τρίτης συνεδόκει καὶ τῷ θειοτάτῳ
Κελεστίνῳ· καὶ τὴν τετάρτην ὁ μέγας σαφῶς συνίστη καὶ διεβεβαιοῦτο
Λέων, οὗ καὶ ἡ πρὸς ταύτην ἐπιστολή, διὰ τὸ πᾶσαν ἔχειν δεικνύναι
20 δογμάτων ἀκρίβειαν, ὀρθοδοξίας στήλη προσαγορεύεται· καὶ τὰς ἐξῆς
μετὰ ταύτας τρεῖς δέ εἰσιν οἱ κατὰ τοὺς καιροὺς ἐκείνους γινόμενοι,
ἤτοι τὴν πέμπτην ὁ θεῖος Βιγίλιος, ὁ ἱερὸς δ' Ἀγάθων τὴν ἕκτην, καὶ
τὴν τελευταίαν καὶ ἑβδόμην Ἀνδριανὸς ὁ θεσπέσιος.

25 Ὅθεν οὐδενί τινι λόγῳ τὰ τῆς εἰρήνης ἡ βασιλεία μου ᾑρετίσατο,
ἵν' ἡ καθ' ἡμᾶς ἁγία ἐκκλησία τῶν οἰκείων μεταβολήν τινα ἢ μετάπτωσιν
καταδέξηταί ποτε στέρξαι εἴτε δογμάτων εἴτε κανόνων εἴτε ἐθίμων
ἐκκλησιαστικῶν, ἐγγράφων τε καὶ ἀγράφων, ἀλλὰ τῶν τοιούτων ἁπάντων
ἀκριβῶς κατὰ τὸ ἀπαράλλακτον φυλαττομένων ἐπὶ τοῖς εἰρημένοις
30 κεφαλαίοις διαμένειν τὴν εἰρήνην τῶν ἁγίων ἐκκλησιῶν ἐπευδόκησε.

Τοίνυν καὶ στέργειν ταῦτα διακελευόμεθα πάντας, τούς νῦν τε
ὄντας τῶν ἀνθρώπων καὶ οὓς ὁ μέλλων οἴσεται χρόνος κατὰ τὰ διωρισμένα
τῷ παρόντι χρυσοβουλλίῳ λόγῳ τῆς βασιλείας μου, ὡς θεμέλιον ἡγου-
35 μένους τὸν τοιόνδε ταύτης χρυσοβούλλιον λόγον καὶ ἀπευθυνομένους
πρὸς τοῦτον, καὶ ἐπιστηριζομένους ἐφ' οἷς τῇ ἡμετέρᾳ βασιλείᾳ καὶ τῷ
ἀρχιερατικῷ συλλόγῳ τῆς καθ' ἡμᾶς ἁγίας ἐκκλησίας συνελθεῖν εἰς

---

4 ἐγκανονικῶς: MS. ἐγκανόνως, corr.

V

Nevertheless, to give assurance in abundance, My Majesty now issues this present chrysobull, by which he recommends and as Emperor exhorts all, when they have rendered the aforesaid honour and the above-mentioned prerogatives, spiritually and canonically, to the most holy and blessed Pope and to the apostolic Roman Church, to cling without change to all the rest of our dogmas and customs, conserving them through life, some as words of God, others as a heritage from our fathers.

Not only the luminaries of other Churches, but above all before them, as being of a superior excellence, also the most holy popes of the various periods, in their office of common teachers of the world, clearly lent support to, lauded and passed these things on to our holy Church. For straightway the saintly Silvester confirmed what the first synod decreed for us; and what the second synod decreed the most holy Damasus sanctioned, for during it he it was who was seated on the apostolic throne. The findings of the third synod met with the approval of the most divine Celestine, and Leo the Great clearly brought together and maintained the fourth — his letter to it on account of its manifesting complete precision of doctrine is hailed as a pillar of orthodoxy. There were three councils after those that took place in those days, namely when the divine Virgilius headed the fifth, the holy Agatho the sixth and the divine-sounding Adrian the last and seventh.

So my Majesty chose the way of peace, most certainly not so that our holy Church should agree to embrace any change or alteration of either our doctrine, our canons or our ecclesiastical practices, whether they be written or unwritten, but with all these preserved exactly and without change, it approved that, on the basis of the aforesaid conditions, the peace of the holy Churches should be permanent.

We, therefore, bid all welcome this, both the men who exist today and those that time will bring in the future, according to the directives contained in this present chrysobull of My Majesty, taking this my chrysobull as a basis and adjusting themselves to it and taking courage from what led Our Majesty and the body of bishops of our Church to approve entry into this peace, with

155ʳ τὴν ‖ εἰρήνην ταύτην συνέδοξεν, εὐδοκίᾳ τοῦ τὰ διεστῶτα συνάπτοντος
καὶ ἀρχηγοῦ τῆς εἰρήνης σωτῆρος Θεοῦ.

Ὑπεγράφη δὲ καὶ κατὰ τὴν συνήθειαν δι' ἐρυθρῶν γραμμάτων
τῆς βασιλικῆς θείας χειρός.

II (8)

5 ⟨Γράμμα τῶν συναθροισθέντων ἀρχιερέων πρὸς τὸν βασιλέα περὶ τοῦ χρυ-
σοβουλλίου αὐτοῦ λόγου⟩

155ᵛ ‖ Ἐπειδήπερ ἅπαντες ἡμεῖς, εἰς ταὐτὸν γνώμης γενόμενοι μετὰ τοῦ
θεοστεφοῦς καὶ κραταιοῦ ἁγίου ἡμῶν αὐθέντου καὶ βασιλέως, τὴν
εἰρήνην τῶν ἁγίων τοῦ Θεοῦ ἐκκλησιῶν τῆς τε ἡμετέρας καὶ τῆς πρεσβυ-
10 τέρας Ῥώμης ὡς ἐπωφελῆ καὶ σωτήριον τῷ ἡμετέρῳ χριστιανικῷ
πληρώματι κατεδεξάμεθα, καὶ τὴν ἕνωσιν ἤδη σὺν Θεῷ ἐτελέσαμεν·
ἐτελέσαμεν δὲ ἐπὶ τούτοις προσδιορισμοῖς· πρῶτον ἀρχιερέα καὶ ἡγεῖσθαι
καὶ λέγειν τὸν ἁγιώτατον πάπαν· εἶναι πρὸς αὐτὸν ἔκκλητον ἐκ παντὸς
ἐκκλησιαστικοῦ προσώπου ἀδικεῖσθαι τοῖς ἐνταῦθα δικαστηρίοις
15 ὑπολαμβάνοντος· καὶ τρίτον ἀναφορὰν ἐν τοῖς ἱεροῖς διπτύχοις τοῦ
ὀνόματος αὐτοῦ ποιεῖσθαι, ὥσπερ ἀνέκαθεν ἔθος παλαιὸν καὶ πατρικὸν
ἐπεκράτησεν.

Ἐπειδὴ ἐπὶ τούτοις συνέβη καὶ τέλος κατὰ τὸ Θεῷ δοκοῦν τὰ τῆς
τοιαύτης ἔσχηκεν ὑποθέσεως, δείσαντες ἡμεῖς ἐπὶ τοῦ μέλλοντος μή
20 τις ἀδείας ἐκ τῆς εἰρήνης δραξάμενος καὶ πρὸς ἄλλο τι ἐπέκεινα τῶν
προσδιωρισμένων τριῶν παρασύραι θελήσειε, χρυσοβούλλιον γενέσθαι
πρὸς ἡμᾶς λόγον τὸν κραταιὸν καὶ ἅγιον ἡμῶν αὐθέντην καὶ βασιλέα
ἐξῃτήσαμεν, διαλαμβάνοντα μὲν ἐπὶ τῆς εἰρήνης ἐπὶ τίσιν αὕτη προ-
βέβηκεν, ὅτι ἐπὶ μόνοις τοῖς εἰρημένοις τρισί, τῷ ἀνήκοντι δηλαδὴ
25 πρωτείῳ τῷ ἀποστολικῷ θρόνῳ καὶ τῇ εἰς αὐτὸν ἐκκλήτῳ καὶ τῇ ἀνα-
φορᾷ τοῦ ὀνόματος· ἐξασφαλιζόμενον δὲ καὶ τοῦ μηδένα τῶν ἡμετέρων
μηδέποτε εἰς ἄλλο τι παρὰ ταῦτα καθέλκεσθαι ἢ πειρωμένου τινὰ καθελ-
κύσαι ἀποπηδᾶν αὐτίκα καὶ τὰ συγκείμενα ἀθετεῖν. Ταῦτα χρυσοβουλλίῳ
λόγῳ τῆς ἁγίας αὐτοῦ βασιλείας τὸν κραταιὸν καὶ ἅγιον ἡμῶν αὐθέντην
30 καὶ βασιλέα περιλαβεῖν ᾐτησάμεθα. Ὁ δὲ καὶ πρὶν ἡμᾶς αἰτῆσαι, ὥσπερ

---

28 χρυσοβουλλίῳ: MS. corr. from χρυσοβούλλιον

the blessing of God our Saviour who joins together what was rent apart and is the prince of peace.

Signed, as is customary, in red ink by the divine imperial hand.

II (8)

⟨Letter to the Emperor of the Assembled Bishops about the Chrysobull⟩

Since we all have come to the same conclusion as our God-crowned and mighty holy Lord and Emperor and have accepted the peace of the holy Churches of God, ours and that of the elder Rome, as useful and salutary for our Christian flock, with God's help we have already effectuated union. We have, however, effectuated it on these specific terms: to consider and speak of the most holy Pope as first bishop; right of appeal to him for every individual ecclesiastic who thinks himself unjustly treated in the tribunals here; and thirdly, the commemoration of his name to be made in the holy liturgy, as was the ancient and patristic custom that prevailed from of old.

Since it was on these conditions that things went forward and, as pleased God, the negotiations about this business reached a conclusion, we were afraid for the future that some one might seize for himself occasion to try to extract something else that goes beyond the three specifying terms, so we besought our mighty and holy Master and Emperor that a chrysobull should be drawn up for us, on the one hand defining in respect of the peace on what conditions it progressed to a conclusion — that it was on only those aforesaid three conditions, namely, the primacy that belongs to the apostolic throne, the right of appeal to him, and the commemoration of his name — and on the other hand giving guarantee against any of ours ever being drawn away to anything beyond these conditions or, if there is an attempt to lead anyone to overstep them, straightway to set the agreement aside. This we asked our holy Master and Emperor to include in a chrysobull of his holy Majesty. But, since before we made our request, as it were of his own intiative, he was intending to do this and to relieve us

V

20

οἴκοθεν ταῦτα τελέσαι καὶ πάντα φόβον καὶ ὑποψίαν ἡμῖν λῦσαι δια-
νοούμενος, παραχρῆμα ἐπευδοκεῖ τῇ ἡμῶν αἰτήσει καὶ τὸν χρυσοβούλλιον, οἷον δὴ καὶ λαβεῖν εὐχόμεθα, ἐπορέγει ἡμῖν.

156ʳ

Ἐφ' ᾧ δὴ καὶ τὸ πλήρωμα τῆς καθ' ἡμᾶς ἁγίας συνόδου τὰ μέγιστα
πληροφορηθέντες ὡς οὐ μόνον ἀζήμια ἀλλὰ καὶ σφόδρα ‖ λυσιτελῆ
τὰ τῆς ἐκκλησιαστικῆς ἑνώσεως ᾠκονόμηται, ἐπασφαλιζόμεθα καὶ
αὐτοὶ διὰ τοῦ παρόντος ἡμετέρου γράμματος τῇ τοιαύτῃ ἀδόλως ἐμμένειν εἰρήνῃ καὶ κατὰ τὸ δυνατὸν ἑκάστῳ τὸν ἅπαντα χρόνον συνιστάνειν
αὐτήν· καὶ οὐκ ἐξέσται τὸ ἀπὸ τοῦδε μετὰ τὴν τοσαύτην πληροφορίαν προ-
10 φάσεις συμπλάττειν καὶ λόγους ἀνακινεῖν κακοτέχνως κατὰ τῆς τοιαύτης
ἐκκλησιαστικῆς ἀποκαταστάσεως· ὃς δὲ ταῦτα διαπραττόμενος φωραθείη
ἀπόνοιαν ἴσως ἔχων τοῦ καλοῦ καὶ συμφέροντος ἢ καὶ ἀπονοίᾳ εἴκων
καὶ ματαίαν δόξαν θηρώμενος, τὸν τοιοῦτον ἅπαντες κοινῇ ψηφιζόμεθα
αὐτοκατάκριτον εἶναι καὶ ἄνευ τοῦ συστῆναι ἐπ' αὐτῷ δικαστήριον,
15 ὡς τῆς οἰκείας ὑπογραφῆς ἀθετητὴν καὶ τὸ ἑαυτοῦ μέρος τὸν τῆς εἰρήνης
σύνδεσμον παραλύοντα, ἣν ὑπέσχετο φυλάττειν ἀπαραποίητον· στερί-
σκεσθαι δὲ πάσης ἀρχιερατικῆς καὶ ἱερατικῆς τιμῆς ὡς ἄνθρωπον ταράκ-
την καὶ τοῦ κοινοῦ ἀγαθοῦ λυμεῶνα.

Ταῦτα ἕκαστος ἡμῶν καθ' ἑαυτοῦ ἀποφαίνεται ἄνπερ ποτὲ παρα-
20 βαίνων εὑρίσκηται τὴν ἑαυτοῦ γραφὴν ἢ ἐπὶ φυλακῇ τῆς ἐπὶ μόνοις τοῖς
εἰρημένοις τρισὶ συντελεσθείσης εἰρήνης ἐνεγράψατο. Ταῦτα καὶ οἰκειο-
χείροις ἐγγραφαῖς ἐμπεδώσαντες τῷ κρατίστῳ καὶ ἁγίῳ ἡμῶν αὐθέντῃ
καὶ βασιλεῖ ἐνεχειρίσαμεν, μαρτύριον βεβαίας καὶ ἀδόλου τῆς ἐπὶ τοιαύτῃ
καὶ μέχρι τοσούτου ἑνώσει τῶν ἐκκλησιῶν γνώμης ἡμῶν καὶ ψῆφον
25 καταδικάζουσαν τοὺς μετὰ τὸ εἰς αὐτὴν ἐγγράψασθαι μενούσης τῆς
αὐτῆς βουλομένους ἀποσκιρτᾶν. Ταῦτα δὲ ὀφείλει ἐγγράφεσθαι
πρότερον καὶ πᾶς ὁ μέλλων εἰς τὸ ἑξῆς εἰς τὸ τῆς ἀρχιερωσύνης προβαί-
νειν ἀξίωμα καὶ οὕτως ἐγκαθίστασθαι εἰς ἀρχιερέα καὶ συντηρεῖν ταῦτα
ἀμετακίνητα, ὥστε, εἴ τις καὶ τῶν τοιούτων τὰ ἐγγεγραμμένα ταῦτα
30 μετὰ τὸ ἐγκαταστῆναι εἰς ἀρχιερέα παραβῆναι θελήσειε, τῇ αὐτῇ
ὑποκεῖσθαι καταδίκῃ ἥτις ἀνωτέρω διείληπται.

III (6)

⟨Πιττάκιον τοῦ πατριάρχου Ἰωσήφ⟩

154ʳ

† Ἐγχωρῶ τοῖς ὑπὸ τὴν ἐμὴν ἐπαρχίαν ἀρχιερεῦσι κατὰ Κύριον
ἀγαπητοῖς ἀδελφοῖς καὶ συλλειτουργοῖς τῆς ἡμῶν ‖ μετριότητος διδόναι

of all fear and suspicion, without delay he acquiesced in our request and presented us with the chrysobull such as we wish to get.

Seeing, then, that the full complement of our holy synod is fully assured that the business of the Church-union has been arranged not only without causing harm but also so as to be extremely advantageous, we also by means of this our present letter certify that we abide without guile in that peace and to the best of each one's ability sustain it for all time. It will not be possible henceforward after such fulness of assurance to fashion excuses and maliciously to start criticisms against this restored ecclesiastical situation. If anyone shall be caught doing these things perhaps in desperation of any good and advantage coming from it or giving way to madness and seeking after vain glory, such a person we all with one voice decree to be self-condemned and that without recourse to a tribunal in his regard, as one who has violated his own signature and who, for his part, has broken the bond of peace which he promised to preserve intact, and to be deprived of all episcopal and sacerdotal office as a turbulent man and a destroyer of the common good.

This each one of us decrees against himself if ever he is found contravening his own written word, which he wrote for the conservation of the peace that has been concluded on only the three stipulations mentioned earlier. Having ratified this with our own written names we presented it to our most mighty and holy Master and Emperor, a testimony of our firm and sincere judgement on such and so great a union of the Churches and a vote condemning those who after signing it wish to evade it while it remains in force. Whoever for the future shall be promoted to episcopal rank must beforehand subscribe to this and so be instituted as bishop and should preserve it inviolate. Therefore, if anyone of these shall contravene this written statement after his institution as bishop, he shall incur the same condemnation as is determined above.

III (6)
⟨The Pittakion of Patriarch Joseph⟩

I allow the bishops of my eparchy, my beloved brethren in the Lord and concelebrants with My Mediocrity, to give their

V

γνώμην τῷ κρατίστῳ μου αὐτοκράτορι ἤγουν ἄδειαν τῶν ὧν ὁ πάπας
ᾐτήσατο τριῶν κεφαλαίων ὅπως πραγματευσάμενος εἰρήνην μετ' αὐτοῦ
ποιήσῃ τὸ βουλητὸν αὐτῷ. Ὑποστραφέντων δὲ ἐκεῖθεν τῶν βασιλικῶν
πρέσβεων, εἴπερ ἀναπαυθῇ τὸ πνεῦμά μου τοῖς πραγματευθεῖσι παρ'
5 αὐτῶν, ἵνα καὶ ἔτι πατριάρχης εἰμί· εἶδ' οὖν, παραχωρήσω τοῖς βου-
λομένοις τὸν θρόνον.

IV (1)

149ʳ

Ἐπειδήπερ ἡ ἱεροαγία Ῥωμαϊκὴ τοῦ Θεοῦ ἐκκλησία, μήτηρ οὖσα
10 πάντων τῶν πιστῶν καὶ διδάσκαλος, κρατεῖ βεβαίως καὶ διαμαρτύρεται
καὶ διδάσκει ὅτι τὸ Πνεῦμα τὸ ἅγιον ἀπὸ τοῦ Πατρὸς αἰωνίως ἅμα τε
καὶ ἀπὸ τοῦ Υἱοῦ οὐχ ὡς ἐκ δύο ἀρχῶν, ἀλλ' ὡς ἐκ μιᾶς ἀρχῆς, οὐ δυσὶν
ἐκπορεύσεσιν ἀλλὰ μιᾷ ἐκπορεύεται, καὶ ταύτην τὴν τῶν ὀρθοδόξων πατέρων ⟨καὶ⟩ διδασκάλων, λατίνων τε ἅμα καὶ γραικῶν πρόδηλον εἶναι γνώμην
15 καὶ ψήφισμα· οὐκ ὀλίγοι διὰ τὴν τῆς ἀναντιρρήτου ἀληθείας ἀγνωσίαν
εἰς πολλὰς καὶ ποικίλας πλάνας περιωλίσθησαν· ἡμεῖς τοιγαροῦν τοῖς
πλανῶσι τὴν ὁδὸν περικλείεσθαι ἐπιποθοῦντες κατακρίνομεν καὶ ἀποδο-
κιμάζομεν καὶ ἀναθεματίζομεν πάντας τοὺς τολμῶντας ἀρνεῖσθαι τὸ
Πνεῦμα τὸ ἅγιον αἰωνίως παρὰ τοῦ Πατρὸς καὶ Υἱοῦ ἐκπορεύεσθαι
20 εἴτε προπετεῖ τόλμῃ διϊσχυρίζεσθαι ἢ διαβεβαιοῦν ὡς τὸ Πνεῦμα τὸ
ἅγιον παρὰ τοῦ Πατρὸς καὶ παρὰ τοῦ Υἱοῦ ἅτε ἐκ δύο ἀρχῶν καὶ οὐ
μιᾶς ἐκπορεύεται.

V (3)

150ᵛ Ἑτέρα ἔγγραφος ἀσφάλεια τῆς δυσσεβείας τοῦ Βέκκου δι' ἧς ἀναθεματίζει
πάντας τοὺς μὴ δεξαμένους τὴν αὐτοῦ δυσσέβειαν εἰς ἣν καὶ ὑπέγραψαν
25 πάντες οἱ τότε ἀρχιερεῖς

Ἦν ὅτε τῆς εὐταξίας τε καὶ ἀληθείας ἐπικρατούσης ἡ κατάστασις
καὶ εἰρήνη καὶ ἡ δεσποτικὴ παρακέλευσις τῷ τῶν χριστιανύμων γένει
ἐπεχωρίαζε καὶ ὁ τοῦ ἀποστολικοῦ διάδοχος θρόνος, ὁ τῆς πρεσβυτέ-

───────────────

20 διαβεβαιοῦν: MS. διαβεβαιῶν, corr.

opinion to my most powerful Emperor, namely freedom in respect
of the three items which the Pope demanded, so that when he has
arranged the peace with him he may do what he wants. But
when the envoys have returned from there, if indeed my soul shall
acquiesce in what has been arranged by them, let me be still
Patriarch; but if not, I shall surrender the throne to them that
want it.

IV (1)

The Synodical Decree which the Bishops then in Constantinople Made about the Holy Spirit.

Cum sacrosancta romana ecclesia, que deo auctore mater est
omnium fidelium et magistra, firmiter teneat, profiteatur et doceat,
quod spiritus eternaliter ex patre et filio non tanquam ex duobus
principiis, set tanquam ex vno principio, non duabus spiracionibus,
set vnica spiracione procedat, et hanc ortodoxorum patrum atque
doctorum latinorum pariter et grecorum constet esse sentenciam,
et non nulli propter hoc huius irrefragabilis ignorancia veritatis
in errores dubios uarios sint prolapsi, nos hiis erroribus uiam pre-
cludere cupientes dampnamus et reprobamus omnes, qui negare
presumpserint eternaliter spiritum sanctum ex patre filioque procedere sive temerario ausu asserere, quod spiritus sanctus ex patre
et filio tanquam ex duobus principiis et non tanquam ex vno procedat.

V (3)

Another Declaration in Writing of the Impiety of Beccus Anathe-matising All Those Who Do Not Accept His Impiety, Which All the Prelates of That Day Subscribed.

There was a time when, in a climate of discipline and truth,
order, peace and the voice of authority prevailed among those who
bore the name of Christian, and the hereditary throne of the Apostolic, the supreme bishop of the older Rome, the shepherd of shep-

151ʳ ρας ‖ Ῥώμης ἄκρος ἀρχιερεύς, ὁ ποιμὴν τῶν ποιμένων, ὁ πατὴρ τῶν
πατέρων, ἡ ἀκρότης ἁπασῶν τῶν ἐκκλησιῶν, ὁ τῶν ἱερέων πάντων
ἐπέκεινα, ὁ κοινὸς ἡμῶν πατήρ, ὁ οἰκουμενικὸς πάπας, τὰ ἀρχῆθεν
ἀπονενεμημένα αὐτῷ πρεσβεῖα ἐκέκτητο. Ἐπεὶ δὲ ὁ τῆς εἰρήνης ἐχθρὸς
5 καὶ πολέμιος, βάσκανον ἐπιβαλὼν ὀφθαλμόν, ταύτην ἐκ μέσου πεποίηκε
⟨καὶ⟩ τὴν μάχην ἀντισῆξε καὶ τὴν ἀπέχθειαν, ἥτις καὶ ἐπὶ μακρὸν ἤδη
χρόνον ἐκράτησε, στέρησις τῶν τοιούτων ὑπεροχικῷ προνομίων τῷ
ἀποστολικῷ ἐντεῦθεν ἐπιγέγονε θρόνῳ

Ἀλλ' ἔδει ποτὲ τὸν τῆς εἰρήνης Θεὸν ταῖς ἐκκλησίαις αὐτοῦ τὴν
10 εἰρήνην καὶ πάλιν ἐπιβραβεῦσαι· ὅπερ καὶ μέγιστον ὂν ἀγαθὸν ἐν ταῖς
ἡμέραις τῶν θεοστεφῶν βασιλέων ἡμῶν γενέσθαι ηὐδόκησε κατὰ τὴν
ἑαυτοῦ καρδίαν τούτους εὑρών. Ἔνθεν τοι καὶ τὸ ἀρχιερατικὸν πλήρωμα
συναθροισθέντες ἡμεῖς κελεύσει τοῦ κράτους αὐτῶν τὸ τοιοῦτον θεοκίνητον
ἔργον ἠνύσαμεν, σπουδὴν μὲν πολλὴν καὶ ἀγῶνα συχνὸν εἰσενεγκάντων καὶ
15 τῶν αὐτοκρατόρων ἡμῶν καὶ ἡμῶν δὲ αὐτῶν τῇ τούτων γνώμῃ ἐξακολου-
θησάντων καὶ σπευσάντων καὶ συναγωνισαμένων αὐτοῖς ὡς εἰκός, ἅτε
δὴ καὶ εἰδότων δίκαιόν τε καὶ ἐπωφειλημένον εἶναι τοῦτο μᾶλλον ἡμῖν,
τὸ ἀποδοῦναι δηλονότι τῇ ἀποστολικῇ καθέδρᾳ τὰ ἀνέκαθεν προσαρ-
μόσαντα ταύτῃ πρεσβεῖά τε καὶ προνόμια. Οὗ δὴ χάριν καὶ εἰς πέρας
20 αἴσιον σὺν Θεῷ τὸ τοιοῦτον θεοφιλὲς ἠγάγομεν ἔργον, τετάρτην ἄγοντος
τότε καὶ εἰκοστὴν τοῦ δεκεμβρίου μηνὸς τῆς δευτέρας ἐπινεμήσεως, κατ'
αὐτὴν τὴν παραμονὴν τῆς σεβασμίας τελετῆς τῆς τοῦ Κυρίου γεννήσεως.

Ἐπεὶ δέ τινες ἀπό τε τῆς βασιλικῆς συγγενείας τε καὶ σειρᾶς, ἀπό
τε τῆς συγκλήτου βουλῆς, τῆς ἀρχιερατικῆς ὁμηγύρεως, τῶν ἐκκλησιαστι-
25 κῶν ἀρχόντων, τοῦ ἱερατικοῦ καταλόγου, τοῦ τάγματός τε τῶν μοναχῶν,
καὶ τοῦ τῶν λαϊκῶν συναθροίσματος, οἷς δῆτα καὶ γυναῖκες ἐναρίθμιοι
φαίνονται (βαβαὶ τῆς τοῦ Σατᾶν ἐπηρείας ὅτι καὶ μέχρι γυναικῶν τὸ
τοιοῦτον κακὸν προβαῖνον ἐχώρησε), πρὸς τοῦτο δὴ τὸ μέγιστον ἔργον
ἀφηνίασαν καὶ ἀπεδυσπέτησαν καὶ τοσοῦτον ἐματαιώθησαν, ὡς καὶ
30 τοὺς ἀκεραιοτέρους καὶ ἁπλοϊκοὺς τῶν ἀνθρώπων ἐξαπατᾶν καὶ διαστρέ-
φειν καὶ τούτους διδάσκειν οἷα τὴν χριστιανικὴν πολιτείαν καὶ διαγωγὴν
ἀνατρέπουσι· μὴ συνάγεσθαι δηλαδὴ πρὸς τοὺς ἱεροὺς καὶ θείους ναούς,
μὴ τοὺς πρεσβυτέρους συνήθως προσίεσθαι, τῶν τελουμένων παρ'αὐτοῖς
151ᵛ ἁγιασμάτων ἀπέχεσθαι, πρὸς τούτοις ἀθετεῖν καὶ ἀποπέμπειν ‖ καὶ τὸ
35 διὰ τούτων ἐνεργούμενον βάπτισμα· ἐξ ὧν πάντων ἁπλῶς ὅσον τὸ
ἐπ' αὐτοῖς παραλῦσαι τὸν χριστιανισμὸν ἐπειράθησαν.

---

6 καὶ: om. MS., addidi

herds, the father of fathers, the very crown of all the Churches, the excellence of all priests, our common father, the œcumenical Pope, was in possession of the prerogatives accorded him from of old.   But when the enemy and foe of peace, having turned a malignant eye, put an end to this and substituted strife and emnity, which has prevailed now for a long time, deprivation of such privileges ensued for the pre-eminent apostolic throne.

Yet the time had to come when the God of peace would again bestow peace on his Churches.   This, a surpassing good, was the blessing he granted in these days of our God-crowned Emperors, whom he found to be after his own heart.   Hence we, the whole body of the bishops, having met together at the bidding of their Majesties, have accomplished this so great, God-instigated work. Our Emperors lavished zeal and unremitting labour on this and we ourselves followed up and furthered their intent and, as was right, added our endeavours to theirs, for we knew that it was just and profitable especially to us to accord to the apostolic See the prerogatives and privileges that of old had been attached to it. For this cause, then, with God's help, we brought this great and God-loved task to a successful conclusion, on 24 December of the second indiction, on the very eve of the devout celebrations of the Lord's birth.

But some of royal blood and lineage, some members of the senate, some of the bench of bishops, of the church officials, of the status of monks and of the assemblage of layfolk, among whom there seems to be a large number of women (alas! for the evil guile of Satan that he has managed to promote such wickedness among women) — these rebelled against and withheld co-operation in this so important work and became so self-conceited that they deceived and corrupted the more guileless and simple and taught them what perverts the Christian way and manner of life, that is, not to frequent the holy and divine churches, not to admit priests into their company as is usual, to shun the sacrifices celebrated by them, and moreover to reject and set aside the baptisms performed by them.   In other words, by all this they tried to the best of their power to bring Christianity to an end.

26

'Επεὶ ταῦτα οὕτω συμβέβηκεν, οἱ θεοστεφεῖς ἡμῶν ἄνακτες, μηδαμῶς τοῖς γινομένοις ἐθινυστάξαντες, ἀθροίζουσι καὶ πάλιν τὴν ἀρχιερατικὴν χορείαν ἡμῶν. Συνοδικὴ πάντων ἡμῶν κροτεῖται συνέλευσις.

5 Συνάγονται οἱ τῆς ἄκρας κακίας εἰσηγηταὶ καὶ διδάσκαλοι καὶ τῆς εἰρήνης ἀντίθετοι· παραστάντες ἐρωτῶνται πολλάκις εἰ τὴν γενομένην εἰρήνην στερεωτέαν ἡγοῦνται καὶ εἰ τῆς μιαρᾶς αὐτῶν καὶ θεομισοῦς διδασκαλίας ἀφίστανται. Οἱ δὲ εἰ καὶ μιᾶς τὸ πρὶν ἐξήρτηντο γνώμης καὶ ἐφ' ᾧ παραλόγῳ τούτῳ πράγματι συνεφώνουν, ἀλλ' ὅμως αὐτῶν δὴ τούτων τινὲς ὅποσοι τάχα συνέσει τε καὶ διακρίσει τῶν ἄλλων ἦσαν 10 ἐπιγνωμονέστεροι καὶ ὀξύτεροι, μὴ δυνηθέντες παρασχεῖν ἀπόκρισιν ἔλλογον, μὴ δὲ πρὸς τὸν τῆς ἀνομίας ἔλεγχον ἀπαντῆσαι, κατὰ πρόσωπον αὐτοῖς παριστάμενον αὐτίκα τε τὴν ἑαυτῶν ἐπιγινώσκουσιν ἀβουλίαν, καὶ οὗ κακοῦ γεγόνασιν ἐπαισθάνονται, καὶ τῆς μακρᾶς καὶ ἀνοήτου πεισμονῆς ἐκείνης ἀφέμενοι, συνέρχονται γνησίως ἡμῖν καὶ τῷ κοινῷ τῆς 15 ἐκκλησίας ἐπισυνάπτονται σώματι. Οἱ δὲ ἄλλα ἐπ' ἄλλοις προφασισάμενοι οὐδὲν ἕτερον ἐκ τῆς ἀπολογίας αὐτῶν ἢ τοῖς προτέροις καὶ πάλιν ἑαυτοὺς ἐμμένειν διὰ τέλους παρέστησαν· πρὸς γὰρ τὸ φῶς ἀληθείας ἅπαξ οἱ δείλαιοι μύσαντες ἀναβλέψαι πάλιν οὐκ ἴσχυσαν, ματαιωθείσης τῆς ἀσυνέτου καρδίας αὐτῶν.

20 Οὐκ ἔδει τοίνυν ἀνέχεσθαι ἡμᾶς, οὐκ ἔδει ἐφησυχάσαι καὶ μὴ πρὸς ἐκδίκησιν διαναστῆναι τοῦ χριστιανισμοῦ. Ἔνθεν τοι καὶ κατ' αὐτῶν τῶν εἰς τὴν τούτου κινηθέντων ἀνατροπὴν καὶ κατάλυσιν δεῖν ἔγνωμεν ἀποφήνασθαι καὶ τῆς αὐτῶν ἀποστασίας καὶ ματαιότητος ἀξίαν τὴν ψῆφον ἐπενεγκεῖν. Διὸ καὶ κατὰ τὴν δοθεῖσαν ἡμῖν ὑπὸ τοῦ παναγίου 25 Πνεύματος ἐξιουσίαν κατὰ μὲν τῶν ἱερωσύνην ἐχόντων ἐν ὁποιῳδήτινι τάγματι εἴτε ἀρχιερατικῷ σεμνύνονται ἀξιώματι, εἴτε πρεσβύτεροι τὸν βαθμόν, εἴτε διάκονοι — κατὰ τούτων πάντων καθαίρεσιν ἀποφαινόμεθα καὶ ἀφορισμὸν καὶ ἀνάθεμα· κατὰ δὲ τῶν ἄλλων πάντων ἁπλῶς ἐν οἱᾳδήτινι τύχῃ ἢ ἐπιτηδεύματι ἢ ἀξιώματι ὑπάρχονται, εἴτε βασιλικῆς οὗτοι 30 συγγενείας εἰσὶ καὶ σειρᾶς εἴτε τῆς συγκλήτου βουλῆς εἴτε μοναχοὶ εἴτε καὶ λαϊκοί — κατὰ τούτων πάντων ἀφορισμὸν ἀποφαινόμεθα καὶ ἀνάθεμα.

Πλὴν οὐχὶ καὶ τὴν τῆς μετανοίας ἀποκλείομεν θύραν οὐδ' οἷον
152ʳ ἀθάνατον αὐτοῖς τὴν ‖ καταδίκην ταύτην ἐπάγομεν· ἀλλ' εἴ ποτε καὶ
35 αὐτοὶ συνιέντες τῆς ματαίας ταύτης γνώμης ἀγαθὸν μετάμελον δέξαιντο καὶ τὸν μὲν τῆς ἐχθρᾶς ἐπιπροσθοῦντα σκοτασμὸν ἀφ' ἑαυτῶν ἐκτινά-

---

2 ἐθινυστάξαντες: so in MS. Meaning? ἔθη νυστάξαντες?   5 εἰρήνην:
MS. εἰρημένην, corr.   6 στερεωτέαν: MS. στερητέαν, corr.

V

Because of this state of affairs our God-crowned lords would in no way tolerate what was being done. Again they bring together the body of bishops. A plenary session of the synod is held. The authors and teachers of that surpassing evil and the opponents of peace are brought before us and are asked repeatedly if they think that the peace that has been made should be confirmed and whether they abandon their foul and God-hated teaching. Some of them, even though they before adhered to the one opinion and concurred in this senseless business, those who in intelligence and judgement were more discerning and cleverer than the rest, unable to furnish a reasonable answer and to reply to the charge of lawlessness laid against them in person, straightway acknowledge their imprudence, realise the evil they have been involved in and, shaking themselves free from the lasting and senseless ideas, genuinely go along with us and join the common body of the Church. Others added one excuse on top of another and offered nothing else in their defence than that they remained right through to the end still set in their previous views, for when once the miserable creatures had shut their eyes to the light of truth, they could not again lift up their gaze, for their foolish hearts had been rendered vain.

So it was not right for us to remain inactive, not right to sit idle and not to rise up to the defence of Christianity. Against those who were busy in its subversion and destruction we realised that we had to make a decision and to pass a decree to meet their apostasy and vanity. Therefore, in accordance with the authority given us by the all-holy Spirit, against those who possess the priesthood in any degree at all, whether they are hallowed with the office of bishop or are in rank simple priests or deacons — against all of these we decree deposition, excommunication and anathema: against all others in whatever station or calling or rank, whether they are of imperial blood and lineage or of the senate or monks or even laymen — against all of these we decree excommunication and anathema.

But we do not shut the door of repentance nor do we impose this sentence as being everlasting, but if at some time even these, coming to their senses from their vain opinions, should really repent and should reject and shake off from themselves the dark-

V

ξαιεν, πρὸς δὲ τὴν τῆς εἰρήνης λάμψιν καθαρῶς ἐντρανίσαιεν καὶ ὅλως
πλάνης τε καὶ ἀπωλείας βαθυτάτου κρημνοῦ τὰς ἑαυτῶν ψυχὰς ὑπεξέ-
λοιεν, τούτους αὐτίκα καὶ ἡμεῖς ὅμου τε τοῦ ἐπενεχθέντος ἀπολύσομεν
βάρους, καὶ ἀδελφικῶς καὶ πατρικῶς περιπτυξόμεθα καὶ ἀγκαλισόμεθα.

5 Οὕτω τοίνυν πάντες ἡμεῖς τὸ τῶν ἀρχιερέων πλήρωμα συλλεγέντες
κατὰ τὸν ἱερὸν καλούμενον οἶκον τῶν ἐν ταῖς Βλαχέρναις θεοφρουρήτων
ἀνακτόρων ἐννέα καὶ δεκάτην τοῦ φευρουαρίου μηνὸς τῆς πέμπτης
ἐπινεμήσεως καὶ τὰ ἐπὶ τούτου γνωμοδοτήσαντες καὶ ἀποφηνάμενοι
καὶ τὴν παροῦσαν τομογραφίαν ἐκθέμενοι ταῖς αὐτοχείροις ἡμῶν ὑπο-
10 γραφαῖς ἐξησφαλισάμεθα καὶ ἐβεβαιώσαμεν.

VI (5)

152ʳ **Ἔγγραφος ἀσφάλεια τῶν κληρικῶν τῆς μεγάλης ἐκκλησίας ἐπὶ τῇ εἰρήνῃ
δῆθεν τῶν ἐκκλησιῶν**

Ἐπεὶ ὁ ἁγιώτατος ἡμῶν δεσπότης ὁ πατριάρχης Κωνσταντινουπόλεως, νέας Ῥώμης, καὶ πᾶσα ἡ τῶν ἀρχιερέων ὁμήγυρις συνοδικῶς
15 ἀθροισθέντες κοινὴν τομογραφίαν ἐξέθεντο δι' ἧς ἀφορισμῷ καὶ ἀναθέματι καὶ καθαιρέσει καθυποβάλλουσι πάντας τοὺς ἀποσχιζομένους
τοῦ κοινοῦ τῆς ἐκκλησίας συλλόγου, καὶ τὸ πρωτεῖον μὴ παραδεχομένους
τοῦ ἄκρου ἀρχιερέως καὶ διαδόχου τοῦ ἀποστολικοῦ θρόνου τοῦ οἰκουμενικοῦ πάπα, καὶ πάντα τὰ ἀπονενεμημένα αὐτῷ πρεσβεῖά τε καὶ
20 προνόμια ἅπερ ἄνωθεν ἐξ εὐαγγελικῶν τε διαταγμάτων καὶ συνοδικῶν
καὶ πατρικῶν παραδόσεων εἴληφε· τὴν τοιαύτην τομογραφίαν στηρικτέαν ἡγούμενοι καὶ ἡμεῖς κατὰ πᾶσαν ταύτης περίληψιν, καὶ κατὰ πάντα
ἐξακολουθοῦντες τῷ ἁγιωτάτῳ ἡμῶν δεσπότῃ καὶ πατριάρχῃ καὶ τῷ
τῶν ἀρχιερέων πληρώματι τὰς οἰκείας ἑαυτῶν παρέχομεν ἐγγραφὰς καὶ
25 ὑπισχνούμεθα δέχεσθαι καὶ φυλάττειν διόλου ἀμεταβλήτως τὸ τοιοῦτον
πρωτεῖον τοῦ ἄκρου ἀρχιερέως καὶ διαδόχου τοῦ ἀποστολικοῦ θρόνου
τοῦ οἰκουμενικοῦ πάπα καὶ πάντα τὰ ἀρχῆθεν ἀπονενεμημένα αὐτῷ
πρεσβεῖά τε καὶ προνόμια, οὐ μόνον ἐπὶ τῆς παρούσης εὑρισκόμενοι
τάξεως, ἀλλὰ καὶ εἰς τελεώτερον τὸ ἀπὸ τοῦδε προαγόμενοι ἕκαστος·
30 τοὺς δὲ μὴ εἰς ταῦτα ἐμμένοντας, ἀλλὰ μᾶλλον ἐντεῦθεν καὶ τῆς τῶν
χριστιανῶν ὁλοκληρίας ἑαυτοὺς ἀποτέμνοντας, τούτους καὶ ἡμεῖς ὁμοίως
ἀποβλήτους ἡγούμεθα καὶ ἐν τῷ τῆς καταδίκης τῶν εἰρημένων ἐπι-
τιμίων, οἷς αὐτοὺς ἡ ἱερὰ καὶ θεία σύνοδος καθυπέβαλλεν.

---

21 στηρικτέαν : MS. στερητέαν, corr.

ness of enmity and, with that, should gaze steadfastly at the light of peace and draw their souls back out of error and the deep chasm of perdition, we for our part will immediately free them from the burden laid on them and at the same time will embrace them and clasp them to our bosoms in a spirit of brotherly and fatherly love.

So then all of us, the full bench of bishops, gathered together in the holy hall of the God-guarded palace called of Blachernae on the nineteenth day of the month of February of the fifth indiction and after discussion and decision on this subject, issued this present Statement in Writing, which with our individual signatures we sanctioned and confirmed.

VI (5)

A Statement in Writing of the Clerics of the Great Church about the So-called Peace of the Churches.

Since our most holy lord, the Patriarch of Constantinople, New Rome, and the whole of the bench of bishops met in synod have issued a common Statement in Writing by which they impose excommunication, anathema and deposition on all those who break away from the common body of the Church and who do not recognise the primacy of the Supreme Pontiff and successor on the apostolic throne, the oecumenical Pope, and all the prerogatives and privileges accorded to him, which from antiquity by reason of precepts of the gospels and synodical and patristic traditions he received and possesses, we also, considering that such a Statement should be upheld in its full scope and following in everything our most holy lord and Patriarch and the whole bench of bishops, register our names and we promise to accept and to preserve completely unchanged the aforesaid primacy of the Supreme Pontiff and successor on the apostolic throne, the oecumenical Pope, and all the prerogatives and privileges which from the beginning were accorded to him, not only when we remain in our present rank, but also if hereafter we are preferred to a higher one; and those who do not abide by this but rather cut themselves off from it and from the whole community of Christians we consider excommunicated and under the judgement of the penalties that have been laid down, which the holy and divine synod imposed on them.

V

30

153ʳ ‖ † Ὁ μέγας οἰκονόμος τῆς ἁγιωτάτης τοῦ Θεοῦ μεγάλης ἐκκλησίας,
Μιχαὴλ ὁ Γεμιστός, ὑπέγραψα

† Ὁ χαρτοφύλαξ τῆς ἁγιωτάτης τοῦ Θεοῦ μεγάλης ἐκκλησίας καὶ
ἀρχιδιάκονος τοῦ εὐαγοῦς βασιλικοῦ κλήρου, Κωνσταντῖνος ὁ
5 Μελιτινιώτης, ὑπέγραψα

† Ὁ δικαιοφύλαξ καὶ σακελίου τῆς ἁγιωτάτης τοῦ Θεοῦ μεγάλης
ἐκκλησίας, Θεόδωρος ὁ Σκουταριώτης, ὑπέγραψα

† Ὁ πρωτέκδικος τῆς ἁγιωτάτης μεγάλης τοῦ Θεοῦ ἐκκλησίας, Στέφανος ὁ Πανάρετος, ὑπέγραψα

10 † Ὁ κανστρίσιος, Νικηφόρος ὁ Γαληνός, συναινῶν ὑπέγραψα

† Ὁ ραιφενδάριος τῆς ἁγιωτάτης μεγάλης τοῦ Θεοῦ ἐκκλησίας,
Μιχαὴλ ὁ Ἐσχαματισμένος, ὑπέγραψα

† Ὁ ὑπομνηματογράφος, Μιχαὴλ ὁ Βαρδαλής, ὑπέγραψα

† Ὁ ἱερομνήμων, Κωνσταντῖνος ὁ Βαλσαμῶν, ὑπέγραψα

15 † Ὁ ἐν πατριαρχικοῖς ἄρχουσιν ἐπὶ τῶν σεκρέτων, Στέφανος διάκονος
ὁ Κοκηνός, ὑπέγραψα

† Ὁ διδάσκαλος τῶν ἀποστόλων, Γεώργιος ὁ Παχυμερής, ὑπεγραψα

† Ὁ πριμμικήριος τῶν λογιωτάτων πατριαρχικῶν νοταρίων, Γεώργιος
ὁ Βέκκος, ὑπέγραψα

20 † Ὁ ἄρχων τῶν ἐκκλησιῶν, Μανουὴλ ὁ Ξιφιλῖνος, ὑπέγραψα

† Ὁ ὑπομιμνήσκων τῆς ἁγιωτάτης τοῦ Θεοῦ μεγάλης ἐκκλησίας,
Ἰωάννης ὁ Φαπῆς, ὑπέγραψα

† Ὁ διδάσκαλος τοῦ ψαλτῆρος, Μανουὴλ ὁ Δυσύπατος, ὑπέγραψα

† Ὁ ἐπὶ τῶν κρίσεων, Ἰωάννης ὁ Χαλκούτζης, ὑπέγραψα

25 † Ὁ ἐπὶ τῶν γονάτων, Μανουὴλ ὁ Ἀκροπολίτης, ὑπέγραψα

† Ὁ ἐπὶ τῶν δεήσεων, Γεώργιος, ὑπέγραψα

† Ὁ ἄρχων τῶν μοναστηρίων, Κωνσταντῖνος ὁ Ἀαρών, ὑπέγραψα

† Ὁ ἐπὶ τῆς ἱερᾶς καταστάσεως, Νικόλαος ὁ Σκουταριώτης, ὑπέγραψα

† Ὁ πρῶτος ὀστιάριος, Κωνσταντῖνος ὁ Γεμιστός, ὑπέγραψα

153ᵛ † Ὁ δεύτερος ὀστιάριος, Γεώργιος ὁ Κλειδάς, ὑπέγραψα ‖

† Ὁ εὐτελὴς διάκονος, Θεοφύλακτος, ὑπέγραψα

† Βασίλειος διάκονος καὶ πατριαρχικὸς νοτάριος, ὁ Φαφωνάς, ὑπέγραψα

† Μαμουὴλ διάκονος καὶ πατριαρχικὸς νοτάριος, ὁ Γεμιστός, ὑπέγραψα

† Ὁ ἐν διακόνοις ἐλάχιστος, Μιχαὴλ ὁ Ἰασίτης, ὑπέγραψα

35 † Ὁ ἐν πατριαρχικοῖς νοταρίοις, Ἰωάννης ὁ Κάλλιστος, ὑπέγραψα

† Ὁ ἐν πατριαρχικοῖς νοταρίοις, Στέφανος Ὑπάτιος, ὑπέγραψα

† Ὁ ἐν πατριαρχικοῖς νοταρίοις, Νικηφόρος ὁ Ζαχαρίας, ὑπέγραψα

---

17 τῶν ἀποστόλων: MS. Probably should be τοῦ ἀποστόλου (cf. note 1
on the following page).

I, the Great Oeconomus of the most holy Great Church of God, Michael Gemistus, signed.

I, the Chartophylax of the most holy Great Church of God and Archdeacon of the sacred imperial clergy, Constantine Melitiniotes, signed.

I, the Dikaiophylax and Sacristan of the most holy Great Church of God, Theodore Skoutariotes, signed.

I, the Protekdicus of the most holy Great Church of God, Stephen Panaretus, signed.

I, the Canstrisius, Nicephorus Galenos, agreed and signed.

I, the Referendarius of the most holy Great Church of God, Michael Eschamatismenus, signed.

I, the private Secretary, Michael Bardales, signed.

I, the Hieromnemon, Constantine Balsamon, signed.

I, Secretary among the patriarchal officials, deacon Stephen Kokenos, signed.

I, the Teacher of the Apostles (1), George Pachymeres, signed.

I, the Primmicerius of the most learned patriarchal notaries, George Beccus, signed.

I, in charge of the churches, Manuel Xiphilinus, signed.

I, the Hypomimnescon of the most holy Great Church of God, John Phapes, signed.

I, the Teacher of the psalter, Manuel Dysypatus, signed.

I, over judgements, John Chalkoutzes, signed.

I, over knees, Manuel Acropolites, signed.

I, over petitions, George, signed.

I, over the monasteries, Constantine Aaron, signed.

I, over sacred discipline, Nicholas Skoutariotes, signed.

I, the first doorkeeper, Constantine Gemistus, signed.

I, the second doorkeeper, George Kleidas, signed.

I, the humble deacon Theophylactus signed.

I, Basil Phaphonas, deacon and patriarchal notary signed.

I, Manuel Gemistus, deacon and patriarchal notary, signed.

I, the least of the deacons, Michael Iasites, signed.

I, one of the patriarchal notaries, John Callistus, signed.

I, one of the patriarchal notaries, Stephen Hypatius, signed.

---

(1) The reference is to the liturgical lectionary called the *Apostle* and should undoubtedly be in the singular. On this title and on the offices and titles of the other signatories listed here, see J. DARROUZÈS, *Recherches sur les ὀφφίκια de l'église byzantine* (= *Archives de l'orient chrétien*) Paris, 1970.

32

† Ὁ ἐν πατριαρχικοῖς νοταρίοις, Γεώργιος ὁ Παλατῖνος, ὑπέγραψα
† Ὁ ἐν πατριαρχικοῖς νοταρίοις, Ἀλέξιος ὁ Ἀγαλλιανός, ὑπέγραψα
† Ὁ ἐν πατριαρχικοῖς νοταρίοις, Θεόδωρος ὁ Ὑπάτιος, ὑπέγραψα
† Ὁ ἐν πατριαρχικοῖς νοταρίοις, Γεώργιος ὁ Βαρδαχλάς, ὑπέγραψα
5 † Ὁ ἐν πατριαρχικοῖς νοταρίοις, Ἀνδρέας ὁ Ὁλόβωλος, ὑπέγραψα
† Ὁ ἐν πατριαρχικοῖς νοταρίοις, Μανουὴλ ὁ Βουρδής, ὑπέγραψα
† Ὁ ἐν πατριαρχικοῖς νοταρίοις, Ἰωάννης ὁ Γλυκύς, ὑπέγραψα
† Ὁ ἄρχων τοῦ εὐαγγελίου, Ἰωάννης ὁ Κυδώνης, ὑπέγραψα
† Ὁ ἄρχων τῶν φώτων, Γεώργιος ὁ Χειλάς, ὑπέγραψα
10 † Ὁ ἄρχων τοῦ ἀντιμινσίου, Μανουὴλ ὁ Μουζάλων, ὑπέγραψα
† Ὁ δομεστικὸς τῆς ἁγιωτάτης τοῦ Θεοῦ μεγάλης ἐκκλησίας, Γρηγό-
ριος ὁ Γλυκύς, ὑπέγραψα
† Ὁ πρωτοπαπᾶς τῶν ἱερέων καὶ δευτερεύων, Ἰωάννης ὁ Θεολόγος,
ὑπέγραψα
15 † Ὁ δευτερεύων τῶν διακόνων, Ἰωάννης ὁ Περιστεριώτης, ὑπέγραψα

VII (4)

152ʳ Ἑτέρα ἔγγραφος ἀσφάλεια τῆς τοιαύτης δυσσεβείας ἣν καὶ ἐλογογράφησεν ὁ
Κύπριος καὶ πάντες οἱ τοῦ παλατίου ἄρχοντες ὑπέγραψαν

Ἐπειδὴ διὰ τὴν κινηθεῖσαν ὑπόθεσιν ἕνεκεν τῆς τῶν τοῦ Θεοῦ
ἁγίων ἐκκλησιῶν ἑνώσεως παρά τινων ἀπαιδεύτων ἀνθρώπων λόγοι
20 ἐκφέρονται ἀπρεπεῖς, καταφρόνησιν μὲν ἔχοντες εἰς τὸ θεῖον ὕψος
τῆς ἐπ' εὐεργεσίᾳ ἡμῶν ἐκ Θεοῦ προβεβλημένης βασιλείας τοῦ κραταιοῦ
καὶ ἁγίου ἡμῶν αὐθέντου καὶ βασιλέως, ἔχοντες δὲ καὶ ὕβριν εἴς τινας
τῶν ὑπὸ τὸ ἔνθεον αὐτοῦ κράτος, οὐ μὴν ἀλλὰ μέχρι τῆς τοιαύτης τῶν
λόγων ἀπρεπείας φθάνουσαν διὰ τὴν ἄκραν τῶν ἀνοήτων μοχθηρίαν,
25 ὡς ἐντεῦθεν καὶ ἡμᾶς κατ' ἀλλήλων γλῶτταν κινοῦντας βάλλειν ταῖς
λοιδορίαις ἀλλήλους καὶ σχισματικοὺς ἀνερυθριάστως ἀποκαλεῖν · τὴν
τοιαύτην βουλόμενοι τῶν κακῶν ῥύμην ἀναχαιτίσαι καὶ ἅπαν μὲν τὸ
μηδεόντως ἐκ τούτων γινόμενον ἀποπαῦσαι, ὁμόνοιαν δὲ καὶ τὴν προσή-
κουσαν εὐφημίαν εἰσηγήσασθαι, κατὰ τὴν δοθεῖσαν ἡμῖν παρὰ τοῦ
30 παναγίου Πνεύματος ἐξουσίαν τάδε γνωμοδοτοῦντες ἀποφαινόμεθα.

Τοῖς μὲν θεοπροβλήτοις ἡμῶν ἁγίοις αὐθένταις καὶ βασιλεῦσι πᾶν
εἴ τι ἀγαθὸν ἐπευχόμεθα, μῆκος βίου, νίκας κατ' ἐχθρῶν, εἰρηναίαν
ζωήν, σωτηρίαν ψυχῆς, καὶ τῆς αἰωνίου ἐν Χριστῷ βασιλείας ἀπόλαυσιν ·
τοῖς δ' ὑπὸ τὴν αὐτῶν βασιλείαν ἅπασι τοῖς τε ἐν τέλει τοῖς τε τῶν
35 στρατιωτικῶν καταλόγων, καὶ πᾶσιν ἁπλῶς τοῖς ὑπὸ τὸ ἔνθεον αὐτῶν

---

24 φθανούσαν: MS. φθανούσης, corr.　　35 αὐτῶν: MS. αὐτοῦ, corr.

I, one of the patriarchal notaries, Nicephorus Zacharias, signed.
I, one of the patriarchal notaries, George Palatinus, signed.
I, one of the patriarchal notaries, Alexius Agallianus, signed.
I, one of the patriarchal notaries, Theodore Hypatius, signed.
I, one of the patriarchal notaries George Bardachlas, signed.
I, one of the patriarchal notaries, Andrew Holobolus, signed.
I, one of the patriarchal notaries, Manuel Bourdes, signed.
I, one of the patriarchal notaries, John Glykys, signed.
I, in charge of the Gospel-book, John Cydones, signed.
I, in charge of the lights, George Cheilas, signed.
I, in charge of the antiminsion, Manuel Mouzalon, signed.
I, domesticus of the most holy Great Church of God, Gregory
   Glykys, signed.
I, Protopapas and Secundarius, John Theologus, signed.
I, Secundarius of the deacons, John Peristeriotes, signed.

VII (4)
**Another Declaration in Writing of that Impiety Which Cyprius
Formulated and All the Officials of the Palace Signed.**

Because of the undertaking now in progress for the union of
the holy Churches of God some ignorant people have spoken in
an unseemly manner, indeed with contempt, against the divine
sublimity of the rule of our mighty and holy Lord and Emperor,
prospered by God for our benefit, also with insolence against some
who are under his godly sovereignty. Not only that, but such a
degree of unseemliness has that insolence reached owing to the
depravity of those senseless people that in consequence we too are
speaking against one another, insulting each other and unblushing-
ly calling each other schismatics. With a view to checking such
a spate of evil and putting an end to all the confusion resulting
from it, also to introduce harmony and fitting good manners in
speech, we, by reason of the authority given us by the all-holy
Spirit, after a free expression of our views, decree as follows.

For our God-appointed holy Lords and Emperors we pray
for every good whatsoever, length of days, victory over enemies,
a peaceful life, salvation of their souls and the enjoyment of the
everlasting kingdom in Christ; for all those under their sovereignty,
the magistrates, the armed forces, and in a word, for all who are

V

34

κράτος τελοῦσι καὶ τὴν ὀφειλομένην πίστιν καὶ εὔνοιαν αὐτοῖς διασώζουσι,
152ᵛ τοῖς τοιούτοις ἅπασι τὴν ἀπὸ Θεοῦ εὐλογίαν ‖ καὶ εἰρήνην εὐχόμεθα
καὶ σωτηρίαν ψυχῆς τε καὶ σώματος· ὡς εἶναι καὶ ἡμῖν εὔκαιρον λέγειν
τὸ γραφικὸν ἐκεῖνο.

5   Θειότατοι βασιλεῖς ⟨ἐν⟩ Χριστῷ Ἰησοῦ καὶ μετὰ Θεὸν καὶ παρὰ
Θεοῦ σωτῆρες προκεχειρισμένοι ἡμῶν, οἱ εὐλογοῦντες ἡμᾶς, εὐλογοῦντες
δὲ καὶ τοὺς πιστῶς καὶ εὐνοϊκῶς πρὸς ἡμᾶς ἀνατεινομένους, εἶεν εὐλο-
γημένοι καὶ παρ' ἡμῶν καὶ παρὰ Θεοῦ· ὅσοι δὲ γλῶσσαν βλάσφημον
τῷ θείῳ τῆς βασιλείας ὑμῶν τολμήσωσιν ἐπανιέναι ὕψει ἢ στόμα λοίδορον
10   διᾶραι κατά τινος τῶν ὑφ' ὑμᾶς, τούτους κατηραμένους ἀποφαινόμεθα
καὶ παρ' ἡμῶν ὑπάρχειν καὶ παρὰ Θεοῦ, τῆς ἴσης αὐτοὺς καταδίκης
ἀξιοῦντες τῶν ἀδικίαν εἰς τὸ ὕψος λαλούντων καὶ τῶν ἐπὶ πᾶσι βλασφη-
μούντων Θεόν.

      Ἐπὶ τούτῳ γὰρ καὶ τὸν παρόντα τόμον ἐκθέμενοι ταῖς οἰκειοχείροις
15   ἡμῶν ὑπογραφαῖς ἐξασφαλιζόμεθα.

VIII (2)

149ʳ **Ἐπιστολὴ τοῦ Βέκκου πρὸς τὸν ἰταλὸν πάπαν δι' ἧς ἀναθεματίζει πάντας
τοὺς ὀρθοδόξους χριστιανοὺς τοὺς μὴ δεξαμένους τὴν ἑαυτοῦ δυσσέβειαν**

      Τοῦ φιλαγάθου Θεοῦ καὶ Σωτῆρος ἡμῶν Ἰησοῦ Χριστοῦ τοῦ κατὰ
τὸ πολὺ καὶ ἄμετρον αὐτοῦ ἔλεος τὰ διεστῶτα πολλῇ τῇ πρὸς ἡμᾶς
20   συμκαταβάσει συνάψαντος, καὶ λόγοις ἀρρήτοις κατ' εὐδοκίαν καὶ
βούλησιν πατρικὴν καὶ συνεργείᾳ τοῦ ἁγίου καὶ ζωαρχικοῦ Πνεύματος
τὰ ἐπὶ γῆς τοῖς οὐρανίοις ἑνώσαντος, τοὺς οἰκτιρμοὺς αὐτοῦ κἂν τοῖς
παροῦσιν αἰῶσι δείξαντος ἐφ' ἡμᾶς καὶ τὴν εἰρήνην τῆς οἰκείας ἐκκλησίας,
ἃς ὁ τοῦ ἀνθρωπείου γένους ἐχθρὸς καὶ πολέμιος διέρρηξε πρὸ πολλοῦ
25   καὶ ταύτην ἐπὶ μακρὸν διαστατὴν πεποίηκεν, ἀγῶσι συχνοῖς τοῦ κρα-
τίστου καὶ ἁγίου μου αὐτοκράτορος ὀλίγῳ πρότερον γενέσθαι καταξιώσαν-
τος, οὐκ ἔστιν εἰπεῖν ὅπως ἔκτοτε καὶ ἡμεῖς πρὸς αὐτὴν διεκείμεθα,
ταύτῃ συνεῖναι καὶ συζῆν ἀδιαλείπτως ἐπιποθοῦντες καὶ ἀποδεχόμενοι
καὶ τῇ ἀποστολικῇ καθέδρᾳ μετὰ χαρᾶς ἀποδιδόντες τὰ ἀρχῆθεν ἀπο-
30   νενεμημένα πρεσβεῖά τε καὶ προνόμια καὶ τούτων διηνεκῶς αὐτὴν
149ᵛ ἀπολαύειν ἐθέ‖λοντες.

_____

5 ἐν: addidi   10 κατηραμένους: MS. κατηρημενους, with ρα written above
19 πολλῇ: MS. πολλαὶ, corr.   29 ἀπονενεμημένα: MS. ἀπονεμήνα corr.

under their inspired rule and preserve to them due faith and good-will — to all these we wish the blessing of God and peace, and the salvation of their souls and bodies. So it is opportune for us to recite that written document.

Most divine Emperors in Christ Jesus, predestined to be our saviours after God and with God, who bless us and who bless those too who are well inclined towards us with faith and good will — may they be blessed both from our part and from God's.   But whoso shall dare to raise a blasphemous voice against the divine highness of Your Majesty or to open a reviling mouth against any of those subject to you, these we decree to be accursed both with us and with God, deeming to be deserving of an equal condemnation those who speak words of injustice against Your Highness and those who speak words of blasphemy against God.

For in this sense we have issued this present statement and confirmed it with our individual signatures.

VIII (2)

A Letter of Beccus to the Italian Pope by Which He Anathematises All Those Who Do Not Accept His Impiety.

The God of goodness, our Lord Jesus Christ, who in his great and infinite mercy and condescension towards us has joined to-gether what was rent apart and with words unspeakable according to the good pleasure and will of the Father and with the co-oper-ation of the holy and lifegiving Spirit has united earth with heaven, in this present time has shown compassion to us and has deigned, through the constant efforts of my most powerful and holy Emperor, to restore peace to his Church, which the adversary and enemy of the human race had long since rent asunder and for long kept divided.   It is not possible to express adequately our disposition towards it, we who unceasingly desire to be and to live in it and who joyfully yield to the Apostolic See the prerogatives and privi-leges ascribed to it from the beginning, in the wish that it may enjoy them always.

36

Νῦν δὲ πρὸς ἡμᾶς καταλαβόντων καὶ τῶν αἰδεσιμωτάτων πρέσβεων τῆς σῆς αἰθριότητος, οὓς ἄνδρας κατενοήσαμεν πάσῃ διαπρέποντας ἀρετῇ, πλήρεις τε συνέσεως φυσικῆς ὁμοῦ καὶ πνευματικῆς καὶ λόγων τῶν ἐκμαθήσεως, ἐξ ὧν καὶ τὰ ἐπὶ τῆς σῆς ἁγιότητος ἐμάθομεν τελεώ-
5 τερον ἀκριβεῖ πληροφορίᾳ σχόντες ὧν ἀκοῇ καὶ πρὸς τῶν μὴ ἰδόντων ἀλλ' ἐκ φήμης καὶ μόνης τὸ λέγειν ἐχόντων πρὶν παρειλήφαμεν, ὡς ἄρα μετὰ τῶν ἄλλων καὶ τῶν κατὰ τὴν ἔκθεον σὴν πολιτείαν καὶ σοφίαν τὴν ὑπερθαύμαστον ἀνεκδιηγήτων ὧν κατ' ἀξίαν καὶ τὸν ὑψηλὸν τοῦτον καὶ μέγαν θρόνον ὁ Θεὸς δεδώρηται κατὰ τὸν θεῖον ἀπόστολον, καὶ
10 τὴν μέριμναν ἔχων διηνεκῶς τῶν ἐκκλησιῶν τῆς εἰρήνης καὶ ὁμονοίας φροντίζων αὐτῶν.

Ταῦτα τοίνυν μεμαθηκότες οὕτω τε ἐπὶ αὐτῶν ἐξακριβωσάμενοι μετ' εὐφροσύνης ἀφάτου τὸν εἰς τοῦτο τὸ μέγιστον ἔργον ζῆλον ἡμῶν καὶ τῇ σῇ μακαριότητι διὰ τοῦ παρόντος ἀναγνωρίσαι διανέστημεν
15 γράμματος, παραστῆσαι βουλόμενοι ταύτῃ σαφῶς ὅπως θερμότητα τῆς τοιαύτης τῶν ἐκκλησιῶν εἰρήνης ἀντιποιούμενοι τὰ ἀνέκαθεν προσαρ-μόσαντα τῇ ἀποστολικῇ καθέδρᾳ πρεσβεῖά τε καὶ προνόμια μὴ μόνον ἀσπασίως ταύτῃ παρέχομεν ἀλλὰ καὶ διὰ παντὸς παρέχειν αὐτῇ προθυ-μούμεθα.

20 Καὶ πρῶτον μὲν ὅτι τὸ σχίσμα τῶν ἐκκλησιῶν ὡς ἀδίκως καὶ παραλόγως πάλαι παρεισφθαρὲν ἐξ ἐπαιρείας σατανικῆς ὅλῃ ψυχῇ καὶ γνώμῃ καταρχὰς τῆς καταλλαγῆς τελείως ἀποβαλλόμενοι στέργομεν ἅπερ ἐκυρώθη τηνικαῦτα διὰ τόμου συνοδικοῦ· καὶ τὸ πρωτεῖον, τὴν ἔκκλητόν τε καὶ τὸ μνημόσυνον τῷ ἀποστολικῷ θρόνῳ προσνέμοντες,
25 ταῦτα φυλάττειν ἀπαραποίητα καὶ εἰς τὸ ἐξῆς ὑπισχνούμεθα, μηδὲν αὐτῶν ἐπαγγελλόμενοι κατὰ μηδένα τρόπον καινοτομῆσαι τὸ σύνολον· ἔπειτα δὲ παραδηλοῦμεν τῇ μεγάλῃ ἁγιωσύνῃ σου ὡς ἐπεὶ τῆς τοιαύτης ἑνώσεως τῶν ἐκκλησιῶν πρόρρησις Θεοῦ τὸν ἀρχαίκακον οὐκ ἦν ἠρε-μεῖν· ὅθεν καί τινων ἡμετέρων τινὰς ἄξια δοχεῖα τῆς ἑαυτοῦ κακίας
30 εὑρὼν τὸν οἰκεῖον ἰὸν τούτοις ἐξεμέσας ἐνέχεεν· οἱ καὶ πλήρεις γεγονότες τοῦ πονηροῦ νόθον διδασκαλίαν εἰσηγοῦντο καὶ παρέγραπτον τῷ τοῦ Κυρίου λαῷ, πείθοντες τούτους διὰ τὴν τοιαύτην εἰρήνην καταφρονεῖν τῶν ἐν τοῖς ἱεροῖς καὶ θείοις οἴκοις συνάξεων, τοὺς πρεσβυτέρους παρὰ πάντα λόγον δίκαιον ἀποστρέφεσθαι, τῶν τελουμένων παρ' αὐτοῖς ἁγιασ-
35 μάτων ἀπέχεσθαι, πρὸς τούτοις ἀθετεῖν καὶ τὸ διὰ τούτων ἐνεργούμενον βάπτισμα· δι' ὧν δὴ πάντων ἐπειρῶντο τὴν χριστιανικὴν ἀνατρέψαι διαγωγὴν καὶ κατάστασιν.

Now the very estimable nuncios of Your Serenity have come to us, men that we perceive to excel in every virtue and to be replete with wisdom both natural and supernatural and with words that flow from learning. From these we have been more fully informed of the state of Your Holiness, gaining from their exact and sure knowledge what before we had gathered from hearsay and second-hand informants who were no more than purveyors of mere rumours, among other things of the inexpressible fruits of your godlike way of life and your marvellous wisdom for which, as says the divine apostle, God, who has a never-ending solicitude for the peace of his Churches and watches over their harmony, has bestowed on you this lofty and mighty throne.

In the light, then, of this knowledge and information, with unspeakable joy we set ourselves by this present letter to acquaint Your Beatitude of our zeal for this so important work, wishing to show you clearly that in our earnestness in seeking this so precious peace of the Churches we not only willingly grant to the Apostolic See the prerogatives and privileges that of old were attributed to it, but that we sincerely wish to grant them always.

First, at the very start of this reconciliation, we reject completely and with all our hearts and souls the schism of the Churches as having been introduced unjustly and against all reason by the machinations of Satan, and we accept what was ratified then by the synodical document. Conceding to the apostolic throne the primacy, the right of appeal and the commemoration, we promise to preserve these unaltered also for the future, declaring that in no point and in no way at all will we instigate any change in their regard. Further, we proclaim to Your mighty Holiness that, after the announcement of this important union of the Churches, the primeval enemy of God could find no peace. So, having discovered among ours some who were worthy vessels of his malice, he spewed out and injected into them his very own venom. They, filled with the Evil One, introduced counterfeit and fraudulent teaching to the Lord's people, persuading them to despise the liturgies in the holy and divine temples because of this peace, against all reason to shun priests, to hold themselves aloof from the sacred ceremonies performed by them, even to reject baptism administered by them. By all these means, then, they were trying to subvert the Christian way of life and its very basis.

Διὰ ταῦτα σπουδῇ πολλῇ τῶν θεοστεφῶν ἁγίων αὐτοκρατόρων
150ʳ μου πᾶσα τῶν ἀρχιερέων ἡ ‖ θεία χορεία καὶ πάλιν ἐπὶ τὸ αὐτὸ συναθροί-
ζεται, σὺν οἷς ἡ μετριότης ἡμῶν μετακαλεσαμένη τοὺς τῆς τοιαύτης
ἀπάτης προστάτας καὶ ἀρχηγούς· καὶ τούτων πολλοὺς διορθωσαμένη
5 διδασκαλίαις καὶ παραινέσεσιν, ὡς εἶδέ τινας ἐξ αὐτῶν τῇ οἰκείᾳ πλάνῃ διὰ
τέλους ἐμμείναντας, ἀπόφασιν κοινῇ τῇ ψήφῳ κατὰ τούτων ἐξήνεγκεν·
ἥτις καὶ πάντας τοὺς οὕτως ἔχοντας ἱερομένους μὲν ὄντας ἐν ὁποιῳδήτινι
τάγματι εἴτε τῷ τῆς ἀρχιερωσύνης ἐνθεωροῦνται σεμνώματι εἴτε πρεσ-
βύτεροί εἰσι τὸν βαθμὸν εἴτε τοῖς διακόνοις συγκαταλέγονται· τούτους
10 πάντας πρὸς δὲ καὶ μοναχοὺς καὶ αὐτοὺς ἱερωσύνης παντοίας περικειμένους ἀξίωμα, καθαιρέσει καὶ ἀναθέματι καθυπέβαλε· λαικοὺς δὲ
καὶ ἄλλως αὖ μοναχοὺς οἵτινες καὶ ἰδιῶται καλοῦνται διὰ τὸ μηδόλως
ἱερωσύνῃ κοσμεῖσθαι· μὴ δὲ κἂν ὁποίας ὦσιν οὗτοι τύχης καὶ καταστάσεως, εἴτε τῶν ὑψηλῶν καὶ μεγάλων τὴν κάτω καὶ κατὰ κόσμον δόξαν
15 καὶ περιφάνειαν, εἴτε τῶν ταπεινῶν τε καὶ χθαμαλῶν, ἀφορισμῷ καὶ
ἀναθέματι καὶ τούτους παρέπεμψεν.

Ταῦτα μετὰ τῆς ἐπὶ αὐτὴν ἀρχιερατικῆς ὁμηγύρεως πάσης ἡ
μετριότης ἡμῶν συνοδικῶς ἐκφωνήσασα καὶ γραφῇ παραδέδωκεν· ἣν
καὶ ταῖς αὐτοχείροις ἡμῶν ὑπογραφαῖς ἐπεκυρώσαμεν ἕκαστος, ὡς ἔχει
20 μαθεῖν ἡ μακαριότης σου καὶ ἀπὸ τῆς τομογραφίας αὐτῆς ἥτις ταύτῃ
διακομίζεται· καὶ ἐπὶ μὲν τῆς εἰρήνης τῶν ἐκκλησιῶν τοῦ Θεοῦ καὶ
τῶν ἀνέκαθεν ἀπονενεμημένων τῷ ἀποστολικῷ θρόνῳ πρεσβείων ὅτι
ταῦτα τηροῦμεν εἰλικρινεῖ διαθέσει ψυχῆς ἀναλλοίωτα καὶ ἔτι τηρή-
σομεν τῇ χάριτι τοῦ Χριστοῦ τοσαῦτα καὶ οὕτω τὸ ἀσφαλὲς δὲ πλου-
25 τοῦντα καὶ βέβαιον.

Ἤδη δὲ καὶ τὴν τῆς πίστεως ὁμολογίαν ἐκθεῖναι χρέων ἵνα ἴδῃ
σαφῶς ἡ μακαριότης σου τό τε φρόνημα καὶ τὴν ἐπὶ τὸ θεῖον γνώμην
ἡμῶν καὶ ὡς τῆς τῶν ἁγίων πατέρων εὐσεβείας ὡς εἰκὸς ἐξεχόμενοι
τὴν ἀποστολικὴν ἐκκλησίαν τῆς Ῥώμης ὀρθόδοξον οἴδαμεν ὁμογνωμο-
30 νοῦντες ταύτῃ κατὰ τὴν ἔννοιαν. Πιστεύομεν γὰρ εἰς ἕνα Θεὸν ἄναρχον
καὶ ἀναίτιον, ἀόρατον, ἀκατάληπτον, ἀναλλοίωτον, τὸν Πατέρα τοῦ
Κυρίου καὶ Θεοῦ καὶ Σωτῆρος ἡμῶν Ἰησοῦ Χριστοῦ, πάντων ποιημάτων
ὁρατῶν τε καὶ ἀοράτων δημιουργόν, ὃς ἐξ οὐκόντων τὰ πάντα ὑποστη-
σάμενος προνοητικῇ δυνάμει συνέχει ταῦτα καὶ διοικεῖ· καὶ εἰς ἕνα
35 Κύριον Ἰησοῦν Χριστὸν τὸν Υἱὸν τοῦ Θεοῦ τὸν μονογενῆ, τὸν ἐκ τοῦ
Πατρὸς γεννηθέντα πρὸ πάντων τῶν αἰώνων, Θεὸν ἀληθινὸν ἐκ Θεοῦ
ἀληθινοῦ, τὸν συναϊδως ὄντα τῷ Θεῷ καὶ Πατρί, καὶ πάντα ὅσα ὁ Πατὴρ
ἀπαραλλάκτως ἔχοντα δίχα μόνου τοῦ εἶναι πατήρ, ὁμοούσιον τῷ Πατρὶ

For this reason at the instigation of my holy God-crowned Emperors, the whole divine college of archbishops met again. With them Our Mediocrity, having summoned the protectors and leaders of such an imposture, converted many of them by instruction and warnings, but when we saw some among them obstinately persisting in their errors, by common consent we passed sentence on all of those who were so disposed — clerics of every rank without exception, whether distinguished with the episcopal dignity or ranked as priests or listed as deacons — on all of these, and besides on monks and on all that have any kind of sacred character, we imposed deposition and anathema. Likewise we assigned to excommunication and anathema laymen and also those monks who are called ' private ' as not having any sacred character, no matter of what fortune or status, whether high and mighty in reputation and external show here below in this world, or humble and lowly.

Our Mediocrity, with all the assembly of archbishops around us, promulgated this in synod and consigned it to writing in a document which we, each of us with his own hand, ratified with his signature, as Your Beatitude can see from the statement that accompanies this letter; and, as regards the peace of the Churches of God and the prerogatives ascribed of old to the apostolic throne, you can see that with sincere disposition of soul we preserve these unchanged and by the grace of Christ will preserve them for the future, many as they are and thus enhanced with assurance and certainty.

It is now high time to state our profession of faith so that Your Beatitude may clearly perceive our thought and mind about the divine and that, while we stand firm in the religion of the holy Fathers as is fitting, we recognise that the apostolic Church of Rome is orthodox, for we are in agreement with it in meaning.   For we believe in one God, without beginning and without cause. beyond our sight and our comprehension, unchanging, the Father of our Lord and God and Saviour Jesus Christ, creator of all things visible and invisible, who from nothing gave substance to all things by his provident power and conserves them and directs them; and in one Lord Jesus Christ, the only-begotten Son of God, born of the Father before time began, true God of true God, coeternal with God and Father, who without change has all whatsoever

40

δι' οὗ τὰ πάντα ἐγέ ||νετο τά τε ἐν οὐρανῷ καὶ τὰ ἐπὶ γῆς · ὃς διὰ τὴν ἡμε-
τέραν σωτηρίαν μὴ λιπὼν τοὺς κόλπους τοὺς πατρικοὺς ἐκένωσεν ἑαυτὸν
καὶ κατῆλθε μέχρι καὶ δούλου μορφῆς · σαρκωθεὶς ἐκ Πνεύματος ἁγίου
καὶ Μαρίας τῆς παρθένου καὶ θεοτόκου καὶ φορεσθεὶς ἀναλλοιώτως τὸ
5 καθ᾽ ἡμᾶς μετὰ τὸ γενέσθαι τέλειος ἄνθρωπος ἔμεινε τέλειος καὶ πάλιν
Θεὸς εἷς καθ᾽ ὑπόστασιν ὑπάρχων ἐν δυσὶ τελείαις ταῖς φύσεσι, θεότητι
λέγω καὶ ἀνθρωπότητι, καθ᾽ ἣν ἀνθρωπότητα καὶ πέπονθεν ἑκὼν ἀπαθὴς
ὢν τῇ θεότητι · σταυρόν τε καταδεξάμενος τῇ οἰκείᾳ σαρκὶ καὶ τὸν
διὰ σταυροῦ θάνατον, ὡσαύτως δὲ καὶ ταφήν · ἀνέστη τριήμερος ἐκ
10 νεκρῶν, καὶ ἀναληφθεὶς μετὰ τοῦ προσλήμματος ἐκάθισεν ἐκ δεξιῶν
τοῦ Θεοῦ καὶ Πατρός, καὶ πάλιν ἥξει μετὰ δόξης κριτὴς ζώντων καὶ
νεκρῶν ἀποδώσων ἑκάστῳ τῶν ἀνθρώπων κατὰ τὰς ἐν τῷδε τῷ βίῳ
πράξεις αὐτοῦ · καὶ βασιλεύσων ἀθάνατα καὶ ἀνώλεθρα · καὶ εἰς τὸ
Πνεῦμα τὸ ἅγιον, τὸ κύριον, τὸ ζωοποιόν, τὸ ἐκ τοῦ Πατρὸς διὰ τοῦ
15 Υἱοῦ ἐκπορευόμενον καὶ αὐτὸ Θεὸν εἶναι γνωριζόμενον ὡς ὁμοφυές τε
καὶ ὁμοούσιον, καθάπερ γὰρ κατ᾽ οὐσίαν καὶ φύσιν ἐστὶν ὡς ἐκ τοῦ
Πατρὸς διὰ τοῦ Υἱοῦ γεννηθέντος ἀφράστως ἐκπορευόμενον · τὸ πάντων
κτισμάτων τελεσιουργόν, τὸ παντοδύναμον · τὸ παντέφορον · τὰ πάντα
γινῶσκον καὶ τὰ βάθη τοῦ Θεοῦ, ὅπερ πρόεισι μὲν ἐκ τοῦ Πατρὸς φυσικῶς
20 καὶ οὐσιωδῶς, πρόεισι δὲ καὶ ἐκ τοῦ Υἱοῦ καθάπερ ἀμέλει καὶ ἀπὸ τοῦ
Θεοῦ καὶ Πατρός · τὸ σὺν Πατρὶ καὶ Υἱῷ συμπροσκυνούμενον καὶ
συνδοξαζόμενον · τὸ λαλῆσαν διά τε τῶν προφητῶν καὶ τῶν κηρύκων
τῆς χάριτος · ἔτι μίαν ἁγίαν καθολικὴν καὶ ἀποστολικὴν ἐκκλησίαν
δεχόμενοι σεβαζόμεθα · καταλογοῦμεν ἓν βάπτισμα τυγχάνειν ἁμαρτίας
25 ἀφιέναι δυνάμενον · προσδοκῶμεν ἀνάστασιν νεκρῶν καὶ ζωὴν τοῦ
μέλλοντος αἰωνίζουσαν.

Ταῦτα πρεσβεύοντες ἄνωθεν καὶ ἐξ ἀρχῆς, ὡς στήλην ὀρθοδοξίας
κατέχομεν, καὶ μετ᾽ αὐτῶν παραστῆναι τῷ βήματι τοῦ Χριστοῦ κατὰ
τὴν ἡμέραν τῆς κρίσεως ἐπευχόμεθα πρεσβείαις τῆς θεοτόκου καὶ
30 πάντων τῶν ἁγίων, ἀμήν.

the Father has except only to be Father, consubstantial with the Father through whom all things whether in heaven or on earth were made, he who for our salvation without leaving the bosom of the Father emptied himself and descended even to the form of a slave, made flesh by the Holy Spirit and the Virgin Mary, mother of God, and clothed with our nature but unchanged, after becoming perfect man he still remained perfect God, being one in hypostasis in two complete natures, Godhead, I say, and manhood, in which manhood, though in Godhead he could not suffer, he also willingly suffered, having accepted the cross for his flesh and by the cross death and likewise the tomb; the third day he rose again from the dead and, having ascended with what he had assumed, sat at the right hand of God and Father, and he will come again in glory as judge of the living and the dead, to render to each of men according to his actions in this life, and will reign immortal and imperishable; and in the Holy Spirit, the Lord, the giver of life, who proceeds from the Father through the Son and is acknowledged also as God seeing that he proceeds in his substance and nature ineffably from the Father through the engendered Son, perfecter of all creatures, almighty, all-seeing, who knows all things, even the depths of God; who indeed comes forth from the Father in nature and substance and comes forth from the Son exactly as from God and Father, who is adored and glorified with the Father and the Son, who spoke through both the prophets and the heralds of grace; also we accept and reverence one holy, catholic and apostolic Church; we profess one baptism capable of forgiving sins; we await the resurrection of the dead and the everlasting life of the world to come.

This we have professed from of old and from the beginning and we cling to it as a pillar of orthodoxy, and we pray that we may present ourselves with this before the tribunal of Christ on the day of judgement, by the intercession of the Mother of God and of all the saints. Amen.

REFLECTIONS

The very strong impression left after reading these official documents (with the exception of Beccus's letter about which something will be said shortly) is that the only thing that bothered the Greeks, faced with the question of the union of the Churches, was the canonical position of the pope — the three points, primacy, appeal and commemoration. Pachymeres's narrative is no different. The Emperor urged this one aspect. Joseph's *pittakion* mentions it. The synodical letter sent to the Pope in Lyons, dated February 1274, mentions only the primacy. The chryso-bull and the synodal acceptance of it refer specifically to no other bar to union and repeatedly insist on these three heads being the only concessions. The *tomographia* of February 1277 decrees penalties against opponents of the union without identifying their errors in detail, but the Statement in Writing signed by the clerics of the Great Church, signifying their acceptance of the *tomographia*, specifies recognition of the three points. None of these documents (or Pachymeres) gives the slightest hint that a basic obstacle to union was the doctrinal difference on the Procession of the Holy Spirit. Yet, when Beccus called the Latins heretics, he was thinking not principally of the primacy but of the *Filioque*, and everybody knew it. And when he was converted to unionism and became a chief supporter of Michael's ecclesiastical policy, it was because by reading the Fathers and writers like Blemmydes he had become convinced that the difference between the Churches over the *Filioque* was more a divergence in words than in doctrine: once again, everybody must have known that. All the same, after the abdication of Joseph I on 9 January 1275, to succeed him Beccus was elected on 26 May by the synod to the great satisfaction of all the bishops ([1]).

The picture that Pachymeres then paints is somewhat strange. The city is in a turmoil; the schism deepens; the populace is divided into small and hostile factions of 'theologians' ignorant of both theology and history. But in the ecclesiastical world there is peace. About the Church he has nothing more to relate than that

([1]) PACHYMERES, *Op. cit.*, p. 403.

Beccus soon has friction with the Emperor as he pleads, almost violently, for imperial compassion on men condemned, till there is a scene when he throws down his patriarchal staff and stalks out of the palace.   He then becomes ill and goes to recuperate to the monastery where the ex-Patriarch Joseph is staying and these two old friends resume their earlier intimacy.   Beccus returned to the city and in 1279 abdicated after further friction with the monarch. In all this narrative of four years of tense Church history, theology is not mentioned. It seems that the bishops and ecclesiastics, having agreed to the union on a canonical basis, deliberately closed their minds — or at least their mouths — on the theologically controversial *Filioque*.   But it peeped up.

While Beccus was still off the patriarchal throne, nuncios came from Rome to ask for palpable signs of union from the Greek Church.   Some of the Greek anti-unionists suggested to them an acid-test — to demand that the Greek Creed conform to the Latin by including the *Filioque*. If the Emperor (so the anti-unionists argued) refused their request, the Romans would realise that the union was a farce; if he acceded to it, he would be unmasked before the Greeks as changing their Creed.   In either case, the union would be ended.   The ruse failed, for Palaeologus harangued the synod, repeated the guarantees given in his chrysobull and persuaded the bishops not to force the issue [1].

Shortly afterwards the theological factor came to the fore again, and it was Beccus who was responsible.   Earlier he had determined, though contrary to his natural inclination, not to get involved in the written polemics by answering the many ill-informed and theologically unsound attacks on the Latin Church.   There came a point when he could stand it no longer. "So he held frequent synods and invited many outsiders also; he set out many old books and put out many other [new] ones, demonstrating, as he was convinced himself, that the peace was sound, and doing this with all earnestness" [2]. The bishops tried to get the Emperor to silence him and failed.   They were furious, especially the Metropolitan of Ephesus who was the Emperor's confessor, for "they had with very great difficulty accepted the peace and had barely yielded and were unionist only in appearance, pacifying

[1] *Ibid.*, pp. 456-7.
[2] *Ibid.*, p. 481.

44

their consciences not from Scripture (for there was no occasion for that) but by economy usual in the Church for the attainment of a greater good" [1]. They were scandalised, "preferring for themselves the lesser evil of sinning by making peace with men who erred in the divine dogmas to the greater evil of seeming to call the dogmas in question" [2].

What the records of Pachymeres seem to say is that the Greek bishops throughout all the negotiations for union and in the years after it closed their minds to the theological question of the Procession of the Holy Spirit. What, then, is the value of doc. IV (1), the translation of the doctrinal decree of the Council of Lyons? The text itself suggests no connection with the Eastern Church except that it is in Greek, it is a literal translation of the original Latin of the decree which the Greek delegates doubtless approved of in Lyons and brought back with them to Constantinople, and it is in a collection of synodal and imperial documents. In addition some one — the first, early compiler or a copyist — added the title: "Synodical decree which the bishops of that day in Constantinople made about the Holy Spirit". They certainly did not "make' it in the sense of 'compose' it. Did they accept it?

Beccus wrote two letters [3] to popes with a very similar content. They both consist of a first part expressing at length the acceptance of papal primacy, the one, doc. VIII (2), mentions the *tomographia* under that name and described the circumstances of its composition — opposition to union from persons of all ranks, clerical and lay, and the imposition of penalties; the other alludes to it without detail. In both there follows a lengthy profession of faith, that of the second letter being the longer and including some direct quotations from the Clementine profession of faith. Doc. VIII (2) was composed (it says so itself) after the papal nuncios had arrived and probably soon after they had arrived. It was meant to accompany and explain the copy of the *tomographia*

---

[1] *Ibid.*, p. 480.

[2] *Ibid.*, p. 483.

[3] One, the earlier one, is doc. VIII (2). The Greek text of the other is in A. THEINER and F. MIKLOSICH, *Monumenta spectantia ad unionem ecclesiarum graecae et latinae* ... (Vindobonae, 1872) pp. 21-8. The Latin text is in *Acta Romanorum Pontificum ab Innocentio V ad Benedictum XI* (1276-1304) (= Pontificia Commissio etc. Fontes, III, V, 2) edd. F. D. DE-LORME and A. L. TAUTU (Città del Vaticano, 1954) no 18, pp. 36-43.

that was being sent to the Pope through them. Later, when the nuncios had stayed on for some time and when, in deference to the Pope's wish, the Emperors had renewed their profession of faith and furnished copies of it in writing with their signatures, Beccus wrote the second letter with the fuller expression of his faith, to emulate them, whose example he refers to in the letter.

It is noteworthy that only in the earlier part of these letters, where he confines himself to the primacy-issue, does Beccus claim the consent of the synod and the Church. Had the synod made a statement accepting the *Filioque*, writing to the Pope he must have recorded that, and in glowing terms. He did not. So one must conclude that the two versions of his profession of faith contained in these two letters are the expression of his personal belief and do not purport to be the mind of the synod and the Church.

VI

JOHN BECCUS, PATRIARCH OF CONSTANTINOPLE
1275-1282

Very little is known about the early life of Beccus. He was born probably in Nicaea — certainly he owned vineyards there and had many relations and dependents in that area [1]. He was appointed chartophylax of the Great Church by Patriarch Arsenius, who had excommunicated Emperor Michael VIII Palaeologus for having blinded the young son of his predecessor, emperor Theodore II Lascaris, so as to bar his succession. As the Patriarch refused to absolve Palaeologus till he did penance, i.e., renounced the throne in favour of the boy, relations between the court and the Church were very tense. One of Beccus's first actions in office was to suspend a palace cleric from his priesthood for celebrating a marriage without the requisite previous consent of the chartophylax. The Emperor fumed. Beccus escaped imprisonment only by apologising [2].

Arsenius was deposed in late spring 1264. He was followed on the patriarchal throne by Germanus (1265-6) and then by Joseph (1266-75). Beccus remained as chartophylax under them all and clearly enjoyed also the confidence of the Emperor who used him for diplomatic missions. With the Patriarch and a number of other personages and a load of rich gifts, Beccus escorted the Emperor's second daughter for her marriage to a son of the Czar of Bulgaria. Appalled by the squalor, misery and barbarity of the Bulgarian court, the ambassadors took her back to Constantinople. A little later, in 1270, with the archdeacon Meliteniotes, he was sent to King Louis IX of France to get him to restrain his brother Charles of Anjou from attacking the Empire. They found Louis in Tunisia desperately ill. His promise to promote peace among Christians was of little avail, for he died the next day [3].

The kind of 'peace among Christians' that Michael Palaeologus wanted was immunity from attack from the west for Constantinople, retaken only in 1261. To achieve this he wooed the Holy See with suggestions of Church union. The popes, who were nearly as afraid of the

---

1. G. Pachymeres, *De Michaele et Andronico Palaeologis*, 2 vols., ed. I. Bekker (Bonn, 1835), esp. I, pp. 227, 494.

2. *Ibid.*, pp. 225-9. This incident dates from before May/June 1264 when Arsenius was deposed.

3. *Ibid.*, pp. 350-5, 361-4.

kings of Sicily as was the Greek Emperor, were (and with reason) only half-convinced that Michael's interest in union was anything more than a camouflage of his political aims. Nevertheless they responded to his overtures. Clement IV, however, in 1264 determined to make pretence impossible. He drew up a detailed profession of faith as held by the Roman Church, which Michael and the Greek Church should accept. But Clement died soon after and the next pope was not elected till nearly three years later.

Palaeologus had more difficulty in persuading his own Church to accept union than he had with the new Pope Gregory X, who before ever he reached Rome to be crowned had sent a message of goodwill to Constantinople. The Emperor tried in every way he could. He brought up the subject frequently in conversations with his clerics, urging the need of union if Constantinople was not again to be bathed in blood from a new Latin invasion. He reminded them that a few years earlier Patriarch Manuel and the synod had agreed to recognise the claims of Rome and that there were documents in the archives to prove it. His chief sympathisers were the archdeacon Meliteniotes, George the Cypriot and George Metochites. One day, when Michael was haranguing the Patriarch and other clerics, among them Beccus, the Patriarch bade Beccus under pain of excommunication reply. He hesitated, caught between the hammer of the excommunication and the anvil of the Emperor's possible displeasure. Finally he said: «Some people are in fact heretics and are said to be such; others neither are nor are said to be; others again are said to be but are not; whereas others are said not to be and are. Among these last the Italians should be classed». His fears were amply justified. He was accused of negligence in carrying out his diplomatic missions. He sought sanctuary in a church. Then, invited to an audience with the Emperor, he was arrested as soon as he emerged «and confined in the Tower of the Anema under the guard of the Celts» [4].

While Beccus was in prison things did not stand still. Palaeologus produced a historico-theological tractate to prove that the Latins were not heretics. The Patriarch answered it, wrote an encyclical letter repudiating union and took an oath personally never to accept it. The Emperor was completely frustrated. But he received an unexpected ally. Beccus in prison was converted to unionism.

When he had called the Latins heretics, it was because of their doctrine on the Procession of the Holy Spirit. They believed that the

---

4. *Ibid.*, pp. 374-8.

Holy Spirit proceeds from the Father and from the Son, and in the Nicene Greed they added the words «and from the Son» after «who proceeds from the Father». The Greek Church of that day professed that the Holy Spirit proceeds «from the Father only» or «from the Father through the Son», and condemned the western addition to the Creed. In prison Beccus was given excerpts from the writings of Greek Fathers and theologians, which rather favoured the Latin view. He was impressed by them. But «being an honest man and passionately devoted to the truth», since hitherto his studies had been more in profane than in sacred literature, he asked for the treatises from which the excerpts had been taken to study them, before making up his mind on the question, for once he had settled his conscience he would steadfastly act according to it. Having studied carefully writings of various Fathers he concluded that the sole difference between Latins and Greeks was the preposition 'from' or 'through', while the substance of the doctrine was the same. His conscience was formed. He approved of union [5].

Beccus's imprisonment took place probably in early 1273. When he was released is uncertain, but he was back in office as chartophylax by February 1274, when he signed a decree of the synod. That decree was the fruit of much activity by the Emperor. When he found his persuasions to win people to his policy unavailing, he had recourse to harassment of one sort or another till, stressing that union with Rome was absolutely essential to save the Empire and at the same time claiming that it was innocuous since it consisted of only three points of canon law — acknowledgement of papal primacy, right of appeal to Rome, and commemoration of the pope in the Liturgy — he prevailed on the synod of bishops to accept it. The synodal statement for Lyons of February 1274 was the document that bore Beccus's signature [6]. Thereupon delegates were sent to the Council of Lyons, where they agreed to union of the Churches. Joseph I abdicated. John Beccus was canonically and unanimously elected as his successor on 26 May 1275 and consecrated and enthroned on 2 June, Whitsunday.

The new Patriarch was as strong a character as the Emperor. On

---

5. *Ibid.*, pp. 381, 383-4; Nicephorus Gregoras, *Byzantina Historia*, ed. L. Schopenus (Bonn, 1829) vol. I, pp. 128-30; George Metochites, *Historia Dogmatica*, ed. A. Mai, *Patrum Nova Bibliotheca*, VIII (Rome, 1871) pp. 41-5. Beccus knew no Latin; cf. G. Hofmann, 'Patriarch Johann Bekkos und die lateinische Kultur', in *Orientalia Christiana Periodica*, 11 (1945), pp. 140, 161.

6. *Acta Urbani IV, Clementis IV, Gregorii X (1261-1276)*, ed. A. Tautu (Città del Vaticano, 1953) doc. 42.

union they saw eye to eye, but on other matters there soon was friction. It was, apparently, part of a patriarch's duties or privileges to intercede with the Emperor for aid for the destitute and for mercy for the condemned. Beccus was never satisfied with 'no' for an answer. If at first refused some request, he returned again and again to the charge in repeated audiences and with other arguments. The Emperor became irritated at his persistence. There were several scenes between them, some of which Pachymeres describes. On one occasion the Patriarch pleaded for someone whom, as it happened, Michael disliked. The requests and the refusals became more and more heated and discourteous till Beccus cast his episcopal staff onto the floor and stalked out, refusing to return though Emperor and imperial lackeys called on him to do so. Another time at the end of a solemn Liturgy he would not allow the Emperor to be offered the blessed bread [7]. The not-unexpected result was that the easy relations between Emperor and Patriarch and the complete freedom of access to the imperial presence that had characterised the early days of Beccus's reign soon ceased. Michael limited his opportunities for asking graces to one day in the week, Tuesday, and Michael Xiphilinus was appointed as secretary to present petitions and receive answers.

As Patriarch, Beccus had other things to do besides squabbling with the Emperor, but Pachymeres relates nothing about these. Fortunately there are other, though very limited, sources. Soon after his consecration Beccus must have sent to inform the Pope of his election and to report on the progress of the union in the east. There was, in fact, a strong and general opposition to it. The chief opponents were the numerous monks, most of whom (the Arsenite faction) were already hostile to the Emperor and the official Church because of the blinding of the boy, John, and the deposition of Patriarch Arsenius who had defended him. They were, however, not the only ones who rejected union. Members of every rank of society and of the Church were against it, including the Emperor's sister and her daughters, senators, bishops, officials of Church and State, priests. To meet this situation Patriarch and synod issued a «tomographia» repeating their acceptance of union and enacting penalties for all who persisted in rejecting it. This document is dated 19 February 1277. It was signed by all the bishops of the synod. Shortly afterwards all the officials for the Great Church had to certify their acceptance of it [8].

---

7. Pachymeres, *Op. cit.*, pp. 405-8.

8. J. Gill, 'The Church Union of the Council of Lyons (1274) portrayed in Greek Documents', *Orientalia Christiana Periodica* 40 (1974), docs. V and VI, pp. 22-32.

Beccus sent a copy of the 'tomographia' to Rome with an accompanying letter of his own, that contained a profession of faith. A little later, perhaps in April, to meet the request made by Pope John XXI through his nuncios then in Constantinople, he wrote a similar letter with a longer profession of faith. In these documents he states very explicitly his acceptance of Roman primacy and of the *Filioque* doctrine as believed by the Latins. It is true that, in respect of the Procession of the Holy Spirit, he employs, not the controversial preposition ἐχ (from), but παρὰ (from). He leaves no doubt, however, that his belief is one with the belief of Rome: «For just as the Spirit is from the substance of the Father by nature, so the Spirit is from the substance of the Son by nature» [9]. A few months later he applied the sanctions passed by the synod against those «who do not accept the holy Roman Church to be the mother and head of all other Churches and the mistress of orthodox belief, and its supreme pontiff to be the first and shepherd of all Christians», to the Greek rulers of Epirus and Thessaly, both of them vassals of Palaeologus, who were making their courts centres of anti-unionism and rebellion [10].

Beccus fell ill, probably in 1278. Against the wish of the Emperor he went to convalesce in the monastery where the ex-Patriarch Joseph was then residing. There he had leisure to read many pamphlets and other works of Greek writers deficient in the theology of their own Church and positively misrepresenting that of the Latins. But, tempted though he was to write answers, he agreed with his friend Xiphilinus that, were he to start writing, it would probably only make matters worse by again opening up debate on what had once been settled.

Beccus had not long returned to Constantinople when some of the clergy preferred serious charges against him to the Emperor, «false and completely baseless, but not difficult for the monarch to credit, for he was very much on the look-out for a means of curbing the zeal of the Patriarch» [11]. An imperial decree was issued removing from patriarchal jurisdiction all monasteries situated outside the diocese of Constantinople, on the grounds that the right claimed by a long line of patriarchs to 'stavropegic' monasteries wherever they were was an abuse. After

---

9. A. Theiner and F. Miklosich, *Monumenta spectantia ad unionem ecclesiarum graecae et latinae* (Vienna, 1872), pp. 21-8; esp. p. 26.

10. *Acta Roman. Pont. ab Innocentio V ad Benedictum XI (1276-1304)* (= Pont. Comm. ad redig. cod. iur. canon. orient. Fontes III, V, II) edd. F. M. Delorme & A. L. Tautu (Città del Vaticano, 1954), doc. 19, pp. 43-4.

11. Pachymeres, *Op. cit.*, I, pp. 449-50.

further provocations Beccus finally reacted (March 1279) by sending
the Emperor notice of his intention to abdicate and by retiring to the
monastery of Panachrantus.

While Beccus was thus in retirement, it happened that four nuncios sent by Pope Nicholas III arrived and were met by the Emperor
near Adrianople. Their purpose was to ask for more copies of the profession of faith of the two Emperors and to get proofs that the Church
was seriously and generally concurring in the union. Michael sent messengers to ask Beccus to take up his duties again. He himself escorted
the envoys to Constantinople and exhorted the Greek ecclesiastics to
give them a friendly reception, saying and doing nothing to upset them.
To impress them with the sincerity of his endeavours for union, he had
them shown round a prison where four generals, all of them relatives
of his, were in chains. Sent against John of Thessaly, instead of fighting
him, they had let him get possession of several strongholds, since he was
anti-unionist and Michael was unionist. They were all in one dungeon,
chained each in a corner.

Beccus re-entered Constantinople with a generous escort on 6 August 1279. Pachymeres records the sequel. «Then having concocted a
letter of reply to the Pope (Urban it was then), they authenticated it
with many signatures (written by one and the same hand) of non-existent bishops and non-existent Sees, as if of many holy and famous men.
But I do not know whether the Patriarch was privy to this, though
certainly the Emperor was, intending with this fictitious multitude of
bishops to make a show of equality between the Churches . . . With man-
y quotations from our Fathers that the Spirit pours forth, comes, is
given, shines forth, appears, from the Son, and the like, they aimed at
lessening the importance of the word 'proceed', and declared also that
'we subject to suitable penalties those who do not agree to observe the
union'» [12]. Such deception, however, (continues Pachymeres) did no
good.

Beccus's defence of the Latin doctrine of the *Filioque* brought on
him and other unionists accusations of all kinds of heresies. To justify
the unionist position he took up his pen and began to write, forgetting,
so says Pachymeres, his promise to Xiphilinus and the virtue of prudence.
Beccus himself later claimed that he wrote those early treatises in a spirit of 'economy', i.e., without asperity and tempering his arguments so as
not to cause unnecessary offence [13]. But his mildness of manner did not

---

12. *Ibid.*, pp. 461-2.
13. John Beccus, 'De libris suis', in PG. 141, 1020-8, esp. 1021 A-C, and 1025 BC.

succeed in disarming his opponents. In particular many bishops were furious with him. It had needed some forcing of their consciences to bring them to accept the union even on the minimal terms proposed by the Emperor. Yet Beccus was «bringing dogma into debate» with impunity, though there was an imperial prohibition against writing about the union. Complaint was laid before the Emperor, but he gave an enigmatic answer, neither exonerating nor condemning.

As opposition to the union did not abate and was intensifying political instability, Michael Palaeologus became increasingly violent and tyrannical. He acted on every denunciation from common informers. He sensed conspiracy on all sides and blinded the suspect. Anyone who wrote a pamphlet against union, who read one, who did not destroy any that came his way, was liable to the death penalty. Monks who told fortunes (to prophecy the Emperor's death) were blinded, mutilated or exiled. Of the four generals chained in prison, one had died, two of the others were blinded for still refusing union, the fourth was intimidated into yielding. Beccus was in a delicate position for, owing to his defence of the Latins, he was blamed by the Emperor «for having lost him his popularity with the people, and by the people for not having let the impact of what had been done diminish with the passage of time» [14].

During all this period the usual multifarious business of the synod and the patriarchal curia must have been carried on, but there is little record of it. A few clerics were censured for misdemeanours; a dispensation was granted for the marriage of Princess Anna with Michael Comnenus, and (on 3 May 1280) the Referendarius, Michael Eschamatismenus, was condemned for having erased the word 'from' in a manuscript of the works of St Gregory of Nyssa because it seemed to favour Latin theology [15]. Pachymeres records that Beccus, at about the time when he had begun to defend the unionistic position in writing, for the same purpose «held many synods, inviting also many non-members, and he read books and brought out many others, using his every endeavour to show that the union was sound and in this he was very assiduous» [16].

---

14. Pachymeres, *Op. cit.*, I, p. 495.

15. Metochites, *Op. cit.*, p. 86. V. Laurent, *Les régestes des Actes du Patriarchat de Constantinople*, I. *Les régestes de 1208-1307* (Paris, 1971) doc. 1447.

16. Pachymeres, *Op. cit.*, p. 481. According to Pachymeres, *Op. cit.* II, p. 32, to preclude accusations of heresy being levelled against him, Beccus added three anathemas to the formula read out on the Sunday of Orthodoxy. The text given by Pachymeres seems unlikely and J. Gouillard, *Le synodikon de l'Orthodoxie* (Paris, 1967) knows nothing about it.

As the cruelty of the Emperor grew, Beccus, knowing also that the bishops were looking for an excuse to effect his own disgrace [17], became more cautious not to give Michael a pretext. When the Emperor crossed the Bosphorus, the Patriarch went with him (12 July, probably 1280). On 16 August Emperor and Patriarch departed again for Asia Minor, Michael towards Nicomedia, Beccus towards Nicaea, but he did not enter that city since he had nothing to give to his relations and friends, a state of things unworthy, so he thought, of his rank. Palaeologus was the first back in Constantinople; Beccus arrived on the eve of the feast of the Holy Cross (14 September) and hastened to the imperial court before ever returning to his own palace. In late spring 1281 Beccus was back again in Nicaea, this time to conduct the obsequies of Anna, wife of the co-Emperor Andronicus. The rich presents he received on this occasion he distributed with great generosity among his kinsfolk. On his way back to Constantinople he had a long conversation with the widower Andronicus, who was very friendly towards him. Having celebrated with him the feast of Sts Peter and Paul (29 June), he returned to the capital.

Next year Emperor Michael led another expedition to Asia Minor, for since regaining Constantinople in 1261 he had neglected the defences there against the Turk in favour of trying to reoccupy all Greece. He was in Brusa when he learnt that the new Pope Martin IV on 18 November 1281 had excommunicated him. A year later, on 11 November 1282 he died while on a campaign in Thrace. His body was taken at night to a neighbouring monastery. According to Gregoras, Andronicus would not be present, «the reason being his [father's] deviation from the doctrine of the Church» [18].

Michael's had been the power that had kept the union in being and that had suppressed opposition. With his death the position of the Emperor Andronicus, who had several times subscribed to the union with the Latins, became extremely delicate. He quickly retracted and began his attempt (which lasted for thirty years) to placate Arsenites and antiunionists and to restore peace and internal unity to the Church. He dared do little to control the monks, who had suffered most from his father's oppression. Just before Christmas, when Beccus was preparing to celebrate the festal services and to perform a memorial ceremony for

---

17. Pachymeres, *Op. cit.*, p. 483.
18. Gregoras, *Op. cit.*, p. 153.

the late Emperor, Andronicus sent Constantine Meliteniotes to ask him to abdicate, and himself did not attend the Christmas Liturgy. Beccus obliged on 26 December by retiring to a monastery, but demanded an escort of soldiers so as not to lay himself open to a charge of voluntarily deserting his post. Four days later, Joseph, «just not dead», was carried back to the patriarchal palace.

With Joseph a «lifeless lump», the monks, claiming to act in his name, took charge. St Sophia was closed till it had been liturgically purified, not by a bishop, but by a mulilated monk. All those tainted with unionism — virtually the whole of Constantinople — had their penalties and their fines assessed by monks. Patriarch Joseph, they said, had suspended from divine services all bishops and clerics. Meliteniotes and Metochites were permanently degraded. George the Cypriot, however, was one of the judges at an assembly that arraigned people, not for the content of what they had written, but for having written at all, about dogma. That was to prepare the stage for the trial of Beccus on whom the general hatred and wrath were concentrated.

A few days later bells sounded throughout the city to summon monks and populace, for Beccus was to be tried. He refused to go unless with an escort of soldiers to control the mob. He was accused of mounting the patriarchal throne while it was still occupied (by Joseph) and of writing on dogma. Realising that it would be impossible to make a reasoned defence before judges so hostile and so undisciplined a mob, he replied only that he wrote because no one else was there to defend the truth and that the synod, which without his knowledge had freely elected him to be Patriarch and then had brought back the former Patriarch, should decide on his present status (i.e. if he was canonically Patriarch still). In the end they persuaded him to go with them to Joseph and there he signed a document containing a «profession of orthodox faith and a rejection of error, together with a renunciation of the priesthood». Metochites (who with Meliteniotes also signed a profession of faith) is vehement in asserting that none of them intended this to be more than a temporary step while the violence of the mob was at its height, though he confesses that it would have been more heroic to stand firm throughout [19]. Beccus was exiled to Brusa with a small pension from the Emperor, who for his part had to agree not to procure any religious commemorations for his dead father.

---

19. Metochites, *Op. cit.*, p. 93. The text of Beccus's profession of faith is contained in the 'tome' of Patriarch Gregory issued after the trial of 1285 — PG. 142, 234-46, esp. 237-8.

On 23 March Joseph I died, but not before a written abdication from the patriarchal throne had been screwed out of him to pacify the Arsenites. To replace him Andronicus appointed George the Cypriot, neither Arsenite nor Josephite, even if ex-unionist. He was consecrated on 11 April with the name of Gregory. During all Easter week with a number of rabid Arsenites he sat in judgement on those suspected of unionism. The widow of Michael VIII, Theodora, had to submit a written profession of faith and a promise not to procure religious services in memory of her dead husband [20]. A decree was passed depriving of their rank all who had been ordained by Beccus or who had favoured union [21].

Meanwhile Beccus had entered the lists again. In early 1284 he wrote an encyclical letter, to be given publicity by his many friends, demanding the right to defend himself against the charge of heresy and to expose the aberrations of the usurper of his throne. The Emperor decided that he should have his way. On 7 February 1285 in the Blachernae palace at a special synod the trial was held before the heads of both State and Church, with numerous bishops, senators and officials and a throng of monks and people [22]. Beccus was brought in, and only when Meliteniotes and Metochites were called out to testify did he know that he had any friends present. The three were arraigned on the same charges. In a sense, Beccus was the plaintiff and the official Church the defendant, for Beccus had provoked the summoning of the synod. But he was not allowed to open the proceedings. The plea of defence of the accused was very simple: it was they who held the traditional faith of the Eastern Church; their opponents had changed it.

---

20. S. Petridès, «Chrysobulle de l'impératrice Théodora (1283)», in *Echos d'Orient*, 14 (1911), pp. 25-8. From a comparison of Beccus's *De depositione sua* (PG. 141, 949-69, written before the flight from Constantinople of the Patriarch of Antioch shortly after Easter 1283) with Pachymeres and Metochites, the chronology of the early trials seems to be: 31 Dec. 1282 Patriarch Joseph returns; 1-3 January 1283 Beccus in fear of death (PG. 141, 956A); 4 January trials by monks (Beccus, 956D; Pach. II, 25-7; Met. p. 91); 7 January synod when Beccus signed the profession of faith (Beccus, 961; Pach. II, pp. 33-6; Met. 92-3); synod in Easter week under Patr. Gregory in church of Blachernae (Pach. II, pp. 52-7; Met. pp. 98-105; Gregoras, *Op. cit.*, pp. 171-3.

21. S. Petridès, «Sentence synodale contre le clergé unioniste» *(1283)*, in *Echos d' Orient*, 14 (1911), pp. 25-8. The date should probably be 1284.

22. Pachymeres, *Op. cit.*, II, pp. 88-103; Metochites, *Op. cit.*, pp. 123-70; Gregoras, *Op. cit.*, I, pp. 169-71. Gregoras's account is very brief and wrong. It ends «When Beccus saw that he would receive no clemency, he openly renounced the union».

Beccus had taught that the Spirit has his existence also from the Son. The logothete, Muzalon, denied that the ancient writers had ever used the actual word 'existence' in that context. A phrase of St John Damascene was quoted in reply, wherein the Father is said to be «the producer (proboleus) through the Son of the illuminating Spirit». Muzalon explained that 'proboleus' in respect of the Father signified that the Spirit «has his natural and eternal existence from him», but in respect of the Son it implied not «existence but eternal manifestation and splendour». He was immediately attacked by Beccus for giving the same word in the same context two different meanings, which none of the Fathers or any sound thinker did. Challenged, the ex-Patriarch reasserted his teaching that, in reference to the Procession, the prepositions 'Through' and 'From' were equivalent, quoting in proof St Gregory of Nyssa and the formula of the seventh council. He declared that he and his companions agreed in all things with the Fathers and averred that their only wish was ever to be in harmony with the orthodox faith of the Church of God. After the fourth session the meetings were prorogued to give time to the authorities to find an answer to Beccus's refutation of their explanation of the Damascene's words. The synod, without however having found the desired solution, met again in July to deliver sentence. The accused were declared guilty of heresy. Andronicus, wanting to avoid harsh penalties, tried to persuade them to adopt a more conciliatory attitude. They all three refused to modify their convictions and were sent to bleak exile in the fortress of St Gregory in Bithynia, this time without any pension.

Despite their condemnation, the trial had been a moral triumph for the three unionists. Patriarch Gregory tried to redress the balance and to rob Beccus of his seeming victory, by producing in August 1285 a 'tome' justifying the synod and giving an explanation of those words of the Damascene that had caused such difficulty. All ecclesiastics were required to sign it. Very few did [23]. They were wise. Beccus very soon obtained a copy of it and wrote a refutation which was widely circulated by his friends. Gregory's enemies prevailed on the Emperor to appoint a committee to amend the 'tome', but it could find no answer to Beccus's argument about the Damascene's words and in the end it cut the Gordian knot by omitting them altogether. Patriarch Gregory abdicated.

---

23. V. Laurent, «Les signataires du second synode des Blachernes (été 1825)», in *Echos d'Orient* 26 (1927), pp. 129-49.

Beccus remained in the fortress of St Gregory till his death. Meliteniotes and Metochites were sent there with him, but after a time the latter was brought back to Constantinople for reasons of health. Gregory's successor, Athanasius, took advantage of a journey to Asia Minor to send Beccus 100 gold ducats and Meliteniotes 50, and also in other ways to modify somewhat the severity of their treatment. The Emperor also went to Asia Minor and all three exiles (for Metochites had asked to rejoin his companions) were taken to Lopadion to meet him, when they had a pleasant conversation together. Pachymeres suggests that the prisoners should have been more accommodating in their attitudes when they learnt of the disgrace of their arch-enemy Gregory. Gratified, he says, they were, but they did not change, and for all his graciousness to them Andronicus, still battling with the Arsenites, was not inclined to bring on himself new trouble by letting them return to Constantinople [24].

In his long years of exile Beccus had plenty of time for writing, and a fair number of his treatises have been preserved and published [25]. Most of them were written before the collapse of the union in 1282 but he rewrote some of them afterwards and also produced new ones including at least three refutations of the 'tome' that Patriarch Gregory had issued after the synod of Blachernae in 1285.

While quite able when necessary to argue metaphysically about the internal economy of the Blessed Trinity, Beccus, like the other theological writers of his day, relied mainly on the authority of Tradition contained in the writings of the Fathers to support his case. That he had read them, not merely in *catenae* or collections of quotations, but had studied the complete treatises for himself is apparent from his handling of them and his clear references to his sources. He was by nature thorough in whatever he did, and so he was thorough in his study of theology.

The first treatise he produced to vindicate his own orthodoxy and to win supporters for it among others was entitled «On the Union and Peace of the Churches of Old and New Rome» [26]. At the very beginning of it he stated very plainly the twofold purpose he had in writing it— to show that the Fathers clearly asserted «that the Holy Spirit has his

---

24. Pachymeres, *Op. cit.*, pp. 103-5.
25. PG. 141, 16-1032.
26. PG. 141, 16-157.

existence from the essence of the Father and of the Son» (i.e., the doctrine of the Roman *Filioque*), and to prove that the objections to that truth were ill-founded. He then quoted many Fathers as stating that the Spirit is substantially from Father and Son, that for them 'From' and 'Through' in the trinitarian context were equivalent, and that 'Through' implied a medial position of the Son between Father and Spirit. The second part of the treatise examined and replied to the arguments of four of the chief adversaries of the *Filioque* doctrine, beginning with Photius, the originator of the controversy.

Beccus's other treatises covered the same ground but in different ways, sometimes answering questions proposed to him, sometimes by countering arguments of influential theologians. The width of his reading on the subject of the Holy Spirit is best shown by the grand collection of patristic quotations that he brought together in his «Epigraphae» [27]. They are arranged under thirteen heads, which build up an argument whose logical conclusion is that, according to the Fathers, the Spirit proceeds also from the Son. Under the several heads there are anything from a dozen to three dozen quotations — a mine of patristic learning that would serve many an advocate of Church union in the years to come. When Beccus, imprisoned by Michael Palaeologus in 1273, set himself to study the *Filioque* question, Pachymeres suggested that his knowledge of theology might be somewhat deficient because till then «he had devoted himself more to profane than to divine literature» [28]. The competence he acquired by that study can be gauged by the reputation he enjoyed with the generation that followed him. «There were some who surpassed him in Greek learning. But in respect of acuteness of natural talents, of fluency of speech and of proficiency in the dogmas of the Church, all others in comparison with him were mere children» [29].

The chief impression that one retains after studying what is reported of Beccus by the three Greek writers who speak of him at some length — George Pachymeres and Nicephorus Gregoras, both anti-unionists, and George Metochites, a confirmed unionist — is his patent honesty of character. Not one of them ever suggests that his conversion to unionism was anything but genuine. Indeed they go out of their way to stress his sincerity. Pachymeres blames him somewhat for riling the Emperor in his way of pleading for the miserable and suggests impru-

---

27. *Ibid.*, 613-724.
28. Pachymeres, *Op. cit.*, I, p. 381.
29. Gregoras, *Op. cit.*, I, pp. 129.

dence when he began to write on dogma. In each case, the fault was perhaps, if anything, an excess of virtue — to force the Emperor to practise Christian charity and to conteract the ignorant travesties of Latin doctrine that were being circulated by exposing and recommending what in his view was the truth. At the mock trial of January 1283 Beccus did, indeed, sign a profession of faith against his convictions. But if he had not done so, he might quite easily have been lynched, and he always intended to reassert openly his unionism when circumstances allowed. He did that by demanding public trial. The ultimate proof of the sincerity of his theological beliefs is his death in 1297 after twelve years of harsh exile in the fortress of St Gregory in Bithynia. A gesture of compromise on his part after the condemnation of 1285 [30] or again in about 1293 when he met the Emperor in Lopadion near Brusa would have gained for him, at the least, considerable alleviation from the rigours of St Gregory or even transfer to a milder and more pleasant locality [31]. He never made any such gesture. A phrase at the end of his last will and testament, a kind of epitaph for himself, explains why. «I, John, by the mercy of God humble Archbishop of Constantinople but, because of the true dogma of the Fathers, that is, the Procession of the Holy Spirit from the Father through the Son, condemned to exile and prison till death, with my own hand write this last will and testament and sign it» [32].

---

30. Pachymeres, *Op. cit.*, II, p. 103.

31. *Ibid.*, p. 105.

32. PG. 141, 1032B. «John Beccus, who once was Patriarch, towards the end of March [1297] died in the prison attached to the fortress of St Gregory and was buried on the spot somewhere in the cell. The Emperor was distressed since it had been settled between him and Beccus with his companions to discuss conditions for an arrangement and agreement to be made with the counsel of wise and spiritual men and not of chance individuals and men of no account whatever, but he did not manage to do it in time. They brought back Meliteniotes and placed him with Metochites in the city and, since these would not agree to the terms proposed by the Emperor's advisers and the Church authorities, they put them in confinement near the Great Palace, where later John Tarchaniotes is confined» (Pachymeres, *Op. cit.*, II, pp. 270-1). So Beccus died in prison in 1297 after 14 years in exile, Meliteniotes in 1307 after 24 years of confinement and Metochites in 1328 after 45 years — for loyalty to the union. Cf. V. Laurent, 'La date de la mort de Jean Beccos', in *Echos d'Orient*, 25 (1926), pp. 316-9.

The memory of John Beccus, however, faded from the memory of the Greeks. Writing in 1452, Gennadius notes that only after his return from Italy in 1440 he had to his surprise learnt of the synod in the Blachernae Palace and of Beccus's condemnation. Thereafter he frequently referred to it in his polemics against the Council of Florence; cf. *Oeuvres complètes de Gennade-Scholarios*, 8 vols. ed. L. Petit, X. A. Sidéridès, M. Jugie (Paris, 1928-36), III, p. 154.

VII

NOTES ON THE DE MICHAELE ET ANDRONICO PALAEO-LOGIS OF GEORGE PACHYMERES

I. THE ARGUMENTS FOR UNION OF PATRIARCH BECCUS

There are extant two fairly long accounts of the trial in 1285 of John Beccus, Constantine Meliteniotes and George Metochites, the one by George Pachymeres,[1] the other by George Metochites.[2] In view of the length of the trial, protracted as it was over four days in February and one in July, neither account is complete and, indeed, it needs careful attention to realise that they are both recording the same events.

Pachymeres devotes nearly a half of his description to a discussion arising out of a quotation from St John Damascene – the Father is "the producer *(proboleus)* through the Word of the illuminating Spirit"[3] and according to him it was Meliteniotes and Metochites who introduced it at the very beginning of the trial to prove the Procession of the Holy Spirit from the Father through the Son. For them "producer" meant "cause" and, to parry an objection against their opinion, they proposed an example – we say that the Father is perfect God, the Son perfect God and the Spirit perfect God, but the conclusion is not that there are three Gods. Their quotation from the Damascene, however, gave rise to an incident that created something of a sensation. Moschabar, the Charto-phylax, on hearing it declared that it was spurious. The Great Logothete, Mouzalon, who was conducting the trial, publicly rebuked him and, on the grounds that it was to be found in the Hoplotheca (a collection of patristic quotations long held in veneration), declared that he accepted it as genuine.[4] He agreed with the defendants that *"proboleus"* in respect of the Father meant "cause", but in regard to the Son he asserted that it meant, not "cause", but "illuminator". They expostulated that the same word in the same context could not have two different meanings, and the argument went on for some time with no conclusion. At this point Beccus took up the defence and, after introducing the metaphor of the sun, the ray and the light, he challenged the Logothete to explain some words of St Gregory of Nyssa that "the one is immediately from the first and the

---

[1] De Michaele et Andronico Palaeologis, 2 vols., ed. I. Bekker (Bonn, 1835), II, pp. 89–103.

[2] Historia Dogmatica, ed. A. Mai in Patrum Nova Bibliotheca, VIII (Rome, 1871), I, pp. 132–68.

[3] De fide orthodoxa c. 13, P. G., 94 849 B.

[4] Pachymeres (II, pp. 108–9) says that another reason why the accusers did not want to jettison the thirteenth chapter of the Damascene was that it contained one of their best quotations against the Latin Filioque: "We do not say that the Holy Spirit is from the Son."

other is from the first through the immediate one".[5] When no convincing answer was forthcoming, asked why he equiparated "from" and "through" in respect of the Blessed Trinity, he replied that that was the only way to peace between the Churches – was the little word "from" to brand a man as a heretic? He continued that he wished to be in communion with all the members of the court and, if they rejected "through" and with it the doctrine of the Fathers, he would agree. That was meant as a challenge to Patriarch Gregory, and it was taken as such.

The Damascene-quotation, however, had been more of a challenge and it led to important consequences. The reason for the prorogation of the trial for four months till July was to give the official Church time to produce a solution to the problem it posed, since the Logothete's explanation was unconvincing. No solution, however, was forthcoming even in July and the three unionists were condemned as heretics with their argument unanswered. Patriarch Gregory determined to remedy the defect. He produced a *'tomos'* in defence of the synod, which all bishops and persons in official positions were required to sign. There was great reluctance, and the *'tomos'* in the end brought about the downfall of its author, who had to abdicate. Pachymeres, the historian, was one of those under obligation to sign, and this fact, together with all the stresses and anxieties connected with the Damascene-quotation, fixed it firmly in his mind and, when twenty years later he was writing his history,[6] led him to allot to it too large a space, not only in his account of the trial but – it is my contention – also in his description of the propaganda for union produced by Beccus well before the trial, during the reign of Michael VIII.

Pachymeres had a very great respect for John Beccus and in his history he describes with some detail the future Patriarch's conversion to, and progress in, unionism. Imprisoned for calling the Latins heretics, Beccus was given a collection of excerpts from the Fathers to read, that favoured rather the Latin doctrine about the Procession of the Holy Spirit (I, pp. 380–1). He was impressed but not overwhelmed. He asked for the treatises from which the excerpts had been taken and became genuinely convinced that "the sum of the Latins' audacity was perhaps the addition to the Creed" and that the only difference in the doctrines of the two Churches about the Holy Spirit lay in two words, "from" and "through" (I, p. 383). So he supported union and in 1275 was made Patriarch. Some years later, perhaps in 1278, appalled at the ignorance shown by Greek polemicists about Latin teaching on the Procession, he began to write. Pachymeres explains that at this juncture there fell into his hands the treatises that Nicephorus Blemmydes had written to Emperor Theodore II Lascaris and to James, archbishop of Bulgaria, and various tractates of Nicetas of Maroneia. Inspired by these, to the intense irritation of the bi-

---

[5] Ep. ad Ablabium, P. G., 45 133 B.

[6] Pachymeres purports to quote from Patriarch Gregory's *'tomos'* but he produces no more than a paraphrase: Pachymeres, II, 113 lines 8–11 and Gregory P. G., 142 240 A.

shops, his colleagues, he produced several compositions (I, pp. 477–8), and that in these he employed the *proboleus*-quotation from the Damascene, about which there was, so Pachymeres asserts, great division among theologians, some rejecting it outright as spurious, others accepting it but substituting *"parocheus"* for *"proboleus"*, others retaining *"proboleus"* and explaining it in the way that Mouzalon did in the trial, as meaning in respect of the Son "illuminator". Beccus also, so writes Pachymeres, followed up the *proboleus*-quotation with the one from Gregory of Nyssa (I, p. 482). All this while he was free to promulgate his views before the death of Michael VIII Palaeologus on 11 December 1282.

After 1282 the situation was radically changed. The anti-unionists were now the persecutors in a variety of 'trials' and the unionists the persecuted. Apropos of disorders in the first months of the reign of Andronicus II (i. e., events two years before the trial in 1285), Pachymeres indulges in a lengthy digression about the theology of the disgraced Patriarch John Beccus. He instances some of the quotations that Beccus used from the Fathers and, among them, the "Immediately from the first, etc." -phrase of Gregory of Nyssa. In that way Beccus, he says, persuaded himself that he reflected the mind of the Fathers. He rejected the Addition that the Latins had made to the Creed but approved of their doctrine, because he was convinced that "from" and "through" in the trinitarian context were equivalent. "The culmination of his audacity was to interpret the Damascene's *"proboleus"* as cause and to allow no other possible meaning, and so to give grounds for the by-no-means light or negligible accusation of making the Son cause of the Spirit along with the Father". To forestall objections he employed the example of the three Divine Persons, each being perfect God yet without leading to the conclusion that there are three Gods; and to prove his orthodoxy he added three anathemas to the formula of the Synodicon of Orthodoxy (II, pp. 27–33).

There are several similarities between these descriptions of the general teaching of Beccus in the days of union and the account that Pachymeres gives of the trial – the strong stress on the *proboleus*-quotation from St John Damascene and the lesser stress on the words of Nyssa; and the example of the three Divine Persons. The explanation may be the not unnatural one that at his trial Beccus employed the same texts and the same arguments that he had thought cogent and had used in his previous discourses and writings on the union. Of his spoken discourses we have no independent record, but several of his early treatises are extant, most of them as rewritten during his exile when he would have tended, not to omit, but to expand arguments that had proved effective in the course of the trial.[7]

---

[7] In his exile Beccus wrote several refutations of the '*tomos*' and of tractates written by Patriarch Gregory about the Holy Spirit. In these he obviously includes the *proboleus* controversy, but these are outside the scope of this 'note', which is concerned solely with his teaching before his fall from office.

The truth, however, is that in his pre-1282 treatises[8] he refers to St John Damascene only rarely and to the *proboleus*-text in particular hardly at all. It does not appear in his long treatise *De unione ecclesiarum veteris et novae Romae* nor in the nearly as long *De Processione Spiritus Sancti*. Of the three *Letters to Theodore of Sugdaea* it is found only in the first, where on one occasion it is the last of a series of quotations from six Fathers, and it is used again shortly afterwards in conjunction with a quotation from Nyssa's *Against Eunomius* (i. e., not the "One immediately from the first etc."), as the basis of an argument to prove "cause". In the very long *Against Andronicus Camaterus* there is a long quotation from St John Damascene that contains the *proboleus*-phrase, but no special attention is drawn to it. Finally, in the immense collection of citations from the Fathers that make up Beccus's *Epigraphae* Damascene's *proboleus*-quotation does not appear at all.

The quotation from St Gregory's *Letter to Ablabius* is found slightly more often — once in the *De unione ecclesiarum*, twice in the *De Processione Spiritus Sancti*, and once in the first *Letter to Theodore of Sugdaea*, in no case with any special emphasis. In the treatise *Against Camaterus* it appears four times and is alluded to still again, but as an explanation of other words of Nyssa and not in conjunction with the Damascene. In the *Epigraphae* it is used once, the thirty-fourth of a series of fifty—one quotations.

The example of the three Divine Persons is not found at all in Beccus's pre-1282 writings.

Pachymeres implies that Beccus was much influenced by Blemmydes and Nicetas of Maroneia. Beccus himself mentions the name of Blemmydes only twice. In his *De depositione sua* II he states that Blemmydes deplored the division of the Churches and that he had written whole treatises to show that the Fathers, when they said "through the Son" in respect of the Holy Spirit, meant "immutable and timeless existence".[9]

Blemmydes himself in the letters to Lascaris and the Archbishop of Bulgaria does not quote the *proboleus*-text and once only the "One immediately from the first etc." of Gregory of Nyssa, and this so as to prove that the Fathers say "through" and not "from".[10]

Of Nicetas Beccus wrote that he favoured the Latin disputant in his *Dialogues* so much that the Greek joyfully embraced union. In those *Dialogues*[11] Nicetas employs once (in the second) the *proboleus*-quotation with a long argument drawn from it. The quotation from Nyssa appears three times, once only with any force — and no more.

---

[8] P. G., 141 16–1032.

[9] P. G., 141 968 A, 992 C.

[10] P. G., 142 537 D.

[11] P. G., 141 169–221. N. Festa published treatises 2 to 4 with a Latin translation, scattered over the issues of Bessarione for the years 1912–1916.

So it seems likely that Pachymeres, when he is describing the unionistic activity of Beccus the Patriarch, fills out from his clearer recollections of the trial the fainter memories of what had gone before. The trial, as he recalled it, almost turned on the Damascene quotation, which indeed entailed momentous consequences. Pachymeres portrays Patriarch Beccus as giving a similar importance to it, though it is hardly to be found in his writings or in what Pachymeres suggests were his sources, the works of Blemmydes and Nicetas. The same can be said for the quotation from Gregory of Nyssa; while the example of the three Divine Persons being one God, which is attributed by Pachymeres to Beccus the Patriarch in one place and in his narrative of the trial is put into the mouths of Meliteniotes and Metochites, is not found at all in the writings of Beccus. Lastly, had Beccus brought the quotation from the Damascene into clear prominence (and contradiction) before the trial of 1285 as Pachymeres implies, or had he used on any large scale the quotation from Nyssa in his writings and his conversations to promote unionism, surely the official Church would not have been reduced to silence and disarray when these arguments appeared in the Blachernae-trial and the Logothete would not have been surprised and shocked when Moschabar muttered that the quotation from St John Damascene was spurious.

So, to appraise the content of Beccus's advocacy for union, his own writings offer safer evidence than do the records of George Pachymeres.

II. THE OCCASION OF THE CONVOCATION OF THE SYNOD OF BLACHERNAE IN 1285

There is no doubt that the exiled Patriarch John Beccus was responsible for the summoning of the synod in Blachernae in 1285, but there are two accounts of how he acted to bring it about. Pachymeres is the source of one of these and his narrative is very detailed. He writes that the new bishop of Brusa, where Beccus resided in exile, whose name when he worked in the imperial kitchens was Nicholas and Neophytus when he became a monk, outraged that the pope had been commemorated in the liturgy, imposed a fast of reparation on his faithful. These were very angry and vented their displeasure on Beccus as the prime cause of their discomfort. In self-defence the ex-Patriarch took his stand in the largest room of the monastery "so as to be heard by everybody", poured scorn on the bishop for his ignorance and turned his attack on George the Cypriot, his successor on the patriarchal throne with the name of Gregory. "What has come over you that you heap reproaches on me and shun me who am a genuine Greek of Greek race, parentage and upbringing, while you welcome and take to your bosoms a man born of and brought up by Italians and a foreigner to our ways, as is shown by his very dress and speech. If it is doctrine you are complaining about, appeal to the Emperor and before all the world listen to my views . . ." It was not long before word of this reached the ears of Andronicus. Nothing was done for some time. Then Beccus was taken to Constantinople.[12]

Metochites also describes the occasion of the summoning of the synod in the Blachernae Palace, but he makes no mention of the bishop of Brusa and of provocative events there. According to him, Beccus felt that it was time he was given an opportunity of vindicating the orthodoxy of his theological teaching. He composed an encyclical letter and had it widely circulated, demanding a public hearing with regard to the accusations of error levelled against him and denouncing the Patriarch for upsetting the Church. This letter was written before the meeting of the Arsenites summoned by the Emperor in Adramyttium, which took place in Lent 1284. The result was an attempt to stop all communication with Beccus, but his letter was already well-known. Public opinion was divided, some for and some against Beccus's demand. The last word lay with the Emperor who was in favour and Patriarch Gregory acceded, once he was convinced that he would be supported and would not suffer from the occasion.[13]

It is *possible* that both Pachymeres and Metochites are right, i. e., that the Bishop of Brusa imposed a fast and that Beccus wrote an encyclical letter. It is *certain* that the account of Metochites is right for Meliteniotes records the same[14] and in a letter to the Emperor Patriarch Gregory complains about the encyclical letter, that Beccus was out only to upset the Church and that people were divided on whether to accede to or to refuse his demand for a public trial.[15]

III. AN ADDITION TO THE SYNODICON OF ORTHODOXY BY BECCUS

Pachymeres reports: "To avoid the charge [of heresy, Beccus] added to and increased the decree read out in the church on the Day of Orthodoxy with three chapters, for he imposed a triple anathema on whoever held that the Son was either cause or co-cause with the Father of the Spirit or who knowingly allowed himself to be in communion with such as spoke or believed in that way."[16]

---

[12] Op. cit., II, pp. 88–9.

[13] Op. cit., pp.121–3. The text of Beccus's encyclical letter is lost, unless, as V. Laurent suggests (Les régestes des Actes du Patriarcat de Constantinople. I. Les régestes de 1208–1307, (Paris, 1971) sub no. 1474, p. 263), it is the treatise entitled De depositione sua I (P. G., 141 949–69), which suggestion could well be accepted except for one element of doubt. The treatise ends with an appeal to the Patriarchs of Alexandria and of Antioch, "whom Constantinople now holds within itself" (P. G., 141 969 C). But the Patriarch of Antioch left Constantinople and abdicated at Easter 1283 to escape being involved in the anti-unionist trials (Pachymeres, Op. cit., II, p. 56), and his successor Arsenius elected in Antioch by the local clergy having died, Cyril was elected (Ibid.), who came to Constantinople only some considerable time after the trial in the Blachernae Palace (Ibid., p. 123).

[14] Laurent, Loc. cit.

[15] Ibid.

[16] Pachymeres, Op. cit., II, p. 32.

This is, I think, the only reference to such an addition to the *Synodicon* by Beccus. No other friend or enemy of his mentions it. It did not survive, and J. Gouillard in his exhaustive book, *Le synodikon de l'Orthodoxie* (= *Travaux et Mémoires* II) (Paris, 1967) knows nothing of it. Nevertheless Pachymeres's clear assertion is categorical and it is supported by what, according to the same Pachymeres, Meliteniotes and Metochites declared in the trial of 1285: "We do not say that the Son is cause in respect of the coming forth of the Spirit from the Father, or even co-cause, but we anathematize and excommunicate any who say so. What we do say is that the Father is cause of the Spirit through the Son, since the word *proboleus* is understood in the sense of cause."[17]

IV. CLERICAL SIGNATURES FOR UNION

Pachymeres reports that Emperor Michael "first having drawn up a '*tomos*' whose purpose was good will to the Emperor, bade people sign it. I do not know for what kind of need, unless it was to seem to have signatures from the men of the Church, even though the topics were at variance . . . Afterwards he sent his agents round and began to examine each house closely, who was innocent and who not. And the excuse was" that the houses were his by right of conquest and he could justly demand arrears of rent from his opponents. He assessed their belongings for sequestration and prepared ships to carry them into exile, and in fact he did banish people to a variety of places. Pachymeres's narrative then recounts at length the maltreatment of Holobolus, which occurred on 6 October. "But the clergy seeing the danger that hung over them implored the monarch to spare them his anger on condition that they remained peaceful till after the envoys had made their return. Yet though they besought him earnestly they failed to persuade him, but they were flatly charged with *lèse majesté* if they would not complete their subscription. As some were alleging as an excuse their fear of being forced to accept even further demands, the Emperor straightway makes a decree and a chrysobull is issued." Pachymeres further says that the chrysobull was "full of the most hair-raising imprecations and replete with the most awful oaths" that he (Michael) would no more use force, that the faith should be untouched etc., "otherwise that he should be utterly destroyed and undergo the most fearsome fate".[18] That, perhaps, was only a way of saying that the chrysobull was a very solemn document indeed. In point of fact, it contained no imprecations and awful oaths. On the contrary it was calm, dignified and persuasive.[19]

---

[17] Ibid. II, p. 91. Metochites makes similar statements in his Historia Dogmatica e. g., pp. 158–9.

[18] Op. cit., I, pp. 390–5.

[19] J. Gill, "The Church Union of the Council of Lyons (1274) Portrayed in Greek Documents", in Orientalia Christiana Periodica 40 (1974), pp. 5–45, esp. doc. I, pp. 12–19.

There are two points that call for clarification in this passage from Pachymeres's history, the date and the historical context of the document requiring signatures that he locates in his narrative before the issue of the chrysobull, and the date of the chrysobull.

1. *The Date of the Document Requiring Signatures*

On 17 February 1277 Patriarch Beccus and the synod of Constantinople issued a *'tomographia'* re-affirming the union agreed to in the Council of Lyons and imposing the penalty of excommunication on all, clerics or laymen, who refused to accept the union. There is extant also the text of a declaration whereby forty-one ecclesiastics of St Sophia (whose names are appended) testified to their acceptance of that *'tomographia'*. This document is not dated but it must be of the period of the *'tomographia'*, viz., about the middle of 1277. There is, too, another document attesting to the loyalty to the Emperor of the signatories, the officials of the imperial court, in view of the divisions that the religious controversies of the day over union were causing among them. No signatures are recorded and no date is given, but most likely it was the palace equivalent of the ecclesiastical document mentioned above, and so would be of about the same date, viz., middle 1277.[20]

Pachymeres in his history says no word whatsoever of these three documents, even though his name is found among the forty-one clerics who signed the certificate required of the patriarchal Curia. Instead he mentions, in a historical context where it fits only with difficulty, a *'tomos'* which demanded loyalty *(eunoia)* to the Emperor and which "men of the Church" were to sign. It seems to me that he is really referring to, and combining into one, the two attestations to be signed by the officials of the Church and the officials of the court separately (these latter to show among other things *eunoia*) and mistakenly is dating this episode in the early part of 1273 instead of in mid-1277.

2. *The Date of the Emperor's Chrysobull*

W. Norden[21] dates this chrysobull from before the sending to Lyons of the Greek embassy, which left Constantinople on 11 March 1274. F. Dölger[22] rejects Norden's date in favour of *ca. Okt. 1274*. Both these authors had to judge on only the data provided by Pachymeres, for the text of the chrysobull and of the documents connected with it had not in their day been published.

---

[20] Art. cit., doc. V, VI and VII.
[21] Das Papsttum und Byzanz (Berlin 1903), p. 521.
[22] Regesten der Kaiserurkunden des Oströmischen Reiches, I, 3, (Munich 1932) no. 2013.

The edition of those documents[23] decides for Norden and against Dölger. The argumentation is briefly as follows. (It is given at greater length in my article just mentioned.) In Pachymeres's account the chrysobull followed closely on the maltreatment of Holobolus on 6 October. Pachymeres adds that the chrysobull had a pacifying effect, for "reassured by this they sign and except for a few, who having been exiled and after a time having assented, are recalled and are reunited with the Church, all the clergy without exception" (I, pp. 395–6). The letter to Pope Gregory in Lyons composed by the Greek synod before the end of February 1274 informs the Pope that the Emperor "now has us all in agreement". So the chrysobull dates from between 6 October and the end of the following February 1274. The year, then, was 1273, and this is confirmed by the synodical decree of 17 February 1277, the 'tomographia', which states that the bishops agreed to the Emperor's union "on 24 December of the second indiction". The chrysobull, therefore, dates from shortly before or shortly after 24 December 1273, according as the synodical decree recording the bishops' agreement dates from the day of the synod or from shortly afterwards.

Apropos of this synodical decree I may add that Fr Laurent in his *Actes des Patriarches* concludes to the existence of a document dated 24 December of the second indiction, which he thinks is lost. That document is, in fact, the decision of the synod expressed in the letter it sent to the Emperor in 1273 (document no. II in my article). Having found the reference to it in the 'tomographia' of 19 February 1277, he was led mistakenly to ascribe to it a content similar to that of the 'tomographia' itself and mistakenly to date it as of 24 December 1276.

This same 'tomographia' was the occasion for him of another error. It is mentioned in both of the letters that Patriarch John Beccus addressed to the Pope in 1277, in that of February/March (*Actes patriarcaux* no. 1432) as "the 'tomographia' that accompanies this" and in that of April (*Ibid.* no. 1433) as the "synodical 'tomos' that will be exhibited to you". Fr Laurent did not observe that it was the document that he had already described in no. 1431, and he mistakenly created an unnecessary no. 1434, a "synodical 'tomos'" expressing the complete submission of the Byzantine episcopate".

V. THE DATE OF THE DEATH OF PATRIARCH ARSENIUS

If my dating of the documents published in my article is correct, it follows that Patriarch Arsenius, whose death occurred on 30 September, six days before the punishment of Holobolus on 6 October, died in the year 1273.

---

[23] Gill, Art. cit.

VIII

Pope Urban V (1362-1370) and the Greeks of Crete

To Our Venerable Brethren, the Archbishop of Crete and his Suffragans, health etc.

It is commonly said and indeed it is in itself very likely that the malice of the monks and the priests, depraving and cunningly deluding the minds of simple layfolk, has strengthened and does not cease to strengthen the damnable schism of the Greeks, from which, since by leaving the Church they contemptuously rejected a Catholic mentor, a multitude of heresies has arisen and does not cease to arise, to such a degree that, when certain laymen — men of importance — wish to enter the bosom of the sacrosanct Roman Church which is the mother and mistress of all the Churches they are prevented by those same monks and priests, in places that are not under the domination of a Catholic power.

Since, therefore, as we have heard with pleasure, in the island of Crete, in which your churches are situated, Our beloved sons the Doge and Commune of Venice have a more complete dominion over Latins and Greeks than is usual and an ecclesiastical censure by the help of the secular arm can better than is usual be put into due execution, and since for this reason the aforesaid schism with God's favour can, as may be reasonably hoped and believed, by suitable means be eliminated from the island in question, We by these apostolic letters enjoin on your Fraternity that each of you in his own city and diocese should by Our authority strictly prohibit that any candidate or lettered Greek layman of the afore-mentioned island should henceforth be admitted to the rank of cleric or henceforward promoted to any other order at all, unless by a Latin or a Greek Catholic bishop, who should by

written document give certification of such promotion. Those
who in this way shall be ordained priests must celebrate Mass
and the other divine offices according to the rite which the
Roman Church observes. In addition, also, to the prohibition
as above, no Greek monk or priest who does not observe the
aforesaid rite shall henceforth dare to hear confessions or
preach to the people, those who contravene being constrained
by ecclesiastical censure with no right of appeal (1).

The editor of the Latin text of this unfortunate letter interprets
it as meaning: " It follows from this way of speaking that only the
Latin rite was permitted in Crete. This is confirmed by what is
said about confessors and preachers " (2). Other writers have expressed a like opinion (3).

I think that such authors misinterpret the letter and draw a
false conclusion.

*　*　*

The religious situation in Crete after the Venetians got possession of the island in c. 1209 is obscure. A Latin archbishop (of

---

(1) " ... inhibeat ne aliquis scholaris seu laicus litteratus graecus
de insula supradicta insignantur decetero charactere clericali vel pro-
moveatur decetero ad quoscunque Ordines, nisi per latinum episcopum
aut graecum catholicum, per cuius litteras de sua promotione faciat
plenam fidem; et hii qui ex talibus fuerint in presbyteros ordinati, Missas
et alia divina officia iuxta ritum quem praefata Romana servat Ecclesia
debeant celebrare, adiiciens quoque inhibitioni iam dictae, quod nullus
calogerorum seu sacerdos graecus, praefatum ritum non servans, decetero
audeat confessiones audire vel populo praedicare... " (28 July 1368,
Acta Urbani PP. V (1362-1370), ed. A. L. TAUTU (Rome, 1964), n. 153).

(2) *Ibid.*, p. 254, n. 4.

(3) " ... et de faire observer par les prêtres ainsi consacrés les rites
de l'Eglise romaine. Ce dernier détail mérite d'être souligné, car il nous
confirme qu'en ce moment le Saint-Siège ne songeait pas à aucune concession en faveur du rite oriental " (O. HALECKI, *Un Empereur de Byzance
à Rome* (Warsaw, 1930), p. 183.

[Urban] " required of Greek priests who wished to become Catholics
conversion to the Latin rite and allowed only those candidates to ordination who were ready to accept this rite. ... [With the abolition of
schism in the island] " also the complete Latinisation of the island would
become a *fait accompli* " (W. DE VRIES, *Die Päpste von Avignon und der
christliche Osten*, in *OCP*, 30 (1964), p. 115).

Candia, usually called 'Archbishop of Crete') and some bishops were found there almost immediately. A document of probably 1224 says that the Greek hierarchy had consisted of an archbishop and ten bishops and that of these 3 had fled the island while the Genoese were still in possession, 3 had died, 2 were vagrant seeking alms and 2 still remained in their dioceses ([1]). According to S. Borsari four Greek bishops were integrated into the Latin hierarchy, at least one of them by appointment by the Latin authorities, where the church "had a Greek Chapter and mixed Latin and Greek faithful " ([2]). Presumably such bishops had accepted the obedience of the Latin Church, for already in 1219 Pope Honorius had authorised the Latin archbishop to "correct and reform" all bishops, abbots and clerics, Latin and Greek, on the island ([3]). But both he and his successors on the throne of St Peter defended against Latin archbishops and bishops the rights and immunities of Greek monasteries, particularly that of Mt Sinai, which had many possessions in Crete ([4]).

The Venetians had no intention of allowing the Church on the island to become powerful. There was soon friction in respect of clerical immunities of Greeks, subjects of the Latin archbishop; of the appointment of abbots; of secularisation of ecclesiastical properties; of paying tithes. "In fine, the religious policy of Venice follows its tradition of caution and relative indifference. It mattered little, at bottom, whether their subjects followed the Latin rite or the Greek rite, provided that they were loyal and faithful " to Venice ([5]). Religion should not upset politics. The Greeks should be left with their liturgical usages and even their priests. But the number of their priests and monks was controlled and Greek religious

---

([1]) G. FEDALTO, *La Chiesa latina a Creta dalla caduta di Costantinopoli (1204) alla riconquista bizantina (1261)*, Κρητικὰ Χρονικά, 24 (1972), p. 152.

([2]) S. BORSARI, *Il dominio veneziano a Creta nel XIII secolo* (Napoli, 1963) pp. 106, 107.

Acta Honorii III (1216-1227) et Gregorii IX (1227-1241), ed. A. L. TAUTU (Città del Vaticano, 1950), n. 219, 11 February 1237.

([3]) 15 March 1219, *ibid.*, n. 59.

([4]) Cf. G. HOFMANN, *Sinai und Rom*, in *Orientalia Christiana*, 9 (1927), pp. 218-99.

([5]) Fr. THIRIET, *La Romanie vénitienne au moyen âge*, (Paris, 1959), p. 403.

464

influences from outside rigidly excluded. So entry to the island of Greek bishops, priests and monks was forbidden and within the island priests were to be ordained only to fill the places of the dead and the chronically sick — such control being in the hands of the Venetian government. Greek priests were, for the most part, not ' free men ' (¹). On the other hand, the Venetian government of the island bought off a particularly dangerous rebel, Alexis Calergis, by giving him ecclesiastical property and conniving at his introducing a Greek bishop into one of the dioceses and enriching himself with both monastic and episcopal property (²).

As a result of various litigations the Signoria accepted, and imposed acceptance on the government of Crete, that the Archbishop of Candia possessed certain villages and other properties and that 130 *papades* (Greek priests) were under him. All other *papades*, the great majority, were under the civilian administration. On 13 March 1324, however, it yielded so far as to allow that these latter *papades* were under the archbishop, but only to the same degree as layfolk. The head of the non-archiepiscopal *papades* was a *protopapas* (an ' arch-priest ', not a bishop), assisted by a *protopsaltis*. There was controversy as to who should appoint them, Latin archbishop or civil power. By a decision of 8 June 1402 the Signoria settled it. It was the right of the Signoria itself, and the nominee should never be drawn from among the 130 archiepiscopal *papades*.

So relations between the Venetian authorities and the Archbishop of Crete (even though almost always a Venetian) were usually strained. But Church and State had some things in common. One was that neither would have a non-catholic Greek bishop at large in Crete. So who would ordain Cretan priests?

Pope John XXII made provision for the ordination of Greek Catholic priests. On 1 April 1326 he instructed the Latin Archbishop of Crete to appoint a Greek vicar who would minister to the Catholic Greeks. His letter is important.

(¹) Fr. THIRIET, *La situation religieuse en Crète au début du XVe siècle*, in *Byzantion*, 36 (1966), pp. 204-5.

(²) Complaints of the Popes to the Doge of Venice, *Acta Clementis PP. V (13031-314)*, edd. F. L. DELORME and A. L. TAUTU (Città del Vaticano, 1955), n. 14; 29 May 1307: Calergis's descendants still held the properties 40 years later, *Acta Clementis PP. VI (1342-1452)*, ed. A. L. TAUTU (Città del Vaticano, 1966), n. 75, 12 July 1346.

We understand that in your cities and diocese and province there are mixed races with different languages, namely Latins and Greeks, who in one faith have different rites and customs, and that, whereas the Latins under the obedience of the Roman Church follow in everything the rites of that Church and are wisely ruled by your government and that of your suffragans, the Greeks have been and are without a Catholic Greek prelate to minister the sacraments to them and to instruct them both by word and example according to the customs of the Roman Church.

We, therefore, moved by Our zeal for souls and earnestly desiring to gain them for the Lord, by these apostolic letters commit to your Fraternity and ordain that, by Our provident authority, you appoint in your diocese situated in the island of Crete some Greek as prelate for the aforesaid Greeks and as your vicar for the said purposes who in all things shall be obedient and subject to you and shall accept obedience to the said Church, shall instruct both by word and example the said Greeks according to the customs of the said Roman Church, shall lead them to obedience of the said Church and shall confer on them all orders and minister confirmation and the other sacraments to them, it being forbidden for the future that these functions be exercised on the island by any schismatical prelate (¹).

Pope John was clearly inspired by the enactment of the Fourth Lateran Council of Innocent III, which prescribed such vicars. In Crete, then, there were different rites (and obviously legitimate rites) with one faith, that there was to be a Greek bishop of Greek rite, a Catholic, and that he was to follow his Greek rite as modified according to Latin customs imposed by the Roman Church — confirmation by a bishop, conferment of all seven orders, anointings.

John XXII did not mean this to be a negative measure to repress the Greeks, but constructive to build up the Church. At the same time he was writing vigorously to Cyprus insisting that certain Greek monasteries should be left in peace and invoking in their favour the penalties of the Church and the help of the king. To the archbishop

---

(¹) *Acta Ioannis XXII* (*1317-1334*), ed. A. L. TAUTU (Città del Vaticano, 1952), n. 81.

466

of Crete he wrote on 17 July 1326 giving him wide faculties " in order that your ministry might prosper the more ", for the Pope "with zeal for souls was moved by an earnest desire to gain them for God " (¹). By that, of course, John meant the winning of all Greeks to enter the Roman Church.

How Greeks who had not joined the Roman Church obtained ordination is not clear, for they were forbidden by the Venetian government to go outside Crete for it except with special leave and Greek bishops were forbidden entry into Crete. In 1335 Pope Benedict XII, informed that a Greek bishop was functioning in Crete, wrote to the Doge of Venice insisting that he be expelled (²). In 1357 a certain Bishop Macarius was there and some time later Bishop Anthemius, but, unlike the regulations limiting the ordinations of priests, the one concerning bishops was, so wrote Pope Gregory XI in 1373, well observed (³).

All this papal vigilance about the Greeks of Crete was intended to lead all Greeks to enter the Roman Church. Ordination to the priesthood conferred, besides the religious character, many material privileges in the way of relief from forced labour and taxes of various sorts, and so it had its attractions and was a desirable way of life. If ordination could not be obtained from a non-catholic bishop, aspirants might be willing to get it from a Catholic source. They would have to promise obedience to the Roman Church authorities, and their ordinations would, as laid down by John XXII, be by a Catholic Greek bishop, according to the Greek rite with its Latin modifications, and in their ministrations to their faithful they themselves would have to observe the modifications of their rite that Rome had from the time of Innocent III insisted on. That was what the Lateran Council enacted, what John XXII enjoined in 1335 and what Urban V repeated in 1368. None of these regulations imposed the Latin rite on Greeks. They imposed the Greek rite with the Latinising modifications.

That such was the case is apparent from the documents. The decree of John XXII has been sufficiently analysed already. The

---

(¹) *Ibid.*, n. 87.

(²) *Acta Benedicti XII (1334-1342)*, ed. A. L. TAUTU (Città del Vaticano, 1958), n. 3, 25 July 1335.

(³) Letter to the Doge, 27 October 1373, *Acta Gregorii P.P. XI (1370-1378)*, ed. A. L. TAUTU (Rome, 1366), n. 91.

letter of Urban V (which is the opening paragraph of this article) envisages a Greek Catholic bishop as prescribed in the legislation of Pope John. He would employ the modified Greek rite in all his ministrations and, hence, in his ordinations, and the priests he ordained would belong to and follow the same rite. What Pope Urban did in addition was to insist that only that modified Greek rite should be used and that only those candidates willing to practise that modified Greek rite should be admitted to ordination.

To encourage in another way the adoption of the Catholic Greek rite, Pope Urban tried to make conversion also materially attractive or at least to stop it being a cause of persecution. He himself helped Catholic *papades* and he urged others to favour them. In the month of July 1368, just before and after making his decree about Greek ordinations, he was writing to Crete about a certain George Rampani, whose case was, perhaps, at least in part the occasion of the decree in question.

Rampani, a convert priest, had been made ' archipresbyter ' (= *protopapas*) by the Archbishop of Candia. The Archbishop had subsequently been transferred to the Patriarchate of Grado. Urban instructed him to examine Rampani (through someone who knew Greek if he [the Patriarch] did not) and to confirm him in office if suitable. Another letter of the same day to the Patriarch bade him restrain Greek priests from acting without due permission from Rampani, if he were judged suitable to be *protopapas*. Still another letter to meet another of Rampani's complaints instructed the Patriarch to substitute Catholic priests for the ' canons who had categorically refused to enter the Roman Church ' at the weekly public procession with an icon of Our Lady through the streets of Candia. A fourth letter of the same date asked the Patriarch to see that Rampani as *protopapas* received his stipend, double that of the other ' canons ', even though he could not officiate in the funerals and other religious functions in question, since he could not take part in them ." on account of the excommunications imposed by apostolic authority on all clerics and laymen, participating in divine services of the Greeks " [1]. The Archbishop of Crete also was bidden by the Pope to favour and help Rampani who was " a true Catholic priest " and very zealous [2].

[1] 23 July 1368, *Acta Urbani V*, nn. 149-52.
[2] *Ibid.*, n. 154.

468

George Rampani actually did very well out of his conversion. He acquired several canonries for himself and others for his sons, the hostility of the Latin Archbishop of Crete and a reputation with the Venetians as a trouble-maker ([1]). Be that as it may, the papal letters show that after his conversion he was a true Catholic priest, he was married (his wife's name was Anna) and of the Catholic Greek rite, unable to function with non-Catholics not because they followed another rite but because they were excommunicated. He and other Greek Catholic priests could conduct the weekly procession of the icon of Our Lady and perform the chants and ceremonies that were part of it. He knew only Greek and so could not celebrate in Latin, and at that time there was no Greek translation of the Latin Mass.

([1]) M. I. MANOUSACAS, Βενετικὰ ἔγγραφα ἀναφερόμενα εἰς τὴν ἐκκλησιαστικὴν ἱστορίαν τῆς Κρήτης τοῦ 14ου - 16ου αἰῶνος, in Δελτίον τῆς Ἱστορικῆς καὶ Ἐθνολογικῆς Ἑταιρείας τῆς Ἑλλάδος, 15 (1961), pp. 154-5.

John V Palaeologus at the court of Louis I of Hungary (1366)

On 18 April 1365 Pope Urban V wrote an optimistic letter to the Byzantine Emperor, John V Palaeologus, announcing an expedition that would free "the city of Constantinople and the other parts of Greece still under your rule from the incursions of the abominable Turks".[1] The expedition never set out. On 25 January 1366 Urban addressed another letter to the Emperor. In it he wrote: "You know that Louis of Hungary has approached the Byzantine frontiers from the land side, that King Peter of Cyprus is powerful at sea and that Amadeus of Savoy, your cousin, is arriving".[2] Alas, what was described as fact was still only a hope, and this letter was already a year old when it reached the hands of Palaeologus. He, in fact, setting out in mid-winter 1365—1366,[3] had gone in person to the court of Louis, king of Hungary, in Buda, who in the spring of the year 1365 in a short campaign of less than three months had occupied a region of Bulgaria round Vidin and captured its ruler Strazimir. It is very likely that the two monarchs in Buda agreed on speedy help for Constantinople, since Louis asked Venice to prepare two to five ships for him to go *per terram et per mare in subsidium imperii romani contra Turchas et quod istud erat de requisitione et beneplacito Domini Imperatoris Constantinopolitani.* Venice's reply, agreeing, is dated 13 March 1366.[4] By early June the bishop of Nyitra for Louis I and George Manicaites for John V were at the papal Curia[5] to learn from the Pope the conditions under which John and the Greeks should be reconciled with the Roman Church. On 22 June 1366 Urban advised Louis that the Greek Emperor seemed to be motivated towards Church union more by political reasons than by religious ones, and he permitted Louis to defer for a year any obligation he might have undertaken in favour of the Greeks.[6] On 1 July the Pope in letters to Louis and to John set as the condition for the Greek reconciliation the acceptance of the Clementine profession of faith as made by Michael VIII Palaeologus in 1274. On the same day in very many letters to Louis and others he authorized the preaching of the crusade against the Turks to be led by Louis and exhorted bishops and barons to be active in its prosecution.[7] A few weeks later (23 July

---

[1] Acta Urbani PP. V (1363—1370) (= Pont. Comm. ad redig. Cod. Iuris Canon. Orient. Fontes III, XI) ed. A. L. Tautu, Città del Vaticano 1964, doc. 74.

[2] Ibid., doc. 90.

[3] Demetrius Cydones, *Oratio pro subsidio Latinorum*, PG 154, col. 1000 D. This speech makes no mention of the capture of Gallipoli by Amadeus of Savoy. So it dates probably from between 27 July 1367 when the Count put in at Negroponte and 23 August when he took Gallipoli.

[4] G. Wenzel, *Monumenta Hungariae historica* II. Budapest 1875, doc. 479.

[5] A petition made by Nyitra is granted by a document dated 12 June 1366 (Acta Urbani V, doc. 102).

[6] Ibid., doc. 105. A. Theiner, *Vetera monumenta historica Hungariam sacram illustrantia* II. Roma 1860, doc. 139.

[7] Acta Urbani V, docs. 107—111.

and 31 July), letters of credence and safe-conducts were issued to two papal envoys sent to a variety of countries on the same business. Louis on 23 July thanked Venice for its agreement about the galleys he had asked for[8] but on 20 September he wrote again modifying his request. He now wanted not fully armed and equipped ships but only hulls that he would fit out for himself.[9] Amadeus of Savoy reached Constantinople on 2 September and on 11—12 October,[10] after being held up for a week by bad weather, he set off to help his cousin John V, who, leaving behind as a hostage his son Manuel at the Hungarian court, had left Buda for home and had been refused passage through Bulgaria. He must have quitted the Hungarian capital in early September.[11] He was allowed to complete his journey on 21 December[12] after several interchanges of messages between Amadeus and the Bulgarian Czar, John Šišman, and some military action. He reached Amadeus in Sozopolis on 28 January 1367 and was back in Constantinople in early April.[13]

It seems clear that the relations between the two monarchs in Buda were at first friendly, indeed very friendly, and then became unfriendly, indeed so very unfriendly that John departed with empty hands, that he had to leave a son behind as hostage, that his host Louis (as far as is known) did not raise a finger to help him in the embarrassing situation caused by Šišman's refusal to give him passage, and that the Hungarian king did nothing whatsoever to help Constantinople against the Turks. Why such a change of attitude?

J. Meyendorff has offered one suggestion, that king Louis, supported by his mother and Hungarian notables, insisted as a condition of military assistance that John, his sons and his people should submit to being rebaptised in the Latin rite and so be reconciled with the Church of Rome. In an account of a meeting between of the Latin Patriarch of Constantinople, Paul, (who had accompanied Amadeus of Savoy on his expedition) and the ex-Emperor of Constantinople John VI, at that time become the monk Joasaph, with three metropolitans representing the Greek Patriarch, in the presence of John V, his wife and two sons (one of them Manuel, the late hostage), held in the spring of 1367, Joasaph is reported as saying to Paul: "This division (of the Churches) has reached such a pitch that some of yours want to rebaptise members of our Church. For the King of Hungary does this shamelessly, since he has rebaptised many, and among them also the son (Strazimir) of Alexander, the king of the Bulgars, as if our baptism were no good. But why must one quote individual examples? When the Emperor, my

---

[8] Wenzel, op. cit., doc. 483.

[9] Ibid., doc. 485.

[10] 11 October — P. Schreiner, Studien zu den βραχέα χρονικά. München 1964, p. 147; 12 October — S. Lambros, Βραχέα χρονικά. Athens 1932—1933, № 47.

[11] After news of John's predicament had reached Constantinople, Amadeus had sent an embassy to the Bulgarian Czar and awaited an answer before sailing north. The Greek Empress Helena gave him 12.000 florins mense septembris for the expenses of the expedition to Bulgaria. (F. Bollati, Illustrazione della spedizione in Oriente di Amadeo VI. Torino 1900, pp. 3—4.)

[12] S. Steinherz, Die Beziehungen Ludwigs I. von Ungarn zu Karl IV. Pt. II, Die Jahre 1358—1373. (= Mitteilungen des Inst. f. Österr. Geschichtsforsch. IX) Innsbruck 1888, p. 368.

[13] E. L. Cox, The Green Count of Savoy Amadeus VI and Transalpine Savoy in the Fourteenth Century. Princeton 1967, p. 229. For a wider exposition of all these events cf. O. Halecki, Un Empereur de Byzance à Rome, Warsaw 1930, pp. 111—137.

son (i. e. John V) was there asking help from the king against the infidel, the king himself, his mother and the political notabilities brought pressure to bear on him in many ways to have him and his sons baptised, saying that otherwise 'We cannot give you help if this is not done first'."[14] Meyendorff makes this statement more credible by quoting from Franciscan sources that, after the capture of Vidin by Louis, within fifty days the Latin Friars had baptised more than 200.000 Bulgars.

Nevertheless it is extremely improbable that the Hungarian court pressed John V to be rebaptised and that the Franciscans deliberately rebaptised members of the Church of Constantinople.

In the first place, whereas the Greeks challenged the validity of the Latin rite of baptism, the Latin Church did not deny the validity of the Greek baptism.[15] Innocent III and Innocent IV both wanted the Greek ceremonies of the sacrament to be supplemented by unctions, but they, with all the popes of the period, did not challenge the basic validity of Greek baptism. It is unlikely, then, that the Hungarian court with its ecclesiastical advisers was so ignorant of the sacramental teaching of its own Western Church as to deny validity to Greek baptism that its Church officially acknowledged.

Secondly, the question that had arisen in Buda between Louis and John was not whether John would or would not be reconciled to the Latin Church, because the papal letter of 1 July 1366[16] records that he had already promised that to Louis on oath,[17] but it was about the mode of the reconciliation. Neither Louis nor John, nor both of them together, could decide that. That was a matter for the highest Church authorities, and quite rightly the monarchs conjointly referred it to the Holy See. Urban proposed as the condition what had been regularly in force over the last century ever since the submission of Emperor Michael VIII Palaeologus in the Council of Lyons — acceptance of the profession of faith that Clement IV had drawn up especially for the Greeks and recognition of papal primacy. He wrote at least five letters on this subject and in none of them does the question of rebaptism ever occur (as it did not in connexion with Michael VIII). It is, then, most unlikely that Louis's envoy in Avignon ever suggested rebaptism as a mode of reconciliation for the Greeks and, consequently, that Louis himself ever seriously proposed it as such.

Thirdly, though there must have been some degree of disorder in the mass-baptising by the Friars, there was no indiscriminate baptising *en masse*. King Louis insisted that the names of all those baptised by the Latins should be registered and so it was done. Wadding reports

---

[14] The text of the anonymous, but on the whole trustworthy, account is published with introduction and commentary by J. Meyendorff, *Projet de concile œcuménique en 1367*, Dumbarton Oaks Papers 14 (1960) 147—177.

[15] The 4th *capitulum* of the IV Lateran Council (1215) forbidding the rebaptism of Latins testifies to this practice. A list of Greek *gravamina* against the Latin Church drawn up c. 1215 or c. 1252 attacks Latin baptism. J. B. Cotelerius, *Ecclesiae graecae monumenta* III. Paris 1686, pp. 495—520, esp. nos. 11—13. Jerome of Ascoli reported to Gregory X that the Greeks baptiset Latins joining their Church. See B. Roberg, *Die Union zwischen der griechischen und der lateinischen Kirche auf dem II. Konzil von Lyon (1274)*, Bonn 1964, p. 230.

[16] *Acta Urbani V*, doc. 107.

[17] Tu et nobiles viri Manuel et Michael nati tui acceptaretis, faceretis et adimpleretis ... omnia quae super reconciliatione praefata tibi et eiusdem tuis filiis mandaremus ...

that "eight Friars Minor ... within fifty days converted over 200.000 men. All their names were entered in registers which King Louis sent to the General of the Minors" to urge him to send more Friars;[18] and he later quotes a letter sent by the Minister of the Province of St. Francis: "And lest it happen that there arise doubts about the number, by order of the king all the baptised were put down in a public register".[19] The relevance of this precaution will be appreciated in the light of what will be said later in this article.

Fourthly. According to the account published by Meyendorff, the monk Joasaph, speaking not later than 4 June 1367 (when Amadeus left Byzantium with Patriarch Paul and a group of Greek envoys), declared that the Czar Alexander's son (Strazimir) had been rebaptised. That between the years 1365 and 1367 Strazimir was rebaptised is most unlikely, for on 1 June 1368 Pope Urban addressed a letter to him and his brothers using the form of address that in curial practice was employed only for those who were not members of the Latin Church: "To the nobles Strazimir, George and Balsa brothers, Zupans of Zente, grace in the present as a promise of future glory". In this letter the pope expressed his joy at the news given him by the Bishop of Sfacia that the three brothers *"intended to enter* the unity of the Church of Rome".[20] They fulfilled their intention in the usual way by formally accepting the Clementine profession of faith on 20 January 1368 and by signing and dating a document to that effect.[21] So it looks as if the account of the discussion between the Latin Patriarch Paul and the monk Joasaph is putting into Joasaph's mouth as spoken in 1367 a statement of what occurred only two years later and an inaccurate statement at that, since Strazimir's formal conversion involved no rebaptism. A reasonable conclusion from this is that the account was not closely contemporary with the events and that, written some (considerable?) time afterwards, it could be as untrustworthy in respect of Louis's supposed pressure on John V as it is with regard to Strazimir's rebaptism.

Further. There was, apparently, some misgiving in the minds of some of the Franciscan missionaries working in Bosnia about the legitimacy and propriety of what they were doing. In consequence, their local Superior, Fra Bartolomeo of Alverna, wrote in 1379 an encyclical letter to them explaining and justifying their activities. Apropos of the baptisms of 1365—1366 he mentions a remark of the Greek Emperor, John V: "Also, John, Emperor of the Greeks, when he came to the king, said in the hearing of many: 'The king does well to baptise those Slavs, because they follow neither the Greek nor the Roman form'."[22] P. Wirth, accepting Meyendorff's conclusion that the king of Hungary was insisting on rebaptism of the Greek Emperor and his subjects, interprets this phrase as meaning that John, realising that by refusing to acquiesce in the rebaptism of Greeks he was ruining his chances of getting help, tried to minimise Louis's displeasure by showing toleration regarding the rebaptism of Bogomils, and Wirth suggests that it was the influence

---

[18] *Annales Minorum*, ed. L. Wadding. Lyons 1637, year 1366, IX, p. 115.
[19] *Ibid.,* 1366, XVI, p. 116.
[20] *Acta Urbani V*, doc. 145.
[21] *Ibid.,* doc. 160.
[22] D. Lasić, O. F. M., *Fr. Bartholomaei de Alverna, Vicarii Bosnae, 1367—1407, quaedam scripta hucusque inedita.* Archivum Franciscanum Historicum 55 (1962) 59—81, esp. p. 75.

of the indignant Bogomils on Šišman that led him to obstruct the Emperor's return.[23] I think that interpretation unnecessary. The Emperor's words just quoted quite clearly testify that he considered both the Greek and the Latin forms of baptism to be valid. So did the Franciscans; and, if the Franciscans did, so must Louis have done who organised the whole process of baptising the Bulgars of the conquered territories, insisting on careful registration of all those baptised.

In 1372 the same Fra Bartolomeo had sent to the Holy See a long list of *dubia* in respect of Franciscan missionary practice and he requested official solutions. The answers to the first three of his *dubia* have some interest for this present enquiry. Fra Bartolomeo had asked whether, as the Friars were too few in comparison with the multitudes around them, they had acted rightly in employing to help them in baptising "those priests of these parts who were willing to follow the Roman formula" even though they were ignorant and not canonically ordained; they were told: Yes. In respect of Greeks and schismatics they had asked if the bishops could "make the chrism" and the priests "consecrate the Body of Christ"; they were answered in the affirmative in both cases. Thirdly they were advised to leave in their good faith the simple faithful baptised in the Greek rite and not bothered by any scruple about their position.[24]

Fra Bartolomeo, in the letter to his Franciscan subjects of Bosnia already quoted, is very revealing on the reasons for the baptising performed by the Friars. He wrote: "(The local priests) have reached such a pitch of madness and ignorance that they have lost the form and way of baptising, some from obstinacy, others from contact with the Paulicians of Vlachia and the heretics of Bosnia, others because they are not among those appointed by their Roman superiors or Hungarian bishops as pastors. Each one makes up a formula for himself just as he likes and, while he pours the water on the head, one says: 'Blessed are they", another: 'Sprinkle me'; another: 'As many of you as have been baptised have put on Christ'; another again says 'Alleluia' three times; another 'The servant of God is baptised in the name of St Peter or Demetrius' according to the name he wants to be known by; and out of twenty of them you will hardly find two who agree in their baptising, but each one boasts of his being better than the rest and they work off so many deceptions in their baptising that for an intelligent Christian it is an abomination to hear".

Later in the letter he answers an objection put by his own Friars. Allowing (they had said) that it is right to bring people back to Mother Church, "what is the reason why Christians already baptised are baptised again, especially as, according to the authorities of the (Roman) Church the Greek form of baptism is not challenged, and it is in that that the people have been baptised or firmly believe that they have been baptised, and that is sufficient for salvation. It should be enough to reconcile them by an imposition of hands as is done by the Greeks". To this Fra Bartolomeo replied "that, if they observed the form of the Greeks, namely, 'The servant of Christ is baptised in the name etc.',

---

[23] *Die Haltung Kaiser Johannes' V. bei den Verhandlungen mit König Ludwig I. von Hungarn zu Buda im Jahre 1366.* Byz. Zeitschr. 56 (1963) 271—273.
[24] There were also 20 other *dubia: Acta Gregorii P. P. XI* (1370—1378) (Fontes III, XII), ed. A. L. Tautu, Rome 1966, doc. 34 a.

never should we baptise anyone of them. But after repeated enquiries made in various ways we have found for certain that these priests of the Slavs, on account of their ignorance and lack of any training, preserve no legitimate and fixed form and what they know they do not apply to the matter. Indeed a year ago when the king baptised 400.000 people, among 400 schismatical priests there were not found any who preserved the form. Also John, the Emperor of the Greeks, ... (as quoted earlier). Besides yesterday in the town of Ceni, in the presence of some of our Friars, monks coming from the territories of Greece said about those priests: 'Those people are not priests but dogs and they do not genuinely baptise. For that reason we baptise them *sub conditione,* because a thing not known ever to have been done cannot be said to be repeated' ".

"One can allow that some of them are genuinely baptised, especially as lately monks expelled from Athos in Greece have taught some in these parts. But, because they are very few, we cannot distinguish them from the rest ...".[25]

One can safely conclude from these various statements of the Franciscan Superior to his scrupulous Friars that the missionaries' policy, founded on theological principles, was to baptise only those who had not been validly baptised and that, as they recognised the validity of the Greek sacrament of baptism, they did not wittingly baptise those who had been baptised in that rite. If some, validly baptised according to the Greek form, were rebaptised, it was by mistake, owing to the inability to distinguish them amidst the mass of the non-baptised. In view of this, it is not credible that king Louis could have demanded rebaptism of the Greek king, his sons and people.

If, then, John's refusal to be rebaptised was not the cause of the disagreement between him and Louis I because the demand was never made, no explanation seems to be left to account for the abrupt change in their friendly relations that occurred in Buda. A letter from Pope Gregory XI to Louis dated 28 January 1375 may offer the solution of the problem. Gregory told Louis that John claimed to have fulfilled the conditions that in 1366 Louis had set for Hungarian help to Constantinople and that he had asked the Holy See to press his claim for that help, as Constantinople was in a very precarious position. "Lately our most dear son in Christ, John, illustrious Emperor of the Greeks, has informed Us that, admittedly some considerable time ago while he was with you in your kingdom, he requested help from your Magnificence and that Your Majesty, out of your reverence towards God and the Catholic faith, (had agreed) graciously to grant him the help he asked for if he would return to the obedience of the Roman Church. Afterwards that same Emperor came in person to the City (of Rome) and there he promised the obedience in question in a solemn ceremony and on oath, according to the wish and demand of Pope Urban V of happy memory, whereupon he straightway requested from you the help treated of before, but he has not yet been able to obtain it." John asked the Pope to plead his cause with Louis, which Gregory did pointing out also to the Hungarian king that the Turks would soon

[25] Lasić, *art. cit.,* pp. 66, 74—75.

be a menace to his own kingdom and that, by defending Constantinople, he would be defending himself.[26]

Palaeologus made his profession of faith in Rome on 18 October 1369, three years after his visit to Buda and the formulation of Louis's condition. But it seems that from the beginning he had intended to meet that condition. The first step towards it was on 29 May 1367 when in Constantinople he signed documents with Amadeus of Savoy promising a visit to the Pope of himself or his eldest son,[27] and probably this act itself was the fruit of resolutions made even earlier — immediately after the return from Bulgaria, when he spent several weeks in the company of Amadeus and the Latin Patriarch in Sozopolis in the early months of 1367.[28]

Postscript

There is still an air of mystery enshrouding all this incident that neither Meyendorff's solution nor mine dissipates — why in 1366 John V had to go through any form of reconciliation with the Church at all, for already in 1357 he had been reconciled with it. Philippe de Mézières, the companion of the apostolic nuncio, Peter Thomas, bishop of Patti, records a letter of John himself dated 7 November 1357, wherein he stated: "With the advice and counsel of our barons we replied to the aforesaid Brother Lord Peter that, as we promised so we will do, to be obedient and faithful and devoted to the Roman Church; indeed We promise and swear and I firmly promise and hold everything without exception that the holy Roman Church holds and in that faith I wish to live and die and never will I diverge from it. And in this way I promised to the said Brother Lord Peter and in the presence of many bishops I swore in his hands and henceforth I shall preserve the faith and loyalty to my lord the Supreme Pontiff that other princes of the Roman Church preserve". The same author recounts that "the Emperor as a faithful and devoted Catholic with great devotion received the Body of the Lord from the hands of the nuncio apostolic, Brother Peter himself".[29]

Pope Innocent VI was informed of that reconciliation, not only by the letter of John V, but also by the apostolic nuncio himself. A papal letter addressed to Bishop Peter Thomas on 11 May 1359 refers to the Emperor's conversion: "Your Fraternity recounted that our most dear son in Christ, John, the illustrious Emperor and governor of the Romaei (*carissimus in Christo filius noster Joannes imperator et moderator illustris*) some little time ago professed and swore in your hands, when as Bishop of Patti[30] you were nuncio of the Apostolic See in those parts, to be always faithful, obedient and devoted to the holy Roman Church and Us and to our successors, the Roman Pontiffs, and will for ever hold what the Roman Church itself holds and teaches and that he will

---

[26] *Acta Gregorii XI,* doc. 137.
[27] *Acta Urbani V,* doc. 172.
[28] Bollati, *op. cit.,* pp. 106, 107, 118—119.
[29] Philippe de Mézières, *The Life of Saint Peter Thomas,* ed. J. Smet. Rome 1954, letter pp. 76—79; quotations, pp. 77—78, 75.
[30] Peter Thomas had been created Bishop of Corone on 10 March, the day before this letter was written.

strive with all his might to bring the Church of the Greeks and the people subject to him to the same devotion and obedience".[31]

It will be noted that the papal letter re-echoes somewhat the terminology of the imperial letter and that the Pope refers to the Greek Emperor with the form of address reserved for members of the Roman Church. Innocent died on 12 September 1362.

His successor, Urban V, wrote several times to the Greek Emperor in the early years of his reign. He never referred to his reconciliation with the Church and he addressed him with the form for non-members. And in 1366 he arranged for John's reconciliation as if he had never been reconciled before. Why?

A not very convincing explanation of this strange situation may be that all the items of correspondence between Pope Urban and Constantinople were not entered regularly in the papal registers. O. Halecki states that in Reg. Vat. 63 (which consists of documents exchanged between popes of Avignon and the East) John's chrysobull of 15 December 1355 is followed by a note: *"Item sequitur alia littera in papiro scripta duabus bullis aureis bullata"*, but this chrysobull is missing. It might have been John's letter of 7 November 1357.[32] The letter of Peter Thomas about the conversion is also missing; and the fact that the letter of the Pope of 11 May 1359 (as also a second letter of the same date on the same subject) is 'Unnumbered', suggests confusion in the registers.

---

[31] Reg. Aven. 141, f. 20 r.
[32] O. Halecki, *op. cit.,* p. 61, n. 2.

X

THE SOURCES OF THE 'ACTA' OF
THE COUNCIL OF FLORENCE

'This conscientious reproduction of the speeches from the Greek records of the sessions in the centre of the above-mentioned history [i.e. the printed 'Acta'], the partisan attitude adopted in favour of the Romanising party and the whole arrangement, but especially the personal remarks introduced—particularly those in the diary-account of the further progress and the conclusion of the negotiations for union that followed the last of the general sessions —of the author who obviously was present and participated in them all up to the end, explain the general esteem that this Greek history of the Council of Florence enjoys in, at least, ecclesiastical circles of the West up to the present day'.[1] In this place and in others, too, Frommann recognises that there are two elements, the speeches and the diary-account, in the Greek 'Acta'[2] of the Council as we find them in the printed editions. He did not, however, follow up the line of investigation that this recognition opened up to him, partly because he did not trace the history of the text he was using back to the manuscripts; partly, I imagine, because he had concluded that the *Memoirs* of Syropoulus were far more trustworthy as a source. The purpose of this article is, first to show that there were two sources of the 'Acta' and secondly to try to determine their nature.

PART I.—THE SOURCES

(a) In the preceding essay I pointed out that there are three large families of Mss. of the Council of Florence: I. Those which contain only the discourses and omit the descriptive accounts of the arrivals at Venice, Ferrara and Florence, the discussions on Purgatory and the events that followed the public sessions in

---

[1] T. FROMMANN, *Kritische Beiträge zur Geschichte der Florentiner Kirchen-einigung* (Halle a. S., 1872), p. 50.
[2] Throughout this essay I use the word 'Acta' to denote the account of the Council of Florence as it is found in the printed editions, and the word 'Acts' in the sense of authoritative proceedings of a council.

Florence: II. Those which, with the discourses, give also the accounts omitted in I, in an ungrammatical and somewhat colloquial Greek—by far the largest of the three families: and III. Those with the same content as II but in a less ungrammatical Greek.

A comparison of the Mss. shows that the differences in the diction in II and III applies only to the descriptive accounts, i.e. to the parts omitted in I. The parts common to all three families, i.e. the discourses, are not only written in grammatically good Greek, but they all derive from the same source. This conclusion emerges clearly from a collation of the Mss. and it is confirmed by the fact that Joannes Plousiadenus, the copyist of a Ms. of the second Family (Cod. Laurenz. Conv. Sopp. 3), was considerate enough to add notes in his text stating that he had taken some of his material from 'another book'.

(b) These notes are not found with every variation between I and II, but there are sufficient of them to show conclusively that one of his books was a Ms. of the first Family (I). For the descriptions of the arrivals of the Greeks at Venice and Ferrara and for the discussions on Purgatory he gives no indication of his source. His first reference to another book occurs in the text at the exact point where Family I finishes its account of the proceedings at Ferrara. It is as follows: 'From this point on we are writing from another copy what was done privately and publicly at this juncture, on account of the transfer of the Council from Ferrara to Florence' (*A.G.*, p. 213).

He does not, however, indicate when he goes back to his first source, but he clearly must have done so, for later he interpolates two passages of unequal length into the text of Family I, noting at the beginning that they are from the 'other book' and at the end that he is returning to the 'first book'. Then, at the very point where all the Mss. of Family I came to an end, Plousiadenus comments in his codex: 'At this point we finish the first copy, the whole book; the following we found in the other copy'. These marginal notes, therefore, leave no doubt that the 'Acta' as we now know them in the printed editions are compiled from two separate sources.

(c) There is a notable difference in the character of the contents of the first Family and that of the additions made to it to form the second and the third Families. The first Family recounts almost exclusively the speeches and discussions of the public sessions. Sometimes these were lively, but the account given of them is a transcript of the words employed, not a general description or a résumé. On the other hand, the added parts are descriptive of scenes and events, somewhat verbose in the introduction, briefer and indeed diary-like in the later sections. Speeches are very rarely given in 'direct' form, usually they are synopsised; and the events dealt with are the relations between the Greeks themselves and their less official contacts with the Latins.

(d) At the same time the diction has changed and even more, judged on classical standards, the accuracy of grammatical construction. The grammar of the sessional accounts is above reproach and the diction is literary Byzantine Greek. The non-sessional sections of the 'Acta' even in the Mss. of the third Family, and much more so in those of the second, abound in unclassical and even ungrammatical constructions and use contemporary words as synonyms for classical words. Like the difference of character of the contents, so the difference of language and correctness between the two parts is obvious even in the printed editions, although editors have removed many of the solecisms and other non-classical usages that are of frequent occurrence even in the most correct of the Mss. of the second and third Families.

(e) The 'Acta' have been frequently condemned as being a 'partisan' account, by writers who thought them the product of one author. T. Frommann, for example, in the quotation already given refers to them as 'Romanising'. A. Warschauer was convinced that they were 'emperorising'.[3] Whether either of these scholars is justified in his contention will be considered in the following essay. What is of interest here is that all the examples and incidents they adduce to prove their views are taken not from the sessional sections of the 'Acta', i.e. the contents of Family I, but from the parts added by Plousiadenus from his 'other book'. There is, in fact, a difference of tone between them. The additional parts are more personal, more Greek; the sessional parts are impersonal, mere transcripts of dogmatic speeches. There is one exception to this. At the end of session VII in Ferrara, a short session in the 'Acta', there is a note to explain

---

[3] *Ueber die Quellen zur Geschichte des Florentiner Concils* (Paderborn, 1891), pp. 9–11.

why it is so short. The three Greek notaries declare that because the Latin speaker was talking only to fill up time, 'We had begun to write, but when we realised that all this was off the subject, we stopped and indeed chiefly because our side did not bother to make any defence in the matter. Therefore, it is not written down in this record, like some other unnecessary items' (*A.G.*, p. 160).

(*f*) The quotation just given indicates that the writers were more than one in number and implies a group. Another remark, found in four Mss. of the first Family, 'These things were written by the principle secretary', with a variation of it in two other Mss., 'These things were written by the three ecclesiastical secretaries', explains who the 'We' were who stopped writing at the end of the seventh session. They were the three Greek notaries whose work it was to write down all the discourses of the sessions and to compare their accounts among themselves and with the Latin record, so as to produce an accurate transcript of the speeches delivered: Being Greeks they would, in any debate with the Latins, tend to be anti-Latin, as the quotation shows. They were not, however, 'authors' of any work, tendentious or otherwise, but as nearly as possible automata recording sounds. The non-session parts of the 'Acta', on the other hand, are plainly and openly the work of one writer describing what he saw and heard.

CONCLUSION OF PART I

There is, I think, no doubt whatsoever that the 'Acta' as we have them are drawn from two distinct sources, the one furnishing the discourses delivered at the public sessions, the other providing the rest. It can still be asked whether there were not even more than two sources, i.e. whether all the rest comes from the same original, seeing that Joannes Plousiadenus makes no mention of his second book till nearly the end of the proceedings at Ferrara and after that point notes his new authority each time he changes over. The answer to this question is, I think, 'No', and for these reasons. The parts unaccounted for are the descriptions of the arrivals at Venice and Ferrara up to and including the discussions on Purgatory. The copyist gives no indications of his source for these, but he certainly did not take them from the Mss. of Family I which have their own very brief introduction. When he does mention a second book, he three times refers to *the* first book and three times to *the* second book, implying that he was using only two, not more. Nor is it likely that he himself is responsible for the introductory pages, for they are the description of a participant and an eye-witness and, more than that, of an archbishop, which Joannes Plousiadenus certainly was not in 1437. Further, the description of the arrival at Florence is so similar, though very much shorter, to that of the arrival at Ferrara—even to a few identical phrases, that one must conclude that they come from the same pen. And the arrival at Florence falls within a part taken from the 'other book'. Whether, however, the 'other book' contained copies of the official Bulls of the opening of the Council and of its transference to Ferrara is an open question. There is no reason why it should not, but on the other hand Plousiadenus might have had easy access to these and so have included them without more ado.

So it seems safe to conclude that there were only two, at any rate, main sources of the 'Acta' and from the arguments put forward it seems likely (personally, I should say, seems highly probable) that the two sources had two distinct authors, or rather that whoever wrote the non-sessional sections did not write the accounts of the sessions. From this it follows that, in judging the historical value of the 'Acta', a distinction should be made between the two parts and that the whole thing should not be lumped together and labelled e.g. a *Tendenzwerk*. The accounts of the sessions give every sign of being what they purport to be, an accurate and impersonal verbatim record of what was said, and as such they should be accepted as the primary historical source for the history of the Council. The other parts are more personal and on these each historian will doubtless have his own opinion. Mine will be found in the next essay in this collection.

PART II. THE NATURE OF THE SOURCES

(*A*) *The Discourses*

The discourses reproduced in the Mss. of the first Family and embodied in the 'Acta' may be the official Acts of the Council (or part of them) or they may be nothing more than a collection of the speeches with no official character. Reasons can be adduced in favour of both of these views.

I. The Discourses are the Acts

(a) All the Mss. of all the families (and all the printed editions) are entitled, *Practica of the Holy and Oecumenical Council held in Florence.* Now the word, Practica, had, at least by the time of the Council of Florence, come to mean official Acts. It is used in this sense several times in the 'Acta' themselves and it is never used in any other sense, e.g. *A.G.* pp. 11, 77, 457. It is used in the same sense by Syropoulus (e.g. pp. 170, 254), who speaks even of the 'Practica' of this council: 'I refer those who want detailed information about what was said in the sessions to the Practica' (p. 118), but as will be noticed later, he calls them also 'Minutes'.

This use, then, of the word 'Practica' in the title of the 'Acta' strongly suggests an official character. Whoever was responsible for the title in the original, knowing full well the connotation of the word, would hardly have had the temerity to label as 'Practica', within a few years or even months of the close of the Council, what was·nothing more than an unofficial collection of speeches —even of speeches certainly made at the Council—put together privately by himself.

(b) It is universally admitted that official Acts were written. For that purpose *notarii* were appointed on both sides and their number was three.[4] References to them in the 'Acta' and in Syropoulus are frequent and, it is to be observed, these references are strictly to the secretaries or to their minutes of the proceedings and not merely to the occasions when notes were exchanged between the Latins and the Greeks, or when meetings were arranged to compare manuscript-books of the Fathers and the Councils to check the accuracy of the quotations made from them. From the 'Acta': e.g., at the end of session 3 in Ferrara, Cardinal Cesarini says: 'But so that you too may give a clear answer to all the points of the speeches, what today has been said and written down by your notaries must be read and compared with the version of ours. In this way, when remembrance of it has been refreshed and agreement reached, we shall in the next session make our reply on all that has been said' (*A.G.*, pp. 87–8); or in the last session at Florence, when the Emperor asked for the Latin books, he was answered by Cardinal Cesarini: 'What we

---

[4] *Tres vero fideles notarii erant constituti pro qualibet parte, qui omnia gesta in latino et graeco fideliter conscribebant* (Fantinus VALLARESSO, *Libellus de ordine generalium Conciliorum et unione Florentina*, ed. B. SCHULTZE (Rome, 1944), p. 21.

have said, the secretaries have noted down: that you have got, so examine that' (*A.G.*, p. 398). From Syropoulus: e.g., describing the scene at the first business session at Ferrara, he writes: (in front of the assembled Fathers were) 'the interpreter and the secretaries of the Patriarch and the Latin ones, writing the words of the speakers' (p. 165); or 'There was said . . . whatever is contained in the minutes which were being written there in detail by the appointed secretaries and, if anyone should desire further information, he will find it there' (p. 217).[5] An official account, then, of the proceedings was written and that by three secretaries on either side. The statement, therefore, already quoted: 'This was written by the three ecclesiastical secretaries,' should, it would seem, be taken as applying to these three official secretaries and as indicating that they wrote the discourses contained in the Mss. of Family I. But, the statements quoted above show that they wrote the official account of the Council or the Acts. Therefore, the discourses of the Mss. of I are the Acts.

(*c*) If the Acts did still exist, what would one expect them to contain? Not descriptions of arrivals and eulogies of towns— for the secretaries would not function officially until the Council was in session. Not private conferences of one side or the other or even semi-official meetings of small bodies of delegates—for the secretaries are officials of the whole Council and should be present in full numbers to note and compare what was said. No, the most natural content for Acts of a Council are the arguments and counter-arguments delivered at the public sessions, recounted in *oratio recta*, and transcribed in full and as nearly verbatim as is possible. And that is the content of the Mss. of Family I, i.e. the discourses.

(*d*) The Florentine Ms. Bibl. Laurenz. Conv. Sopp. 3 is one of the few dated Mss. of the Council. It was 'The property and product of John Plousiadenus, priest, head of the churches'. Plousiadenus was 'head of the churches' from 1463–70,[6] which means that some Ms. of Family I was certainly in existence at least before 1470.

It is most likely that a Ms. of that same family was in exist-

---

[5] Similar references are to be found in the account of Andrea da S. Croce, e.g. *Quia placet, ut breviter respondeatur et distinctim, ut vobis morem geramus, videtur, ut per vos relata per notarios adscripta auscultentur* (*A.L.*, p. 45); *Placeat plane dicere ut scriptores possint scribere* (Ibid., p. 197).
[6] A. PETIT, *Joseph de Méthone*, in D.T.C. VIII 2, c. 1526.

ence before c. 1444, the date which most critics assign for the composition of Syropoulus' *Memoirs*. Syropoulus himself indicates that he wrote not from notes taken during the council but from memory (cf. pp. 231, 345). He would then have been the more ready to avail himself of any documents he could find in Constantinople. It is, in fact, highly probable that he constructed his account of the public sessions from the Practica that he refers to so often, because his synopsis contains phrases and combinations of words found in the Mss. of Family I and repeated in the 'Acts'—e.g. SYR. p. 169, *A.G.* pp. 65–6; SYR. p. 174, *A.G.*, p. 160; SYR. pp. 175–6, *A.G.*, pp. 212–3; SYR., p. 216, *A.G.*, p. 242.[7] The obvious answer to this is that one would naturally expect a similarity of phrase and word when the one source gives an account *in extenso* and the other a précis of the same speeches—both could be drawn directly from the words of the speaker. But three of these examples are not of speeches, but of explanatory narrative. One of them is the account of the incident referred to earlier, when the secretaries stopped writing the Latin speech (*A.G.*, p. 160, SYR. p. 174). The Greek of Syropoulus has words and phrases that correspond so closely to the narrative of the Mss. that the conclusion of dependence is inescapable. Yet the account of the Mss. was obviously composed first, and so must antedate the *Memoirs*. Was, possibly, the copy that Syropoulus consulted the original, authentic Acts that the three secretaries produced for the Greek Church? That is quite possible, for that copy would have been consigned to the Emperor.

2. The Discourses are only a Collection

(*a*) While it is true that Syropoulus on one occasion refers to the proceedings of the council as 'practica' (p. 118), on two others he calls them 'minutes' (pp. 167, 217), i.e. by the same word that he twice uses for the reports of the discussions on Purgatory (pp. 118, 132), which were in fact the written statements read at the meetings of the committees of ten a side by each side in turn and delivered later to the other. Not only that, but the very secretaries, too, who were employed in recording the discourses in the council call their production, not 'practica', but 'minutes' (*A.G.* p. 160).

[7] For other similar passages cf. L. MOHLER, *Kardinal Bessarion* Bd. I, (Paderborn, 1923), pp. 73–4, n. 2.

But the force of the argument in the previous section lay in the use of the title at all, seeing (it was suggested) that that word had come to have a distinctive meaning. That the secretaries, writing while the Council was still going on, should call their work 'minutes' is easily understood, for it would hardly merit the title of 'practica' till it was complete and had received the approbation of the authorities. In any case, that both the Secretaries and Syropoulus do on occasion employ another word does not weaken the argument. In English, I could call e.g. the Acts of the Council of Chalcedon by some wider term—the 'minutes', the 'records', the 'proceedings'—without being understood to deny that I recognise them as the Acts in the narrower, official sense.

(b) There is a widespread opinion that the 'Acta' are untrustworthy as history. The main reason for this is that all the writers about them up to date have taken them as the work of one author and have judged them as a whole. One of the purposes of this article is to show that that is wrong, that they should be judged in parts—discourses and descriptions—and each part assessed on its own merits.

The Manuscripts

(c) It can be urged that the Mss. of Family I omit certain official items that Practica should contain and so they cannot be Acts. Such items would be the Bull for the opening of the Council and the Pronouncement of the Patriarch, which were read publicly on April 9th, 1438, and the Bull for the transfer of the Council from Ferrara to Florence.[8] To these might be added the *cedulae* exchanged between the Greeks and the Latins in the months April to June 1439 preceding the close of the Council, and the speech made by Bessarion before the Pope on the eve of the solemn declaration of the Union. The Mss. of I are silent, too, on the preliminary conferences between the two parties of delegates and on the discussions about Purgatory.

There is no real difficulty in the omission of the records of the committee meetings of May–July 1438, because these were not public sessions and the three secretaries did not function at them at all. As regards the other items mentioned, authentic copies of

[8] The Mss. of Family I contain the Decree of Union but without the signatures.

the Bulls must have been given to the Greek Emperor at least, possibly also to the Patriarch; the *cedulae* were certainly delivered to the Greeks; and presumably Bessarion left in the Emperor's hands a copy of the official statement that he made in the name of his Church. All these must have been taken back to Constantinople and would undoubtedly have been deposited in the imperial archives and possibly also in the chancery of St. Sophia.

Complete Greek Acts, with all the relevant documents, must have existed in Constantinople; it is inconceivable that the Emperor would have returned without them. How, then, do the Mss. of the first Family compare with those Acts? They contain almost none of the items of which the original could well have been preserved. They give only those parts in which the official secretaries were engaged, with the exception of the last sessions both of Ferrara and Florence—this will be discussed in the next section. The Mss. we have do not include the autograph document that resulted from the secretaries' combined work, but there is every likelihood that some of them are copies made from it and made either while the Council was still sitting or very soon afterwards. If, therefore, one takes the Acts to include all the official documents issued during the period of the Council, the Mss. furnish only an incomplete version of the Acts. If, however, the term is restricted to the events of the public sessions where the arguments were propounded and the Fathers discoursed, then there is every likelihood that the first Family furnishes a complete version of the Greek Acts.

(*d*) All the Mss. of Family I end abruptly with the arrival of the Burgundian envoys at Ferrara and in the sessions at Florence in the course of the last session but two, in each case without comment. The proceedings at Ferrara are continued in the 'Acta' with a session on December 4th, where it is mentioned that Ephesus spoke and that Cesarini 'began to speak a thousand words for every one of Ephesus's and he never stopped talking'— the whole session is dismissed in half a page. Two pages follow with a single heading: 'On December 8th, Thursday, there took place session 15', which one session corresponds to two sessions in the account of Andrea da S. Croce, those of December 8th and 13th. All these three sessions, omitted in the Mss., are given at great length by Andrea. Their tone is very acrimonius and, particularly in the first of them, there is a great lack of courtesy, mostly on the part of Cesarini who is not only abrupt but positively rude to the Emperor and to Ephesus. That the *notarii* were present and fulfilling their duties is attested by Andrea (*A.L.*, p. 124) who reports Ephesus as saying: '*Dicatis plane propter notarios*' and Cesarini's curt reply: '*Faciam.*' Why, therefore, no Greek record of these sessions is included in the Mss. is not easy to explain, unless they were omitted because they went over the same old ground again (all the sessions at Ferrara were on the one point of the addition to the Creed of the *Filioque*) and were of a tone offensive to the Greeks.

Where the Mss. cease their record of the proceedings at Florence, the 'Acta' continue the same session (No. 7) with short speeches for two more pages and record another two sessions in direct speech but at no great length—2 pages and $1\frac{1}{4}$ pages respectively. In the Latin *Acta*, after the end of the last session but two (the latter part of which corresponds only vaguely to the account of the 'Acta'), there are also two more sessions, given at great length. In these the Greek contribution to the debate is six lines by the Emperor at the beginning of the first and twenty lines by Isidore of Kiev at the end of the second, the whole of the rest being the eloquence of John of Montenero. In the first of these sessions Andrea da S. Croce notes the presence of the *notarii*: '*Interpr.: Placeat plane dicere ut scriptores possint scribere*' (p. 197). In the second it is possible that neither the Greek interpreter, Nicholas Secundinus, nor the secretaries were present, for Andrea remarks: '*Lecta est in Graeco per Generalem Camaldulensem qui has omnes auctoritates hoc die in Graeco legit*' (p. 216). Ephesus was not present at these last two sessions, having been forbidden by the Emperor to attend in the hope of avoiding argument and of reaching a conclusion: the Greek prelates were generally tired to death of debates. The silence, then, of the Greek secretaries may have been due to the fact that these two sessions were a Latin monologue and it seems to reflect the general feeling of futility.

There is now-a-days a general consensus of opinion that the Greek Acts of the Council, like the Latin, have been lost. The capture and sacking of Constantinople make it understandable that any copy that was taken there by the returning Greek delegates should have perished. It is, however, inconceivable that at least one copy was not left in the papal archives in Italy but, if the Latins could lose their own Latin official reports, they could undoubtedly lose also the Greek ones. Nevertheless Abrahamus Cretensis and later Caryophilus, who produced the second Latin translation of the 'Acta', believed that they possessed the Greek Acts. In this they were mistaken to this extent at least, that they took as the Acts the version that contained, besides the discourses, the descriptions and the diary-notes that certainly were not part of the official Greek Acts. That there existed within their reach Mss. containing only the discourses which, more than the longer version, give the impression of being Acts may have escaped their notice, or they may have concluded that the longer version, containing as it does the discourses, was the original whole and the Mss. of Family I were merely deficient.

To me, the arguments in favour of the discourses being the Greek Acts, or at least the sessional parts of the Acts, are very strong. They are entitled Practica. It is stated in them that they are the work of the three ecclesiastical secretaries and one copy was made by the 'principle secretary' (hypomnematographos). They contain matter characteristic of Acts and, if they show any prejudice, it is for the Greeks and not the Latins. (The Mss. we have go back to a very early archetype and themselves show signs of being of an official character.) They correspond in content, even in what they omit, to the records at Constantinople that Syropoulus terms 'Practica' and 'minutes' and show verbal similarity with the text he consulted there. That text must have been written before 1444, the date of Syropoulus's work, and may even have been the original, the archetype, from which our Mss. were taken, for where else would the original have been, if not in Constantinople?

(B) *The Descriptions*

All I propose to do here is to try to determine the content of the second source.

From the notes added to his text by Joannes Plousiadenus, it is clear that the 'other book' contained (1) a description of the conferences among the Greeks with regard to the transfer of the Council from Ferrara to Florence, (2) some speeches in session 6 in Florence that were omitted from Family I, (3) some speeches at the end of session 7 where Family I finishes, (4) a little of what was said in the last two sessions and (5) the account of the negotiations from then on up to the departure of the Greek delegates.

In this last section a certain number of short speeches are recorded in *oratio recta* but most are in résumé. To the above we may safely add, I think, (6) the description of the arrivals at Venice and Ferrara and (7) the résumé of the discussions on Purgatory, that occupy the early pages of the 'Acta'. Besides this, the second source, seeing that it is so detailed on the less official events, must have contained also (8) a more or less complete account of the speeches of all the public sessions, but whether they were in full and in direct speech or only in résumé is not clear.

That, I think, is as far as the material at our disposal allows us to go. Of the second source there is, as far as I know, no extant Ms., and so one can argue only from the parts included in the Mss. of the second and third families (II and III), both as regards authorship and as regards the nature of the original. Frommann's description of it as *tagebuchartiges* is, I think, amply justified, though to demonstrate that beyond fear of contradiction would take too long to do here and can fitly be left to another occasion. Frommann, however, meant his description to apply generally to the 'Acta' or, at any rate, far more generally than the text warrants, with the consequence that he sadly underestimates their historical worth. He recognised that the 'Acta' contain at least elements taken from the Acts,[9] but failed to realise that these elements are more than two-thirds of the whole, and that they are not cut up piecemeal and scattered throughout the work but are grouped in two solid, unadulterated parts, the one containing the discourses delivered at Ferrara, the other those at Florence. The diary-element is confined strictly to the sections drawn from the second source. The rest, the discourses, have no diary-character at all. Their characteristic is rather that of Acts, though whether of the official Acts of the Eighth Oecumenical Council or only of something like official Acts the reader may judge for himself from the considerations here proposed.

[9] Indess lässt sich dieser Verlust einigermassen verschmerzen, da die Acten zum Theil im Werke Syropuls, und in noch grösserer Vollständigkeit in dem erwähnten Geschichtswerk Aufnahme gefunden haben (FROMMANN, Op. cit., p. 48).

ADDITIONAL NOTE: Since articles X and XII were first written V. Laurent A.A. had published a new edition of the *Memoirs* of Syropoulus: *Les Mémoires de Sylvestre Syropoulos sur le Concile de Florence (1438-1439)* (Paris-Rome, 1971). The Greek text of his edition differs only very slightly from the edition of R. Creyghton used in these articles. As Laurent has everywhere noted in the margins the pagination of Creyghton, the reader of these articles can, if he wishes, check the accuracy of the references they contain.

XI

A New Manuscript of the Council of Florence

Professor Egidio Mioni, in the course of his meticulous labours in cataloguing the Greek MSS of the Marcan Library of Venice came across a large fragment of a MS treating of the Council of Florence. He not only had the courtesy to draw my attention to it, but also most graciously he has sent me photographs of the folios in question. I am pleased to have this opportunity to thank him for this liberal act of kindness.

The fragment, of the latter half of the XVth century, occupies fol. 209 to 236^v of the Greek MS I 29 (= 949). It is written in a regular hand very easy to read except when the pages have been damaged apparently by water. Both the beginning and the end are now missing, so there is no title and no colophon or signature. All information about the character, authorship, value etc. of the MS must be sought from its content, which is interesting enough.

The MS is, in fact, nothing less than a copy of the ' Second Book ' that John Plusiadenus (Joseph of Methone) utilised in writing Conv. Sopp. 3 of the Mediceo-Laurentian Library of Florence and Fond. gr. 423 of Paris, to fill out the Greek protocol of the Council of Florence in order to produce what has since been generally known as the *Practica* or Acts of the Council of Florence ([1]). He himself in several marginal notes of Conv. Sopp. 3 informed his readers that he was copying this ' From the First Book ' or that ' From the Second Book '. The ' First Book ' was the official Greek Acts, composed of the minutes written down during the sessions by the three Greek secretaries appointed for that purpose. The ' Second Book ', or as I call it elsewhere *The Description*, was an account written by

---

([1]) References in this short article to the *Practica*, the « Acta » or *Acta graeca* are to *Quae supersunt actorum graecorum Concilii Florentini*, ed J. GILL (Roma, 1953).

a Greek metropolitan participant in the council, covering the events from the arrival of the Greeks in Venice till their departure from the same place. Plusiadenus, to give a more complete picture of the council, combined these two sources.

He took his narrative of the events of February to September 1438 from the 'Second Book', of October and November from the 'First Book', of December 1438 and January 1439 from the 'Second Book', of March from the 'First Book' and of all subsequent events till the Greeks left Florence in August 1439 from the 'Second Book'. In other words, the only element of his account that is not taken from the 'Second Book' is the text of the speeches made in the public sessions (which actually constitutes more than two-thirds of the *Practica*), or, to express this in another way, the only part of the 'Second Book' that has not been preserved to us in the *Practica* is whatever its anonymous author wrote about the speeches delivered in the public sessions (if we presume, as I think we may, that the 'Second Book' began with the arrival in Venice and ended with the departure thence, as Plusiadenus records it).

Content of the Fragment.

Actually this Fragment of the Greek MS. does not quite complete those parts of the 'Second Book' that were omitted by Plusiadenus, and what it does give is very inadequate, since a debate that in the *Practica* occupies anything up to thirty pages is finished off in the Fragment in a single page or less. Indeed, the sessions in Ferrara are so confused that the impression is left that the author was writing some time after the events, though, as will be seen later, this criticism should perhaps be modified. The Fragment begins in the middle of what is probably the description of session IV of 20 October 1438. The next session mentioned is dated 1 November, but the account probably covers, besides session VI of 1 November, also session V of 25 October, and Cardinal Cesarini is the only speaker named, though Andrew of Rhodes held the floor for most of session V and Bessarion for the whole of session VI. Sessions VII and VIII are omitted entirely, and sessions IX and X seem to be compressed into one with no date mentioned.

At this point interest quickens, for with the close of session X the protocol of the 'First Book' ends (so Plusiadenus declares in a note in Cod. Conv. Sopp. 3) and he therefore turned to the 'Second

528

Book ' to continue his narrative. From this point onwards, therefore, the ' Second Book ' as printed in the ' Acta ' and as found in the Fragment of Cod. gr. I 29 should agree. They do, but only in part. A comparison of the two texts immediately discloses a characteristic of the writer of the Fragment — he was an editor, not just a copyist, that is, he selected bits here and there, leaving out the rest, and added a word or two to connect up his selected passages into a continuous narrative. The result reads smoothly and, if there were no other text of the ' Second Book ' extant, one could easily conclude that the Fragment contained the whole of the original. For his résumé of the sessions there is indeed no other text, and therefore there is no certainty that what we have in the Fragment is the whole of what the unknown Metropolitan wrote. It may be nothing more than a facile concatenation of extracts put together by the copyist of the Fragment. Hence the reserve attached earlier to the criticism of the résumé.

The printed ' Acta ' narrate the events between the session of 13 November and the arrival of the council in Florence in about fourteen columns, from which passages that together occupy about three columns are found in the Fragment. There are other passages in the Fragment, amounting to about another three columns in length, that have not been utilised in the *Practica*. To these I shall return later to describe their content. In addition, both Plusiadenus and the Fragment give verbatim the peroration of Ephesus' last speech in Ferrara, but locate it differently. Reference to this also will be made later.

Between the history of the events in Ferrara and those in Florence, the scribe of the Fragment included a brief tractate: " An Answer to those who say that Christ said: ' Whom I shall send ' and ' Receive the Holy Ghost ', and for this reason that the Holy Spirit proceeds also from Him ", which occupies one and three-quarter folios (213ʳ-214ᵛ) and is incomplete. This seems to be an interpolation. It has the usual triangular diagram to illustrate the relations within the Blessed Trinity. It does not read like part of a speech. There can be little doubt that it is an addition made by the scribe to underline Latin errors.

There follows the account of the activities in Florence, which opens abruptly, so abruptly that it presupposes some previous narrative, that is in fact not given. " On the second day of the week, therefore, the second of March, another full session was held in Florence ". This and each subsequent session is recorded separately, though very briefly, and session V of 14 March contains, as was to be expected, the two short interpolations from the ' Second Book ' that Plusiadenus introduced into the protocol (*Acta graeca* pp. 345-6, 351-2) in the *Practica*. Where the ' First Book ' ends (p. 387) the *Practica* and the Fragment become identical, except that the Fragment omits many passages ranging in length from a few lines to several pages. The last events recorded in the Fragment occurred on Wednesday, 10 June (*Acta graeca* p. 442). The rest is lost.

Conclusions.

1. From what has already been noted, it is obvious that the Fragment is neither the original ' Second Book ' nor a copy made from the *Practica*. A comparison of the Fragment with the text of Plusiadenus demonstrates that the latter is far and away the better and that, whereas there is an occasional reading where the Fragment is patently more correct, there are very many where it is manifestly wrong. Plusiadenus, however, made two copies of his extracts from the ' Second Book ', the one in Conv. Sopp. 3, the other in Paris. gr. 423. Where these two differ (not often and only in non-essentials) the Fragment agrees with the Medicean MS. much more often than with the Parisian. This fact confirms what I have suggested elsewhere, viz. that Plusiadenus wrote first Conv. Sopp. 3 and then Paris. gr. 423, and that he composed these codices separately, each from the original ' Books ', so that the one was not copied from the other (cf. *Acta graeca* pp. xxix-xxx). It indicates also that Plusiadenus was the first of a long series of editors of the *Practica* to ' improve ' the text by arbitrary alterations, though Plusiadenus did it on a very minor scale (cf. ibid. p. xxx).

2. The Fragment gives very little new information. The résumés of the sessions whether in Ferrara or in Florence add nothing new to the full-length protocol contained in the *Practica*. For the rest, both the *Practica* and the Fragment for everything after session VII in Florence are copies of the same source, and the *Practica* are more complete and more accurate: only very rarely does the reading of the Fragment for an occasional word seem more probable. There remains the narrative of the last sessions in Ferrara and here the Fragment supplements the text of the *Practica* in two points:

it gives something more of the background of Greek irritation and frustration in December 1438 and it distinguishes between sessions XII and XIII, rightly, whereas Plusiadenus fused both into one by omitting a couple of lines of introduction to session XIII: " On 13 December, therefore, Saturday, the Emperor came once more and a session was held, in the absence again of the Patriarch, away ill ".

Certainly, also Plusiadenus refers to the distress and disillusionment of the Greeks at their ill-success in debate, but only after the last session in Ferrara. The Fragment (which relates nothing more after the last session than a speech of the Emperor, rather out of context) puts in a relatively long lament already after session XI of 4 December and asserts that the Emperor imposed the subsequent sessions: " When, therefore, we saw that the only result we were getting out of it was trouble and idleness, we were unwilling to attend any more sessions. So we said to the Emperor: ' What good shall we do to others or receive ourselves by holding sessions and assisting at them? The Latins will never yield to the truth but, with their facility for words and their readiness for debate, they produce on every point a thousand slick answers. We hoped to prove by crystal-clear arguments that it is unlawful to add to the Creed, and that, when this was once demonstrated, they would remove the Addition from the Creed, which would then be preserved undiminished and intact, as our Fathers transmitted it to us. But since the Latins in season and out of season insist on this and are neither persuaded by the decrees nor inclined to be restrained by all the forceful arguments that they have heard from us, Scripture says: " Have no word with a disobedient and contradicting people ". So, as Emperor, decree that there shall be one more session and also bid them come to the truth and, if they do not obey, after a first and a second warning according to the Apostle, give it up '. But the Emperor put pressure on us yet again to convince them once more by further proofs. He said in the words of the Apostle that he ' wished to be an anathema ' for them as he [the Apostle] for his brethren, the Israelites. So again there was a debate and we met together, unwillingly, without our patriarch ".

The session of 7 December is followed by another bit of local colour, that is omitted by Plusiadenus: " But he [Cesarini] could not prove his case and make us convinced that they had not contravened the decrees of the Fathers. How could he, when obviously the letter of the blessed Cyril cries aloud and ratifies that the symbol of the faith should in no way be upset? When these things had been said in this way, the session was dismissed. All of us, therefore, went off as usual to our Patriarch and began to argue among ourselves, saying: *To what purpose is this waste?* When we declare the truth, we do not persuade them; when we bring forward the saints, we are not credited. Why do we still go on wasting time and not depart for whence we came? This we brought to the notice of the Emperor (for he was in a monastery at a distance of about three miles outside the city). He answered that there should be discussion with them on the Addition in still one more session and after that no more.

" On 13 December, therefore, Saturday, the Emperor came again and a session was held, once more in the Patriarch's absence, for he was ill " ([1]).

These quotations do not change in any essential way the picture we already have of the council in the month of December 1438. They do, however, offer an explanation of why the Greek Acts have no protocol of the last sessions in Ferrara and they make a little more reasonable the exaggerations of Syropoulus' history of the period. They leave no doubt that the Greeks at that time were thoroughly disillusioned and tired of fruitless discussions, that they despaired of ever persuading the Latins and that they themselves, unmoved by the arguments of their adversaries, remained firmly convinced of the illegality of the Addition. They were also, apparently, oblivious of any other consideration. There is no hint of distress at failing to unite the Churches, no sigh of regret that their threatened city of Constantinople would go unaided. They wanted to go home — give a last chance to the Latins and, if that fails, home. To the historian this is not brand new information, but it adds security and depth to his knowledge for it is a strong and clear statement, it spreads the disaffection over a longer period than was before envisaged and it brings out into greater relief the patience and wisdom of the Emperor.

3. This same account throws some light also on the mentality of the author of the ' Second Book '. There is no doubt that by the summer of 1439 he was a convinced unionist, persuaded of the orth-

---

([1]) The Greek text of these quotations, as of the rest of the Fragment, will soon be published as an appendix in the reprinted edition of *Quae supersunt actorum graecorum Concilii Florentini* and separately for acquisition by those who have the first edition.

odoxy of Latin doctrine. That conviction, however, came slowly. He began, it is true, full of marvel at the material grandeur of Venice but, when the sessions in Ferrara ceased, he was as anti-Latin as the bulk of his colleagues, and he showed no sign of change perhaps till Mark Eugenicus was reduced to an embarrassed silence in session V in Florence. It is obvious that his change of attitude really began with Montenero's masterly exposition of Latin doctrine on the *Filioque* in session VII and VIII of Florence and developed thereafter. This should check the facile accusations made against him of ' Latinising ' or ' Emperorising ', as if an honest change of opinion after learned discussion and sincere consideration were a thing impossible or immoral.

4. The collation of the Fragment with the *Practica* shows that the writer of the Fragment edited his copy (i.e. selected some passages and rejected others and to some small degree rearranged the narrative by linking together what was really separate), and this in respect of the events of December 1438 and January 1439, and also of those that followed the session of March 1439 in Florence: it is not unlikely that he did as much for the sessions in Ferrara. Plusiadenus also is convicted by this same collation of editing his narrative for December 1438, but he is completely exonerated of any accusation of editing the history of the events after March 1439. In point of fact, his account of this period is so completely chronological that any editing is *a priori* unlikely, but it is useful to have also an independent proof of the integrity of his text.

5. Unfortunately the Fragment does not make it possible to give a definitive answer to the query that concerns all the verbatim statements reported in the non-protocol part of the *Practica* — the peroration of Mark Eugenicus, the *vota* of the Patriarch, Scholarius, and the Emperor concerning the *Filioque* doctrine, and the written declaration of the dying Patriarch — whether all or any of these were included in the original ' Second Book '. The Fragment gives only the first of these, but it has so many long (and intentional) *lacunae*, compared with the text of Plusiadenus, that one cannot say whether the verbatim statements are omitted for brevity's sake or because they were not in the text he was copying. The diversity, however, in the use made by the Fragment and by Plusiadenus of the peroration of Ephesus makes the following suggestion at least plausible. The Fragment gives first a synopsis of that peroration

that is obviously taken from the 'Second Book', and then, after finishing everything connected with Ferrara, it includes the full text as a kind of addendum. Plusiadenus omits the synopsis and gives only the full text but places it at the end of the penultimate session: he then has to run the account he found in the 'Second Book' of the last session into the previous one, thus fusing two sessions into one. Obviously both copyists had the synopsis in their 'Second Book'. They had too the original full text, but separately. Probably they had all the other verbatim statements in a similar way, not within the 'Second Book', but separately, and Plusiadenus incorporated them aptly into the narrative of the 'Second Book', whereas the writer of the Fragment, already looking for passages he could easily leave out, omitted them all. Also Syropoulos, who reproduces very few documents, gives most of these verbatim statements, which suggests that copies of them were not hard to come by.

* * *

This Fragment lifts some of the mystery that has hitherto surrounded the 'Second Book' without, however, completely satisfying our just curiosity. It makes us reasonably certain that we now know its full content — the arrivals at Venice and Ferrara and the discussions on Purgatory as reported by Plusiadenus; the résumés of the sessions in Ferrara contained almost complete though perhaps edited in the Fragment; the events connected with the transfer of the council to Florence described much more fully by Plusiadenus but to be supplemented by the Fragment; the synopsis of the sessions in Florence as in the Fragment; the events of the spring and summer of 1439 found both in the *Practica* and, with many *lacunae* and no ending, in the Fragment. Even if the original of the 'Second Book' in all its completeness should some day come to light, it would not, I think, spring any surprises on us, unless it stated the name of the author. The Fragment gives no fresh clue on this point, except that it strengthens the feeling that, all arguments to the contrary notwithstanding, Dorotheus of Mitylene, owner of manuscripts, theologian, reader of both Greek and Latin Fathers (*Acta graeca* pp. 402, 427), often messenger between Emperor and Pope, could not possibly have written such bad Greek.

XII

THE 'ACTA' AND THE MEMOIRS OF
SYROPOULUS AS HISTORY

There are two main sources for the history of the Council of Florence, the 'Acta' and the *Memoirs* of Syropoulus. Of these the former is not to be judged as a single work, but as divided into 'Discourses' and 'Descriptions', and since the Discourses have been discussed at some length in the previous essay, here we are concerned only with the Descriptions, i.e. the account of the arrival of the Greeks at Venice and Ferrara and the debates on Purgatory, the negotiations for the transfer of the Council from Ferrara, and the events after the close of the public sessions in Florence that culminated in the official union of the two Churches —in all, some 120 of the 472 pages of the 'Acta'. What value have these 120 pages historically? Unlike the Discourses they have no official character, still they are the work of an eye-witness and an active participant in the events they describe, particularly in those of the last few months before July 1439. Yet the picture they convey of the situation is so different from that offered by Syropoulus that the student is constrained to chose either the one or the other—he cannot wholeheartedly accept both. The 'Acta' are in favour of union and are conciliatory in tone to the Latins: the *Memoirs* are opposed to union and hostile to the Latins and the Greek 'Latinisers'. This gives rise to another difficulty for the student, for he himself comes to the question predisposed to the one attitude or the other and it is hard not to be influenced by one's sympathies.

Though the purpose of this article is to assess, as far as may be, the historical value of the Descriptions of the 'Acta', that cannot be done without at the same time passing judgment on the *Memoirs*, for the two accounts must be compared and in many cases an acceptance of the one necessarily involves a rejection of the other.

A. General Account of Both Sources

The Descriptions of the 'Acta'. So accustomed have historians become to thinking and judging of the 'Acta' as a single whole, a lengthy work of 472 columns, as long as, if not longer than, the *Memoirs*, that it will be hard for them to appreciate how short is the personal part of it, the Descriptions. These, let it be repeated, occupy only about 120 columns and for the most part they are only brief diary-notes. They give the impression that the author set out to do something on a larger scale, for his account of the arrivals at Venice and Ferrara are fairly elaborate, but he soon desisted from that and in the 94 remaining pages he contented himself with short résumés of the more notable events. His narrative, with one or two exceptions, of the various conferences and meetings that took place just before and just after the public sessions at Florence is in parts almost schematic. That in itself determines the kind of record he can give. It leaves no room for personal impressions, for behind-the-scenes incidents, for gossip, and in fact his account deals only with public or semi-public conferences and meetings between the Greeks and the Latins or among the Greeks. Doubtless his picture of the situation would have been more complete if its background had been fuller, but part at least of that background does appear in so far as it colours the attitude and words of the participants in the conferences. He shows that certain Greeks were actively disposed for union and among them he himself is to be numbered. He mentions that certain others voted against union and that Ephesus was to the end hostile to it but, except in one phrase, he expresses no animus at all against any of these. He speaks of the Patriarch's illness, but only to account for delays in conferences or for the fact that meetings were held in his and not in the Emperor's apartments, and he portrays the Patriarch as generally conciliatory to the Latins and increasingly in favour of union. The Emperor is particular about the honours to be shown to himself but is not above appealing to the hardships undergone to persuade the Greeks to consider favourably the transference of the Council to Florence. When the Patriarch, towards the end, was too ill to direct, and especially after his death, the Emperor took the lead in all the Greek negotiations, patiently striving to bring the Greeks to agreement among themselves and then to union with the Latins. When he lost heart, the leading Greek unionists threatened to unite without him. The Pope is spoken of always with respect and reverence. His financial difficulties at Ferrara are given as the reason for the need to move the seat of the Council and for the straitened circumstances of the Greeks who had been 5 months without their grants for maintenance. All this is background, but not background put in for its own sake. It appears incidentally, one might almost say accidentally, with the notices of the events. The author was favourable to union and does not attempt to disguise it, and the tone of his work is friendly to the Latins, but, apart from the five words mentioned above, it is no less friendly to all the Greeks. He indulges in no adulation of the Latins nor in any back-biting of the Greeks. For one thing, a bare diary-account of events does not lend itself to that kind of treatment; for another, the impression is given that the author was not interested in it.

The Memoirs of Syropoulus. Compared with the Descriptions, Syropoulus' work is very much longer. Some 230 columns of the *Memoirs* deal with the history of the events from the arrival of the Greeks at Venice to their departure from the same place—the period covered by the 'Acta'—of which only about 20 columns are devoted to official discussions, while most of the rest is background. To assess this justly, the situation in Constantinople must be taken into account. The Emperor on his return had been met with the news that his wife was dead and in his grief he neglected to take any measures to establish and promote the union. This neglect gave the anti-unionists among the returning Greek delegates the opportunity to get hold of the popular ear, an easy enough proceeding as the populace was already anti-Latin and, even in the most favourable circumstances for making the union a reality, would have been hard to persuade. As it was, a lively propaganda was begun and the majority of the Greek delegates, faced with popular hostility, changed position and recanted. But at Florence they had all signed the Decree. Some reasons had to be adduced to account for their acceptance of Union in Florence and their rejection of it in Constantinople and, the more they were suspected of treachery to Orthodoxy, the stronger those reasons had to be or, at least, to seem to be. It was being said that their concurrence had been bought. So the misery and poverty in which they had been left by the Latins— in part, at least, true—was pictured as a deliberate policy of duress. The Emperor's management of affairs was not merely undue, but overwhelming, pressure. No validity at all could be allowed to any of the Latin arguments at the Council, but the

Greek delegates had been ill-supported by the dead Patriarch and deceived by the wiles of Bessarion and the cunning of Gregory, the imperial confessor.

Syropoulus, too, had signed the Decree, probably very much against his will as he himself declares a thousand times, but nevertheless he had signed and he was having, it would seem, some difficulty in accounting for it and in living it down. His two solemn asseverations that the subscriptions to the Decree were not bought clearly implies that he, too, had had this accusation thrown at him: 'This He knows, who examines reins and hearts and who will give just judgment on the slanderers of those who signed—that they signed on asking for and receiving money' (p. 292) and on p. 307 he calls on God to witness the truth of a similar protestation. The atmosphere of suspicion is illustrated by a letter to Syropoulus from John Eugenikus, Mark of Ephesus's brother, who had left Ferrara secretly on September 14th, 1438, and reached Constantinople in the middle of the following year —he, of course, had not signed the Decree. The date of the letter is not determined but it was written after George Scholarius had become the monk Gennadius, 'the honest and noble, to me the completely venerable in fact and in name', i.e. after 1450. In the letter John hopes that God 'has firmly corrected Your Honour so that having got back your former, reverent and holy way of life after the terrible fall in Italy. . . .' He reminds him of Peter's repentance and David's sorrow, and exhorts him: 'just as you have already before made good and atoned for the fall in Italy, so by many a token you have shown most clearly in works and words both there and after that and constantly the soundness of your opinion. . . .'[1]

Syropoulus then, had to prove his orthodoxy: he had to defend himself for his signing, perhaps also to himself, certainly to others. He may have signed only under strong pressure from the Emperor, but he had signed. He was not of the stuff that martyrs are made of, not the equal of a Mark of Ephesus. He was writing largely from memory (apart from the dates of the sessions, taken probably from the Practica deposited at Constantinople, and the occasions when the Greeks received grants of money from the Latins, he gives very few other dates) and his memory was embittered by what he honestly conceived to be his treachery to his faith and by

[1] LAMBROS, I, pp. 191–5.

remorse for the guilt that that involved. This does not, of course, mean that everything he says is false or even that in the passages where he most shows his feelings there is no solid fact, but it does mean that one has to be constantly on one's guard against accepting what he says at its face value and in all its details, especially when he is speaking of the Latins, the 'Latinisers', the Emperor or even the Patriarch—and these make up a fair proportion of the leading personalities of the history. One has to be on one's guard even when he is speaking of himself, for it is then that his defence of himself mostly comes in—'He lets his own person play a large rôle in the forefront of events, so that at times one is in doubt whether he really acted the part that he ascribes to himself'.[2]

B.   More Detailed Examination

The above general account of the two sources may appear too lenient to the 'Acta' and too severe on Syropoulus, and the reader may conclude that, in fact, here is another case of prejudice upsetting historical impartiality. What has been stated, then, must be substantiated from the works themselves. This can, perhaps, best be done by contrasting the treatments accorded by the two authors to the personages or parties involved in the negotiations at the Council.

(1) *Diary-character of the 'Acta'*. But first of all the diary-character of the Descriptions must be demonstrated, for in my view it gives an *a priori* probability of veracity to the 'Acta'. The primary purpose of exposing in detail this characteristic is not to argue whether the Descriptions or Syropoulus is right on this or that date where they happen to disagree, but to show the detail of the Descriptions and the almost continuous chain of events they narrate, which in itself suggests a day-to-day diary-entry contemporaneously with those events and so less likelihood of slips of memory, not only as to the dates but as to what took place on those dates.

The date of composition of the Descriptions is not known but that they were written partly during the sittings of the Council can be inferred. Where the writer recounts the death of the Bishop of Sardis (*A.G.*, p. 26), who according to Syropoulus (p. 112)

---

[2] Mohler, *Kardinal Bessarion*, I, p. 70.

was buried on April 24th, 1438, he adds: 'This frightened us not a little, but by the grace of God only he instead of all of us, up to the present, departed to the eternal abodes'. The phrase 'up to the present' suggests that this first part of the Descriptions was written while the Greeks were still at Ferrara and the plague still rampant. The diary-character of the events between the sessions of Ferrara and Florence and, even more so, of those that followed the public sessions of Florence also leads to the same conclusion. The work was possibly finished and perhaps re-written in Constantinople for the Mss. end: 'All this being finished, we left Florence and went to Venice and leaving there went to Constantinople and there each one to his own abode'.

The date of the *Memoirs*, on the other hand, has usually been regarded as known. Mohler[3] considers that the last chapter was a kind of appendix added later to the main work, which itself was written before 1443.

Memory, however, can mislead. An example of how it can create a false impression, is Syropoulus' account of what purported to take place in the interval between the last session at Ferrara and the Greek resolution to go to Florence. The point here is not so much the definite events reported as having occurred, but the impression of a long period of frustration, misery and oppression, which the reader cannot help but get and which Syropoulus himself probably retained. Yet the period in question lasted for not more than 18 days and included the feasts of Christmas and the New Year, which, being spent away from home, may have increased the Greeks' longing to return, but which must have helped at least to fill in the time by the celebration of their Liturgies. Syropoulus does not even refer to them.

Here is a synopsis of the account. Every day without exception Cristoforo [Garatoni] came to the Patriarch in the morning and Andrea in the afternoon to persuade him to debate dogma (p. 185). We go to the Patriarch to complain about our empty idleness, our being on a foreign soil and the lack of victuals: the Patriarch made no answer at all (p. 185). We went to him the next day and the day after that and urged the same: in the end the Patriarch rounded on us (p. 186). 'On that we went away, but on many occasions and over many days having gathered together before the Patriarch and having sung the same song of misery and

[3] Ibid., p. 74.

heard the same [reply] from him, finally' he sent them to the Emperor who only roughly told them that they could not expect to achieve any success without some difficulties (p. 187). But 'after the passage of days, distressed at so much idleness and neglect' they approach the Patriarch again (p. 187). 'And after many days' supplication, he sent us with seemingly kind words to the Emperor. But he again scoffed at us and was angry and with the aforesaid words dismissed us. And that we endured for the two months during which there were no sessions' (p. 188). Then the Staurophoroi summon all the Greeks to 'force the Patriarch to busy himself with the Emperor and free us from misery in a foreign land'. The Patriarch 'pretended to receive their words with joy' (p. 188) and sent a committee of them to the Emperor, but the Emperor went to visit the Patriarch before the committee arrived. On the next day the Greek dignitaries visited the Patriarch to learn what had been arranged, but the Patriarch urged that they ask the Emperor, who would more readily yield to the opinion of the majority (p. 189), so the committee approached the Emperor who was very angry (p. 190): 'the dignitaries therefore were very annoyed with the Patriarch, thinking that so monstrous a thing had been done by him on purpose' (p. 190). 'Again we were in distress at our idleness and attacked the Patriarch', who defended himself (p. 191). Later the Patriarch summoned most of the Greeks to a meeting: 'It does not seem to me to be of any benefit to you to sit idle and to put up with all that I hear of at the hands of the Latins, for they are at home and act as they please, but mine are miserable in a foreign country and oppressed by want . . . . (p. 192). 'I know that ours proposed many strong arguments about the addition to the Creed and almost unanswerable . . . but what the Latins said was rotten and weak . . .'(p. 193). The Patriarch proposed an ultimatum of 15 days to be presented to the Pope, within which time the Latins should agree to give up the Addition, otherwise the Greeks would return home. Mitylene and Syropoulus carried this decision to the Emperor (p. 194). In a long discussion with the Emperor, Mitylene softened and 'in everything agreed with the Emperor', but Syropoulus was firm (p. 195-6). The next day the Emperor visited the Patriarch (p. 197). 'Some days went by' and the Emperor wished to convene a meeting of the dignitaries and 'draw them willy-nilly to debate on dogma'. But he was ill and so was the Patriarch. The latter, therefore, was carried in a litter and next day there was a general meeting of the Greeks.

That day was December 31st at the latest, as can be gathered from the 'Acta' (p. 218 ff.), according to which for 16 days after the last session both the Emperor and the Patriarch had been ill and then the Patriarch was carried in a litter to the Emperor. On the next or the second day after, there was the meeting. The Emperor recovered and on Friday, January 2nd, there was another meeting in the apartments of the Patriarch who was too ill to move. The Emperor spent Saturday and Sunday in discussion with the Pope (Jan. 3rd and 4th): on January 6th the Feast of the Epiphany was celebrated, after which the Emperor showed them the written agreement arrived at. On January 10th the Decree of transfer was promulgated. The account of the 'Acta', then, hangs together and fits in with the date of the Decree known from other sources. Syropoulus is, therefore, recording the events of the period between December 13th, the date of the last session, and, at the latest, December 31st—an interval of 18 days. Even though the Greeks after the last session must have waited for some days —a week or more—before they decided they were wasting their time in idleness, he gives no indication of that in his narrative, because he had a general recollection of long periods without public discussions, which he wanted to make the most of, and transferred inaccurately his general impression to each particular occasion. And the casual reader he carries with him.

To return to the more immediate purpose of this section, here is a table of the events after the last session in Florence according to the two sources. The days (first column) or dates without brackets are stated in the narrative: the days or dates in brackets are arrived at by calculation.

EVENTS BETWEEN MARCH 24TH AND JULY 6TH

	DESCRIPTIONS		MEMOIRS	
March		*page*		*page*
T	24 Last session	397	2 other sessions ...	217
Th	(26) Meeting to compare			
	texts	399		
M	30 Meeting with Pat. ...	399		
T	(31) Emp. to Pat. in rain.			
	Schism among Greeks	401–2		

XII

152

XII

154

DESCRIPTIONS			MEMOIRS	
June cont.		*page*		*page*
Th	(4) *Vota* written ...	438	Syrop. discusses with Protosyn-	
		275	kellos	275
			Syrop. with Pro- tosynkellos ...	275
F	(5) and sent to Pope ...	439		
Sa	(6) 10 delegates to Pope	439		
S	(7) *Vota* clarified ...	439		
M	8 We went to Pope: at late hour Gk. com- munication read in Latin	440		
T	(9) Bess., Isid. and Mityl to Pope	440		
W	(10) Summoned to Pope: Pat. dies	442–5	10 Pat. dies, 8 days after his *votum* ...	276
Th	(11) Pat. buried	445		
(F)	(12) Pope summons Bess., Isid. and Mityl ...	446		
Sa	(13) Emp. summons full meeting	447		
M	(15) Emp. summoned to Pope	448		
T	(16) Emp. and some Metrops. to Pope: dis- courses on Primacy and Eucharist ...	448–50	Emp. and we (exc. Eph.) to Pope: discussions on Eu- charist	278–9
W	17 Dirge for Pat. (9th day). Emp. summons proxies	450		
Th	(18) Pope summons all Greeks: discourses on Primacy and Eucharist	450		
F	(19) Meeting with Emp.	451		
Sa	(20) Meeting with Emp.	451		
S	(21) Accept papal claims	451		
M	22 Visit of 3 Cards. ...	452		
(W)	(24) Feast of S. John Bapt.	452		
(Th)	25 General despair ...	452		
F	(26) 4 delegates from either side meet	452–3		
Sa	(27) Dirge for Pat.: Isid. and Mityl. to Pope: agreement on union	453–4		
(S)	(28) Committee for Decree	454		
T	(30) Dismay: meeting with Emp. and Cards. ...	455		

An examination of the above table confirms the statement that the Descriptions give a diary-account of events. The days and dates correspond exactly, which is all the more striking as the author gives a wealth of days and not many dates, but they are never at variance. Further, his days are usually even more exactly stated than appears from the table, because he defined many by their incidence in this or that week of Lent, of Holy Week, or by their falling within the week following the Sunday of Thomas, of the Blind Man, etc., names taken from the Orthodox liturgical year. So consecutive is the list that it would be difficult to transpose any event without upsetting the whole sequence, and one must conclude that the Descriptions furnish an accurate chain of events. On the other hand, the account of individual incidents is, with very few exceptions, extremely brief—another indication that they are diary-entries—but they convey an idea of what took place.

In the corresponding account of Syropoulus there are only four fixed dates, two of which would be well-known (the death of the Patriarch and the date of the promulgation), a third was for a money-grant (for which he always gives a definite date), and the last is June 2nd when the most important voting took place. Syropoulus' account here will not fit in with that of the 'Acta'. For the business recorded in the 'Acta' as having occurred on May 29th and 30th, Syropoulus, in vague phrases like 'two days later', postulates a period of twelve days ending on June 2nd, when he narrates what the 'Acta' assign to May 30th. He must, presumably, have had some reason for asserting this isolated definite date (the only private Greek meeting in this whole period that he does date), but what that was we are not in a position to

156

know. Were there extant in Constantinople the dated *vota* of the Patriarch and the Emperor?—Gennadius in a list of signatories to the Decree (which, incidentally, omits the name of Monembasia) says that the '*votum* of the Patriarch is still preserved nor is it altogether without malice'.[4] Or was Syropoulus only arguing from a current opinion that the Patriarch died within eight days of giving his treacherous *votum*? Until his reason can be indicated and assessed, preference must be given to the 'Acta', where days and dates are expressly mentioned in sequence.[5]

(2) *The Voting in the private Greek Conferences.* The author of the Descriptions is accused, not only of colouring his account to give a wrong impression, but of downright falsification of facts, which is proved, it is said, by comparing him with Syropoulus. The main instance 'sufficient in itself to undermine conclusively the trustworthiness of the "Acta"'[6] concerns the voting in the private Greek conferences. That voting was important, for on it the fate of the Council would, in the event, depend—whether it should continue its sessions at Florence and, once there, whether agreement could be reached on doctrine. With regard to the first question, there is no opposition between the two authors. It is on the second question that irreconcilable differences are alleged, but, before examining the sources, it will be well to see what the voting was about and why.

What was the situation? The Greeks as a whole were not, as it were, professional theologians. They could grasp the substance of the Greek argument against the addition to the Creed, for it rested on a categorical prohibition of apparently any and every change, but they were out of their depth in the theology of the Trinity. So the Emperor felt constrained to apologise: 'Even if ours do not express it clearly because of the ignorance of individuals' (*A.G.*, p. 418) and Scholarius, addressing the Greeks themselves, blamed them: 'How do you think they will regard us . . . (we) who are always at loggerheads and thinking that ignorance or 'many say so' or 'so-and-so denies it' suffices for the examination of the dogmas, shutting out learning and intelligence and wisdom,

---

[4] SCHOL., III, p. 194.

[5] There is extant the *votum* of Manuel Boullotes, and it is dated 3 June. Cf. V. LAURENT, *La profession de foi de Manuel Tarchaniotès Boullotès au Concile de Florence*, in *Revue des Études Byzantines* X (1952), pp. 60–9.

[6] A. WARSCHAUER, *Ueber die Quellen zur Geschichte des Florentiner Concils* (Paderborn, 1891), p. 11.

while the Latins cleave to them'.[7] That accounted for their refusal to re-open the public sessions, though urged thereto time and time again by the Latins (e.g. SYR., pp. 220, 229, 230, etc.), because they were consistently defeated in argument. Mark of Ephesus was the only speaker on the Greek side throughout all the Florentine sessions—the sole defender of the faith[8]—yet of him Scholarius declared: 'Our common teacher and master says all the argument must rest on two or three texts and that the political law establishes it', though the Latins bring forward the six greatest writers common to us both and expound and harmonise them with the Scriptures, 'and nothing has been said by us to them, to which they have not clearly answered with wisdom, honesty and truth'.[9] Bessarion said the same thing to the Greeks also during the Council: 'And we have replied through our experts to what they have said, by complete silence on some points and by an answer of no value at all on others'.[10]

Greek theological training and mentality were patristic and so the question at issue finally resolved itself into: 'Are the writings of the Latin Fathers genuine i.e. unfalsified?' and 'Do they agree with those of the Greek Fathers?' The latter question was really unnecessary, because it was an axiom that Saints cannot contradict each other in matters of faith; nevertheless much time was spent in comparing texts, and Scholarius asserted to the Greeks that he could demonstrate agreement within the space of two hours, if need be.[11] If the answer to these two questions was in the affirmative, then the solution was found and the 'through the Son' of the Greeks meant the same thing as the 'from the Son' of the Latins. The most important voting, therefore, of the Greeks (and the voting where Warschauer found falsification in the 'Acta') was on these two questions. Here are the relevant passages from both the 'Acta' and the *Memoirs*.

(a) *Conference to discuss the genuineness of the Latin texts: A.G.*, pp. 425–7; Thursday (May 28th); SYR., pp. 251–4; no date.

'*Acta*': Isidore, Bessarion and Mitylene read various passages from the Latin Fathers. The Greeks exclaim: 'Never (before) have we known the western Saints, never read them. Now, then, we know them, have read them and accept them. . . . The Emperor

---

[7] SCHOL., I, p. 303.　　　　[8] Ibid., II, p. 493.
[9] Ibid., I, p. 297.
[10] *P.G.* 161, 549A. Cf. also 416D, 422B, 424C.
[11] SCHOL., I, pp. 299, 304, 324, 356, 367.

enjoined: If you accept them, all of you give your votes. All gave their votes with the Patriarch, that they accepted the western Saints and that their writings were genuine and not falsified.'

Memoirs: 'The first 5 or 6 having declared their votes, it was enjoined on the rest to say briefly, if each deemed the sayings of the Westerns genuine or false.' Syropoulus, nevertheless, spoke at length and concluded that, not knowing the western writings, he took as a criterion that those of them that harmonised with the letter of St. Maximus and the words of St. Cyril were genuine, the rest false. 'Those who followed me took my opinion. All the same, the majority of the votes were positive, and these were accepted as genuine' (pp. 252–3). 'The Emperor, therefore, perceiving that, except four or five of the higher clerics, the rest followed Russia and Nicaea and took them as guides, but that those after us for the most part attached themselves to our reasons and took their lead from us . . ., determined to exclude us from the voting and for that end had the Acts of the Councils brought in and read to see who exercised a vote in them. Only bishops and archimandrites had signed the Acts, and so he ordered only such to speak now and at the proper time to sign, all the rest to keep silence. And so he made us be silent or rather freed us from speaking' (p. 254).

(*b*) *Conference on the truth of the Filioque:* The two authorities record different meetings. The 'Acta' give the reading of the Greek Fathers for morning and afternoon of Friday, May 29th, and a full meeting on Saturday, May 30th, at which George Scholarius, the Patriarch and the Emperor gave their solemn *vota* and other Greeks voted, ten of them in favour. The Emperor, pleased at the progress towards union sent Isidore to the Pope. On the Monday of All Saints (June 1st) Isidore brought three Cardinals to the Emperor. 'After these events, Tuesday, which was June 2nd, passed and on June 3rd Wednesday', there was another meeting when the Patriarch gave another public opinion and 'all concurred in it and voted that the Holy Spirit proceeds also from the Son', Ephesus excepted. Syropoulus gives one date, June 2nd, for the meeting where both the Patriarch and the Emperor gave their solemn *vota*. He precedes this by another meeting two days before, i.e. May 31st, where a vote was taken too—this meeting has no parallel in the 'Acta', just as the meeting of the 'Acta' of June 3rd is not mentioned in the *Memoirs*.

(i) *Memoirs:* Meeting of May 31st (pp. 259–262). The Patriarch 'gave his *votum* though shadowed over and submerged, and he seemed to most not to accept the *Filioque*. Then the higher clerics gave their votes and with them the hegoumenoi. And there were 10 for and 17 against' (pp. 259–260). There followed two days, records Syropoulus, of remonstrance by the Patriarch to some that had not voted as he did (so clearly he voted 'for'), of dinners given by Isidore to cajole others and of similar action by the Emperor. Then came the meeting of June 2nd which corresponds to the entry in the 'Acta' of May 30th.

(ii) *A.G.*, pp. 428–36; Saturday (May 30th): Syropoulus, pp. 262–8; June 2nd.

'Acta': Speech (*in oratio recta*) of George Scholarius, not mentioned in Syropoulus. 'When Scholarius had said this, he went out. We, taking the books of the eastern teachers into our hands, read many passages of the Saints. So an end was put to the business. Votes were asked for; differences of opinion were disclosed; the truth was openly declared. First spoke the Patriarch' (p. 431) and then the Emperor, the 'Acta' and the *Memoirs* being in full agreement on both of the texts except for a few words of no importance: Syropoulus states that the Patriarch gave his opinion in writing. Then Isidore and Nicaea spoke. 'The opinions being put forward in order were not given in one sense. But Antonius of Heraclea, Mark of Ephesus, Dositheus of Monembasia and Sophronius of Anchialus opposed the opinion for union in everything' (p. 434). Then Dorotheus spoke. 'The higher clerics being asked their views, so as not to protract the account, some openly spoke out our view, others otherwise. Yet ten higher clerics were in agreement. They are as follows: Russia, Nicaea, Lacedaemon, Mitylene, Rhodes, Nicomedia, Drista, Gannus, Melenikus and besides . . . Gregory the confessor, proxy of Alexandria, and from the hegoumenoi, Pachomius the monk. Later were added to us Cyzicus, Trebizond and Monembasia, who was the procurator of the patriarch of Jerusalem' (p. 436).

Memoirs: The Emperor spoke to Cyzicus and won him over. The Patriarch gave his opinion in writing. The votes of the rest were written down. Heraclea said 'No': Gregory the confessor said 'Yes'. 'Then the rest of the higher clerics gave their opinions', but Trebizond was absent ill and refused to give an opinion. 'Except, therefore, for Heraclea, Ephesus, Monembasia, Trebizond and Anchialus, the rest of the higher clerics gave their opinions in favour of the *Filioque* and union with the Latins. The favourers were, therefore, 13 and they disassociated themselves from the 6' (p. 263). The emperor was then asked if he wished the hegoumenoi to vote. He replied that he believed the Patriarch was opposed to it as they were not ordained, and the Patriarch confirmed this. They did not vote. The Emperor then gave his *votum* and his dog whined all the time, and 'immediately some noted this as an unpropitious portent'. The Emperor's brother, though importuned, refused as a layman to express any opinion and the representatives of the eastern Sees agreed with the Emperor.

(iii) 'Acta' (*A.G.*, pp. 437-8). On Wednesday, June 3rd, there was a full meeting of higher clerics, the philosophers, the Staurophoroi and the hegoumenoi with the Emperor in the apartments of the Patriarch, who was ill. The Emperor spoke first, that as a majority accepted the *Filioque* and all accepted the Latin writings, and as 'the majority had written and delivered their opinions before yesterday, I say that the others must be asked and the vote of the majority prevail' (p. 438). The Patriarch gave his opinion first and 'all concurred in it and gave their opinions that the Holy Spirit proceeds from Father and Son. . . . These opinions having been written down, Mark of Ephesus did not wish to give his opinion on this and so the meeting closed. On Thursday, therefore, having met together, we gave our opinions and a document was made and written in three copies. And we sent one to the Pope, the Emperor took one and the Patriarch the third. . . On Friday we sent the document to the most blessed Pope. . . .') (p. 438).

The accusation against the author of the Descriptions is that in the votes of May 28th (*A.G.*, pp. 425-7; Syr., pp. 251-4), (a) the 'Acta' record an acceptance of the Latin Fathers by general acclamation and make no mention of the opposition which Syropoulus says consisted of four or five higher clerics and the three Staurophoroi; and (b) the 'Acta' do not refer to the exclusion of the Staurophoroi and the hegoumenoi from subsequent voting.

(a) It is not unlikely that the Greeks would have voted on some occasions by acclamation (cf. Syr., p. 223 for another instance), and acclamation does not necessarily mean unanimity. But Syropoulus says that there was an individual vote and division of opinion. The 'Acta' also record the individual vote ('The Emperor enjoined: All of you give your votes') but. do not mention the result or suggest divided opinion, though it can be taken for granted that at least Eugenicus did not agree. There is, unfortunately, no court of appeal, no third source apart from these two. But that there was general agreement on the subject of this conference, viz. the genuineness of the Latin texts, is asserted by Amiroutzes in his *votum* delivered during the meeting: 'Further the whole of this holy Synod has agreed on the two points—I say those too who deny the Holy Spirit to be from the Son—that the citations that the Latins bring forward in proof of this truth are genuinely of the Saints and there is no doubt about it, and that one must obey in all things the Saints in what they say'.[12] And Mark of Ephesus, referring apparently to this occasion, records: 'But they said they did not doubt about the citations whether they were genuinely of the Teachers', though he goes on to deny agreement on the truth of the *Filioque*.[13]

(b) Mark does not refer to the exclusion from voting of the staurophoroi, though he apparently speaks of the occasion of it. Neither does any other of the anti-unionist writers, Syropoulus apart. They frequently urge that opinions were not free, but they lay the blame for this on the Latins and do not adduce this instance to prove it. Gennadius in his 'Answer to the Discourse of Bessarion' declares that before any one could reply to him: 'the Emperor imposed silence' (even though it was on the same occasion that he delivered his 'Exhortation'), but he adds no reference to the Staurophoroi to illustrate further the Emperor's tyranny. It would seem, then, that the exclusion of the Staurophoroi did not strike others as forcibly as it did Syropoulus, who had a very exalted idea of the importance of his position and was aggrieved that, in the arrangement of the seating for the public sessions, the Staurophoroi, 'the 5 senses of the Patriarch', were not given places close to the Patriarch, who did nothing to meet their frequent complaints about it—'doing it on purpose, I think, and putting a distance between us and him' (SYR., p. 108). Whereas he refers to the exclusion time and time again, particularly when he is recounting how he was forced to sign the Decree (where, of course, it makes a very good argument), others of his own party, who would have welcomed so apt a demonstration of injustice,

[12] *E.O.*, 36 (1937), p. 177.
[13] *Relatio de rebus a se gestis*; PETIT, *Docs.* p. 448.

162

if it had struck them as such, pass it over. In any case, it was not unreasonable. The Staurophoroi were only deacons and three of them were consistently blocking agreement among the Greeks. The responsibility of deciding questions of doctrine rested with the bishops only, and there seemed a fair chance of their reaching agreement, and that chance would be the more likely to be realised the less the number of discordant voices. Voices that had a right to be heard were not impeded. There is no sign whatsoever in either the 'Acta' or in the *Memoirs* (apart from the last two sessions at Florence, which the Greeks endured rather than participated in) that Mark of Ephesus was ever hindered from saying whatever he liked in public sessions, private Greek conferences or casual meetings—on the contrary, a special meeting was convened to persuade him (*A.G.*, p. 450) and, when he still remained unconvinced, he was subjected to no reprisals. The most one can say is that, if the three were silenced as Syropoulus says, it was then unfair to force them to sign the Decree of Union.

That there was, not merely a majority, but an overwhelming majority in favour of the truth of the *Filioque* is not open to question. Gennadius, after his change of heart, refers to Mark as the only defender of the faith, the only true archbishop. Mark himself says: 'When I saw them now enthusiastically rushing towards union and those who before had stood by me now fallen to them' he did not hand in his prepared, written *votum*, and this on the occasion when the *Filioque* was the question at issue.[14] It is apparent in the 'Acta' and in the *Memoirs*. The 'Ayes' according to the 'Acta' have already been given. Syropoulus agrees in substance. He records that Ephesus, 'when he realised that almost all were traitors and ready for acceptance of Latinism, was silent' (p. 258). In the final voting on the *Filioque* of June 2nd (according to the *Memoirs*), with Bessarion, Isidore, Mitylene and Gregory the confessor, who throughout were prime movers for union (cf. Syr., pp. 221, 223, etc.) and Lacedaemon (cf. pp. 238, 256, etc.), went Tornobus, Amaseia, and Moldoblachia won over by the Patriarch; Melenikus, Drama, Dristra and others beguiled by a good dinner with Isidore; and the legates of Trebizond and Moldoblachia and, later, Cyzicus, gained in pretty much the same way by the Emperor (pp. 260–1); and, the most important person of them all, the Patriarch. On the same side went the weight of

[14] Ibid.

the theological advisers, Scholarius[15] and Amiroutzes.[16] 'Apart from Heraclea, Ephesus, Monembasia, Trebizond and Anchialus, the rest of the prelates voted to accept the *Filioque* and union with the Latins', (SYR. p. 263), i.e. 5 against, presumably supported by Gemistus; 16 for, together with the Patriarch, and supported by Scholarius and Amiroutzes. Neither the list of the 'Acta' (p. 436) nor that of Syropoulus (p. 262) of those in favour is complete, but between them they account for 15 out of the 16 'Ayes'—neither list mentions Stauropolis, whose name also is not included in the signatures to the Decree (*A.G.*, pp. 465-7) nor in the list of signatories given by Gennadius. Syropoulus' explicit declaration that only 5 were unfavourable removes any hesitation in accepting these statements. In addition, the 'Acta' relate that later were added to the 'Ayes' Trebizond (who, being ill, did not vote in the meeting: SYR., p. 263), Monembasia (who had voted 'No' in the meeting: SYR., p. 263, but who was selected to go with Bessarion, Isidore and Mitylene to the Pope on June 9th: *A.G.*, p. 440), and Cyzicus. Bessarion, however, later asserted: 'For all these reasons union rightly followed and all, without any violence, freely and voluntarily, assented to it. Those who were unwilling to assent (there were only two, not more) were left in their own view without violence or any oppression and returned to their own abodes with honour and charity and at the expense of the Roman Church'.[17] That gives, out of the higher clerics, 2 against and 19 for. Of the Greek theologians, Ephesus was against union, with Gemistus; Bessarion, Gregory the confessor, Isidore, Mitylene were for union, with Scholarius and Amiroutzes.

(3) *The Enforced Idleness and the Poverty of the Greeks.* That the Greeks were not given the agreed maintenance but were left in poverty and misery is a constantly recurring theme of the anti-unionists. Mark of Ephesus (referring to the period after the Greeks had voted for the *Filioque* and union, i.e. after June 2nd): 'A long time passed after this and ours were bearing the delay hard and lamenting their poverty and were being forced towards famine. And indeed this was plotted against them, to give no one anything of the agreed maintenance-grants, so that, being forced by this, they might by degrees yield to them'[18] Scholarius: 'And

[15] SCHOL.., I, p. 374.
[16] *E.O.*, 36 (1937), pp. 177–8. Cf. also SYR., pp. 175, 239, 257, etc.
[17] *Epistola ad Al. Lascarin*; *P.G.* 161, 424CD.
[18] PETIT, *Docs.*, p. 447.

in all, partly by promises, partly by pretended necessities in which he (i.e. the Pope) had the Greeks shut in, he persuaded them, though unconvinced, to agreement with the decision'.[19] John Eugenicus (referring to the period September 1438): 'With famine on top of plague, as by degrees practically the very necessities were lacking, since for four months we had had to live on our own resources'.[20] Syropoulus, it need hardly be said, is not silent on it; it would be too long to give here the 34 references I have collected from the *Memoirs*. Quite obviously, the Greeks did suffer both from enforced idleness and poverty. But the period of the Council—February 1438 to July 1439—should be divided into two periods, the first at Ferrara when long intervals passed with no business done or even attempted and when the maintenance-grants were very badly in arrears, the second at Florence when the Greeks had little excuse for idleness and were less hard-pressed by poverty.

That the Greeks had little to do from February to October 1438 at Ferrara is apparent from both Syropoulus and the 'Acta', and the fault was their own. The Pope wanted to get down to business immediately (e.g. *A.G.*, pp. 19, 422–32: SYR., pp. 99, 113, 115, etc.), but the Emperor insisted on a four months' delay. In June and July the Latins managed to arrange the semi-informal conferences but the Greeks would not touch dogma in spite of Latin pressure (SYR., p. 118 sq.). The sessions began in October only after strong Latin insistence (SYR., pp. 148, 158). One reason for urgency from the Latin side was that the Pope was paying for the upkeep of the Greeks during all this period and he was finding himself more and more pressed for money (*A.G.*, p. 220; SYR., p. 205). The result was that he could not provide for them as had been arranged. He paid the clerics 691 fl. on April 2nd, 689 on May 12th, 685 on June 30th and 1215 fl. as the maintenance of two months on October 21st. By the end of 1438 he was five months in arrears in his payments to them (*A.G.*, p. 222, SYR., p. 205). For that reason and because he feared the depredations of Nicholas Piccinino, who had captured some papal towns and might even attempt an attack on Ferrara itself, and because Florence promised financial aid (much of the money spent on the Council at Ferrara was borrowed from Florence), he pressed for

---

[19] SCHOL., II, p. 260.   [20] LAMBROS, I, p. 275.

the transfer of the Council from Ferrara to Florence (cf. *A.G.*, p. 220; SYR., p. 205).

In his account of the situation at Florence, Syropoulus continues in the same strain—idleness, misery and want. He alleges enforced idleness shortly after the last session of March 24th, 1439 (p. 231); about the Feast of St. George, April 23rd, (p. 225); after the reception of the Latin reply to the Greek answer, about May 10th (p. 249). A glance at the table (pp. 151–5) will show that there was plenty of activity among the Greeks at these times. With regard to money, in accordance with the agreement made about the transfer, on January 12th the Greeks received 2412 florins for four months' back-money—five months' was owing—(p. 211), as well as 340 fl. (2 each) for the journey, for which, in addition, the Latins paid the expenses (p. 212). By the Feast of St. George they were more than three months in arrears (p. 225). A few days later the Patriarch agreed that an end should be made to their distress (p. 227). Shortly after the Latin answer (circa May 10th) they are all upset about 'their misery, want and separation from their families' (p. 249), for now they were four months in arrears in respect of the money-grants (p. 250) and Mitylene addressed himself to the Pope's Camerarius about it, who said he was ready to order it to be given. 'The delay comes from the negligence of those appointed to ask for and receive it. We answered that from the time when Cristoforo had arranged a day and bidden us come to him to get the florins, we had been to him seven times and always it was put off till tomorrow. We were by no means negligent in going and asking for it.' The Emperor, however, was angry that they had approached the Camerarius (p. 250). Finally, on May 22nd, 1205 fl. were given for two months; 'Cristoforo saying on this, that nothing should be given to Ephesus as eating the bread of the Pope like a Judas' (p. 251). On the day after the voting (June 2nd) the Patriarch said to the three recalcitrant Staurophoroi 'that the Pope already is providing what (money) is short, viz. he is disbursing for the five and a half months and for five ships and another for the Emperor' (p. 271). Referring to the period during which the Decree was being written (i.e. after June 28th), Syropoulus notes: 'There was no mention of maintenance. For after the May grant no maintenance whatsoever was given to anyone, except when we were leaving to return to Venice, namely after doing everything the Latins wanted'

(p. 282). Mitylene, however, Cristoforo and Ambrose gave money from the Pope to some of the lower-ranking (poorer?) prelates and the Skevophylax cunningly managed to tap all three sources (p. 283). By July 5th the maintenance was five months in arrears: 'I call God to witness, who is over all, that no mention of it was then made by anyone, nor any request however slight by any of ours, or promise by the Latins. But even if we all were gripped by want, still, though lamenting and weeping in the hidden places of our hearts, the majority signed'—this with a view to the accusation that their compliance was bought (p. 292). After the signing the Emperor encouraged them to endure till they received the five and a half months' maintenance (p. 302), but the Pope was adamant till five copies of the Decree had been signed, though five and a half months' maintenance was due to all (pp. 305-6). 'Two days after the signing [which according to the 'Acta' was on Monday, July 20th], the first of the prelates departed and set out on the road to Venice. On the very day of their departure, not earlier, maintenance for five months was given only to those who were leaving': the rest received theirs similarly on their departure (pp. 306-7).

Syropoulus, it will be noticed, gives precise dates only for the payment of the maintenance grants. He probably was employed by the Patriarch to distribute the money and had preserved the accounts he had then made. Both his dates and the sums received from the papal treasury are correct as far as can be checked by the registers of the *Camera Apostolica*, which recorded not the sums paid directly to the Greeks but the refunds it made months later to the individual Italians who had lent money for the occasion. The truth was that the papal treasury was living from hand to mouth and that from at least April 1438 onwards it was existing mainly on borrowed money. That explains the irregularity of the payments to the Greeks in Ferrara. In Florence, however, the Commune had undertaken to provide for their upkeep (against future repayment from the Holy See), and why there was delay in delivering the stipulated sums there on the agreed days is very difficult to understand. Certainly that was not the Pope's fault. Whoever was responsible, it was hard on the Greeks, and Syropoulus is not unjustified in complaining about poverty and hunger, though the humanist citizens of Ferrara, and much more so those of Florence, must have been generous in their gifts and invitations.

At any rate, when the Patriarch died, 500 florins, the equivalent of twenty months' maintenance-grants, were found in his effects (SYR., p. 318); Cyzicus in July 1438 had plenty of silver articles (SYR., p. 313); the metropolitans did not return to Greece poor and so were accused of having bartered away their faith.[21]

The 'Acta', on the other hand, do not descant on the poverty and idleness of the Greeks, but references to these are not lacking when they arise naturally out of the context. When Denis of Sardis died in April, panic fell on the rest, for the Metropolitan's death was an early case of the plague that later did, in fact, infest the city. Apropos of the transfer of the council to Florence, it is noted that 'there was never a mention of the maintenance-grants', which serves as an introduction and explanation of the Pope's request for the transfer on the grounds that, with the loss of Bologna and of much of his revenues, he was quite unable to support the council in Ferrara, whereas Florence promised ready means (*A.G.*, p. 220). The Greeks accepted, but on conditions, and the conditions that they set reflect also their circumstances. That the arrears of five months' grants should be paid off was one condition; four months was fixed as the maximum stay in Florence; payment there should be made to them through a bank, i.e. not through the papal treasury; freedom of movement was also to be guaranteed (p. 222)—implying their poverty, their nostalgia and previous restrictions on their liberty (Syropoulus says that in Ferrara they were not allowed to go beyond the gates of the city).

The writer's account also of the sojourn in Florence gives here and there a glimpse of some of their hardships. It is not that he is deliberately suppressing knowledge of them; he is recounting in diary-like notes the stages of union, and other things are mentioned only by accident if they happen to be closely connected. For instance, the picture drawn of the weeks from Easter till the end of May 1439 is eloquent. The Greeks were tired to death of public discussions on the grounds that they were both endless and ineffective. They refused point blank to endure any more and, practically speaking, to bestir themselves at all; the Latins were to devise an expedient that would lead to union, or the council should finish and its participants go home. Later the Latins presented them with a statement on the Procession of the Holy Spirit; the Greeks changed it and returned it. The Latins were

[21] Ducas, Op. cit., p. 216.

dissatisfied and wanted explanations. 'We began to complain and to set about putting an end to it all' (p. 416)—on 10 May. Seven days later (it was also five days before the first maintenance-grant in Florence was forthcoming), they were asking the Patriarch how they were going to support life while the talking went on and on (p. 419). When the Patriarch died (10 June), the prelates found in that a ready excuse to press the Pope to bring things to an end (pp. 445–6). Even after agreement on the question of the Procession of the Holy Spirit, which for the Greeks was the fundamental difference dividing the Churches, there were moments when the Emperor gave up hope and demanded ships to take them all back home (pp. 449, 452) and when the prelates also were thoroughly despondent (p. 452).

(4) *Motives*—Money, according to Syropoulos, was never given without an ulterior motive, and he manages to suggest some 'concession' made by the Greeks for each particular occasion (pp. 105, 125, 139, 172, 211). He is free also in ascribing deceit. The delay of four months after the inauguration of the council on 9 April 1438 was agreed to, so that they *might pretend* to send ambassadors to the western courts (p. 104); yet a little later (p. 112) he records that the Pope did send letters to all the Latin nations. The Pope urged the preliminary conferences only to impress the Council of Basel (p. 115). Some of ours would not eat a meal provided by the Pope, fearing hemlock (p. 143). The fourth session in Ferrara (the only session that Syropoulos does not date and that is recorded neither in the 'Acta' nor by Andrea da Santacroce (in the '*Latin Acts*')) was hastened on because the Latins were afraid that some of their simpler followers were too much impressed by what Ephesus had said in the previous one (p. 171). Several times the Patriarch is said *to have seemed* to receive complaints sympathetically and then to have informed the Emperor with a view to having the complainants punished (pp. 188, 190, 248–9). Later to persuade them to compliance he showed them what purported to be a promissary note of the Pope and Cardinals about aid to Constantinople (pp. 271–2). The transfer of the Council to Florence was a plot of the Emperor and the Patriarch. After Heraclea, Ephesus and the Nomophylax had tried to return to Constantinople, 'from then on the Emperor and the Patriarch considered together and took counsel in private how they might lead us further inland and to a greater and safer

confinement. Therefore they secretly arranged with the Pope the journey to Florence' (p. 153, repeated on p. 184); so the Pope sent Ambrose Traversari 'who was clever and cunning, clothed in an outward appearance of reverence, not without some education in Greek letters, and a confidant of the Pope', with one of ours, the Cretan monk Macarius, to arrange matters at Florence: the Patriarch, on being questioned, said that Ambrose had gone only to obtain more books. Such is Syropoulus' version of the events, but the truth is that Ambrose got leave of absence from the Pope in the beginning of September for a fortnight to visit his mother who was sick[22]; that Cardinal Cesarini in a letter of October 17th urged him in the Pope's name to return, as his presence was needed, and to bring what books he could[23]; and that finally he received a peremptory order to return in a personal letter from the Pope, dated November 3rd.[24]

The 'Acta' relate the events and assign no motives.

In a similar way Syropoulus would seem to have had an uncanny insight into what was said when he was not present, and what was not likely to have been divulged to him by the participants. For example, he records (pp. 152–3) Bessarion's arguments to the Patriarch for the recall of Heraclea, Ephesus and the Nomophylax; he relates a plan that Isidore of Kiev proposed to the Patriarch to silence the opposition, together with the Patriarch's answer (p. 260); he informs us of the content of the Patriarch's expostulations to win over some of the archbishops to unionism and their replies (pp. 250–1); it was Mitylene, he says, who suggested the device put forward by the Pope of demanding opinions on oath (p. 230). His own speeches which, of course, he was in a position to know of in detail he records at great length, but, as most of them were made on the spur of the moment, he is not likely to have had them prepared in writing and so what we read in the *Memoirs* is the speeches as reconstructed after a lapse of years—may be as many as twelve. In them he appears always as being as uncompromising as Ephesus, on occasions even more so, e.g. p. 203–4. Yet in the end he yielded and signed. It is somewhat hard to reconcile the picture he gives of himself and of his relations with the Patriarch and the Emperor with other information narrated in the *Memoirs*. The impression got from reading the

---

[22] Trav., no. 53.   [23] Ibid., no. 848.
[24] Ibid., no. 846.

Memoirs is that the Patriarch was unsympathetic, as definitely unionist as Syropoulus was anti-unionist and, at least at the end, completely hostile to him, and that Syropoulus was one of those who most complained about conditions and who was a rallying point for the opposition; yet the Patriarch made him a member of all the delegations he sent to the Emperor (pp. 187, 189, 194, 227). The Emperor, he says, was forced to silence him in the Greek meetings because of his hostility to union, and that only after long argument, expostulation and entreaty (pp. 287–291) did he sign the decree: yet the Emperor appointed him to accompany Bessarion to the Pope on July 5th and, a few days later, with Bessarion, Isidore and the Great Chartophylax, to try to arrange with the Pope for the celebration of a Greek Liturgy. It is doubtful if the Patriarch and the Emperor considered him quite as uncompromising, as he would make himself out to have been, and the 'Acta' too suggest a doubt on the same score: 'What we have done has been a great deal and, besides, against the opinion of the three of our proxies. For Heraclea, Ephesus, Monembasia and Anchialus gave no votes for the letter of agreement that was sent, and also from the clerics the Great Chartophylax and the Protekdikos' (416–7). Is the omission of an express mention of the Great Ecclesiarches just an accident, or does it imply that, contrary to the impression repeatedly given by himself (SYR. pp. 204, 242, 253, etc.), Syropoulus was not the most ardent anti-unionist of the Staurophoroi, but the least?

(5) *The Emperor*. The picture given by Syropoulus of the Emperor is not very attractive. He upheld the honour of the Greek Church when he strengthened the Patriarch's opposition to following the Latin custom of kissing the Pope's foot (p. 94) and when he prevailed on the Pope and the authorities of Ferrara to provide maintenance in money and not in kind (p. 104). But generally speaking, he was unsympathetic and indifferent to Greek wants. After three months' sojourn at Ferrara (i.e. in the beginning of June) he went off to live in a monastery about six miles outside the town, so as to be able to hunt (p. 142). He remained there till at least the middle of December, in spite of requests from the Marquis of Ferrara to spare the game (pp. 144) and of complaints from the country people about damage to property (p. 191), and returned only because some Greeks were embroiled with the Ferrarese in a riot (pp. 191–2) 'and the trouble

of the son of Novacus was more powerful than the entreaties of the
Marquis, the Patriarch and the Pope' (p. 192). His absence from
Ferrara rendered it difficult to make arrangements and checked
easy Greek access to him (pp. 146, 147, 150–1). It seems, however,
that the Emperor must have been frequently in Ferrara, for he
directed the Greek conferences to discuss what subject should be
dealt with in the public sessions, to settle how the voting should
count and to supervise the seating arrangements (pp. 153–163).
He rode in to the first session and he was present at all the others,
so that his living in the monastery would not seem to have been
much of an inconvenience and, after all, six miles is only about
half-an-hour's distance on horse back. He often received complaints harshly (pp. 187 seq.) and was very severe even with the
most venerable and aged (pp. 223–4), and it is implied that he
was little concerned with underlings (p. 225). On the other hand,
he was considerate in offering to take with him to Florence some
of the older prelates (pp. 211) and was always kind to Ephesus
(p. 303) who, though with the Emperor's approval he did not sign
the Decree (p. 284), was defended by the Emperor from being
censured (though Syropoulus says that the Pope urged that he
should be) (p. 299) and was guaranteed safe passage back to
Constantinople (p. 284). He was vain and had a special door made
for his entry to the sessions at Ferrara (p. 167 seq.) and accepted
what all knew to be fictitious letters from the Burgundian envoys,
to save appearances (pp. 176–7). He was insincere: 'As long as the
city (i.e. Constantinople) remains in its present state, I accept the
union of the Churches; if anything else happens, I think it
immaterial whether there is union or not' (p. 128)—this in a
private conversation with the Pope: another example of Syropoulus' uncanny insight. He lied when he denied that negotiations were in progress about sessions (p. 148). He lied when he
said that a messenger had arrived announcing a large embassy
from France (p. 146), and again when he disclaimed any knowledge
of the proposal to move the Council to Florence (p. 203). He
cajoled some of the prelates and the embassies of Trebizond and
Moldoblachia to vote for union (pp. 261–2). He tricked the
Greeks into giving countenance to Bessarion's discourse of July
5th, 1439 (p. 293). He did all the managing of affairs with the
Latins. Though Greek representatives were chosen by free
election (p. 155), they had to report to him each day what had been

done (p. 116): 'Everything depended on his opinion and counsel, and without the will and mandate of the Emperor nothing ecclesiastical was done' (p. 123). Negotiations for the public sessions at Ferrara were made with him, perhaps because the Patriarch was passive: 'For they observed that the Patriarch contributed very little to this, but that everything was arranged through the Emperor' (p. 159). He persuaded the Greeks to discuss dogma (p. 201) and to go to Florence (p. 205). He presided at numerous meetings held by the Greeks after the close of the sessions at Florence, ordered them to give their opinions in writing and, in general, managed everything, partly because the Patriarch was very ill during most of the time. The Emperor, however, was himself frequently ill (cf. p. 199) and directed one meeting at least from his bed (p. 237). After the sessions at Florence he realised that there would be no result from more public discussions (pp. 229, 232, 233, etc.) and so tried to find other means such as the conferences of representatives (p. 234 seq.). He arranged the various meetings of the Greeks to try to achieve unity first among them: (after the Greek meeting of June 2nd) 'Behold with the help of God it has appeared that the belief of the Latins is good and the synod (i.e. meeting) has declared this and has come to the opinion that we should unite. No one, therefore, should dispute further about this. For before the decision of the synod everyone had freedom to say what he wanted, but after the decision no one has freedom to say anything other than the decision of the synod' (p. 271). He ordered that written votes should be given because 'I wish to have the written opinions of each, so that it may not be possible for any to change later' (p. 238). He silenced the Stauro-phoroi in the Greek meetings and his presence checked freedom of speech: 'no one had freedom to say what he wanted, not being able to stand up to the Emperor' (p. 163; cf. also p. 238). He urged that, till the Council had decided, all should keep their judgements on both the Latin faith and the Greek faith in suspense, but once it had spoken 'you must accept unhesitatingly what the Council has determined. For I have so disposed myself as I have said, though I am Emperor and I convened the Council' (pp. 285–6). In his formal *votum* of June 2nd he acknowledged the present Council to be oecumenical and therefore unerring, and 'it is necessary that we should follow it and its decision and especially that I, decked by the grace of God in imperial robes, should support and defend it' (p. 265). He forced the three Staurophoroi very much against their wills and convictions to sign the decree (pp. 287–291).

The picture of the Emperor given by the 'Acta' is not as full as that of the *Memoirs*. The 'Acta' begin with a glowing account of the arrivals at Venice and Ferrara, but omit the questions of kissing the Pope's foot and the arrangements about maintenance. The Emperor is meticulous that the Pope's throne should not be centrally placed, 'this befits the Emperor rather than the Pope' (p. 11), and is grieved over the lack of honour paid him by the Burgundian envoys (p. 213). He presided at Greek meetings (pp. 25, 390, 425, 428, 437), but all of these, when the Patriarch was too ill to move, were held in the Patriarch's apartments. After the sessions at Ferrara the Greeks were set on returning to Constantinople, and it was only the Emperor's patience and persuasion that prevailed on them to remain ('Acta', p. 217, confirmed by Bessarion *Ad Alex. Lasc.*; P.G. 161, 422 CD). He won them over to discuss dogma (pp. 218–9) and to go to Florence (pp. 221–3) by urging that, having already overcome the dangers and labours of the long journey, they should not now easily yield to circumstances and return empty-handed. He refused to entertain the suggestion of further public sessions (pp. 409, 410) and proposed that other means be found, so representatives were elected (p. 411). He encouraged the Greeks when they were downcast (p. 417) and, in his turn, was subject to pressure from Greek prelates when he was inclined to lose hope (pp. 425, 450, 452, 456). He declared to the Pope: 'I am not lord of the synod nor do I wish that union should be imposed by force, but our synod agreed of its own free will and sent this profession of faith' (p. 418 and again 421). He stood fast on Greek terms: 'We do not write or say anything else, except that we will unite if you accept that we have given you' (p. 420 cf. also pp. 447, 449, 452, 455) and several times yielded only after pressure from some of his prelates (pp. 450, 452, 456). He had several private colloquies with the Pope (pp. 417, 420, etc.) and reported to the prelates later what had been said (e.g. p. 419). He urged that the majority vote in the Greek meetings should prevail (p. 438). In his final *votum* he acknowledged the Council as oecumenical and that it was his duty to obey it (pp. 432–3). The only actions that might be considered as limiting freedom of speech were his approving the absence of

174

Ephesus and Heraclea from the last two sessions at Florence (p. 393), his demanding written *vota* from the prelates, and his suggesting that they bear in mind also the needs of Constantinople, though they must give 'votes that do not harm the soul nor harm the body' (p. 426).

Can these two pictures be harmonised? The Emperor's insistence on the honours to be paid to him was, doubtless, due to his considering that, even though the Pope was paying the expenses, he, as Emperor and successor of Constantine the Great, had convened the Council and was its head. The same reason, together with the Patriarch's chronic illness, would account for his managing Greek affairs, though it is to be noted that he always held the meetings in the sick Patriarch's rooms, asked his opinion first on the questions under review, and reported any private conversations of his own with the Pope to his clergy. His going out to the monastery, which according to Syropoulus was after the close of the Conferences on Purgatory and so some time after July 16th (A.G. p. 25) and not in the beginning of June as is roughly calculated in the *Memoirs*, was probably due to a desire to escape from plague-ridden Ferrara in summer when no business was on hand, as much as to his love of hunting. In both accounts he is shown as trying to put an end to internal squabbles and frictions and as endeavouring to achieve unity—a well-nigh impossible task if even only the half of Gennadius' criticism was true[24a]—and to that end he ordered *vota* in writing. In both he expresses no opinion on doctrine in any meeting and only urges that the majority vote should prevail and be loyally accepted by all. In both he gives no *votum* himself till the last occasion and after the Patriarch, and then only to declare that in his opinion the Council was oecumenical and that it should be obeyed in whatever it decided, even by those not convinced by the arguments. But in the 'Acta' he is not portrayed as harsh, indifferent, vain, deceitful. That on occasions he was sharp (he was often ill) and

[24a] 'The Latins won by numbers, money and words. . . . And that nothing humane, nothing Christian, right from the beginning, was done by us, but everything was open betrayal of the truth, contempt of God, luxury, trifles in what was not trifling, and quarrels and wars and jealousies and ignoble slanders of each other and shame and jeers and confusion, from which some shamefully became traitors, others, as it were in a cup of friendship, for too easily gave away the faith of our Church—all this I pass over . . . those of higher rank early betrayed everything and all the rest, some from simplicity others from fear, followed.' Schol. II, p. 259.

diplomatic with so many vain, obstinate and often petty individuals can be taken for granted, but that such was his general disposition, as Syropoulus would have us believe, is at the least open to serious doubt. In spite of Warschauer's confident assertion that the 'Acta' are 'emperorising', it does not seem to me that this close examination of their account bears out the accusation. The 'Acta' do not recount all Syropoulus' censures of the Emperor and they portray him as patient and as striving for unity rather than union, but he is less persuaded of the possibility of union than many of his subjects and needed to be forced to agree on several occasions, which is probably a truer picture of the reality than Syropoulus' account.

* * *

We are now in a position to be able to sum up the evidence proposed and to draw some conclusions on the relative historical values of the *Descriptions* and the *Memoirs*. The *Descriptions* are documents contemporaneous with the events and, apart from the earlier pages recounting the arrivals at Venice and Ferrara, show every sign of being a diary written up daily. By contrast, the *Memoirs* are the recollections of Syropoulus composed some years after the end of the Council. Both authors were present at the events they describe. The writer of the *Descriptions* is more informative on relations with the Latins; Syropoulus on what took place within the Greek community in Italy. Their accounts of the voting in the private Greek sessions have been made out to be utterly opposed, but, apart from Syropoulus' declaration that the Staurophoroi were silenced, examination shows that there is agreement and that the actual number of votes and the names of the voters tally in both records.

Whatever be the truth about freedom of speech, the *Memoirs*, even more than the 'Acta', make it plain that apart from at the last two sessions at Florence there was no check at all on the liberty of Mark of Ephesus, who was the outstanding—in fact the only real—antagonist of union, to say whatever he wished both in the public sessions and in the private Greek meetings. Force is freely alleged by all anti-unionist writers, force exercised, so it is said, by the Latins through the withholding of the grants for maintenance. The only suggestion, that occurs in the copious writings of Gennadius that the Emperor used his authority unfairly is found in his *Against the Discourse of Bessarion*: 'This discourse those present did not criticise but, before they could do that, the Emperor enjoined silence, and he convicted them of great audacity, if they ventured anything about union that had not previously been approved by him, and enjoined penalties, if ever they managed to contravene his orders. Neither was it at all easy for them to contradict you without his previous knowledge; nor, if he knew, would he allow it'.[25] Yet Gennadius on this same occasion (i.e. the three days' interval of April 12th–14th) addressed his Exhortation to the same Greeks and in the same sense as Bessarion, and challenged them to disprove his assertion: 'I will show this not in long discourses, but two hours will suffice for me to convince all of you no longer to hesitate over the agreement of the Fathers'.[26] The latter quotation is of Scholarius the unionist: the former of Scholarius hesitating between Unionism and anti-Unionism. Which more reflects the truth?

The *Descriptions* say very little about the hardships endured by the Greeks, though they do not deny them: Syropoulus refers to them at length and repeatedly, and, as far as can be checked, he is accurate in his statements about money. Syropoulus is free in assigning motives, some certainly incorrect, others dubious: the 'Acta' give a simple recital of facts. The Emperor is differently portrayed in the two versions, though there is much agreement on his managing of affairs, the view he took of the Council and his endeavours to achieve unity of opinion and subsequent acceptance of it among the Greeks. That he possessed all the faults of character that Syropoulus ascribes to him is improbable.

In general, the *Descriptions* are too brief to be tendentious. Their omissions are to be ascribed, not to a desire to alter unpleasant facts, but solely to the diary nature of the work: they do not hesitate to mention those facts when they crop up naturally in the course of the narrative, but incidents and circumstances outside of the main course of events are not treated of for their own sakes. Syropoulus' *Memoirs*, on the other hand, do not purport to be a continuous narrative of even all the official or semi-official occurrences. The table given above shows that he records practically nothing of the relations with the Latins in the last months at Florence. They are recollections, and recollections almost entirely of inter-Greek relations. They err as much as, if

---

[25] Schol., III, p. 113.
[26] Ibid., I, p. 299. Cf. also pp. 304, 356, 367.

not more than, the *Descriptions*, for, though the latter give little of the Greek background, the *Memoirs* give too much—they are all background with all the elements that might have relieved it a little and modified its sombre hues omitted, background that is in effect a treatise to prove, not just to record, that (as Creyghton entitled his edition) it is a *Vera historia unionis non verae*. The historian, therefore, when the sources are opposed should prefer the 'Acta', remembering, however, though never fully trusting, Syropoulus' description of the situation behind the scenes.

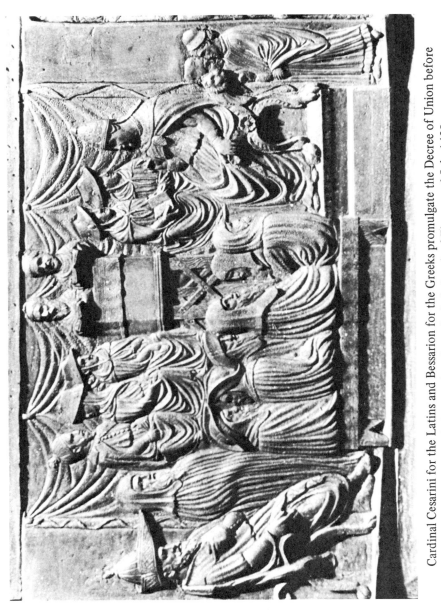

Cardinal Cesarini for the Latins and Bessarion for the Greeks promulgate the Decree of Union before the assembled council in the cathedral church of Florence, 6 July 1439

XIII

THE SINCERITY OF BESSARION THE UNIONIST

AFTER roughly three and a half centuries of schism the Churches of East and West, Latins and Greeks, met in the Council of Florence in the years 1438 and 1439 to discuss unity. Why they met at that time and in Italy was the result of many factors. On the Latin side there was a genuine desire to end the schism and, in an age of Latin councils (Pisa, Constance, Basle), a council seemed an apt means. On their side, the Greeks had the same genuine Christian desire for Church union and had always insisted that only a council could achieve that. What made them accept the West as the venue of the council, instead of holding out for Constantinople, was the fact that Constantinople was then nearly in its death throes, since the Turks had conquered most of its ancient empire and, surrounding it on all sides, were only awaiting opportunity to deliver the *coup de grâce*. The Byzantine Empire was in most urgent need of help to be able to defend itself. Hope for that lay only in the West. The one institution there that might channel effective aid was the papacy which had launched and directed so many crusades of European Christianity. The best way of winning papal support would be union of the Churches. So the Greeks came first to Ferrara and then to Florence to a joint council with the Latins to treat of unity.

Indeed it was not only the Greek Church but the Oriental Church, for the Council of Florence was, materially so to speak, the most ecumenical of all ecumenical councils. The Patriarch of Constantinople was present in person, and with him there were twenty Greek metropolitans, as well as bishops from Russia, Georgia, and Moldowallachia. Add that five of the Greeks were procurators of the other oriental patriarchates, nominated by the Patriarchs themselves.

Among the Greek metropolitans was the archbishop of Nicaea, Bessarion. Born on 2 January 1402 in Trebizond, Bessarion was educated in Constantinople. He took the monastic habit on 30 January 1423 and soon made himself a name as a preacher. Ordained priest in 1431, he studied at Mistra in the Morea under the Platonist, George Gemistus Pletho, and five years later he become abbot of the monastery of St. Basil in Constantinople. Shortly afterwards he was elected to the see of Nicaea, when three other monks with a reputation for learning

378

were also consecrated bishops, Mark Eugenicus for Ephesus, Isidore for Kiev and all Russia, and Dionysius for Sardis. The election of all these was not unconnected with the negotiations for a council of union between East and West, then reaching their climax, for they were outstanding among the Greek clergy for their philosophical and theological ability, whereas the general level of learning of the oriental hierarchy was not very high.

The Greeks reached Venice on 8 February 1438 and Ferrara in the beginning of March, but serious theological discussion did not start till 8 October 1438. The matter most debated was the *Filioque*, a word that the Latins had added to the Nicene–Constantinopolitan Creed to express their belief that the Holy Spirit proceeds from the Father and from the Son. The Greeks declared that addition to be both illegitimate, as having been the act of only the Western Church and not of the whole Church, and doctrinally unsound, since they taught that the Spirit proceeds from the Father only or from the Father through the Son. The legitimacy of the addition of the *Filioque* was the subject discussed in Ferrara; its orthodoxy as a doctrine in Florence. Bessarion in Ferrara began by opposing the Latins vigorously but was gradually shaken by their arguments. In Florence, he ended by being convinced of the soundness of their belief and was an open advocate of unity between the Churches.

The title of this present article is itself significant. It suggests a doubt about what should be unquestioned, namely, the sincerity of Bessarion's acceptance of the union of Florence and of what that union implied, namely, the orthodoxy of western doctrine on the *Filioque*. It is true that there were also other questions involved in the union, but the *Filioque* doctrine was far and away the chief cause of division between the Churches and, therefore, the chief subject of debate. What in these days looms larger in ecumenical conversations, the primacy of the See of Peter, was considered then as of relatively minor importance: it was one of the differences that could have been discussed between Greeks and Latins in June 1438 in Ferrara, when theological disputation was barred.[1]

Latin Catholics, both then and now, have never doubted the sincerity of Bessarion's adherence to the union. With Eastern Christians it is different. In the fifteenth century the union was immediately challenged in the East, and a number of those who in 1439 had accepted it in

---

[1] S. Syropoulos, *Les 'Mémoires' de Sylvestre Syropoulos sur le concile de Florence 1438–1439*, ed V. Laurent (Paris–Rome, 1971), p. 237 (hereafter Syropoulus). Cf. J. Gill, 'The Definition of the Primacy of the Pope in the Council of Florence', in *Personalities of the Council of Florence* (Oxford, 1964), pp. 264–86.

Florence rejected it a short time afterwards in Constantinople. Obviously, they could not look on unionists with a favourable eye. To defend their own double action, they had to plead duress. To explain away the 'defection' of others, they alleged venality and ambition. Bessarion, when he was on the high seas returning to the east, was created cardinal. It was, doubtless, a reward for his part in promoting the union of the Churches, but the Greek anti-unionists of his day concluded from that, that the prospect of reward had been the constant and chief motive of his unionism and that he had, indeed, been a willing tool in the hands of the pope. That he might have been sincere in his actions, innocent of ambition, and unaware of the pope's intention was discounted. That, in naming two Greeks (and the obvious choice among them was Bessarion and Isidore) among seventeen new cardinals, Eugenius IV might have wanted to bring into relief the new union of the Churches was not taken into consideration. Yet both of these explanations might be true and, if one assesses the characters of both Eugenius and Bessarion from the general tenor of their lives, they almost certainly are true.

The Greek world of today judges Bessarion with divergent voices. Some condemn him outright. In 1968 the holder of the chair of Byzantine History in the University of Athens, Professor Tomadakis, in a paper read in Venice professed to show that all those among the Greeks of the fifteenth century who favoured union with the Latins were humanists, and that all such humanists were freethinkers. 'Pletho was a real unbeliever and his pupil Bessarion, dressed in the habit of the Greek clergy, was a humanist and at bottom was no more a believer than his master. He was great as a politician admittedly, an ecclesiastic certainly, but not a true believer. Bessarion is a humanist in the sense that, faced with a choice between the faith and learning, he chose the philosophy of the Greeks.' A few years earlier (1953) Tomadakis had written: 'Elected cardinal after having placed his high political abilities at the service of the See of Rome, he did not rank his religious faith above political aims and ambitions.'[1]

Other Greeks, perhaps most, have a sympathy for Bessarion as a man of great learning who put patriotism above religious conscience. The Archimandrite Parthenius in the beginning of his brochure on Bessarion writes: 'He is the symbol of the patriot who for the sake of his country

---

[1] N. Tomadakis, 'Oriente e Occidente all'epoca del Bessarione', in *Studi bizantini e neoellenici*, N.s. 5 (xv) (1968), p. 33; 'Répercussion immédiate de la prise de Constantinople', in *1453–1953, Le Cinq-centième anniversaire de la prise de Constantinople* (Athens, 1953), p. 61. A. N. Diamantopoulus wrote of the 'measureless ambition of Bessarion', Μάρκος ὁ Εὐγενικός (Athens, 1899), pp. 15 f.

denies everything, even his very faith': towards the end he asks: 'Will he remain for ever the great patriot and the great renegade? I am afraid so, because I could not find anything to justify his change.'[1] One of the latest appreciations of Bessarion from an Orthodox pen is the article of C. G. Patrinelis in the new Greek Ecclesiastical Encyclopaedia.[2] In his view Bessarion was aware of the dangers overhanging Byzantium and proffered counsel to the royal Despots indicating 'as the only way of salvation the orientation of the policy of the Empire towards the West'.[3] In Italy 'little by little he began to adopt conciliatory positions or to accept Roman Catholic opinions' or else he avoided committing himself. In an exchange of unpleasantries, Mark Eugenicus called him "κοπέλλιν" τοῦ πάπα.[4] 'His conversion to the Roman Catholic Church had no small motive, but it was the price he believed should be paid when the issue was through alliance with the West to save the political independence of the race, because Bessarion could not understand how it was possible for an enslaved people to preserve a free Church.' He had other motives beside these political ones; 'he seemed to be really persuaded that the expression met with in some Greek Fathers, *Through the Son*, was not far removed from the Latin *Filioque*', and he had a great admiration for Latin humanism.

The upshot seems to be once more: 'Great patriot, great renegade'. Great patriot he assuredly was. Great renegade, for these writers, implies at least subordinating theological and religious convictions to political ends. Is this conclusion justified and just? The question is worth examining.

First, however, it will be helpful to consider Bessarion's background. In the century before his birth the Greek Church had been divided over the theology of Palamism,[5] to such a degree that the names of its

---

[1] *Βησσαρίων ὁ Καρδηνάλιος* (Alexandria, 1957), pp. 5, 31.

[2] *Θρησκευτικὴ καὶ Ἠθικὴ Ἐγκυκλοπαιδεία*, iii (Athens, 1963), 847–51.

[3] In a letter from Rome written towards the end of 1444, Bessarion suggests the sending of a few Greek youths to Italy to learn skills needed to exploit the resources of the Morea, whither they should return to train others. Cf. L. Mohler, *Kardinal Bessarion als Theologe, Humanist und Staatsmann*, iii (Paderborn, 1942), pp. 448–9.

[4] Syropoulus (p. 446) records that Eugenicus called Bessarion a κοπέλλιν but Eugenicus did not add, as the Greek Encyclopaedia does, τοῦ πάπα or imply it. There is a great difference between saying: 'You are a child and you acted like a child' and 'You are a minion of the pope and you acted like a minion of the pope.'

[5] Gregory Palamas in his theological defence of the practice of Hesychastic Prayer taught that, since the divine essence is utterly unattainable by man yet man is deified, that deification is accomplished by the divine energies that act upon the soul, and that these divine energies, which he also calls 'divinities', are indivisible from the divine essence yet are really distinct from it.

opponents Barlaam and Akindynus had been added to the list of heresiarchs anathematized on the Sunday of Orthodoxy. Palamism had, at least for a time, been a touchstone of orthodoxy and a weapon against *Latinophrones*—Latinizers. But it had also been the reason why some of those who had not been able to accept it had abandoned the Greek Church to join the Latin, among them people of theological merit and political position. Manuel Calecas and the three brothers Chrysoberges all became Dominicans; Demetrius Cydones and Manuel Chrysoloras with many others remained laymen. Their names are less important than what they symbolized. They were, in fact, a challenge to the Greek Church. They had rejected what that Church had solemnly proclaimed as true to seek the truth elsewhere. Their example cannot have been lost on the Greek thinkers of the day, theologians, philosophers, and inquirers.

That the question of Palamism was not dead is clear from an anguished request made on the eve of the Council of Florence by Bessarion, Metropolitan of Nicaea, to Andrew Chrysoberges, O.P., archbishop of Rhodes. Bessarion's letters are lost. Andrew's answer is extant.[1] Bessarion had posed a definite question. Andrew in his reply, happily for us, repeats his actual words, which are very illuminating. The quotation opens: 'The root of *our* difficulty is as follows'; it ends: '*I* desire to have your answer.' Was Bessarion writing only for himself (using the editorial 'we') or was he expressing the uncertainty of a group? An interesting question, to which no answer can be given. Certainly he discloses at least his own genuine doubts.

'The root of our difficulty is the question of divine essence and operation about which Your Reverence knows that in our Church a variety of answers have been put forward, and it was stated and decreed that the divine essence should be held to be distinct from its divine operation.' St. Thomas Aquinas replies differently and Bessarion wants answers to queries he proposes on Aquinas's arguments. The quotation continues: But 'first, if you will, let us consider with reverence how that body of Christians can be and be called the catholic and apostolic Church which on the foremost article of the faith has expressed itself contradictingly and has patently determined that everyone should express it in the same way. How can such a Church urge and direct in the name of the Author of truth, when it has itself taught falsehood about Him? A contradiction cannot be true—such is the common opinion of all men. There was a time when our Church used to say that

---

[1] E. Candal, 'Andreae Rhodiensis, O.P., inedita ad Bessarionem epistula (De divina essentia et operatione)', in *Orientalia Christiana Periodica*, iv (1938), pp. 329–71, text pp. 344–71.

382

there was nothing uncreated except only the divinity in three Persons; all its perfections were identical with that. Afterwards, and not very much later, persuaded by I do not know what reasons, it decreed the opposite and imposed a belief as if it were a pillar of the faith', declaring not only the Trinity uncreated but also a host of some other kind of divinities. 'Since it has once fallen from the truth, it seems that it is not the Church with which Christ promises to abide to the consummation of the world, for that abiding cannot be understood otherwise than as its being preserved by Him always on the foundation of truth. And again, since it has once erred, now it is doubtful for us whether it abides in the truth. I beg, most excellent Father, to hear from you on this subject something new and striking and replete with wisdom.'[1]

There follows Andrew's long answer of philosophical commentary in defence of St. Thomas's teaching, with an occasional quotation from the Fathers. Whether Bessarion was convinced by the reply cannot be said. But the tone of his query leaves little doubt: he already not only hesitated about the truth of Palamism, but rejected it. His rejection brought doubts about the claims of the Church which had approved Palamism to be the true Church of Christ. If the Eastern Church was not the true Church, the Western Church must be—such was the logic of those days.[2] The letter that Andrew was answering had been dispatched by Bessarion from Methone,[3] repeating his request made, but not answered, some time before. So, even before the Council of Florence Bessarion already viewed the Latin Church with reverence and was inclined to think its claims to truth more valid than those of the Greek Church.

Bessarion had been made Metropolitan of Nicaea in about 1436 with a view to the council of union shortly to be held in the West. He was consecrated at about the same time as Isidore of Kiev, Mark of Ephesus, and Dionysius of Sardis—all 'to be present as champions of the synod',[4] which meant, not that they were all unionists before ever there was a council[5]—Eugenicus never was and never pretended to be—but that they were the best theologians among the oriental clergy. In Italy six orators were elected by the Greek synod to speak on behalf of their Church. Bessarion was one of them with Eugenicus and Isidore.

[1] Candal, art. cit., pp. 346, 348.
[2] 'Let us see which is that Church. It is either that of the Latins or that of the Greeks. There is no other than these', Bessarion, *Encyclical Letter 'ad Graecos'*, *P.G.* clxi. 460A.
[3] i.e. on his way to Italy for the council and so between 21 Dec. 1437 and 3 Jan. 1438. Cf. Gill, *The Council of Florence* (Cambridge, 1959), p. 89.
[4] Syropoulus, p. 184.
[5] This is commonly said of Bessarion and Isidore, without any proof offered.

(Dionysius died in Ferrara soon after his arrival.) The public sessions of the council began only in October, and the Greeks were given the honour of choosing the subject to be discussed and of opening the debate.

To decide on the subject the Emperor invited six of the leading prelates, two Stavrophoroi-deacons, three abbots, and the three lay philosophers to a meeting. There was no hesitation about the general theme for the forthcoming debate: it should be the *Filioque*. But opinion was divided as to whether to begin by challenging the Latin *Filioque* as addition to the Creed or as doctrine. The majority voted for the addition, led by Mark Eugenicus and Gemistus, on the ground that it had been the origin of the schism; the rest, with Bessarion, Scholarius, and Amiroutzes (these last two lay philosophers) voted for the dogma. The Emperor accepted the opinion of the majority.[1] Bessarion narrates some details of the meeting. Once the subject had been decided upon, there was talk of method. Eugenicus wanted to found the Greek case on St. Paul's prohibition to his converts: 'If anyone preach to you a gospel besides that which you have received, let him be anathema',[2] and a similar phrase from the Pseudo-Denis. With difficulty Bessarion convinced him that thereby he would be conceding the Latin case. For, if these prohibitions forbade the addition of what was true, they condemned also the Fathers of Nicaea and of Constantinople I; if they forbade the addition only of what was false, they tacitly allowed the addition of the truth, which was precisely the Latin claim. So it was decided to make the canon of the Council of Ephesus (A.D. 431), which forbade 'another faith' than that of Nicaea, the basis of the Greek position.

The discussions began in earnest on 8 October 1438. In the beginning the Greeks, so reports Bessarion, were in the ascendant, because the Latin syllogistic arguments to show that the *Filioque* was not an addition but only a clarification were beside the point, and his own discourse on 1 and 4 November contributed not a little to their discomfiture.[3] In those sessions Bessarion argued loyally for the Greek position and was

---

[1] Syropoulus, pp. 316, 318. Bessarion Nicaenus, *De Spiritus Sancti processione ad Alexium Lascarin Philanthropenum*, ed. E. Candal (Roma, 1961) (= Concilium Florentinum, Documenta et Scriptores, vii. 2), pp. 18–22, written *c.* 1445. The names of the voters as above are supplied by Syropoulus; the rest by Bessarion.

[2] Gal. i. 9.

[3] *Quae supersunt Actorum Graecorum Concilii Florentini*, ed. J. Gill (Roma, 1953) (= Conc. Flor., Doc. et Script. v. 1–2) (hereafter, *AG*), p. 160; Andreas de Santacroce advocatus consistorialis, *Acta Latina Concilii Florentini*, ed. G. Hofmann (Roma, 1955) (= Conc. Flor., Doc. et Script., vi), p. 51: both record the embarrassment of the Latins.

very forthright.[1] Then spoke Cardinal Cesarini with an array of cogent arguments and one final one that shattered Bessarion. Cesarini produced a document to show that the Council of Nicaea had forbidden 'another faith' in almost the same words as the Council of Ephesus.[2] So the Greeks were on the horns of the dilemma that Bessarion had foretold to Eugenicus, for Constantinople I had both added to and subtracted from the Creed of Nicaea. There could be only one conclusion, that legitimate authority could add truth to the Creed. Bessarion was not the only Greek who was convinced of that. Scholarius wrote towards mid April 1439: 'If the decree is understood as it should be, the Latins would not rightly be censured for having added the truth.'[3] In fact the generality of the Greeks was shaken and discouraged. The Latins began to urge them to leave the secondary question of the addition and to tackle the chief controversy, the doctrine of the *Filioque*. They pressed their demand with such an air of confidence in their ability to produce many telling arguments that the Greeks were disconcerted still more. They felt that they would be reduced to silence over the Procession as they had been over the addition. 'We shall never persuade the Latins nor they us; we ought to go home' became the current sentiment, which only the insistence of the Emperor stopped being put into effect.[4]

In a meeting of the clerics, when it was proposed to give an ultimatum to the Pope that the Greeks would leave for home unless the Latins cancelled the *Filioque* from the Creed, 'Bessarion alone did not agree but said that there should be discussion on the Procession. For we can say a great deal and say it well about the faith, and we ought not to cower down before the Latins. Cabasilas wrote only four pages on the addition, yet what we have said about it [here] would fill a book. On the doctrine he wrote a whole book and so surely we shall be able to say a very great deal and say it well.'[5] The synod with some reluctance

---

[1] 'We wish Your Reverence to know that we withhold this permission from every Church and synod even oecumenical and not from the Roman Church alone, since no matter how great is the Roman Church, it is notwithstanding less than an Oecumenical Synod and the universal Church; and we withhold it from the whole Church, much more so then from the Roman Church do we withhold it. But we withhold it not as by ourselves, but we consider that this has been forbidden by the decrees of the Fathers' (*AG*, p. 159).

[2] It was a spurious document, but neither Cesarini nor Bessarion knew that: they thought it was genuine: Bessarion, *Ad Lascarin*, pp. 33–4.

[3] *Orationes Georgii Scholarii in Concilio Florentino habitae*, ed. J. Gill (Roma, 1964) (= Conc. Flor., Doc. et Script. viii. 1), p. 73. For a longer quotation cf. Gill, *The Council of Florence*, pp. 166–9.

[4] That such was the situation is attested by every source: Bessarion, *Ad Lascarin*, pp. 34–5 (= *P.G.* clxi. 353–6); *AG*, p. 217; Appendix to *AG*, pp. 490–1; Syropoulus, esp. pp. 358, 364, and also 346, 352, 354, 356, 360, 362, 366.

[5] Syropoulus, p. 362.

acquiesced in the inevitable. The Greeks went to Florence and there in eight sessions Mark Eugenicus for them and John of Montenero for the Latins argued and counterargued. By the end of those sessions Bessarion had changed. He no longer accepted the refutation of western doctrine that was the theme of Cabasilas's book on the Holy Spirit[1] but the work of another Greek, John Beccus, who had been condemned in a synod in Constantinople in 1285 for his adherence to the union of Lyons.

Nilus Cabasilas (†1363) was a prolific writer in favour of Palamism. At one time an ardent admirer of St. Thomas Aquinas, whose works he knew through the translations of Demetrius Cydones, he later was a firm opponent, and his treatise on the Holy Spirit was an answer to one after another of Aquinas's arguments for the Latin doctrine of the Procession. So, with Cydones's translation and Cabasilas's refutation at their disposal, studious Greeks in Italy had every opportunity of acquainting themselves with Latin thought. As a preparation for the council, Scholarius and Eugenicus had been assigned the task of studying Cabasilas's tractate.[2] Bessarion obviously was thoroughly conversant with it. Eugenicus made good use of it in the sessions in Florence.

The treatise of John Beccus was in a different style. Cabasilas's work, being an answer to a metaphysical treatment, is very largely metaphysical in character; quotations from the Fathers are comparatively rare. Beccus's book is nothing more than a vast collection of quotations from Greek Fathers divided into thirteen sections in support of thirteen assertions whose general conclusion is that the traditional doctrine of the Greek Church on the Procession of the Holy Spirit coincides with the Latin: expressions differ; the substance is the same. In the difficult months of April and May 1439 when the Greek synod was divided over the *Filioque* question as doctrine and desired nothing more than to go home and leave it unsolved,[3] Cabasilas was in the hands of Eugenicus and the antiunionists, Beccus in those of Isidore of Kiev and the unionists.[4]

By that time a considerable section of the Greek prelates had accepted the orthodoxy of the Latin doctrine—the Patriarch, Bessarion, Isidore,

---

[1] *Nilus Cabasilas et theologia S. Thomae de Processione Spiritus Sancti*, ed. E. Candal (Studi e Testi, 116) (Città del Vaticano, 1945).

[2] Syropoulus, p. 170

[3] Cf. two ultimatums to the Pope, 10 April (*AG*, p. 403) and 21 May (*AG*, p. 420).

[4] Cf. Syropoulus, pp. 446, 448. Syropoulus rarely gives a date, but the altercation in question was probably at about the end of May: cf. Gill, 'The "Acta" and the Memoirs of Syropoulus as History', in *Personalities*, p. 153.

Dorotheus of Mitylene, Methodius of Lacedaemon, with Gregory the Confessor, Scholarius, Amiroutzes, and others. The reason was Beccus and the fact that John of Montenero in the last two sessions of March had marshalled a long array of Doctors of the Latin Church who were Doctors and saints also of the Greek Church, and an even longer one of Greek Doctors, whose words either stated or implied that the Spirit is produced also by the Son. That argument, apodictic in itself, was rendered absolute for the Greeks by an axiom which all the Greek theologians in Italy accepted, that saints, just because they are saints and therefore inspired by the Holy Spirit, cannot disagree in the faith. If their expressions of it differ, their meaning is the same. Bessarion delivered a long discourse to the Greek synod in mid April 1439 whose introduction was an affirmation of the axiom and whose body a collection of quotations from the Greek Fathers, all taken from Beccus.[1] Scholarius in a lengthy address on the same occasion and in his Profession of Faith at the end of May[2] enunciated the axiom and the agreement of the saints, and counselled union. Mark Eugenicus also believed in the axiom, but he evaded its logical conclusion by declaring that later Latins must therefore have falsified the writings of their own Fathers because these, as saints, could not have taught what was not true—that is, what Mark believed to be untrue.[3] That was an explanation that was neither complimentary nor convincing. Scholarius rejected it with scorn.[4] Bessarion in a heated argument replied to Mark's suggestion: 'But who would dare to suggest such a thing—complete homilies, commentaries on the gospels, whole theological treatises—

---

[1] Bessarion Nicaenus, *Oratio dogmatica de unione*, ed. E. Candal (Roma, 1958) (= Conc. Flor., Doc. et Script. vii. 1) (= *PG* clxi. 543–621). His dependence on Beccus is clear because occasionally he even includes the short phrases by which Beccus linked some of his quotations, pp. 50, 57.

[2] *Orationes G. Scholarii*, pp. 5–20; *AG*, pp. 428–31.

[3] *Profession of Faith*, in Petit, *Œuvres anticonciliaires de Marc d'Ephèse* (= *Patrologia Orientalis* xvii. 2), p. 438. The rest also accepted the axiom: the Patriarch, *AG*, p. 432; Isidore, *AG*, pp. 400, 426 and *Sermones inter Concilium Florentinum conscripti*, ed. G. Hofmann and E. Candal (Roma, 1971) (= Conc. Flor., Doc. et Script. x. 1), pp. 65 ff.; Mitylene, *AG*, pp. 402, 403; Metrophanes of Cyzicus (later Patriarch of Constantinople), *Orientalium documenta minora*, ed. G. Hofmann (Roma, 1953) (= Conc. Flor., Doc. et Script. iii. 3), p. 47; Gregory the Confessor (Patriarch of Constantinople after Metrophanes), ibid., p. 44; G. Amiroutzes, ibid., pp. 38–9; Boullotes, V. Laurent, 'La profession de foi de Manuel Tarchaniotès Boullotès au Concile de Florence', in *Revue des Études Byzantines*, x (1952), p. 68.

[4] 'Who is so simple-minded as to believe that the Latins wish to destroy the faith and to adulterate the trinitarian theology of all the Doctors? Surely a man who affirms this deserves nothing but ridicule, for no accusation would be disproved by more numerous, more weighty and more truthful arguments than this one' (*Orationes Scholarii*, p. 9).

why, if we remove these from their books, nothing will remain but blank pages.'[1] It is to be noted that all the 'intellectuals' among the Greeks except Eugenicus accepted the orthodoxy of the Latin *Filioque* doctrine.[2] Further, it is to be noted that of the Greek metropolitans, not one changed his view after the council, when several of the older and less theological prelates yielded to popular pressure.

If Bessarion's honesty is to be impugned for his adherence to the union, that of the archbishops who signed with him and of the Patriarch, Scholarius, and Amiroutzes should be denied as well. His opponents are fond of quoting a phrase in the peroration of his *Oratio dogmatica*: 'For who does not know that the only refuge left to us in our dangers was the Latin race and union with them, our hope in their help to protect us and to repel the enemy.' They see in it a blatant affirmation of Bessarion's noble–ignoble patriotism. They should, however, continue reading some five lines further on:

But if we had discerned error in the doctrine of the Latins or distortion in their faith, not even I would have counselled you to embrace union and agreement with them in that case, that for fear of bodily ills you should prefer the values of the present world to spiritual values, the freedom of the body to the betterment of the soul, but I myself would have undergone all that is worst and I would have exposed you to it before I would have urged you to union with them and have recommended such action.[3]

Nilus Cabasilas had opposed not only St. Thomas but also Beccus. He had written a short commentary on each of the positions of Beccus's *Epigraphae*, naturally always negative. Bessarion studied these in Florence. As a result he wrote an answer while he was still only

---

[1] *AG*, p. 401, on 31 March 1439.

[2] Bessarion, Isidore, Cyzicus, Mitylene, Lacedaemon, Monembasia, Rhodes, with Gregory the Confessor, Scholarius, and perhaps Gemistus, since Syropoulus does *not* mention him as against the union in the crucial days at the end of May. There were 20 Greek prelates in Italy in July 1439, of whom 18 signed the decree of union.

[3] Bessarion, *Oratio dogmatica*, pp. 70–1. Bessarion continues: 'But now there is danger, and great danger, that we choose what will damage both body and soul if, when the Latins along with our Fathers and their Doctors believe what is true and orthodox and err in nothing of the faith and agree with our Church and the saints and Doctors of the East, we shall think fit to our own great harm to be separated from such men. . . . I beg of you, yes all of you, to share this decision with me; or, if not all, the majority. If not, I for my part call to witness God, who is over all, and all of you here present and generations to come, that from the beginning and consistently to this day, without passion or guile but with truth, I have never ceased to say what I believed to be true and right and beneficial, that I have never hesitated to declare what I thought right, that never did I put my own safety before the common good . . .' (p. 72). Note that Bessarion was addressing the Greek synod that knew him.

Metropolitan of Nicaea and after he had become convinced of the soundness of the faith of Beccus and of the Latins, i.e., in the second half of 1439. He quotes in turn each proposition, then the commentary of Cabasilas, and finally he replies with his refutation of the commentary.[1] Cabasilas produced the regular Greek objections against the Latin doctrine. Bessarion rejects them all with serious arguments. In his answer about the ninth proposition he puts forward a basic and crucial consideration that Montenero had often insisted on in his debate with Eugenicus in Florence. Greeks and Latins were agreed that everything in the Blessed Trinity is common to all the three Persons except only their personal relations. What were these? What precisely distinguishes Father, Son, and Holy Spirit, each from the others? The Father is He who-is-not-from-another: the other two Persons are both from-another. So this difference cannot be the 'property' that distinguishes the three, since two share it. But there is only one Son, one Father; so 'fatherhood' is the 'property' of the Father, 'sonship' of the Son who receives from the Father everything that is not the Father's 'property', i.e., 'fatherhood', and so receives power to produce with the Father the Holy Spirit.

The Greeks, to preserve the truth that the Father is the prime source of all divinity (which the Latin doctrine does not deny), accounted that primacy as his 'property', and hence as excluding the co-spiration of the Holy Spirit by the Son. In his answer to Cabasilas Bessarion does little more than assert the Latin theory and support it by a few patristic quotations. In a later work he will dilate on this fundamental issue at greater length.[2]

That later work, the *On the Procession of the Holy Spirit, written for Alexius Lascaris Philanthropenus*, was elaborated probably in 1445 when Bessarion had had time to reflect. He had not changed. The treatise begins with a short review of the events that had culminated in the union of Florence. The part that refers to the discussions on the *Filioque* as addition has been utilized in the earlier part of this article. What treats of the *Filioque* as doctrine is relevant here. Bessarion recalls that in Florence there had been acrimonious discussion between Eugenicus and Montenero about the genuine text of St. Basil's *Adversus Eunomium* lib. v. In Florence of the six manuscripts used in the council, five had the text favoured by the Latins. Eugenicus, on the other hand, had claimed that in Constantinople there were 'more than a thousand

---

[1] *PG* clxi. 244–88 with Bessarion's own Latin translation, 287–310. In Bessarion's treatise only 12 propositions are dealt with: no. 5 of Beccus is omitted.

[2] Bessarion, *Ad Alex. Lascarin*, pp. 42–6.

like our codex'.[1] Bessarion on his return to the Byzantine capital visited the libraries of nearly all the monasteries to settle what was in fact the correct reading. He found that manuscripts written after the schism had the 'Greek' text, but that all the more ancient manuscripts written before the schism, as numerous as the others, had the 'Latin' text. To his distress he found also two manuscripts in the monastery of Christ the Saviour Pantepoptes, the one of parchment undated, the other of paper dated to some three hundred years earlier, in both of which the peculiarities of the 'Latin' text had been effaced, but so imperfectly that they could still be discerned. No wonder that he exclaims against the hypocrisy of Greeks who accuse the Latins of corrupting codices. No wonder, one may add, that he himself was confirmed in his conviction that the Latins were right also in their main contention. 'So no one any more can with any show of justice censure Beccus and those like him, since books from long before Beccus's day proclaim the truth.'[2]

There is no need here to retail the conclusions drawn by Bessarion for Lascaris from Basil's text. He does no more than repeat what Montenero had several times urged in Florence and adds nothing new except to give to us a proof that he is convinced by it. More interesting is his more personal defence of the dogma. It opens with a bird's eye view of the arguments.

We put forward our saints none of whom (except perhaps the Damascene, but we never used him) says 'From the Father only'. With our 'From the Father' the Latins agreed: they added 'and from the Son', which does not contradict 'From the Father'. This they proceeded to prove from saints and Fathers, Greek as well as Latin. To which we had no other reply except that they were falsified, and falsified by the Latins. They quoted our Epiphanius—'falsified', we said; Basil, 'interpolated'; Latin Doctors, 'corrupt'. Having no text to disprove their case, we refused to talk. A few said that the Latin saints are in error; but that would mean the end of the faith. I send you the texts [he added to Lascaris]; you can judge for yourself.[3]

Lascaris, it seems, had asked also for some philosophical arguments on the subject of the Procession. Bessarion devoted the second half of his treatise to that. At great length and by an argumentation by exclusion he shows that 'Fatherhood' is the distinguishing 'property' of the Father, as generation is of the Son and spiration of the Spirit, and the spiration, like the generation, should issue from the constitutive 'property', 'fatherhood', and hence via the generation, i.e., the generated Son, since the Son must possess all that the Father has except the

[1] *AG*, p. 386.
[2] Bessarion, *Ad Alex. Lascarin*, pp. 5–11.
[3] Ibid., pp. 36–41, 87.

sole distinguishing 'property'. The Spirit also would co-spirate, were it not that 'A property cannot be its own principle (cause)', and He cannot be a co-producer with the Father of the Son, for so He would be also 'Father', and 'fatherhood' is the constitutive 'property' of only the First Person.

This philosophical position is not only metaphysically defensible, but it can be supported from the saints and Fathers. It is consonant also with the words of such Doctors as spoke of the Father as 'sole source of divinity', whom Eugenicus and earlier Greek controversialists usually quoted to vindicate their views against the Latins. After some twenty considerations, Bessarion ends his work by meeting objections. These are mainly two, that the Latin doctrine either confuses the Father with the Son or postulates two causes or principles in the Blessed Trinity.[1] Insistence on the 'properties' of the three Persons solves the difficulties. Finally Bessarion moves on to a more delicate task, the explanation of texts from St. John Damascene and the pseudo-Denis that at first sight seem to deny any place to the Son in the Procession of the Holy Spirit. Bessarion argues that in the Procession there are two aspects, the equality, even identity, that reigns between Father and Son in respect of the production of the Holy Spirit, and also a certain order in that the Son has received this power of spiration from the Father. 'From' expresses the former aspect; 'Through', the latter. Many saints of both Churches include both aspects in their trinitarian expositions, but others, mainly Latin, stress the former idea exclusively, and still others, mainly Greek, the latter idea. This is what the Damascene was doing when he said: 'We say the Spirit of the Son; but we do not say "From the Son".'[2] Scholarius had proposed a more radical solution: 'We have not one single saint who is clearly in opposition to them and, if there were, we should with greater justice in some way or other bring him into harmony with them than force so great a multitude of Doctors to agree with that one.'[3]

One more work of Bessarion on the *Filioque* question deserves to be mentioned, his *Reply to the Propositions of Mark of Ephesus*.[4] It adds nothing new to what he had written before, as he himself remarks. But, whereas in his refutation of Cabasilas he had noted the Latin (and his own) explanation of the constitutive properties of the three Divine

---

[1] These were arguments proposed by Photius and repeated by Cabasilas.

[2] Bessarion's explanation is not far-fetched. Cf. 'He is the Spirit of the Son not as proceeding from Him, but as from the Father through Him: for the Father alone is cause' (St. John Damascene, *De fide orthodoxa* i. 12; *PG* xciv. 849B).

[3] *Orationes G. Scholarii*, p. 7.

[4] *PG* clxi. 137–244; written probably c. 1450, cf. Mohler, op. cit., p. 235.

Persons and in his treatise to Lascaris had developed this at length, here he treats of it at even greater length so as to write a small but concentrated tractate on the nature of the Blessed Trinity.[1] His answers to Eugenicus's objections are all based on this.

So it appears that the more the Metropolitan of Nicaea studied the question of the Procession of the Holy Spirit, the deeper was his understanding of the Latin doctrine and the firmer his conviction of its orthodoxy.

When Bessarion was already old and, as he thought, not far from death, he wrote his *Encyclical Letter to the Greeks*, for he had been created Patriarch of Constantinople by the Pope.[2] It is a mild letter of affection, exhortation, instruction, and self-revelation. He was not writing to justify his own past action, but incidentally he does so. To recommend to his faithful the Council of Florence, the *Filioque*, and the primacy of the pope of Rome, he refers them to his treatises and mentions some of the arguments there contained. They are the reasons that a quarter of a century previously had convinced him that there was no longer any good reason why the Churches should remain divided and that of the two the claims of the Latin Church to be the depositary of divine faith were the stronger. His own Church had stumbled over Palamism. It had made the addition of the *Filioque* into a major difficulty and in Ferrara had been unable to make good its case. Though no Doctor of the Church had written 'From the Father only', it had adopted that as its doctrine, but in Florence the whole Greek synod with hardly an exception had accepted the Latin *Filioque* as orthodox. In Florence, too, though after some hesitation the Greek synod had acknowledged papal primacy, at least in the sense of a right of universal appeal;[3] also Christ had told St. Peter: 'On this rock I will build my church.' His conscience was no trouble to him; he had always followed the truth as he saw it. Tranquilly he records the promise of his early life, when he sought ever to advance in orthodoxy and to dedicate himself to the truth of the faith.

Now more than ever do I put that in the first place. The more that age advances, the more do diseases of various sorts daily threaten me with death and make life unlivable. I know full well, brethren and fathers, I know and I am in no way deceived. I have not much longer to live, and 'the time of my resolution is at hand', when there comes on men no small fear about what before caused them but little fear: they see the time at hand when they will give an account of their lives. But me, the closer creeps death, the more the purity of the faith consoles me, in the hope

[1] *P.G.* clxi. 153–65.
[2] Written in 1463; Bessarion died in 1472.
[3] Cf. Gill, 'The Definition of the Primacy', pp. 264–86.

392

that my lack of works will be compensated for to my salvation by my belief in sound doctrine, for whose sake I put honour on one side to cleave wholly to this truth. [Honours he might have had, perhaps more in the East than in the West.] But what I might have had with you, I held in little regard and the things of the present world—may God bear me witness—'I counted but as dung' and would have cast them all away had they been many times greater and would have gone off to you, never turning back, if I had not been conscious to myself that I was choosing what was nobler and more conducive to salvation, if I had not been convinced that the holy Roman Catholic Church was teaching and believing what leads to eternal life.[1]

[1] *PG* clxi. 461 B–C, 464 A–B.

XIV

WAS BESSARION A CONCILIARIST OR A UNIONIST BEFORE THE COUNCIL OF FLORENCE ?

Platina in a panegyric on Bessarion delivered in the latter's lifetime declared : " For he, while the power of Constantinople was not yet overthrown, never abandoned his efforts to win over the Eastern Church to the point of view of the Western, until, by beseeching and advising the Greek Emperor and the princes, he had after a most impressive discourse induced them to come to Italy and Eugenius the Supreme Pontiff " [1]. Two centuries later A. Bandini adopted Platina's statement [2], and H. Vast on Bandini's authority repeated it in his noteworthy Le Cardinal Bessarion [3], and E. Candal followed Vast [4]. L. Brehier echoed the same idea, but transformed Bessarion from a conciliarist into a unionist, when he wrote : " C'est probablement parce qu'il [Bessarion] se déclare alors partisan de l'union avec Rome qu'il gagne la faveur de l'Empereur Jean VIII Paléologue " [5]. J. Irmscher, though on somewhat different grounds, reaches a like conclusion : " Bessarion gehörte, solange er auf byzantinischen Boden wirkte, zu der Partei der Latinophilen, welche allein von den abendländischen Mächten Hilfe gegen die Türkengefahr erwartete und daher die kirchliche Union mit dem Katholizismus als unumgängliche Notwendigkeit betrachtete " [6]. D. Nicol broadens the field : " The most intelligent and outstanding clerical delegates [to go to Florence] ... included some who were already intellectually predisposed towards a liking for western culture and even for Latin theology. Bessarion ... was one confirmed advocate of union with the Roman Church " ; in

---

[1] Panegyricus in laudem amplissimi patris D. Bessarionis, PG 161 p. cvi. The ' impressive discourse ' at least is pure imagination. Platina mistakenly may have had in his mind Bessarion's inaugural address in Ferrara in October 1438.

[2] PG 161 p. vii.

[3] Le Cardinal Bessarion (Paris, 1878) pp. 28, 35, 48.

[4] ' Bessario Nicenus in Concilio Florentino ', in Orientalia Christiana Periodica (hereafter OCP), 6 (1940), pp. 417-66.

[5] DHGE 8, 1182.

[6] ' Bessarion als griechischer Patriot ', in Miscellanea Marciana di Studi Bessarionei (hereafter Misc. Bess.) (= Medievo e Umanesimo 24) p. 176.

Constantinople he had met Francesco Filelfo and through him
" had learnt of the exciting new intellectual developments in the
revival of classical learning in the west. ... Bessarion was in love
with Italy before he even got there " [7]. X. F. Patrinelis does not
make Bessarion, still in Constantinople, a unionist, but he portrays
him at that time as seeing salvation only in " the orientation of
the policy of the Empire towards the west ", in proof of which
he adduces the letter that, five years *after* the council (i. e., 1444)
and after some four years' domicile as cardinal in Italy, Bessarion
wrote to Constantine, Despot in the Peloponnesus [8]. L. Mohler
says nothing about any conciliarist activity of Bessarion before his
leaving Constantinople, but he dates Bessarion's *Defence of Beccus
against Palamas* as from pre-council days, which in effect makes
Bessarion already before the council, not only a unionist, but a
believer in the *Filioque* doctrine of the Latins [9]. All these authors
imply that from before leaving Constantinople for Italy Bessarion
was outstanding among the Greeks for his enthusiasm for the
council and even for union.

On the other hand, A. Sadov writing in 1883 affirmed that
Bessarion resolutely rejected the *Filioque* doctrine, and hence
union, till at least the end of 1438. E. Candal agrees with him,
and V. Laurent quotes Candal with approval [10].

In view of this division of opinion, it is worth while to try
to establish the truth about Bessarion's attitude. Evidence is
scarce, but what there is will repay examination.

First a *curriculum vitae* of Bessarion's early years from trustworthy sources. Nicholas Capranica in his funeral oration at
Bessarion's obsequies stated that Bessarion († 18 November 1472)
had lived 69 years 10 months and 16 days; so he was born (in

---

[7] *The Last Centuries of Byzantium* 1261-1453 (London 1972) pp. 370-1.

[8] Θρησκευτικὴ καὶ 'Ηθικὴ 'Εγκυκλοπαιδεία III (Athens, 1963) 848.

[9] *Kardinal Bessarion als Theologe, Humanist und Staatsmann* I (Paderborn 1923) pp. 96-7. His opinion is followed by H.-G. Beck, *Kirche und
theologische Literatur im byzantinischen Reich* (Munich, 1959) p. 767, and
A. LEIDL, *Die Einheit der Kirchen auf den spätmittel alterlichen Konzilien
von Konstanz bis Florenz* (Paderborn, 1966), p. 105.

[10] A. SADOV, *Bessario Nicenus. Eius actio in Concilio Ferrariensi-Flo-
rentino, opera theologica et momentum in historia humanismi* (in Russian)
(St Petersburg, 1883), quoted by E. Candal, ' Bessario Nicenus ', pp. 431-2
with full approval : V. LAURENT agrees with CANDAL, *Les Mémoires du
Sylvestre Syropoulos sur le Concile de Florence* (1438-1439) (hereafter SYR.).
(= Concilium Florentinum Documenta et Scriptores : IX : hereafter CFDS)
(Rome-Paris, 1971) p. 448, n. 1.

Trebizond) on 2 January 1402 [11]. Entrusted as a child to Dositheus, archbishop of Trebizond, and taken by him to Constantinople when he went there, Bessarion was " brought up and educated in Constantinople ". He entered a monastery early — 1417-1418 [12]. He received the monastic habit on 30 January 1423 and the tonsure on 20 July of the same year. Before he was 24 years old he had attracted the attention of the imperial court as a preacher. On 8 December 1425 he was ordained deacon and afterwards was employed on diplomatic missions by the Emperor. On 8 October 1430 he was ordained priest and was consecrated archbishop of Nicaea on 11 November 1437.

Most of the above information is taken from categorical statements made by Bessarion himself [13]. It can safely be filled in from allusions in his letters and other writings, from the funeral oration of Capranica and from other sources. Dositheus was appointed to Trebizond in 1415 but had to resign in 1416 [14]. He (and Bessarion) must have gone to Constantinople soon after his resignation, when Bessarion would have been about 13 or 14 years

---

[11] Bandini gives 2 January 1403 on the grounds that Francesco BONAVENTA MALVASIA, *Compendio historico dell ... basilica di SS. Dodici Apostoli di Roma* (Roma, 1665) p. 235, published a version of the funeral oration of Capranica, which was preceded by a note : " Vixit Nicenus 69 annos 10 menses 16 dies ", and he accuses Bandini, who had used the same source, of deliberately suppressing this quotation.

MOHLER in his first volume dated 1923 follows Vast, but in a footnote adds : " Voraussetzung ist freilich dass Capranica in seiner Angabe zuverlässig ist, denn erfahrungsgemäss stimmen derartige Epitaphien vielen Fällen nicht ". However the edition of the funeral oration which he published twenty years later in *Bessarion's Gelehrtenkreis* (Paderborn, 1942) does not mention the note " Vixit ...". So presumably the MS he used did not contain it ; i.e., the note was never a part of Capranica's oration but an addition by Malvasia drawn from some, to us, unknown source.

R.-J. LOENERTZ gives the date 2 Januarý 1402 with no proof (*Enciclopedia Cattolica* XI [1942]) : presumably he depends on Vast.

H. D. SAFFREY, ' Recherches sur quelques autographes du cardinal Bessarion et leur charactère autobiographique ', in *Studi et Testi* 233 (Rome, 1964), pp. 263-97, esp. pp. 272-4, dates his birth as at the very end of 1399 or the beginning of 1440. His chief reason is that, if Bessarion had been born in 1403, since he certainly was ordained deacon and priest in 1425 and 1430 respectively, he would not have reached the canonical age for either of these orders.

[12] SYR., p. 276.

[13] Introduction to cod. marc. gr. 533 ; note in cod. marc. gr. 14, both cited by E. MIONI, *Bessarione scriba e alcuni suoi collaboratori*, in *Misc. Bess.*, pp. 263-318, esp. pp. 267, 271 ; Bessarion's *Encyclical Letter to the Greeks*, PG 161 461.

[14] V. LAURENT, *Dositheus*, in DHGE, 14 (1946) 700-701.

old. The boy soon entered a monastery. He was put to study literature in the school of John Chortasmenus, who became bishop of Selymbria in c. 1415 (Mark Eugenicus had frequented the same school a decade or so earlier), and afterwards he studied under another well-known master, George Chrysococces, when the Italian humanist, Francesco Filelfo, was a fellow-student of his. After his ordination to the priesthood Bessarion went, probably in 1431, to Mistra in the Peloponnesus, to study under the polymath George Gemistus Pletho, famous in particular as a Platonist and a mathematician. (Mark Eugenicus also studied under Pletho.) As in Constantinople, so in Mistra Bessarion was well known in court circles, this time of the Despot Theodore Palaeologus, the death of whose wife Cleopa († 1433) he celebrated in verse. His studies in Mistra made him for the rest of his life a devoted friend of Pletho and a confirmed Platonist. Capranica relates that Bessarion's persuasiveness in dissipating friction that had arisen between Emperor John and Despot Theodore earned him the gratitude of both the brothers Palaeologus, which resulted in his being called back to Constantinople by John and made abbot of the monastery of St Basil (1436) and a year later (14 November 1437) in his being by Theodore's influence elevated to the See of Nicaea [15].

Nothing in this *curriculum vitae* connects Bessarion with Italy and the Western Church or indicates any immediate subjection to unionist pressures.

He may, however, have been influenced in his more formative years towards unionism by his venerated master Chortasmenus and by his student-acquaintance Filelfo.

, In one of the many private meetings of the Greeks in Florence during the council (May 1439) Bessarion, speaking to the Emperor, declared : " I knew Chortasmenus, bishop of Selymbria, who was one of the great educators and a fine teacher, and I am quite sure that he also praised union " [16]. There is, however, nothing in the published writings of Chortasmenus to support that opinion : just the opposite. In the words of H. Hunger : " He was a defender of orthodoxy. From his correspondence, his letters, particularly to Manuel Chrysoloras and to Joseph Bryennius, are noteworthy. In the first he urges the addressee, suspected not unjustly of ' Latinophrony ', to make an open profession of faith

[15] *Nicolai episcopi Firmani oratio in funere Bessarionis*, in MOHLER, *Gelehrtenkreis*, pp. 404-414, esp. p. 407.
[16] SYR., p. 450.

in writing to put his orthodoxy beyond all doubt. In the second letter he sides wholeheartedly with Joseph Bryennius who after the failure of his Cyprus-mission (to combat the Latin Church there) wished to submit himself to only the orthodox faith and his conscience " [17]. Similarly his highest praise for his deceased friend Theodore Antiochites was Theodore's " firm attachment to the Creed " and his consistent opposition to " novelties against the divine Spirit " and to such as promoted them [18]. There is no extant correspondence between Bessarion and Chortasmenus, who died while Bessarion was in Mistra as can be deduced from phrases in two highly laudatory and affectionate encomia of Chortasmenus that Bessarion wrote from the Morea to friends [19].

Fifelfo went to Constantinople in 1419 as secretary to the Venetian baillie and studied first under John Chrysoloras whose daughter he married in early 1424, and later under George Chrysococces. He was employed on diplomatic missions by John VIII, accompanying him on his voyage to Hungary, 15 November 1423 to late October 1424. On 12 August 1423 George Chrysococces finished copying a manuscript for him, and on 13 November 1426 he completed another. Filelfo returned to Venice in 1427, went to Bologna and Florence, and in 1440 took up long and not very happy residence in Milan. Much (if not all) of his voluminous correspondence has been published [20]. It contains a number of letters to Bessarion on business connected mostly with manuscripts. In these there are only two references to their earlier acquaintance. One of these, dated 23 January 1448, is a polite refusal to lend, send or sell (it is not quite clear which, but probably ' sell ') a manuscript of Homer that he had had copied for himself by Theodore of Gaza : " I am very greatly suprised that you, most reverend Father, who knew me from the days in Constantinople ... where after the death of my father-in-law Chrysoloras we were fellow-students under Chrysococces, should think that with age I

---

[17] *John Chortasmenos (ca. 1370 - ca. 1336-37)* (Wien, 1969), p. 17. Texts of letters, no. 29, pp. 179-80 ; no. 11, pp. 161-2. These letters date from between 1403 and 1407.

[18] Ibid., p. 148. Antiochites died probably on 4 January 1407.

[19] MOHLER, *Gelehrtenkreis*, letters 9 and 11, pp. 431-3, 435-7, taken from cod. marc. gr. 533, an autograph of Bessarion, assembled before 1449 (probably before 1444), containing a selection of his early literary activities that he particularly wanted to preserve : cf. Mioni, ' Bessarione scriba ', p. 271. It contains no letter to Chortasmenos.

[20] E. LEGRAND, *Cent-dix lettres grecques de François Filelfe* (Paris, 1892) : *Francisci Filelfi viri grece et latine eruditissimi epistolarum familiarium libri cccvii ex eius exemplari transumpti* (Venice, 1502).

have changed my ways " : he was, he said, open-handed in giving, but he never sold anything, especially books [21]. It is noteworthy that this, the earliest of his (published) letters to Bessarion, yet is dated from 1448 — eight years after Bessarion's arrival in Italy as cardinal — which does not suggest that there had ever been any close bond of friendship between the two or long-standing reciprocal influence. Six years later Filelfo does speak of affection : " My affection for you dates from the time when, both of us, then young men, attended the school of Chrysococces " [22] In 1464 Filelfo was asking a favour from Bessarion, " to snatch me out of the miseries of the court of Milan " where he was very unhappy.

When Bessarion was living in Mistra almost all of the Peloponnesus was in Greek hands after victorious campaigns of the Palaeologan brothers over the decade before 1432. " Thus after 227 years the Morea was once more entirely under Byzantine control, except for the Venetian establishments in Messenia and the Argolid " [23]. The Venetian establishments were small — Coron and Modon with Naupactus in the south-east and Argos with Nauplion in the north-west. Bessarion's contacts with Venetians could have been very few and far between. Indeed there is no positive evidence that he had any contacts with them at all, and so one should not too easily take for granted a softening influence of Venetian culture attuning his mind to admiration of the West and of the Latin Church.

How much, while he was in the Morea, he knew of the activities in Constantinople for union cannot be assessed. He must have heard of them. Indeed, he asked Scholarius for information, but he was told little [24]. At least till he returned to the capital he

---

[21] *Libri cccvii*, p. 41.

[22] LEGRAND, no. 64, p. 112. Filelfo wrote also two laudatory poems to Bessarion, ibid., pp. 195-8, one of which at least dates from after the death of Nicholas V, 1455. The date of the other, I do not know.

[23] P. Topping, ' The Morea, 1364-1460 ', in SETTON, *A History of the Crusades*, vol. III *The Fourteenth and Fifteenth Centuries* (Univ. of Wisconsin Press, 1975), p. 165.

[24] " I would have told you about the so-called council, about which you desire to hear. But you know quite well the things of the past, so why must you be told things you know ? Of the present situation we [Scholarius] know as much as the draught-animals of the people who come here. So why should I labour to bring you *au fait* with what is obvious. But in respect of the future they see in their dreams what their desires suggest, but only He who makes everything and moves everything would know ", letter of Scholarius to Bessarion in *Oeuvres complètes de Gennade-Scholarios* IV, ed. L. PETIT, X. A. SIDÉRIDÈS, M. JUGIE (Paris, 1935), pp. 419-22.

could have taken no active part in them. Even after his return, there is no evidence to suggest that he was involved in the preparations. We know of others who were. John of Ragusa with the other two envoys of the Council of Basel reached Constantinople on 4 September 1435, and thereafter many court officials and prominent churchmen were in frequent conference with them. Many ecclesiastics, including Antony of Heraclea, Mark Eugenicus, Gregory the confessor, Kritopoulus, the stavrophori and others, were brought together by the Emperor to plan Greek action at the future council in a meeting when Scholarius made an impressive speech and he and Eugenicus were deputed to synopsise the anti-Latin treatise of Cabasilas for general use. In all this Bessarion's name nowhere appears. Mark Eugenicus, Gregory the Confessor, Antony of Heraclea, Denis of Sardes and Isidore of Kiev were appointed proxies of the other three eastern patriarchates. Not so Bessarion[25]. When Syropoulus wrote his *Memoirs* he had no love for Bessarion, so that, had Bessarion in any way been an active unionist before the council Syropoulus would have said so — and scathingly. The first time that Bessarion is mentioned in the *Memoirs* is apropos of his consecration to the See of Nicaea : " At that juncture there were consecrated as archbishops, of Ephesus Mark, of Sardis Denis and of Nicaea Bessarion [note the order] to be present as champions in the council " [26]. What Denis's attitude to union was is unknown : he died shortly after reaching Italy. Mark of Ephesus was the only Greek prelate who was consistently and adamantly opposed to union. It seems likely, then, that the Emperor approved of those three candidates as bishops for their intellectual qualities and their suitability to rule a diocese, not for their enthusiasm for union. In any case, Capranica relates that Bessarion's preferment to the See of Nicaea was the result of the influence of Despot Theodore, not of John VIII, and Theodore as far as we know had no special interest in union.

At some time in his early theological training Bessarion had studied the doctrine of Palamism, a subject of bitter controversy after 1341 but declared in a synod of 1351 to be authoritative teaching of the Greek Church — and had rejected it. From Modon (presumably in 1437 when the Greeks on their way to Italy arrived there and stayed from 21 December for a fortnight [27]) he wrote

[25] SYR., pp. 168, 170, 172 and n. 2, 164.
[26] SYR., p. 184.
[27] SYR., p. 204 and n. 2.

to Andrew Chrysoberges [28], a Greek bishop of the Roman Church,
asking for counsel on the grounds that his own Church in teaching
Palamism had gone astray and he queried whether such a Church
could be the Church of Christ which must teach only the truth [29].
Palamism was not concerned directly with the *Filioque* clause, so
his doubts on Palamism will not have necessitated his subscribing
to the Latin doctrine of the *Filioque*. They may, however, have
made him distrust Gregory Palamas, the prime exponent of Palamism, and inclined him to be critical of other products of his
pen.

Palamas had, in fact, written a *Refutation of the Epigraphae
of John Beccus* Patriarch of Constantinople 1275-82, and an active
promoter with Emperor Michael VIII Palaeologus of the union of
Lyons of 1274. Bessarion wrote an answer to Palamas's *Refutation* [30]. The most authoritative writer on Bessarion's life and
works, Ludwig Mohler, dates this treatise of Bessarion as from
before the Council of Florence, which, seeing that Beccus was
defending the orthodoxy of the Latin doctrine of the *Filioque*
defined at Lyons and hence asserting the justification of the union
of Lyons, and Bessarion was vindicating Beccus against the attacks
of Palamas, means that, according to Mohler, Bessarion also recognised the orthodoxy of the *Filioque* doctrine and of union, and did
this before the council even opened. Mohler bases his dating on
two statements made by Bessarion himself — one, that he wrote
the treatise at the request of Gregory, the Emperor's confessor
(PG 161 140D); the other that Palamas's *Refutation* came into
his hands while he was still " Nicenus ", i.e., simple archbishop
of Nicaea and not yet cardinal (PG 161 288C). The first statement
has no probative value whatever for Mohler's dating, for it does
not give any indication as to when Bessarion first got the book;
and besides, nothing is known of Gregory's theological views till
well on into 1439 when he was in Florence: Mohler is gratuitously
presuming that Gregory was an active unionist in pre-council days

[28] Andrew Chrysoberges, one of three brothers, Greeks, who joined the
Roman Church and became Dominicans. He was sent as envoy by Martin V to the imperial court in Constantinople where he stayed for some
time in 1426-7. Later he became archbishop of Rhodes.

[29] E. CANDAL, *Andreas Rhodiensis, O. P., inedita ad Bessarionem epistula
(De divina essentia et operatione)*, in OCP, 4 (1938) pp. 329-71.

[30] PG 161, 244-310. In an earlier article entitled ' The Sincerity of
Bessarion the Humanist ' I inadvertently attributed this refutation of Beccus to Cabasilas and not to Palamas, an error that happily made no difference at all to the argument of the article.

in Constantinople. The second statement implies no more than that Bessarion wrote his answer before 18 December 1439 (or, perhaps more accurately, 10 December 1440, when he received the insignia of the cardinalate) [31].

Mohler, I feel sure, is wrong. Bessarion was consecrated bishop of Nicaea, i. e., became " Nicenus ", on 11 November 1437. He boarded ship for Italy (and a very overcrowded ship [32]) thirteen days later, on 24 November [33]. He can hardly have written a long treatise with many patristic quotations in the first busy fortnight after taking over the responsibility for a large archdiocese. Further, there are several indications that in the earlier period of the council, i. e., when he was already in Italy, he was opposed to the Latin doctrine. It is quite certain that he utterly rejected the *Filioque* as Addition — see his incisive speech in Ferrara of 1 and 4 November 1438 [34] — and he did not change his mind on that point till 10 June 1439 [35] and probably not even then. That speech in Ferrara was directed solely to the question of the Addition and in it he insisted on remaining within the bounds of that question against Andrew of Rhodes, the previous speaker for the Latins, whom he accused of illegitimately going outside them and of introducing the doctrinal issue. A reader of his convincing refutation of all of Andrew's arguments cannot escape the impression that then Bessarion was adamantly opposed not only to the Latin Addition to the Creed, which is the central theme of his speech, but to the totality of their position on the *Filioque*. Occasional phrases emphasise the negative tone of the whole. In reference to Andrew's foray into *Filioque* doctrine, Bessarion refuses to follow him, but warns : " we shall examine that later by itself, for we have many and various things to say about it " [36]. " From the Father " and " From the Son " have different meanings [37]. " We assert that what you say is not only different words but different things and hence also different meanings, for each proposition has its own meaning. For ' to proceed

---

[31] MOHLER, *Kardinal Bessarion*, pp. 96-7.

[32] SYR., pp. 198, 206, 610. Syropoulus's account of the voyage, pp. 198-214, makes it quite clear that Bessarion could not have written it aboard ship during the voyage.

[33] SYR., p. 196.

[34] *Quae supersunt actorum graecorum Concilii Florentini* (= CFDS V) (hereafter *AG*) ed. J. GILL, (Rome, 1953) pp. 138-60.

[35] *AG*, p. 443.

[36] *AG*, p. 140.

[37] *AG*, p. 149.

from the Father' is one proposition; 'from the Father and the Son' is another — two propositions with a conjunction — so it has two propositions negatively opposed " [38].

Bessarion would have preferred that the *Filioque* as doctrine, and not the *Filioque* as Addition, should have been the subject of the initial theological debates in Ferrara. When the Greeks had met to decide on the theme of the first theological sessions, he had proposed and urged that it should be the *Filioque* as doctrine, on the grounds that, if that was proved false, there would be no need to spend time on it as Addition : but he was outvoted [39]. After the inconclusive debates in Ferrara on the Addition the Latins began to press for discussions on the fundamental theological issue that divided the Churches — the *Filioque* doctrine. In a meeting of the Greeks by themselves about plans for the future " The Bishop of Nicaea alone did not agree but urged that the doctrine should be discussed. For we have (he declared) many excellent things to say about the doctrine and we ought not to run away from the Latins. Why! to the Addition Cabasilas dedicated only four pages and what we have said about it would fill a whole book ; what he wrote about the doctrine was a complete book, so surely we can say a very great deal about it and to the point, too. Nicenus's remarks displeased his hearers but he insisted on discussion of the doctrine. All the same, they took no notice of what he said " and voted for the opposing view [40]. That incident occurred in December 1438, till which time at least Bessarion clearly shared Cabasilas's anti-Latin attitude [41].

The doctrine of the *Filioque* was, in fact, discussed in Florence, when Mark Eugenicus was the sole spokesman for the Greeks. It was these discussions, especially the exposition in the last two sessions of the Latin position by John of Montenero, O. P., basing his arguments on Scripture, on the Latin Fathers and especially on the Greek Fathers, that caused Bessarion to change his mind. He declared to his friend Alexius Lascaris : " It was not the syl-

---

[38] *AG*, pp. 149-50.

[39] SYR., p. 316 ; BESSARIO, *De Spiritus Sancti processione ad Alexium Lascarin Philanthropenum* (= CFDS VII) ed. E. CANDAL (Rome, 1961) pp. 20-2.

[40] SYR., p. 362.

[41] Cf. E. CANDAL, *Nilus Cabasilas et theologia S. Thomae de processione Spiritus Sancti* (Città del Vaticano, 1945). Cabasilas's treatise is based on and in part is a copy of a treatise on the Holy Spirit composed by Barlaam the Calabrian ; cf. G. SCHIRÒ, *Il paradosso di Nilo Cabasila*, in SBNE 9 (1957), pp. 362-88.

logisms or the cogency of proofs or the force of arguments that led me to believe this, but the plain words of the Doctors. For when I saw and heard them, straightway I put aside all contention and controversy and yielded to the authority of those whose words they were, even though till then I had been not a little active in opposition. For I judged that the holy Fathers, speaking as they did in the Holy Spirit, could not have departed from the truth, and I was grieved that I had not heard their words before " [42]. Others, too, were similarly convinced — Gregory the Confessor, Scholarius, Isidore of Kiev and several more. In mid-April 1439 Bessarion delivered a long discourse to the Greek Synod to show on the authority of the Greek Fathers that in respect of the Trinity " Through " and " From " are synonymous and hence that agreement in faith of Greeks and Latins was not only possible but obligatory in conscience.

I believe that Palamas's treatise came into his hands at this period and that he wrote his answer to it some time afterwards, and that it was through this work of Palamas that he became acquainted with the *Epigraphae* of Beccus, a collection of Greek patristic quotations to prove the orthodoxy of the *Filioque* doctrine.

In the light of the above considerations the conclusion seems inevitable that there is no evidence at all concerning Bessarion's attitude about union of the Churches and the orthodoxy of Latin doctrine before he left Constantinople for Italy. His behaviour in Italy seems to indicate that till the discussions on the *Filioque* doctrine were nearly finished in Florence he was not convinced of its orthodoxy and so of the legitimacy of union with the Western Church. In March-April 1439 he changed and thereafter was a protagonist for union. A like phenomenon can be observed in the Descriptive-part of the Greek *Practica* (i. e., the Greek Acts of the Council of Florence) written by an unknown author who was certainly not Bessarion.

However, very recently a new line of enquiry has opened out. Professor Elpidio Mioni, the leading authority on the manuscripts of Bessarion, in his illuminating article, ' Bessarione scriba ' has described the contents of a manuscript of Bessarion, an autograph (Cod. marc. gr. 523), which contains a treatise on the Blessed Trinity under the title : ἔτι ἑρμηνεία ἡμετέρ(α) μέρ(ους) τοῦ πρώτου βιβλίου τ(ῶν) ἀποφάσε(ων). There are ten other items in the codex

---

[42] Pp. 40-1.

besides this treatise and all of them are transcriptions, five of
them autographs, of excerpts from authors, mainly philosophers :
no item is an original composition [43]. The same, then, is likely
to be true also of autograph item no. 6 on the Trinity, that it,
too, is a copy. And it is. The whole item no. 6 is a Greek
translation (as it says) of part of the first book of Peter Lombard's
Sententiae, and it deals with the Blessed Trinity. Professor Mioni
is convinced that this codex and also Cod. marc. gr. 526 " are
closely bound up with the teaching of Pletho whose methods they
follow in collecting the various excerpts, especially from Plutarch
and the historians " [44]. In his opinion the autograph items were
written by Bessarion during the period of his studies under Pletho.
This treatise of the Holy Spirit, then, dates, one would say, from
between 1431 and 1436.

The translation is good and is no more than a translation ;
it is not a commentary or a paraphrase. Very occasionally un-
important words are omitted. Rarely a few words are added to
clarify the sense. Where relevant, " We " is changed to " The
Latins " and " Greeks " to " We ". A few times " Heretics ",
when in the context it might have reference to the Greeks, becomes " Some people ".

The part that is translated is rather less than a third of the
whole of Book I, 94 pages out of 274 (Edition Grottaferrata,
1971) ; 18 Distinctions out of 48 (but it ends abruptly in the
middle of a paragraph) ; about the half of the 34 Distinctions that
refer more or less directly to the Holy Spirit since the last 14
Distinctions deal with God's ubiquity, knowledge, will, etc. The
Lombard's Latin is not difficult. His sentences are short, his
arguments usually straightforward. Nevertheless a translator
would need a good knowledge of Latin [45].

Was Bessarion himself the translator ? At the beginning of
the text there is no title, only a space for a later insertion in red
ink, which was never done. The title given above is taken from
the index of all the items contained in the MS, written by Bessarion on the verso of the sixth folio of flyleaves (the rest are blank)
that precede the numbered pages of the MS proper [46]. Ἑρμηνεία

[43] E. MIONI, *Bessarione scriba* pp. 269-70.
[44] Ibid., p. 270.
[45] Cf. appendix.
[46] I owe this information to the very great courtesy of Professor Silvio
Bernardinello of the University of Padua, to whom I proffer my most
sincere thanks.

ἡμετέρα would seem to indicate that this treatise on the Holy
Spirit is Bessarion's own translation. He must, then, have had
quite a fair knowledge of Latin, because the translator was no
mere beginner. Yet no single one of the many friends and enemies
of Bessarion who have mentioned his name in their writings has
gives as much as a hint of it. To have reached such a degree of
proficiency in the Latin language he must have spent much time in
study. He could hardly have concealed from so many intimates in
Greece — Pletho, Scholarius, Syropoulus, the brothers Eugenicus,
Amiroutzes, Isidore of Kiev, Gregory the Confessor —, during years
of study devoted to the language, his interest in it and his acquired
skill : yet not one of them ever makes even a passing reference
to it, not even Syropoulus or Eugenicus or other anti-unionist who,
at least after the council and Bessarion's cardinalate, could have
been expected to forge from it another argument for his alleged
insincerity. During his many years in Italy none of the numerous humanists who knew him well — Traversari, Andrew of Rhodes,
Perotti, Poggio, Valla and the rest — no Capranica, no Michael
Apostolis, no Platina — does other than marvel at his prowess in
acquiring a competent knowledge of Latin in the early years of
his sojourn there [47].

-----

[47] Bessarion twice at least refers to the learning of Latin. In the
dedicatory note attached to his translation of St Basil's *De Nativitate*,
which he addressed to Thomas of Sarzana, Master of the Sacred Page,
Bessarion declared that it had never entered into his head to publish what
" in the beginning of my studies in Latin I had translated from Greek
as an exercise of my intellect, in so far as the little knowledge of that
language that I then had allowed me, lest the lack of skill and the ignorance of the translator should be attributed to that marvellous doctrine
and reputation of the most eloquent Doctor ", who had himself written
with such elegance and perfection of style : but he had yielded to Sarzana's
importunity. This dedication must be dated from before 27 November
1444, when Sarzana was nominated bishop of Bologna. (MOHLER, *Gelerh-
tenkreis*, pp. 452-3).

The other reference is in his treatise *Ad Alex. Lascarin* (p. 9). In
connection with the controversial text from St Basil's *Adv. Eunomium*,
Bessarion states that no Latin could have changed Basil's text in so perfect a Greek style as not to let it be apparent, " just as also it is impossible for ours to write anything in the Latin language with grace and style
equal to the Latins, no matter how much Greeks have become proficient
in Latin and Latins in Greek. Of this both I and others of ours are
trustworthy witnesses, for though our understanding of the Latin language
surpasses mediocrity, yet we can write nothing that is really elegant and
Latin ".

E. Candal dates the Greek text of this treatise as from between 1443
and 1446, with the probability that it is from before June 1445. The

Can, then, ἑρμηνεία mean not translation but ' explication ' ?
But there is no explication. There is only the Greek translation
of a Latin text. Can he have made this translation in Italy as
an exercise when he was learning Latin in the years after 1440,
and included it among other student-exercises when he had them
bound together to form Cod. marc. gr. Z. 523 ?[48] But all the
other items in the codex date, in the view of Professor Mioni,
from his days in Mistra, so why an exception for this one ?

I still am of the opinion that Bessarion did not know Latin
when he came to Italy in 1440, yet the title of this treatise about
the Holy Spirit seems to imply that he did. This creates for me
a mystery, which at present I cannot unravel.

The part of the treatise that deals most immediately with the
Filioque doctrine is contained in Distinctions XI and XII (pp.
114-21 ; ff. 94v-96v). Briefly his argument for the double Procession (Dist. XI) is a simple catena of N. T. texts — Gal 4, 6 ; Rom.
8, 9 ; John 15, 26 ; Rom. 8, 11 ; Math. 10, 20 ; John 14, 26 ; John
15, 26. Greeks (he goes on) reject it because the N. T. mentions
only the Father (John 15, 26), because Pope Leo placed a " golden "
plaque behind the " altar of St Paul " engraved with the old
form of the Creed, and because councils forbade teaching and
preaching anything other than the Creed. That difficulty is met
by distinguishing between " contrary " and " adding " ; also the
Gospel does not say " From the Father only ". Indeed the Greeks
agree with us in meaning and differ only in words, and Greek
Fathers (Athanasius, Didymus, Cyril, John Chrysostom) state this
double Procession.

Latin translation by Bessarion himself was made probably between 23
April 1449 and 1450 when Bessarion was made governor of Bologna.

A student exercise of Bessarion's has been accidentally preserved in
Marc. gr. 186. It is described by H. D. SAFFREY, *Un exercise de latin philo-
sophique, autographe du Bessarion*, in *Misc. Bess.* pp. 371-9. According to
the author this MS was copied and put together between 1440 and 1450.
On a fly-leaf it contains a phrase by phrase comparison of part of Plato's
Timaeus and Cicero's translation of it. There are enough blunders in the
Latin (not Cicero's) to show that the compiler of this student exercise,
following a characteristic method of the time, was still by no means competent in Latin.

[48] Cod. marc. gr. 523, like other codices that contain Bessarion's earliest writhings, was put together and bound, not when he was in Mistra,
but after he had been established in Italy ; cf. MIONI, Bessarione scriba
pp. 269ff.

Distinction XII asks : " Whether the Holy Spirit proceeds earlier or more fully from the Father than from the Son ". The Lombard, relying on St Augustine, replies, not earlier because there is no time element in God. More fully ? No ! (says St Augustine) but *principaliter* from the Father because the Son receives from the Father the power to produce the Spirit, but equally from both. St Hilary in several places had written of the Holy Spirit being and being sent " through the Son ". Peter Lombard with a slight hesitation applies Augustine's *principaliter* and concomitant " equally ". The Distinction ends with a quotation from St Augustine to assert " neither earlier nor more fully ", the final reply to the question posed in the title.

One wonders why Bessarion translated — copied out — a part of the Lombard's *Sentences* (and broke off before ending the paragraph). Was it because interest in Constantinople about union had incited his curiosity to see what the Latins said about the Holy Spirit, and the Lombard's exposition of the question, meagre though it was compared with St Thomas's erudite treatment of it in the translation of Demetrius Cydones, was the only thing at hand ? Did Pletho propose it as an example of pedagogical method? One can ask many such questions but can give no convincing answer, because there is nothing to suggest what the answer should be. A perusal, however, of the treatise itself makes it plain that Bessarion will not have got much theological profit from his task.

Bessarion may, or may not, have been impressed by Peter's method : he never imitated it. He was not likely to have been influenced by Peter's arguments about the Procession, for they were not pressed with any force and he would have heard them all before — and much more — and have been acquainted with the usual Greek reasons for rejecting them : on the Addition he showed himself in Ferrara a well-prepared and most capable adversary. In his little excursus on " Through the Son " Peter Lombard seems unhappy and as if forced into including it only because Hilary, unwisely, had used the phrase, not once only but often. He does not try to explain and justify it. He is content to repeat Augustine's words. There is nothing here that would have inspired Bessarion to produce the full and flowing discourse on *Dia* and *Ek* that he made before the Greek synod in mid-April 1439 and whose theme he repeated in various later writings.

So this seemingly promising new line of approach does nothing to illuminate our enquiry but leaves it where it was before, and does not change the conclusion, that for lack of evidence it is unwarrantable to state that before the council Bessarion was either an ardent conciliarist or, still more, a confirmed unionist.

Campion Hall
Oxford

APPENDIX
LIBER PRIMUS
DE MYSTERIO TRINITATIS

Distinctio I (Grottaferrata edition, p. 55)

Veteris ac novae legis continentiam, diligenti indagine, etiam atque etiam considerantibus nobis, praevia Dei gratia, innotuit sacrae paginae tractatum circa res vel signa praecipue versari. Ut enim egregius doctor Augustinus ait in libro *De Doctrina Christiana* : « omnis doctrina vel rerum est vel signorum. Sed res etiam per signa discuntur. Proprie autem hic *res* appellantur, quae non ad significandum aliquid adhibentur ; *signa* vero, quorum usus est in significando ». — Eorum autem aliqua sunt quorum omnis usus est in significando, non in iustificando, id est quibus non utimur nisi aliquid significandi gratia, ut aliqua sacramenta legalia ; alia quae non solum significant, sed conferunt quod intus adiuvet, sicut evangelica sacramenta.

Distinctio XI, paragraph 2 (Grottaferrata edition, p. 115)
Quod Graeci non concedunt Spiritum Sanctum procedere a Filio.

Graeci tamen dicunt Spiritum Sanctum tantum procedere a Patre, et non a Filio. Quod ideo dicunt, quia Veritas in Evangelio fidem integram continente, de processione Spiritus loquens solum Patrem commemorat dicens : « Spiritus qui a Patre procedit ». Et ideo etiam, quia in principalibus conciliis quae apud eos celebrata sunt, ita Symbola eorum subiunctis anathematibus sancita sunt, ut nulli de Trinitatis fide aliud docere vel aliter praedicare quam ibi continetur liceat. In quibus quidem Symbolis cum Spiritus commemoretur procedere a Patre, et non a Filio, quicumque, inquiunt, a Filio eum procedere addunt, anathema incurrunt ; unde et nos arguunt anathemati reos.

paragraph 5 (Grottaferrata edition, p. 120)

Forte etiam iuxta hanc intelligentiam dicitur Spiritus Sanctus a Patre mitti per Filium et a Patre esse per Filium. Unde Hilarius ad Deum Patrem de Spiritu Sancto et Filio loquens in XII libro *De Trinitate* ait : « In Spiritu Sancto tuo, ex te profecto et per eum misso ». Item, « Ante tempora unigenitus tuus ex te natus manet, ita quod ex te per eum Spiritus Sanctus tuus est ; quod etsi sensu non percipiam,

tamen teneo conscientia. In spiritualibus enim rebus tuis hebes sum ».
— Item in eodem : « Conserva hanc, oro, fidei meae religionem, ut quod
in regenerationis meae symbolo professus sum, semper obtineam : Patrem scilicet te, Filium tuum una tecum adorem, Spiritum Sanctum
tuum, qui ex te per unigenitum tuum est, promerear ». Ecce aperte
dicit Spiritum Sanctum a Patre per Filium et mitti et esse.
Quod non
est intelligendum, quasi a Patre per Filium minorem mittatur vel sit,
sed quia ex Patre et Filio est et mittitur ab utroque ; sed hoc ipsum
habet Filius a Patre, ut ab ipso sit et mittatur Spiritus Sanctus. Hoc
ergo voluit significare Hilarius, distinctionem faciens in locutione, ut
ostenderet in Patre esse auctoritatem.

75r   Τὴν θείαν γραφὴν παλαιάν τε καὶ νέαν ἢ περὶ πραγμάτων ἢ περὶ
σημείων τὴν πραγματείαν ποιεῖσθαι τῷ μακαρίῳ δοκεῖ Αὐγουστίνῳ ἐν
τῷ Περὶ Χριστιανικῆς Διδασκαλίας βιβλίῳ οὑτωσὶ λέ-
γοντι· « Πᾶσα διδασκαλία ἢ πραγμάτων ἐστὶν ἢ σημείων, τά γε μὴν
πράγματα διὰ σημείων γινώσκεται, πράγματα μὲν οὖν κυρίως καλοῦνται
τὰ μὴ πρὸς τὸ σημαίνειν τι παραλαμβανόμενα, σημεῖα δὲ τὰ ἕτερόν τι
σημαίνοντα »· καὶ τούτων τὰ μὲν σημαντικὰ μόνον εἰσὶ καὶ οὐδαμῶς
δικαιωτικά, ὡς τὰ νομικὰ μυστήρια, τὰ δὲ οὐ σημαντικὰ μόνον ἀλλά τι
καὶ συντελοῦντα πρὸς τὴν τοῦ εἴσω ἀνθρώπου βοήθειαν, ὡς τὰ τῆς
χάριτος μυστήρια.
94v   Οἱ μέντοι Γραῖκοι φασὶ τὸ Πνεῦμα τὸ Ἅγιον ἐκ τοῦ Πατρὸς
ἐκπορεύεσθαι μόνον καὶ οὐκ ἐκ τοῦ Υἱοῦ· ὁ διὰ τοῦτο φασὶ διότι ἐν τῷ
τελείαν περιέχοντι τὴν πίστιν εὐαγγελίῳ ἡ Ἀλήθεια τὸν λόγον περὶ τῆς
τοῦ Πνεύματος ἐκπορεύσεως ποιουμένη τοῦ Πατρὸς μνημονεύει μόνον,
λέγουσα « Τὸ Πνεῦμα τὸ Ἅγιον ὃ παρὰ τοῦ Πατρὸς ἐκπορεύεται »· οὐ
μὴν ἀλλὰ καὶ διὰ τὸ ἐν ταῖς παρ' αὐτοῖς συγκροτηθείσαις οἰκουμενικαῖς
συνόδοις ἀναθήματι ἐν τοῖς συμβόλοις καθυποβληθῆναι τοὺς ἄλλο διδά-
σκοντας ἢ ἄλλως φρονοῦντας περὶ τῆς πίστεως τῆς Τριάδος ἢ καθὼς ἐν
ἐκείνοις περιέχεται.
96v   Καὶ κατὰ ταύτην ἴσως τὴν διάνοιαν λέγεται τὸ Πνεῦμα τὸ Ἅγιον
ἐκ τοῦ Πατρὸς πέμπεσθαι διὰ τοῦ Υἱοῦ καὶ ἐκ τοῦ Πατρὸς εἶναι διὰ τοῦ
Υἱοῦ, ὅθεν ὁ Ἰλάριος πρὸς τὸν Θεὸν καὶ Πατέρα περὶ τοῦ Πνεύματος
τοῦ Ἁγίου καὶ τοῦ Υἱοῦ ἀποτεινόμενος λέγει· « Ἐν τῷ Πνεύματί σου
τῷ Ἁγίῳ τῷ ἐκ σοῦ προϊόντι καὶ διὰ τοῦ Υἱοῦ σου πεμπομένῳ ». « Ἔτι
πρὸ χρόνων ὁ μονογενής σου Υἱὸς ἐκ σοῦ γεννηθεὶς μένει καὶ τὸ Πνεῦμά
σου τὸ Ἅγιον ἐκ σοῦ ἐστι δι' αὐτοῦ, ὅπερ εἰ καὶ μὴ καταλαβεῖν τῷ νῷ
δύναμαι κατέχω ὅμως τῇ πίστει· ἐν γὰρ τοῖς νοητοῖς τούτοις σου πράγ-
μασι ἀναβλέπειν ἀδυνατῶ ». Καὶ αὖθις ἐν τῷ αὐτῷ· « Φύλαξον ταύτην
ἱκετεύω τῆς ἐμῆς πίστεως τὴν θρησκείαν ἵν' ὅπερ ἀναγεννώμενος ἐν τῷ
συμβόλῳ τῆς πίστεως ὡμολόγησα ἀεὶ βέβαιον κατέχω, καὶ ἵνα δηλαδὴ
σὲ τὸν Πατέρα καὶ τόν σον Υἱὸν μετὰ σοῦ καὶ τὸ Ἅγιόν σου Πνεῦμα
τὸ ἐκ σοῦ διὰ τοῦ μονογενοῦς σου Υἱοῦ ὃν ἀξιωθῶ προσκυνεῖν ». Ἰδοὺ
γὰρ σαφῶς φησι τὸ Πνεῦμα τὸ Ἅγιον ἐκ τοῦ Πατρὸς διὰ τοῦ Υἱοῦ καὶ
πέμπεσθαι καὶ εἶναι, ὅπερ οὐχ οὕτω νοητέον ὡς ἐκ τοῦ Πατρὸς διὰ τοῦ
Υἱοῦ ὡς ἐλάττονος πεμπομένου ἢ ὄντος τοῦ Πνεύματος, ἀλλ' ὡς ἐκ τοῦ

Πατρὸς καὶ ἐκ τοῦ Υἱοῦ καὶ ὄντος καὶ πεμπομένου, τοῦτο μέντοι τοῦ Υἱοῦ ἐκ τοῦ Πατρὸς ἔχοντος, τὸ καὶ ἀπ' αὐτοῦ καὶ εἶναι καὶ πέμπεσθαι τὸ Πνεῦμα τὸ "Αγιον. Τοῦτο τοιγαροῦν ἐβουλήθη σημάναι Ἱλάριος ἐν τῇ τῆς προφορᾶς διαφορᾷ τὸ ἐν τῷ Πατρὶ δηλαδὴ ἀρχὴν εἶναι.

XV

THE FREEDOM OF THE GREEKS IN THE COUNCIL OF FLORENCE

The Need of Help for Constantinople

ON 5 July 1439 in the cathedral of Florence on behalf of the oriental Churches the Emperor of Constantinople, four procurators acting for the patriarchates of Alexandria, Antioch and Jerusalem, eighteen metropolitans (counting again the three bishop procurators), the Russian bishop, three procurators of bishops, five Stavrophoroi-deacons of the Great Church of St. Sophia, Gregory the protosyncellus (a fourth procurator of the patriarchs) and seven abbots or delegates of monasteries signed the decree of union of the Greek and Latin Churches. The patriarch of Constantinople had died on 10 June: had he lived he also would most certainly have signed. Only two Greek members of the Council of Florence entitled to sign did not sign, Mark Eugenicus, Metropolitan of Ephesus and procurator of the Patriarch of Antioch, and Isaias, Metropolitan of Stavropolis. The Greeks arrived back in Constantinople on 1 February 1440 and were faced with the disapproval of the monks and of the people at large. Some of the returned prelates began to have second thoughts and denounced the union. Of the twenty oriental metropolitan-archbishops in Florence, nine did not change their decision. Mark Eugenicus and Isaias opposed the union. In favour of it were Bessarion, Isidore, Mitylene, Cyzicus, Lacedaemon, Monemvasia, Rhodes and perhaps also Moldo-Wallachia. These included all the younger prelates, who were also the only theologians of merit among the Greek bishops.[1] It is, then, an exaggeration to say, as it is frequently said, that the Greek Church accepted union in Italy and rejected it in Constantinople. There is, nevertheless, an obvious element of truth in the statement, that deserves consideration.

Externally the Council of Florence was the most ecumenical of all ecumenical councils. The four oriental patriarchates were represented by a numerous array of prelates: the Western patriarchate was headed by the Pope himself. Both East and West firmly believed that definitions of ecumenical councils were for ever binding in conscience. Florence

---

[1] Of the three lay 'theologians' in the suite of the Emperor, two at least had in public written statements accepted union and given their reasons why.

produced definitions contained in the decree of union with the Greeks about the Procession of the Holy Spirit, the after-life, the Eucharist and papal primacy. The East just as much as the West should have concurred in these definitions. In Florence it did: in Constantinople it did not. To justify their *volte face*, the Greeks denied that Florence was an ecumenical council, not because both Greeks and Latins were not adequately represented there but because (so it was alleged) their bishops had been subjected to duress, such duress that they had not been free to refuse assent.

Silvester Syropoulus was the first to defend that position at length. He did it in his *Memoirs*, written probably about the year 1444, his *apologia* for the recanting bishops — and for himself.[2] As the means of the duress he alleged the poverty of the Greeks in Italy, the long duration of the council, fear that there would be no means of return home unless union was accepted, the domination of the Emperor and the imperative need to obtain help to save Constantinople from capture by the Turks. The Orthodox Churches still repeat Syropoulos's defence and perhaps the majority of historians elsewhere have accepted it. General views need re-examination from time to time in the light of more recent research and one such is the defence proposed by Syropoulus.[3] In this article only one point of it is being investigated, duress from the imperative need to help Constantinople; but if that should prove unfounded in history the other points should then be reassessed and all of them weighed together to see if they can fairly be said to amount to such duress as to have forced bishops of a Church to be untrue to their faith by formally accepting what they thought to be heresy.

I

By 1437 the once vast Byzantine Empire had shrunk to a diminutive size. It consisted only of the city of Constantinople and its *hinterland*, a few towns on the Black Sea, a few islands in the Aegean, and the Peloponnesus; and these only at the price of paying an annual tribute to the Sultan. From 1394 till 1402 Constantinople had been besieged by the Turks and had been relieved only because the Mongols defeated and captured the Sultan. In 1422 it was besieged again and saved by an insurrection in Turkish Asia Minor. Having no territories worth speaking of, the Empire had little in the way of taxes and so no means of paying a mercenary army. Worse, the Venetians and Genoese monopolised its

---

[2] Silvester Syropoulus, *Memoirs*, ed. R. Creyghton under the title *Vera historia unionis non verae*, (The Hague, 1660). Hereafter referred to as *Syr.*
[3] For a discussion of the historical trustworthiness of the different sources cf. J. Gill, *Personalities of the Council of Florence* (Oxford, 1964) pp. 144-77.

trade to such a degree that the provisioning of the capital city itself depended on foreign ships. Help could come only from the West. But there all was in turmoil; England and France were at war, Hungary was split by the Hussites, the German Electors were hostile to King Sigismund, the Italian states were permanently fighting among themselves. For the Greeks, to look to the West was to look to the Pope, for he was the head of the Western Church, he was the only one there who had a certain supra-national character capable of commanding general respect, and he could by ecclesiastical taxation raise money over Europe to pay a crusading army. So the Emperor and the Patriarch listened to the overtures of Pope Martin V (1417-31) and of Pope Eugenius IV (1431-47) about unity of the Churches.

II

Fear, then, of the Turks and the need of obtaining immediate help to defend Constantinople and the remnants of the Empire against their further encroachments were a dominant motive in Greek minds, prompting them to thoughts of union of the Churches. It was not the only motive or the highest motive. The Greeks desired union of the Churches for its own sake, because the Church of Christ should be one and not divided. But what made the Greeks accept negotiations for union at that time and made them agree to pursue them in Italy was the perilous state of their homeland. (That union should be sought through a general council was a condition that they had set and that the Latins with some reluctance had accepted.) It was no secret. In Italy the Emperor made this plain from the outset when he stipulated that there should be an interval of four months before there was any doctrinal discussion[4] to allow time for western princes or their representatives to come to Ferrara. He referred to it in his addresses to the Greeks. In Ferrara on 2 January 1439 when urging them to continue the council in Florence, he bade them: 'either accept this proposal of the Pope and go to Florence, or reject him and return home. Only—think how we shall get away, whether we shall have the means and whether Constantinople will get any help.'[5] The prelates finally agreed to go to Florence but on certain conditions, one of which was 'that our city shall receive help for eight months.'[6] On

[4] *Quae supersunt actorum graecorum Concilii Florentini* (ed. J. Gill, Rome, 1953), (= *Concilium Florentinum Documenta et Scriptores*, V) p. 10. Hereafter referred to as *AG*; *Syr.*, p. 104.

[5] *AG*, p. 222.

[6] *AG*, p. 222-3. The other conditions were 'that we shall receive the five months' subsistence allowance owing to us, that for the future in Florence we should be paid through a bank, that we shall go there and nowhere else, that we shall spend there four months and no more, that we shall be our own masters with freedom to go in and out of the city at will, that the prices of foodstuffs shall not be increased above what they are now'.

another occasion, in Florence he told them (28 May 1439): 'Remember also help for our house, the refuge of Christians, the hope of the faith, the salvation of all—I mean Constantinople. So make a wise decision that harms neither soul nor body.'[7]

The Pope used the same considerations when speaking to the Greeks. In Ferrara, he urged them: 'Come with me to Florence and I promise to give in help to Constantinople 12,000 ducats and two ships, and to you what I owe.'[8] Later, in Florence 'We all shall be delighted and shall have a great desire to help you. Our help will bring great relief to the Christians dwelling in the east and those in the grip of the infidel.'[9]

Others referred to it publicly also. Scholarius, in an impassioned address usually entitled *On the Need to Help Constantinople*, told his fellow Greeks among other pungent remarks (c. 15 April 1439): 'You know very well, all of you, that fear of the infidel and the fact that our situation is desperate chiefly induced us to desire and to strive for union of the Church of Christ, though this would have been sought for by everyone for other and better reasons.'[10] At about the same time Bessarion ended his *Dogmatic Address*: 'For who is there who does not know that the last refuge left to us was help from the Latins and a future union with them'.[11] When union seemed at last probable (1 June 1439), the Emperor immediately sent Isidore of Kiev to the Pope to ask for details of what help would be forthcoming.[12]

III

Granted that there was a need of helping Constantinople and that everyone was aware of it, when and how did the consciousness of that need modify the behaviour of the Greek ecclesiastics in Italy? There were two occasions in particular when one might have expected to see the Greeks act under the influence of that need. The one was towards the end of the formal sessions in Ferrara, the other after the sessions in Florence.

Ferrara

The subject of discussion in the fourteen public sessions held in Ferrara was the legitimacy of adding the *Filioque* to the Creed. The reasons for and against were few and simple, but neither side could persuade the other.

---

[7] *AG*, pp. 425-6.
[8] *AG*, p. 220.
[9] *AG*, 28 May, p. 424.
[10] *Patrologia graeca* . . . , (ed. J. P. Migne) CLXI, col. 293BC; hereafter referred to as *PG*.
[11] *Oratio dogmatica de unione* (ed. E. Candal, Rome 1958), (=*CFDS*, VII) p. 70; *PG*, CLXI, col. 699.
[12] Cf.: J. Gill, *The Council of Florence* (Cambridge, 1959), p. 263-4.

The sessions went on with, towards the end, one speaker of each side endlessly repeating the same arguments. The Greeks, already a year away from home and short of money because the Pope was going bankrupt and could pay their allowances only when he could borrow, were disillusioned, weary and discouraged. They wanted to finish with it all and go home.

In the twelfth session on 5 December: 'Cardinal Giuliano replied to every word with ten thousand and never stopped talking.'

> When we realised that we were succeeding in getting nothing but toil and boredom, we determined not to meet with them again. For we said to the Emperor: "What do we gain and what shall we gain meeting together and holding useless sessions? The Latins will never yield to the truth . . . The Scripture says 'With a perverse and contradictory people let there be no speech'. So, as Emperor, command that there be one more session and once more bid them accede to the truth and, if they do not obey, then according to the Apostle after one warning and a second be finished with them."[13]

But the Emperor said 'No'. Hence there were more sessions.

In the thirteenth session of 8 December, Mark Eugenicus spoke at length. Cardinal Giuliano Cesarini replied, dividing Eugenicus's speech into twenty-eight heads, but with no effect on the Greeks. Afterwards in the Patriarch's apartments they lamented: 'Why this waste? We put forward the truth and they will not accept it. . . . Why then waste more time and why do we not return whence we came?'[14] But the Emperor insisted again on more discussion.

On 13 December in the fourteenth and last session in Ferrara Eugenicus again spoke at length and Cesarini replied: 'If you propose ten arguments, I shall propose ten thousand'. No wonder the Greeks complained: 'We are not likely to persuade them nor they us; so we should go back to our own land.'[15]

Syropoulus, the other chief witness to the events, records: 'We kept on asking the Patriarch to see to our return home,'[16] and he narrates the meeting of a committee of the Greeks with the Emperor: 'We urged him to look to the support and help of the city, which will be effected principally by our return, for we do not see that there will be any correction of the errors of the Latins'. The Emperor replied 'Have we come here to go back with nothing achieved? . . . with no word yet on doctrine?'[17]

But the Greeks did not want to embark on a discussion of the doctrine of the *Filioque*. They had come to Italy sanguine that they could easily

[13] *AG*, pp. 214, 490.
[14] *AG*, p. 491.
[15] *AG*, p. 217.
[16] *Syr.*, pp. 187-8.
[17] *Syr.*, p. 190.

prove the Latins to be in the wrong about the Addition.[18] Instead they
had been faced with a multitude of confident arguments.[19] Now the
Latins were urging them to leave the Addition and go on to the doctrine,
and were openly claiming that they could make out a very good case for
their western faith.[20] But the Greeks once bitten were twice shy and,
not wanting to repeat the experience they had had over the Addition, tried
to evade discussion of the *Filioque* doctrine.

Syropoulus tells how they endeavoured to persuade the Patriarch to
stand up to the Emperor who was pushing them to face the doctrinal
question 'You ought to make a real stand against him, since they [the
Latins] have some solid support, as they think (so we have been told) from
the Latin Fathers. For the Addition they haven't. So we must oppose
that move [of leaving the discussion on the Addition and going on to
discuss the doctrine].'[21] When the question was put, only Bessarion was
in favour of discussing the doctrine.[22]

When in December 1438 the ecclesiastics were pressing to return home,
the Emperor asked Syropoulus why the prelates did not want to discuss
the dogma. Syropoulus told him that their reason was that:

[18] 'I, too, know well that there are some among you who thought you could overcome the wisdom of the Latins and persuade them to rest in the positions as of old,
and I marvel at them exceedingly that, though in other respects of sound common
sense, in this point they have been so far mistaken. . . . Let it be granted, then, that
all were of the same opinion and came in the hope of proving that the Latins knew
nothing and did not hold to the truth and that they would persuade them willy-nilly
to abandon their doctrine and that so they would effect union with them. . . . But
you all see that the Latins have defended their opinions brilliantly, so that any one
who desires to be just can have no cause to say a word against them.' (Scholarius,
'On the Need to Help Constantinople', *PG*, CLX, col. 388BCD.)

[19] 'When the Latins had produced these and similar arguments and we had nothing
to reply to them . . . we kept silent. But the Latins, having proved that it was
permitted to add truth to the Creed, naturally promised to prove that the doctrine
added to the Creed was true, namely, that the Holy Spirit proceeds from both Father
and Son, and they summoned us forth to the combat. But ours, beaten in the first
encounter and put to flight, shrank from entering the arena again. . . . So they were
afraid and were very loath to stay on. . . .' (Bessarion, *De Spiritus Sancti Processione
ad Alex. Lascarin*, (ed. E. *Candal*, Rome 1961) [= *CFDS*, VII], pp. 34-5; *PG*, CLXI,
col. 354CD.)

[20] 'The Greeks for their part were strong to put an end to discussion but the Latins
insisted that the sessions go on and that faith and dogma be investigated. They said:
"We are not interested in the Addition nor how it was added to the Creed, for it has
been added and now it cannot be expunged, unless you can show that it is blasphemous.
So let it be examined, and if it is blasphemous let it be banned, but if sound, what
grounds have you of accusation against us. . . ." [Cesarini] "Let it be examined,
Father, let it be examined, and if the *Filioque* shall be found to be blasphemous it
shall remain neither in the Creed nor anywhere else, for what is blasphemous may
never be said at all; but if it is orthodox, it is justified everywhere and most of all in
the Creed".' (*AG*, pp. 217-8).

[21] *Syr.*, p. 190.
[22] *Syr.*, p. 193.

if on this question [the Addition] where we have so great and irresistible a strength of argument, they [the Latins] weave together refutations and think that their answers are good and maintain that the decrees [of the councils] are not opposed to them, if we should proceed to discussion on the doctrine on which, so we hear, they are boasting that they have solid support from the western Fathers (though we do not yet know what), they will say whatever they want and, since the strength and power of the Pope are behind them, they will spread it abroad that 'we have proved brilliantly that our doctrine is sound'. If on this question, though they have proved nothing, they are still not ashamed to say such things and much beyond what is justified, how much more then will they broadcast it. But for us, if we say anything at all, it will be counted as nothing by them and we shall find ourselves frustrated since we have no one [as a third party] who will judge between us.[23]

When they finally agreed to discuss the doctrine of the *Filioque*, they laid it down as a condition that it should not be done in public and in session, but between committees of twelve on each side.

Bessarion summed up the situation of the end of 1438 in these words:

So they were extremely perturbed and were afraid and absolutely unwilling to remain any longer, but all of them kept on asserting that they should be parted from the Latins and return to their Fatherland. . . . After some time and with difficulty, when they had realised the rashness of this plan, persuaded by reasons put forward by the Emperor and their own common sense, they ceased from their ridiculous insistence.[24]

Florence

The discussions on the *Filioque* doctrine took place in Florence whither the council moved in January 1439. There were eight sessions on the subject from 2-24 March, and they failed to produce agreement. The Latins, therefore, insisted that the Greeks should decide among themselves which of the Latin arguments they could not accept and should then discuss them further in session till concord was reached. The Greeks refused absolutely to attend any more sessions and wanted to return home. Syropoulus records of early April: 'We brought pressure to bear on the Patriarch and implored him to advise and beg the Emperor to get something done and especially with regard to our return, since we saw that it was useless to expect any conclusion from the Latins.'[25] The Patriarch did what they asked and the Emperor replied at length about their return saying that in the circumstances it was both impracticable and dishonourable.

---

[23] *Syr.*, p. 195.
[24] *Ad Alex. Lascarin*, p. 35; *PG*, CLXI, col. 356AB.
[25] *Syr.*, p. 227.

Urged by the Latins to continue the debate, on 10 April they sent a deputation of four members to the Pope to say:

> We will have no more discussion, because discussion produces nothing but confusion. For when we speak you have a superabundance of answers. When we listen to what you say—and it is never-ending—but who can listen and talk without ever stopping? So if there is some other method of union, take counsel and inform us of it. If not, we have said what we can. What we believe is the tradition of our fathers and what has been handed down by the seven councils, and we are satisfied with that.[26]

When Eugenius replied proposing four points in particular to be answered, after another meeting among themselves the Greeks through the same deputation repeated the ultimatum: 'Let your Holiness consider, and if there is some other way of union [apart from discussion] we will unite: but if not, we shall return home in charity.'[27]

Meanwhile rumours of an impending Turkish attack on Constantinople had reached Florence and occasioned Scholarius's harangue on *The Need of Helping Constantinople*, wherein he had painted the dangers resulting from a Turkish victory in vivid colours.[28] Nevertheless, when on 15 April cardinals in the Pope's name still pressed for discussion, the Emperor himself retorted: 'We have had enough with what we have said and heard. So what now? Either let there be found some other method of uniting or we say no more.'[29]

The consequence was an impasse and, to solve it, the Emperor suggested meetings between small committees. These, however, effected nothing but they were the cause of the Latins delivering to the Greeks for their consideration and approval a precise theological statement on the *Filioque* that combined both their own and the Greeks' point of view. After acrimonious discussion about it among themselves the Orientals composed another version of it that was deliberately ambiguous,[30] and, of course, the Latins requested explanations of the ambiguities.

---

[26] *AG*, p. 403. Syropoulus says the same: 'It has been clearly shown that union will not follow from discussions in session; we therefore ask that you will make arrangements for our departure home' (p. 229).

[27] 12 April; *AG*, p. 407.

[28] 'You must put before your eyes the slaughter, the chains and the lashes, the insults, famine, thirst and being dragged miserably from place to place, pitiless servitude, rape of children, the strangling of the aged, and, what is the most woeful of all, families rent apart, the desecration of churches, blasphemy cast in the face of the most high God. . . .'. (*PG*, CLX, col. 398BC).

[29] *AG*, p. 409.

[30] Mark Eugenicus later described it as deliberately equivocal, 'as holding a middle ground and capable of being taken according to both doctrines, like an actor's boot . . .' "Relatio de rebus a se gestis", ed. L. Petit in *Patrologia Orientalis*, XVII, p. 447.

The Greek reaction was irritation and a demand to go back to Constantinople:

> And so we began to speed our return. We met together and put the whole question before the Patriarch and the Emperor, saying: 'Why do we sit so long idle? Let there be an end of it', adding that if there is no end of it and that quickly, we cannot sit about any longer; so let there be a way of departing.

The Emperor rejected their demand and asked for their reasons. 'They replied and said to him: "We are afraid, most serene Emperor, that we may pass all the summer here and the autumn as well, and going away in the winter may run into danger".'[31] But cardinals called on the Emperor and still insisted on clarifications. The Emperor replied: 'We do not write or say anything more except that, if you accept what we have given you, we shall unite; if not, we shall leave.'[32] This was the general situation till nearly the end of May. On 28 May Pope Eugenius addressed the Greeks, and his discourse set in motion activity that ended in agreement over the dogmatic question of the *Filioque*.[33] The Greeks would have been content to end the council with that and to go home.[34] But the Pope insisted that union demanded agreement on other points of difference too. Over the question of the primacy there was difficulty and three times there was a breakdown in the discussions and a demand for the means of leaving for home. On 16 June at a public meeting the Emperor addressed the Pope: 'We say nothing except that time presses and preparation for our departure should be made. . . . All that we have to say we have said to the cardinals and we have nothing more to say. Time presses and we cannot waste any more of it.'[35] When, on 22 June, in reply to a compromise suggested by the Greeks, Eugenius insisted on full privileges of the primacy, the Emperor asked him: 'Make arrangements for our departure, if you will be so kind.'[36] Four days later the Greeks offered another formula: 'Having written this, we resolved never

---

[31] 10 May, *AG*, p. 417.

[32] 21 May, *AG*, p. 420.

[33] This is not the place to relate how this came about or to give reasons why it should be judged a genuine agreement. For that cf.: Gill, *The Council of Florence*, pp. 227-66; *Personalities*, pp. 254-63

[34] 'That ancient father of venerable aspect and sorely ill, the Patriarch of Constantinople, longed for the session [of union] to be held. But there were many among us who declared that the difficulty about the primacy and the doctrines of the Eucharist and of Purgatory should first be agreed to by the eastern Fathers before they entered into union with the Roman Church . . .' *Andreas de Santacroce, advocatus consistorialis, Acta Latina Concilii Florentini* (ed. G. Hofmann, Rome 1955) (= *CFDS*, VI) pp. 224-5.

[35] *AG*, p. 449.

[36] *AG*, p. 452.

to write or do more, but, if the Pope did not accept this, nothing else
would be done.'[37] The Pope did accept, and so the promulgation of the
union became possible.

*   *   *

It will perhaps have been noted that in this rather schematic account
of the reaction of the Greeks to some of the situations that they were faced
with in Italy only Greek sources have been quoted. They are all in
agreement; the anonymous archbishop whose description was utilised
by the scribe Plousiadenus to supplement the Greek Acts, Syropoulus,
Scholarius, Bessarion. They all affirm that at the end of the sessions
both in Ferrara and in Florence the Greeks, weary, disillusioned and
overwhelmed by Latin fecundity of argument, wanted to escape home,
though that meant no union.

Nevertheless it is said that the Greeks had to agree to union because
union was a condition of their getting help for their country and getting
help for their country was of such importance and dominated their minds
to such a degree that they had to obtain it at all costs, at the cost even of
betraying their faith. That is the meaning of duress that takes away
liberty. Yet according to the sources, in their various laments over their
misery (only a few of which have been reported here) and in their
ultimata to the Latins, they mention help for Constantinople only twice,
once to say that the best way of securing it would be for them to go back
there and the second time as one of six conditions for their going to
Florence. Union of the Churches is not merely never mentioned—it is
seemingly rejected, although it has been maintained that it was a necessary
condition for help, to be obtained at all costs: 'If there is some other
way of union, we will unite; but if not, we shall return home'. Even
the Emperor, who by the theory of duress is supposed to have been driving
his subjects to accept union at any price, was not himself prepared to
sacrifice his faith and honour to obtain it.

Had the need of winning aid for their country dominated their minds
as overwhelmingly as is suggested, the Greeks both in Ferrara and in
Florence would with regret, with sorrow, and even with tears, have
suppressed their natural feelings and religious convictions and have
accepted, outwardly at least, the Latin explanations of the *Filioque* as
Addition and as dogma, so as to achieve union, and with union, help.
That is not what they did. They acted quite differently. In December 1438
they still asserted that the Latin arguments on the Addition were futile
and that the Addition was illicit. For months after the dogmatic sessions
of Florence, till a new approach to the subject won their free approval,

they still condemned the Latin doctrine and refused to discuss it further. That does not indicate a mentality cowed by any outward circumstance whatsoever, but on the contrary a high degree of independence of spirit and freedom of decision. The need to help Constantinople was a motive that facilitated their coming to Italy for the council. In Italy, far from making them sacrifice their faith, seemingly it did not make them willing to sacrifice even their comfort.[38]

Campion Hall, Oxford.

[37] *AG*, p. 453.

[38] Syropoulus recounts that in May 1438 rumours of danger to Constantinople from the Turks made the Emperor appeal to his prelates for money to arm a ship in its defence. 'So the first of the archbishops said that, had they then been in Constantinople they would have contributed even beyond their means, but being in a foreign country and ignorant of what the future had in store for them, if some of them did have a little money, they should keep it because of the uncertainty of the event and against an emergency in a foreign land; but they said that they would each give fifty aspri.' [These rich archbishops had an annual income of over 1,000 aspri (*Syr.*, p. 65).] Bessarion said that he had spent his few resources obeying the imperial command to leave the Peloponnesus for Constantinople, but of three chalices that he had he would give two. Another offered one of his two cloaks. 'When the Emperor had listened so far, he let it all drop, realising that he was building on empty hopes . . .' (*Syr.*, p. 127).

XVI

AGREEMENT ON THE *FILIOQUE*

Everyone knows that the Council of Lyons, though it seemed to the Latins of that time to promise union of the Churches, was doomed to failure from the start. The acceptance by the three Greek delegates (there were not more) of the Latin *Filioque* indicated that Michael VIII, the Greek Emperor, was willing to pay a high price for protection against the eastern ambitions of Charles of Anjou; it did not mean that the Greek Church was willing to pay the same price. Before the council, the Emperor had tried to persuade it to accept the idea of union: it had refused. After the council, it met with an uncompromising rejection the union that the delegates brought back.

It is sometimes said that the Eastern Church was no more behind the Council of Florence than it was behind that of Lyons. Such a judgement cannot be supported by history. Before ever they set off for the West, the Greek ecclesiastics were on the whole in favour of the encounter with the Latins and of union. That does not preclude the other motive of finding help for their fatherland, but neither does it allow that the political motive was the only one, or even necessarily the chief one, that moved them.

The letters of the western envoys from Basel, who had gone in 1435 to Constantinople to implement the agreement made between that Latin council and the Greeks, bear ample and eloquent witness to the desire for union. John of Ragusa especially describes the processions, prostrations and protracted prayers offered for that end by Patriarch and people, and he assured the council that had sent him of the good will and, indeed, enthusiasm of the Byzantine capital for the speedy and successful fulfilment of the decree *Sicut pia mater*.[1] Scholarius' letter to Pope Eugenius is sanguine of happy results and his letter to a scholar of his, if not optimistic, is hopeful.[2]

In the event the Orientals went to Ferrara in Italy and not to Basel. There things did not go as smoothly and quickly as they had hoped. First, there were long delays, mostly due to the

[1] CECCONI, doc. LXXVII.   [2] SCHOL., IV, pp. 414–5.

Emperor's desire to allow time for the envoys of the western princes to arrive, since he much wanted to meet them to obtain military aid for his Empire. The protracted delay produced difficulties for the Pope, for he was paying some 1700 florins a month for the maintenance of his guests and he soon was dependent on borrowing. His payments were, in consequence, irregular. The Greeks began to feel the insecurity of it, the lower-ranking clergy and court servants even the pinch of poverty. The discussions were long drawn out and the Latins had much more to say for themselves than the Greeks, surprisingly, had anticipated. Neither side would admit defeat. There was an atmosphere of stalemate, frustration and a growing nostalgia among the Greeks, especially when rumours reached Italy of dangers impending over Constantinople. When a year had passed after the solemn inauguration of the Council on 9 April 1438 with union apparently no nearer, the Greeks were almost in despair.

It was at this stage, when things seemed so bad that they could hardly have been worse, at the end of May 1439, that unity was achieved on the chief point of difference between the Churches. That was such a surprising and unexpected turn of events that one is tempted to conclude that the unity thus arrived at was not genuine, that on the side of the Greeks it was the result of the hardships they were enduring, in particular of their longing to be finished with it all and to return home to country and kin. Here, however, instinct is at fault. The documents, on which we must rely for the history of the Council, describe the various, though rapid, stages of this concord and show that it was sincere on the one side as on the other.

The point at issue was the Procession of the Holy Spirit, not as an addition to the Creed, but as a dogma. It was, then, a purely theological question, devoid of complications of prestige and authority in so far as it did not immediately implicate the further question of the primacy of Rome. It had been the subject of discussion during the eight sessions in Florence, five of which were largely wasted in squabbles about the genuine reading of a few texts. In the sixth session Mark of Ephesus had expounded at length the Greek arguments from Scripture, councils and Fathers in favour of his view—Procession from the Father only: in the seventh and eighth, John of Montenero had done a like service for the Latins.

These last three sessions had brought the argument to the domain where the greater part of the Greek ecclesiastics (and probably the greater part of the Latins too) could understand—the domain of patristics. The metaphysics of the Blessed Trinity, especially with the subtle differences of terminology and of outlook between Greeks and Latins confusing the issue further, were beyond the capabilities of most of the audience. The Greeks distrusted syllogistic reasoning, particulary in connection with 'Theologia', the knowledge of God. Montenero's arguments, therefore, in the first five sessions had probably done more harm than good to his cause, for they made his Greek hearers more suspicious of him. In the last two sessions, however, he showed a mastery of patristic learning. He quoted freely from Councils and from Latin Fathers venerated also in the Greek Church, and in particular from Greek Fathers, to show that these nowhere denied the Latin doctrine, but rather implied it by their less precise, more metaphorical phrases. He ended by asserting roundly that the Latins, like the Greeks, held that there is only one cause and principle in the Blessed Trinity and anathematised those who held two.

Montenero's words, of the latter part of the month of March 1439, did not bear immediate fruit, but were a seed. Bessarion, in his *Oratio dogmatica*, delivered before the Greeks probably in mid-April 1439, and Scholarius, with his Exhortation of about the same time, followed the same general lines as Montenero, the harmony of the Latin and the Greek Fathers. Again there was no immediate result. As a last resort to solve the deadlock, the Pope, Eugenius IV, addressed the Greeks and the Latins, exhorting, chiding, encouraging. His speech was the stimulus needed. The Greeks set themselves to new efforts, and the seed sown by Montenero, Bessarion, Scholarius and others began to bear fruit.

The soil in which the seed was set (if I may continue with the same metaphor) was an axiom, that saints cannot contradict each other about the faith, because they are all inspired by one and the same Holy Spirit. To say otherwise would be to assert that the Holy Spirit can contradict Himself. All the Greeks admitted this axiom. Bessarion, Isidore of Kiev, Dorotheus of Mitylene enunciated it. Scholarius stated it positively both in his Exhortation and his written judgement about the Procession of the Holy Spirit. George Amiroutzes included it no less in his written judgement. Mark of Ephesus, as much as the rest, granted its truth, but, when the axiom was applied to the question of the patristic evidence for the Procession of the Holy Spirit, he was in a quandary. Bessarion, Scholarius and others argued that, though Latin saints and Greek saints expressed themselves differently about the Procession, yet as saints they were inspired by the same Holy Spirit and must have said the same thing about the faith. Their expositions of doctrine, therefore, must have the same general content, though couched in different terms. In respect of the Holy Spirit the Latin saints assert that He proceeds from the Father and from the Son; the Greek saints, that He 'comes forth', 'issues forth', 'bursts forth', etc., 'from the Father' or 'from the Father through the Son' or 'from both' etc. Whatever the expression, the meaning is the same, more or less clearly expressed, and therefore the doctrine taught by the Latin Fathers and by the Greek Fathers is the same.

For the Greeks in the Council of Florence there was no refuting that reasoning. The axiom was universally admitted. Quotations from the Latin Fathers and the Greek Fathers had been provided in abundance by Montenero and Bessarion. Mark of Ephesus, to avoid the obvious conclusion, was reduced to having recourse to what Scholarius called 'the height of stupidity'. Unable to challenge the quotations made from the Greek Fathers, he was forced to assert that the Latin Saints could not have said what Montenero and his associates declared they had said—that is, he accused the Latins of falsifying their own Fathers, or, an even weaker defence, he refused to accept the quotations from the Latin Fathers because he personally, not knowing Latin, could not check their accuracy, though Scholarius and probably others, well versed in Latin, could have set his doubts at rest in a minute and probably did try to persuade him.

But Mark was in a minority. Because of his intransigence on that point, the first question to be settled among the Greeks was precisely the question of the genuinity of the quotations from the Latin Fathers. There was no argument against the genuinity except Mark's bare assertion, and it is an indication of his influence that the question was ever seriously raised. Mark himself, in his *Relatio de rebus a se gestis*, says that the majority was in favour of the genuinity. The *Description* (i.e. the addition to the protocol in the *Practica*) and the anti-unionist Syropoulus both say the same. The vote was taken on 28 May and, that point settled, Greek acceptance of the orthodoxy of the Latin doctrine of the Procession of the Holy Spirit was a foregone conclusion. The Latin saints said 'from': the Greek saints said 'through' and a variety of other expressions. Latin saints and Greek saints must declare the same doctrine, so that 'from' and 'through' in respect of the Procession of the Holy Spirit mean the same. There was no way of escaping the conclusion and only two or three of the Greeks tried to do so.

There are, in the different sources, different accounts about the voting on this point of the orthodoxy of the Latin doctrine about the Procession of the Holy Spirit, but the facts related in all of them are substantially the same. The *Description* narrates that ten prelates voted in favour and four against, and that later three more joined the 'Ayes'. Syropoulus puts six as voting against the Latin doctrine (one of whom was sick and did not vote at all) and thirteen in favour. Mark Eugenicus in his *Relatio* does not give numbers, but records that when he saw all those who before had supported him gone to the other side, he discreetly suppressed his written, negative judgement. Certainly at the signing of the decree on 5 July 1439, only two Greek prelates did not append their names, the indomitable Mark and Isaias of Stauropolis. Of the Greek Church in Italy the Patriarch, four out of five procurators of the other eastern Patriarchs, all the bishops but two, the five Staurophoroi (three of them, so says Syropoulus, only under pressure), and half a dozen superiors or representatives of monasteries signed the decree of union that was at the same time a statement of faith. The Emperor signed it also, and George Scholarius and George Amiroutzes, the 'philosopher' counsellors of the Emperor, gave written judgements in public approving the Latin doctrine. Syropoulus in his *Memoirs* does not mention this fact. Neither does he make any note of Gemistus's decision, so that one is inclined to conclude that Gemistus, who certainly would have recorded a vote, also was in favour of Latin orthodoxy on that occasion.

In view of the basic harmony of the documents and of the logical march of events, the only conclusion to be drawn is that at the end of May and the beginning of June the Greek bishops, with hardly an exception, were genuinely and freely in favour of accepting the orthodoxy of the Latin doctrine about the Procession of the Holy Spirit and did in fact freely accept it. A little more than a month later they all, with only two exceptions, signed their names to the dogmatic statement.

What, then, is to be said about the duress that their prolonged separation from home, their distressing financial condition, and their sense of frustration and waste of time certainly exercised upon them? It can without difficulty be admitted that it made them most desirous of returning home and ready to accept the first honourable solution that offered. But, in face of the documents on which our knowledge of the Council rests, it cannot be admitted that it took away their liberty and that it forced them to give approval of the Latin doctrine against their wills. Such a theory of yielding under coercion is disproved by the events of the months March to June 1439.

The public sessions on the Procession ended on 24 March with no union achieved. The Greeks asked for time to consider their answer and, after Easter, on being pressed for a reply, twice sent an ultimatum to the Pope: 'We will undergo no more public sessions, which are a waste of time. We have the seven councils with us. Do you find some other way out of the impasse, otherwise we go home.' There is no sign of fear or of cowering under the force of threats or circumstances. That situation continued till the end of May. Various expedients were tried to find a means that would lead to union. The Emperor addressed his subjects. Bessarion delivered his *Oratio*. Scholarius exhorted. Meetings were arranged between committees of ten from each aside. The Latins presented a concise and carefully worded theological statement about the Trinity and the Greeks returned an amended and imprecise version of it. Subsequently, harrangued by cardinals, they refused either to endure fresh public sessions or to clarify their theological statement. Urged by some cardinals in the name of the Pope, John VIII replied: 'We neither write nor say anything more, except that, if you accept what we have given you, we will unite; if not, we shall go home'.[3] That was on 21 May 1439.

In all this there is not the slightest sign that the Greeks were wilting, hesitating, yielding under pressure. On the contrary, they were consistently firm, even stubborn, in refusing to give way to the insistence of the Latins. The Latins wanted more sessions, as

---

[3] *A.G.*, p. 420.

union had not been achieved: the Greeks said, 'No', and stuck to it. The Latins then urged a clarification of their theological statement, several of whose phrases were designedly ambiguous: the Greeks would not, and did not, accede. Then the meaning and application of the axiom about the saints came home to them, and they were relieved to find that the long-hoped for key to union had been discovered.

It is said that Greek freedom was impaired in another way, that they were not allowed to say what they wanted. The *Greek Acts* (which are the official Greek protocol compiled by Greeks) show conclusively that in the public sessions the visitors enjoyed equal rights with the Latins, so that in the public business of the Council their liberty was not curtailed by any action of the Latins. But Syropoulus asserts that the Emperor restrained free expression of views among themselves, because he was determined to bring about union of the Churches as a means to gaining western help for his Empire.

The best comment on this accusation is the history of Mark Eugenicus. Mark was the only consistent and noteworthy opponent of union among the Greeks. From his first contact with the Latins, his panegyric to the Pope, to his refusal to sign the decree, he was openly and eloquently the adversary of union. Yet he was the speaker for the Greeks in all but one of the private sessions on Purgatory, in all but two of the public sessions in Ferrara on the addition of the *Filioque*, and in all without exception of the public sessions in Florence. He declared his mind freely in the subsequent private meetings of the Greeks and he asked and received imperial protection when he feared that reprisals might be taken against him for refusing to sign the decree. If John VIII, who after all was Emperor and a Byzantine Emperor, was as determined as Syropoulus suggests to have union at any cost, he would have replaced Eugenicus by Bessarion or Isidore, who were both good theologians and, at any rate by the end, sincere upholders of union. That the Emperor allowed Mark, the only serious threat to the union, to continue as public orator and private speaker to the very end disposes of any accusation that he stifled freedom of speech.

By 8 June, then, real concord had been reached on what was the chief difference between the Churches, the doctrine of the Procession of the Holy Spirit. The Patriarch, by then a very sick man, would have been satisfied with that. He wanted the agreement to be proclaimed in solemn session and the council closed. But the Latins insisted on agreement also over the other controverted points. Between 11 June and the end of the month, these were considered, in public session and out of it, and formulas acceptable to both sides were found. We know little in detail about the process, but it followed the pattern adopted by the Latins for the question of the Procession. A very carefully and precisely worded Latin formula was presented; it was discussed and perhaps amended, and then became the mutually accepted formula, ultimately incorporated into the decree. To dispose of Purgatory, the Eucharist, the primacy and the question of the addition of the *Filioque* to the Creed in three weeks, after a year of haggling, seems incredible and a *prima facie* proof that the Greeks had given up struggling and would admit anything at all so as to get home. But it should be borne in mind that, once they had admitted the orthodoxy of that 'rock of offence', the Latin doctrine on the Procession of the Holy Spirit, the ice was, so to speak, broken. They must have been more receptive of the idea that the Latins could be right also on other points and they had no longer to bring themselves to a first recognition that they had misjudged the Latin faith. Besides, on Purgatory, Greek doctrine was altogether vague and fluid. The main point of controversy with the Latins in the discussions in Ferrara had been about the punishment of fire, and nothing on that was included in the decree. Similarly, about the Holy Eucharist, the definition was restricted to the uncontroversial points of matter, minister and rite: the necessity or not of the *epiclesis* was not mentioned. The question of the primacy caused more trouble but, though the decree and the exposition of it given by Montenero in public session were uncompromising about the Pope's position (as one might have expected in view of the opposition of the 'Council of Basel'), the difficulties against the formula raised by the Greeks in the second public session touched mainly one point, the question of appeal to Rome from a decision of a patriarch, and the jejune account of the *Description* records the gradual Greek softening on that point. Acknowledgement of the legitimacy of the Latin addition of the *Filioque* to the Creed 'for the sake of making the truth better known and under the spur of necessity' was added presumably because the Greeks, having agreed on so much, could hardly refuse that

262

last *amende honorable*. So all things considered the mutual acceptance of the common formula of faith on the points of controversy
within so short a time, though admittedly surprising, is not quite
so astounding as at first sight appears.

The decree was signed on 5 July and promulgated on 6 July.
The Greeks reached Constantinople on their return on 1 February
1440 and had already, according to Syropoulus, Ducas and others,
begun to repent of their acceptance of union. That was not true
of all of them. At least eight of the prelates[4] with Gregory the
Confessor and the monk Pachomius, remained ever faithful to the
union; perhaps even others. The defection of the rest can easily
be explained without accusing them of either cowardice or
duplicity. In Florence they had come to a point of great boredom
and depression when an argument in favour of Latin orthodoxy
was put before them and pressed home, an argument which, on
their own accepted principles, was really unanswerable. A wave of
enthusiasm and rejoicing swept over them, for this meant release
and return, with the truth not betrayed. Mark of Ephesus,
however, stood out. However illogically, he refused to change
from the opinion he had always had and that they too hitherto had
had. His intractability was a challenge and a mute accusation of
treachery to their traditional faith. Though their heads were
convinced at least temporarily of Latin orthodoxy, they felt
unhappy about it. Sentimentally they could not rid themselves
of a feeling of instability and disloyalty, and that perhaps the
ascetic Eugenicus was right. When, then, the atmosphere of
Florence that favoured rapprochement changed to the hostile
atmosphere of Constantinople, intellect yielded to sentiment and
those who needed to be led in Italy followed the lead again in their
homeland, only this time it led the other way. They were not men
of strong intellect or strong character, but average men placed in
very difficult circumstances.

To say otherwise is to judge that a large proportion of the
metropolitans of the Greek Church was so lacking in moral
stamina, that in the face of moderate hardship they accepted what
was to them heresy, and that out of them all one alone, Mark
Eugenicus, was found with sufficient moral courage and spiritual
hope to be ready to face the consequences of fidelity to his Church.

[4] Bessarion, Isidore, Dorotheus of Mitylene, Cyzicus, Lacedaemon, Rhodes,
Moldo-Wallachia, Monembasia.

I do not think that that was the case. What documents we have show clearly enough that, on the question of the Procession of the Holy Spirit, the Greek prelates joyfully, freely and honestly admitted Latin orthodoxy, and that on the other questions, where documentation is scarce, there is nothing to indicate dishonesty on their part.

XVII

THE DEFINITION OF THE PRIMACY OF THE POPE
IN THE COUNCIL OF FLORENCE

The ecclesiastical question of first importance in the first half of the fifteenth century was undoubtedly the position of the Pope within the Church. But it was primarily a Latin question, because first the residence of the popes in Avignon and then, and to a much greater degree, the Great Schism of the West had brought Conciliarism into being, which was a theory (also put into practice) that declared nothing less than that, by the ordinance of God Himself, the highest authority in the Church was a general council and that a pope was merely the council's chief executive officer. The principle of the superiority of a council, and so of the inferiority of a pope, was first officially enunciated in the Council of Constance (6th April, 1415). It reached the climax both of its success and of its vociferous publicity in the Council of Basel. It received its *coup de grâce* in the Council of Florence in that part of the decree of union with the Greeks—an infallible document—which treats of the papacy:

Item diffinimus sanctam apostolicam sedem et Romanum pontificem in universum orbem tenere primatum, et ipsum pontificem Romanum successorem esse beati Petri principis apostolorum et verum Christi vicarium totiusque ecclesie caput et omnium christianorum patrem et doctorem existere, et ipsi in beato Petro pascendi, regendi ac gubernandi universalem ecclesiam a domino nostro Iesu Christo plenam potestatem traditam esse, quemadmodum etiam in gestis ycumenicorum conciliorum et in sacris canonibus continetur.

Also in the same way we define that the holy, apostolic See and the Roman Pontiff holds the primacy over the whole world and that the Roman Pontiff himself is the successor of blessed Peter prince of the Apostles, and that he is the true Vicar of Christ, head of the whole Church and father and teacher of all Christians, and that to the same in blessed Peter was given plenary power of feeding, ruling and governing the whole Church, as is contained also in the Acts of the oecumenical councils and the sacred canons.

In formulating that decree the Latins in Florence had their eye as much on the rump-council of Basel as on the Greeks, for Basel at that moment was still carrying on relentless war against Pope Eugenius and had just declared him contumacious and deposed. One may doubt if there would have been quite so much detail in this part of the Florentine decree, if only the Greeks had been envisaged. Not that that makes any present difference about its import also for the Greeks. The position of the Pope there defined is thus defined for Latins and Greeks, no matter who it was that was being chiefly considered.

Whatever the Greeks of today may think, the Greeks in the Council of Florence did not consider the primacy of the Pope as the difference between the churches of the greatest theological importance. That for them was the question of the Procession of the Holy Spirit. Given the choice of subject for the doctrinal debates, they chose to discuss in Ferrara the legitimacy of the addition of the *Filioque* to the Creed. In Florence, after the transfer of the Council, all the public sessions (March 1439) were about the doctrine of the Procession. In 1444–45 the anti-unionists in Constantinople had the opportunity of debating with a Latin theologian in fifteen public conferences: the subject throughout was the Procession. Again in 1449 similar public discussions in Constantinople revolved again about only the Procession. The argument must have continued there, because Pope Nicolas V replied on 12th, April 1450, to Bartolomeo Lapacci, O.P., Bishop of Cortona (the Latin speaker, incidentally, in both sets of conferences mentioned above), to resolve doubts put to him about the decree of Florence, but not about all of it, only about the definition of the Procession. Almost at the same time, or perhaps in 1448, Isidore of Kiev, newly returned from Greece, made a report for the Pope on the reception of the union in the East and on the best means to promote it—to send good preachers who would with arguments drawn from the Fathers, and especially from the Greek Fathers, explain the Procession; and he himself wrote a short treatise on those lines. Finally (lest it be thought that the absorbing interest in the Procession after the Council was due only to the fact that it had been the chief topic of debate in the Council) Syropoulus, who wrote *Memoirs* of the Council, that give much interesting detail not recorded elsewhere, recounts an illuminating event of May 1438, before any public session at all had been held.

The Emperor John VIII had stipulated for a wait of four months between the solemn inauguration of the Council on 9th April, 1438, and any discussion about 'doctrine'. After a time it was decided to hold some conversations between committees of ten a side. Cardinal Cesarini enumerated as 'the more important and the greater differences between the Churches, the Procession, the use of leavened and unleavened bread, Purgatory, the primacy of the Pope'. The Emperor insisted on the observance of the condition that had been mutually agreed on, and so the Procession was ruled out; since the question of leavened and unleavened bread 'seems to be a very big difference', that too had to be deferred; 'but about Purgatory and about the primacy of the pope let them propound whichever they prefer from these two, and we will hear them and reply'.[1] The Latins chose Purgatory, which was discussed on and off for about two months.

All the same the question of the primacy of the Pope, even if it was not the biggest of the obstacles to union between the churches, was one of the obstacles to union. The Greeks did not accept the supremacy of Rome in the Church. They believed in the theory of the Pentarchy, that the five patriarchates of Rome, Constantinople, Alexandria, Antioch and Jerusalem were all substantially equal, even if in practice Rome had a predominance in the West and Constantinople in the East. They resented that Rome did not abide by that equality but had arrogated to itself a supremacy over the rest, which it tried to impose on them. Mark Eugenicus, the Metropolitan of Ephesus, in his speech in the first dogmatic session in Ferrara (8th October 1438) formulated the Greek accusation:

> The Roman Church disregarded and lightly valued one of these, the love, I mean, that it ought to have shown towards its sister Church of the East; for it sanctioned and put forward on its own account a dogma that is neither expressly found in the Holy Scriptures, nor acknowledged by the oecumenical councils, nor approved by the more eminent among our Fathers.[2]

The Greek case against the legitimacy of the addition of the *Filioque* to the Creed, as put forward in Ferrara, rested on the prohibition of the Council of Ephesus, but it was always coloured by the attitude to Rome. Bessarion expressed this concisely:

[1] SYR., pp. 123–4.   [2] *A.G.*, p. 52.

About the authority of the Western Church much could be said, if we had not another subject at present under discussion. We are, indeed, not ignorant of the rights and privileges of the Roman Church; but we know too the limits set to these privileges. We wish your Reverence to know that we withhold this permission from every Church and synod, even oecumenical, and not from the Roman Church alone, since no matter how great is the Roman Church, it is notwithstanding less than an oecumenical synod and the universal Church: and we withhold it from the whole Church, much more so then from the Roman Church do we withhold it. But we withhold it not as by ourselves, but we consider that this had been forbidden by the decrees of the Fathers.[3]

Aloysius of Perano, O.F.M., who spoke after Bessarion, vindicated for 'the Church and its head who enjoys every power and right over the universal Church' the right of modifying the Creed if circumstances demanded; and Cardinal Cesarini, arguing with Mark Eugenicus, several times alluded to the same authority so that Mark in the end proposed that the question be discussed at length and disposed of in the next session ('for we have many, forceful arguments in support of our right'),[4] but Cesarini preferred to finish with the one topic of the addition first, before embarking on another.

As things turned out, it was some considerable time before the formal discussions about the primacy began, because the doctrine of the *Filioque* occupied the minds of the Council till 8th June, 1439. No sooner, however, was the subject settled than Pope Eugenius, somewhat to the discomfiture of the Greeks, who had thought that they could consider the Council over and that they could go home, began to press them to bring the other points of difference to a harmonious conclusion, and he instanced as still outstanding differences the primacy, Purgatory, the Eucharist and the question of the divine essence and operation, i.e. Palamism. The four Greek metropolitans to whom he was talking replied:'As regards the primacy of the pope, at any rate, it was arranged in this way, that he should have whatever privileges he had from the beginning and before the schism'. Two days later (10th June, 1439), again in conversation with the Pope, they answered:

[3] Ibid., p. 159.   [4] Ibid., p. 211.

We say that the first point is most wicked, for how may we affirm that the Roman Church has the power of adding or taking away without its brother patriarchs? So, though what was added is orthodox, all the same he who dared to do it without conciliar approval will not be accounted guiltless. But, if you wish, admit that you acted wrongly and agree not to do it again, and so you will gain pardon. . . .[5]

—they were not answering officially when they said this, but were offering their comments 'as friends'. This time, however, it must have been the Pope who was disconcerted, for their comments 'as friends', not put forward to plead any cause but expressing the inmost conviction of four of the most convinced unionists among the Greeks, showed the degree to which the theory of the Pentarchy was taken for granted. Again on 12th June the Pope urged the settlement of the remaining differences, and the next day the Greeks decided to discuss with the Latins in public session the questions of the primacy, the Eucharist and the addition.[6]

The Latin method of reaching union, at least in the months that followed after the dogmatic sessions of March 1439, had been to prepare a carefully worded theological statement, a *cedula*, about each of the theological differences and to present it to the Greeks for their consideration. The queries and objections that arose were then discussed either informally or formally or both, in public session or in committee. This method was followed duly in the case of the primacy, though quite when the *cedula* about it was delivered to the Greeks is not clear. At any rate, by the time that the Greek decision to discuss this problem synodically was put into practice on June 16th, the Greeks already had it, for the Latin orator, John of Montenero, O.P., contented himself with taking the *cedula* and explaining and proving each of its phrases.

The *Description* does not mention any *cedula* on this subject, and about Montenero's speech it gives nothing more than the bare information that he spoke. The *Latin Acts* fortunately give both what purports to be the very *cedula* and a full synopsis of Montenero's speech.[7] But if the formula given as the *cedula* is compared with the phrases explained by Montenero, differences appear. It would seem that the text that Andrea of Santacroce gives in the *Latin Acts* is the text as it emerged with certain emendations from

[5] Ibid., p. 443.   [6] *A.G.*, p. 447; *A.L.*, p. 231.
[7] *A.L.*, pp. 231–6.

the discussion, and this conclusion is confirmed by comparing it with the decree of union, which is nothing else than the catena of the *cedulae* prefaced by an introduction. The text originally offered to the Greeks can easily be reconstructed from the Latin orator's explanation. It read as follows:

Also in the same way we define that the holy, apostolic and Roman Pontiff is the successor of Peter and Vicar of Jesus Christ, head of the whole Church and father of all Christians, our teacher too, and that he holds the primacy over the whole world, and that to the same See and Roman Pontiff in St. Peter, the Prince of the Apostles, there was given plenary power of feeding, convening, ruling and governing the whole Church.

Montenero drew his proofs from the Holy Scriptures and the councils with a few quotations from the Fathers. Very briefly they were as follows. *Successor of Peter:* Pope Adrian's letter to Constantine and Irene (VII Council, II actio; *Mansi* XII, 1057 CD). *Head of the whole Church:* Adrian's letter to Tarasius (*Mansi* XII, 1081E; PL96, 1240A); Council of Chalcedon (*Mansi* VI, 579D, 147A–D, 154C). *Father of all Christians:* the same Council (*Mansi* VII, 106C); St. John Chrysostom (PG 59, 480); the synodical letter of Pope Agatho to the VI Council (*Mansi* XI, 242D). *Teacher:* the letter of the pseudo-Athanasius to Pope Felix (PG 28, 1475A). *He holds the primacy over the whole world:* Adrian's second letter to Tarasius (*Mansi* XII, 1081E); the decretal letter of the pseudo-Anacletus quoting: 'Thou art Peter', etc. (PG 2, 813B); the letter of the pseudo-Julius to the oriental bishops (PG 28, 1452B). *Feeding:* Jn 21:17; Adrian to Tarasius (*Mansi* XII, 1081B); Agatho's letter to Constantinople quoting Lk 22:31-2 (*Mansi* XI, 239DE). *Convening:* the Council of Chalcedon to Pope Leo (*Mansi* VI, 150B). *Ruling:* words from the pseudo-Anacletus (PG 2, 815A); a sermon of Leo I (PL 54, 149C–150A). *Governing:* the same sermon of Leo I (PL 54, 145C–146A). *Plenary power:* Mt. 16:19; Jn 21:17; Leo's words commenting on these texts (PL 54, 146BC). Cardinal Cesarini added that oecumenical councils, which included Orientals, had approved the letters of Popes Adrian and Agatho.

This skeleton of Montenero's speech will give an idea of his line of argument, a line suited to the patristic preferences of the Greeks that, so it would seem, achieved its object in persuading many of them. At any rate, the *Description* reports that after it they went to the Emperor's residence 'and examined the demands of the Latins and found that they were five and all of them just and good'. Whereupon they pressed the Emperor to concur: 'We accept them all; let there be an end of the business. . , . But he would not'.[8] The *Memoirs* of Syropoulus, the third chief source for information on the Council, are very confused about this period, recounting episodes and remarks haphazard, and stressing the disagreement (everything is disagreement in Syropoulus) of Latins and Greeks about the *epiclesis*-question, in particular between the Emperor and Cesarini, and the convocation of general councils, almost to the exclusion of everything else.[9] The *Latin Acts* record that, on the day following this first explanation, Cardinals Capranica and Condulmaro with a number of theologians visited the Emperor apropos of the expositions of Latin doctrine about the primacy and the Eucharist that John of Montenero, O.P., and John of Torquemada, O.P., had made the previous day. In the discussion that ensued the Emperor, both personally and by the mouth of Bessarion, made several objections to the teaching and perhaps some positive suggestions. The upshot was that on Thursday, 18th June, there was another public session when Montenero and Torquemada replied to the objections made and clarified the Latin doctrine further. This second speech of Montenero about the primacy is of particular interest, as from it we can gather the nature of the difficulties that his first exposition had aroused in the minds of the Greeks.[10]

Before tackling the specific objections that had been urged against the Latin *cedula*, Montenero wished first to dispose of a general difficulty that clearly had been aired at length by Bessarion. The Greek had suggested that the three conciliar letters that Montenero had made so much of in his first discourse were no sure foundation for dogma, for the effusive approvals they contained were probably the expression more of oriental politeness than of interior conviction, and he had demanded a basis of proof taken from the canons of councils. Montenero replied that the letters of Chalcedon to Leo and of Popes Adrian and Agatho to the councils were synodical letters, i.e. letters approved by the councils. The definitions and canons of councils are the result of study of the writings of the Fathers and the letters quoted in the

[8] *A.G.*, p. 450. [9] Syr., pp. 277–81. [10] *A.L.*, pp. 240–7.

councils, which therefore have at least equal authority with the canons. Agatho, for instance, imposed his letter on the sixth Council (*Mansi* XI, 235E), that is, imposed the decision of a Roman synod, and the Council obeyed (*Mansi* XI, 666CD). The Fathers recognized the authority of papal letters; St. Augustine, for instance, put them among the catholic scriptures (PL 34, 40D).

After this justification of his method, the Dominican orator approached the first objection, which had been proposed by the Emperor apropos of the phrase: *Successor of Peter and vicar of Christ and father and teacher of all Christians.* Bessarion in the Emperor's name had asked if this meant 'a certain reverence' as first among all the patriarchs, or something more. Montenero replied: 'Not only reverence, but a certain power of a certain obedience' and proceeded to prove, first that St. Peter was 'head' with the implication that 'head' meant also power, and then to inquire what that power was in the case of St. Peter and his successors. 'Feed my sheep' (Jn 21:17) shows that Peter was head with authority, and Chrysostom's commentary (PG 59, 478) and the *allocutio* of the Council of Chalcedon to the Emperor Marcian (*Mansi* VII, 455C) leave no doubt as to the fact. All the Fathers, e.g. Leo I in sermon 73 (PL 54, 395B), agree. Agatho quoted the testimony of the Byzantine Emperor Justinian I (*Mansi* XI, 270CD), who among other things had called the Roman Pontiff 'head of all the Churches'.[11] What then is the 'power' of this 'head'?

Hence this power, which is in Peter and his successors, is called a power of spiritual jurisdiction, which is directed to the salvation of the souls of all Christians, so that by means of this power the sacraments may be administered duly to the faithful, and in respect of this power all, whether clerical or lay, are subject—laymen in what concerns the salvation of their souls, e.g. if they have committed mortal sin, it belongs chiefly to the spiritual shepherd to correct them and bring them back, as a father, and so if they should act against the faith, like some of the emperors who were heretics and persecuted metropolitans, and there was need to have recourse to the apostolic See, and in similar cases, since the aim of the apostolic See is the peace of the ecclesiastical order, so that by this peace it may arrive at heavenly glory.

[11] *Corpus Iuris Civilis*, vol. II, *Codex Iustiniani*, ed. P. KRUEGER, p. 11.

272

For this reason Christ said: ' To thee I will give the keys' and made him shepherd, to lead the sheep to the pastures of the heavenly life, and all councils are full of examples of this kind.

Athanasius, Chrysostom, Flavian had recourse to popes as heads of the Church, and this without prejudice to the authority of emperors which is over civil and temporal affairs, whereas papal authority is over things spiritual. The ecclesiastical and civil powers are likened to the sun and the moon, the sun meaning the spiritual which is the more sublime, the moon the temporal.

The next objection proposed by the Emperor was about the power of convoking synods. Montenero repeated the testimony of Chalcedon to Leo I 'who had hastened to unite together the body of Christ' (*Mansi* VI, 150B) and added another from the supposed letter of Pope Julius to the Orientals (PG 28, 1452A), arguing from these that the Pope's authority to feed the flock inevitably involved the power to bring the flock together to be fed.

> And these convocations are not made except in times of the greatest need for the whole Church, as when great heresies arise, since it is the business of the pope, who has authority over the [whole] earth and over the Church, and the other patriarchs not so, except over only a certain area.

Two difficulties (he said) have been raised, the first in respect of emperors, the second as regards other patriarchs on the supposition that the Church is founded on five patriarchs. To the first difficulty he replied 'that though emperors brought the councils together, since they had the sole power of dominion, this we say they did, putting that into execution which had the consent and authority of the pope', and he instanced the action and words of Pope Leo both before and after Chalcedon (PL 54, 899AB; 1029AB). About the second difficulty 'as regards the other patriarchs, I never read in any book or council that the government of the Church is in three or five patriarchs', but the Church must have the best government by Christ's ordinance, viz. the monarchical, as He put the power in one apostle, not in four or five. Then quoting and paraphrasing the decretals of the pseudo-Anacletus he referred to the history of patriarchates—Alexandria instituted by St. Peter and held by Peter's disciple, Mark; Antioch, Peter's first See: later Constantinople and Jerusalem were introduced but, in reverence to the canons of Nicaea, Rome did not acknowledge them till Pope Leo consented, and later Justinian embodied the new dignities in a law, so that by ancient right even Constantinople (like Alexandria and Antioch) is the daughter of Rome, which is 'the origin of the laws, the culmination of the high priesthood and the source of priesthood' as Justinian wrote.[12]

It was then asked by my lord of Nicaea whether this power, which is given to the head, is such as is given to a metropolitan in his province or a patriarch in his patriarchate. I reply that it is not such, because the powers of the metropolitan churches [and] of patriarchs are limited to certain areas, in such a way that one patriarch has no power in the territory of another and *vice versa*. But the successor of Peter has the immediate power of a superior over all, but he has it so that all may be done with order, as when cases of greater importance and difficulty arise . . . recourse can always be had to the apostolic See, and doctrine, decision and judgement obtained. . . .[13]

Leo (PL 54, 671B), the pseudo-Anacletus and the pseudo-Clement lend their corroboration.

When Montenero ended, a Greek commented: 'No one among us denies that without the authority of the Roman Pontiff a council cannot be summoned; but on the other hand the Pope cannot do it without the patriarchs.' Cesarini retorted: 'And if others deny that in their canons, will it then be convoked if the Pope so orders?' The Greek replied: 'On that ground they could not stop it from being a council.' The Cardinal: 'And without the Pope there will be no council. . . . Have you not got the Donation of Constantine which he made to Sylvester?' Whereupon the Donation was read out and with that Torquemada took Montenero's place to speak again about the Eucharist.

The history of the agreement must be continued from the *Description* for it gives the chronology of the progress made, even if it adds little detail to the story.[14] Friday, 19 June, was passed studying the 'books' (presumably the Acts of the councils) and Saturday, after a meeting with the Emperor, was passed in the same pursuit, but without result. On Sunday morning

we wrote and approved of the privileges of the Pope, save two: he should not convene an oecumenical council without

---

[12] Ibid., vol. III, *Novellae*, ed. R. Schoell and G. Kroll, Nov. CXXXI.
[13] *A.L.*, p. 247.   [14] *A.G.*, p. 451 seq.

the Emperor and the patriarchs, if they would come; but if they are informed and will not come, the synod should not be held over for that reason: and secondly, if someone should consider himself unjustly treated by one of the patriarchs and should come lodging an appeal, the patriarchs should not come answering and being judged, but the Pope should send examiners to the spot and there, where the business is, give justice locally to the injured.

The Emperor took this decision to the Pope on Sunday evening, who deferred his answer till Monday, 22 June, so as to have time to consult his synod.

The Pope's reply was taken to the Greeks by three cardinals. He insisted on all papal privileges without limitation. The Emperor was in despair and bade the cardinals have ships made ready for the Greeks' departure. Tuesday passed without any contact between the churches. Wednesday was a great day in Florence, for it was 24 June, the feast of St. John the Baptist. Isidore of Kiev, Bessarion, Dorotheus of Mytilene and others urged both Pope and Emperor not to give up, with the result that a meeting of six delegates from each side was arranged for Friday, 26 June. Details of that meeting are lacking, but on the evening of the same day the Greeks agreed upon another formula, which they wrote and sent to Eugenius:

About the primacy of the Pope, we profess that he is supreme Pontiff and representative and guardian and vicar of Christ, shepherd and teacher of all Christians, that he directs and governs the Church of God, without prejudice to the privileges and rights of the patriarchs of the East, he of Constantinople being second after the Pope, then the Alexandrine, and after him the one of Antioch, then the one of Jerusalem.

That was really an acceptance of the Latin *cedula* with the addition of the order of the Patriarchates. However the account continues: 'When we had written this we determined neither to write nor to do anything else, but if this should not be accepted by the Pope, nothing further would be done. And having sent it on the evening of Friday we learnt that he had received it with pleasure and then we were relieved'.

Cesarini in a speech before the Latin synod, convoked on 27 June to approve the various *cedulae* before they were incorporated into the definitive decree, recounted briefly the history of the negotiations with the Greeks. Apropos of the primacy he said:

> The last difference was about the primacy and this seemed to surpass human possibilities, because subjects stray from their head, and in point of fact till now they have not been well disposed about the power of the Roman Pontiff, saying that he was like the head of some one entity, like a dean. And after an exposition of the Holy Scriptures and the sacred councils, the truth appeared, that the apostolic See and the Roman Pontiff is the successor of St. Peter; then by the disposition of the divine goodness it was brought about that the Greeks agreed to the *cedula* presented by the Latins. Finally they said that we should make some deliberation about the patriarchal Sees, viz., that Constantinople should be second, etc., as had been determined in the constitutions of the councils and, in the Lateran Council when Alexander III presided, he renewed the privileges of the patriarchal Sees.[15']

The phrase in the Bull, therefore, about the order of the patriarchal Sees was inserted at the instance of the Greeks, and the omission from it of *convocandi* (which Cesarini forgot to mention) was presumably in deference to the Emperor's strong objection.

The Latins approved. Twelve representatives from each Church met to formulate the decree, and all seemed about to end peacefully. But there were more difficulties yet in store. The decree was drawn up in the Pope's name only, without mention of the Greek Emperor and the Greek Church. John VIII objected strongly. Also the section of the decree that treated of the primacy ended that to the Pope 'in Blessed Peter full power was given by our Lord, Jesus Christ, of feeding, ruling and guiding the universal Church, *as is contained also in the sacred Scriptures and the words of the saints*'. These last words probably had not been in the original *cedula*. At least they did not figure in Montenero's first speech when he explained the *cedula* phrase by phrase. In his second speech he had preluded his replies to the objections raised by the Emperor by disposing of a fundamental difficulty, which was precisely what is contained in this phrase, and so it seems most likely that the Latins, having once found the Greeks rather hesitant on this point, added it to the *cedula* without further

---

[15] *A.L.*, p. 255.

consultation, as being, after Montenero's exposition, mutually acceptable, and then automatically included it in the decree.

Montenero's explanation, however, had not dispelled the Emperor's prejudices, and he still objected that 'if any one of the saints shows respect to the Pope in a letter, is he to take this as a privilege?' Eugenius sent cardinals. They agreed without much difficulty to add in the preamble of the decree 'with the assent of . . . John Palaeologus, Emperor of the Greeks . . . and the others representing the Oriental Church', but they stood out for retaining the offending phrase about the primacy. The Emperor was equally determined. The cardinals with his permission addressed the Greek synod which, so reports the *Description*, took common counsel and wrote: 'that the Pope should have his privileges in accordance with the canons, and the words of the saints, and the Holy Scriptures and the Acts of the councils'. The *Description* is here clearly wrong, for according to it the Greek prelates conceded what the cardinals were demanding, with the addition of two more sources—the canons and the Acts of the councils. It must have been these last two, and not the 'Holy Scriptures and the words of the saints', that they were insisting on, because the Bull of union reads: 'as is contained in the Acts of the oecumenical councils and the sacred canons', and it is inconceivable that the Latins, if they had been given what they were demanding with so much persistence, would then have declined to avail themselves of the concession.

The solution of the difficulty may be hidden in the next paragraph of the *Description*: 'Next day, Wednesday, the cardinals went to the Emperor and said to him: "The Holy Father has received the two documents and has bidden us choose one out of the two. So let the statement be read and examined so that a final decision may be given to the question"'. What happened, perhaps, was that the Greeks offered two variations of the phrase in dispute and that the Latins, really wanting neither of the forms presented, chose the less objectionable, the one later inserted into the decree, 'as is contained in the Acts of the oecumenical councils and the sacred canons'. In this, then, the Pope gave way to Greek opinion.

The result, of course, was that the decree had to be engrossed afresh. That was done on Thursday, 2 July, and the parchment was taken to the Pope and the Emperor for inspection and approval. It was the Pope's turn this time to object. By mistake the word 'all', not in the *cedula*, had been inserted in the Greek text before 'privileges and rights' of the oriental patriarchs. Eugenius was for having it deleted. Presumably the Emperor refused, for it is still to be found in the final decree, which is the result of another rewriting, on Saturday, 4 July, to include *omnibus* in the Latin text, since both texts had to correspond exactly. That was the end of the alarums and excursions. The decree was signed by Latins and Greeks on 5 July and promulgated in both languages on 6 July.[16]

Two reflections come to the mind after studying the history of the primacy-debate in Florence. The first is that the Latins did not put before the Greeks a minimalist, but rather a maximalist, interpretation of the primacy. Montenero was almost brutally frank—'not reverence, but a certain authority of a certain obedience'; Peter was head and that meant authority; the Pope is successor of Peter and head with a like authority; it is a 'spiritual jurisdiction'; the pope convokes synods and the emperor (even a Byzantine emperor) executes; 'I have never read that the government is in three or five patriarchs' but in one; the Pope is not like a metropolitan with a limited power 'but the successor of Peter has the immediate power of a superior over all'. The Pope was no less uncompromising. When the question could have been settled by his accepting the relatively small limitations to his prerogatives in respect of the convocation of general councils and the exercise of his rights as court of appeal, though he must have been strongly tempted to yield so as to bring the discussion to an end, an action that would at once have gratified the Greeks and have assured

---

[16] The decree of union also declares: 'We also define that the explanation of the words *Filioque*, for the sake of clarifying the truth and under the impulse of necessity at the time, was licitly and reasonably added to the Creed.' How the metropolitans, who, speaking 'as friends', had earlier condemned the addition wholesale, came to accept this cannot be said for lack of documents. The *Description* says no word on this point. The *Latin Acts* give a *cedula*, in the words of the decree, and Cesarini's remarks in his recapitulation of negotiations, which do not really add very much light either: 'Then, when this subject was settled, the next came up, because ever since the subject of the addition was moved, it seemed right to define synodically that the addition was licit; and in this there was great difficulty, which four hours would scarcely suffice to narrate. Finally it was agreed to profess that that addition was justly and rightly made' (pp. 230, 254). The illegitimacy of the addition obviously died hard, and one may be justified in thinking that the Greeks consented because, once they had accepted papal primacy in the words of the *cedula*, they could less easily refuse the addition, but that it went sadly against the grain to break with their traditional attitude towards it—and, with the agreement of the Latins, they did not insert it into their Creed.

278

him of the union of the Church which was his chief boast against the Council of Basel that was still hanging on and about to elect an anti-pope, he refused that easy way out and instead threw everything back into the melting-pot by insisting on all or nothing. The Greeks, therefore, were left in no doubt as to what papal primacy meant. There was no deception, no ambiguity, no understatement. When in the first place by their various written answers, they agreed as a Greek synod to the Latin *cedula* on the primacy and its explanations, and then when they signed the decree, they were accepting something whose terms were plain.

But (and this is the second reflection) they brought a Greek and not a Latin mentality to their appreciation of the question. For the Latins (as has been said) the great question of Church polity was the position of the Pope within the Church, which for them was coterminous with what the Greeks called the Western patriarchate.[17] The Greek difficulty was with the position of the Western patriarchate itself, the Latin Church, whose patriarch was the Pope, within the whole Church, composed, in their view, of the five patriarchates. When they spoke of the *Filioque* and the right (or not) of introducing it into the Creed, they blamed 'the Roman Church' (also perhaps because no one was quite clear as to which pope was responsible). So Mark of Ephesus in his speech in the first dogmatic session and later when arguing with Cesarini; so Bessarion denying to the Roman Church what he denied to the universal Church. Even after agreeing with the Latins about the Procession, the four Greek prelates, speaking 'as friends', could tell the Pope: 'How can we say that the Church of Rome had the power of adding or subtracting without its brother patriarchs?'; and a few days later: 'We will never accept [the addition].' Later the difficulties raised by the Emperor and Bessarion against the Latin *cedula* all reflected the same preoccupation with the position

---

[17] That is, the relations between Pope and general council. An illuminating side-light on the primacy-definition in the decree of union is given by some words contained in a speech to demolish the pretensions of Basel, delivered months after the promulgation of the definition about the primacy by John of Torquemada in the presence of the Pope: 'If indeed the case should occur that the totality of the Fathers meeting in a universal synod should unanimously make some definition of faith and that the person of the Pope alone should contradict it, I should say, in my judgement, that one should stand by the synod and not the person of the pope. For the judgement of so many Fathers of a universal synod in a matter of faith seems rightly to be preferred to the judgement of a single man' (JOANNES DE TORQUEMADA, O.P., *Oratio synodalis de primatu*, ed. E. CANDAL, (Rome, 1954), p. 58).

of the other patriarchates in relation to the Roman Church—the Pope a *primus inter pares?* the power of convoking councils independently of emperor and the other patriarchs? papal power like that of a metropolitan or a patriarch? Greek hesitation after Montenero's speeches to accept the Latin claims stemmed from the same cause—reserve with regard to the convocation of councils without emperor or patriarchs; reserve in respect of appeals to Rome; later insistence on a clause to safeguard in some way the 'privileges and rights' of the other patriarchs, which was added to the *cedula*; the Emperor's demand for mention of the Greek Church in the Bull of union; and the limitation of the grounds of papal prerogatives to councils and canons of the councils; finally the intrusion of the word 'all' before 'privileges and rights' of the patriarchs.

This attitude of thinking almost exclusively in terms of the 'Roman Church' led the Greeks to concentrate their attention on one aspect of Montenero's explanation of the primacy to the exclusion of another—to stress the jurisdictional authority and to neglect the teaching authority of the Holy See. It is true that the *cedula* (and also the decree) was couched in terms that more readily suggested jurisdiction, and that Montenero had expatiated at length on that aspect of it though he had also introduced the teaching authority into his explanation of several of its clauses. The one phrase that clearly refers to teaching, 'teacher of all Christians', was indeed the subject of the Emperor's first difficulty, and that the Dominican solved in his second speech. But John VIII saw no query in it about a primacy of teaching:

You say that he is 'father and teacher and master of all Christians'. We should like to know if by these words there is signified a certain reverence, because he is the first among all the patriarchs, as we pay honour to a great lord, or if there is implied some power beyond reverence, because in the *cedula* he is said to be 'head of the Church'.[18]

Montenero's reply was to prove that Peter was head with an authority to which all were subject, i.e. jurisdiction as 'head', not as 'teacher'. And all the other difficulties and hesitations of the Greeks (as far as the documents disclose them) were of a like nature.

Two possible conclusions could be drawn from this observation, that the Greeks raised no objection about the teaching

[18] *A.L.*, p. 243.

280

authority of the popes, either because they accepted it or because, owing to their absorption in the aspect of jurisdiction, they had not realized that it was being taught by the decree on the primacy. The second of these alternatives is the more probable, and for this reason. The Greeks at that time looked on the whole question of the western patriarchate's relations to the other patriarchates as a canonical one, and not as a dogmatic one. Being canonical, it ranked less highly than the doctrinal questions of the Procession and of the Eucharist, and in the Emperor's opinion, when in May 1438 Latins and Greeks were looking for a subject of discussion between their committees, it did not fall under the ban that forbade all dogmatic discussion in the four months' interval of waiting. The Greek case against the Latin addition to the Creed rested, not on a definition, a 'horos', but on the prohibition, a canon, of the Council of Ephesus. The bishops later expressed their horror and amazement that the western patriarch had acted without his brother patriarchs, whose existence and rights were established by the canons of Nicaea, Constantinople and Chalcedon. The objections the Greeks made to the *cedula*, which Montenero answered in his second speech on the primacy, were all jurisdictional, i.e. canonical, and they demanded from him proofs from the canons, and insisted on the insertion in the decree of 'as is contained in the Acts of the oecumenical councils and in the sacred canons'.

Surprise is nowadays often expressed that the Greek prelates in Florence accepted the primacy at all, but, even more, that they accepted it with relatively little debate and in so short a time— eight months for the Procession: one month for the primacy, the Eucharist and Purgatory. The explanation is that the Procession was the dogmatic question *par excellence*—it was debated at great length in Italy, and interminably and exclusively afterwards; on the question of the Eucharist, the *epiclesis* was not defined and the other points were of very minor importance; about Purgatory the Greeks had no very clear views[19]—Mark Eugenicus to some extent made up his theology about it as he went along; the primacy was canonical, not doctrinal—it had not yet entered into oriental dogmatics about the Church, that the Church must not have a visible head on earth.[20]

[19] *A.G.*, pp. 25, 447; Syr., p. 130.
[20] 'Therefore the principle of 'Autocephalous Churches' . . . is the very essence of Catholicity itself. Where is the Catholic Church? . . . *the Catholic Church is there where is the equality of local churches, their full communion with*

However, even if what is here suggested is true, that the Greeks thought 'Roman Church' where the decree read 'Roman Pope', it makes no substantial difference to the Greek understanding of what they were accepting when they discussed the primacy and signed the Bull of union. If they failed to grasp the full import of the Latin formula, it was not (let it be repeated) for lack of lucid explanation and intransigent insistence from the Latin side. What they could not fail to understand on any hypothesis was that the Roman Church was, not the equal, but the head of the other Churches, because founded on St. Peter, the Christ-appointed head of the Apostles; that it had the right of governing the rest, and that with authority; that it had a universal jurisdiction and was therefore a court of appeal from all the world. If the separated Churches of the East would now accept as much as did their fathers at Florence, the end of the schism would be in sight, for the transition from 'Roman Church' to 'Roman Pope' would not be insuperable.

APPENDIX

THE PRIVILEGES AND RIGHTS OF THE PATRIARCHS

The phrase in the decree of union, 'Renewing also the order given in the canons of the venerable patriarchs, that the Patriarch of Constantinople should be after the most holy Roman Pontiff, third he of Alexandria, fourth the Antiochene, and fifth he of Jerusalem, namely without prejudice to all their privileges and rights', was unquestionably added to the original Latin *cedula* to meet the Greek request for mention of the order of the patriarchates, and was modelled on a formula proposed by the Greeks to the Latins on Friday, 26 June 1439 (cf. above p. 274). The words 'without prejudice to the privileges' are found both in the Greek proposal and in the decree of union. The question arises, what was meant by them.

Probably Greeks and Latins did not mean the same thing, and probably neither party could have defined on the spot exactly

each other, and their unbroken communion and link with the Apostles, under one Head—Christ' (Vladimir RODZIANKO, One and Catholic, in Barriers to Unity, ed. M. BRUCE (London, 1959), p. 38).

what it did mean. If asked, both would perhaps have explained the phrase as referring to such privileges as had existed in history, the idea, that is, that they had of the situation before the schism; but Greek ideas and Latin ideas on that were not the same. The formula in which the Greeks proposed the order of the patriarchs and their privileges begins: 'About the primacy of the Pope, we profess that he is supreme Pontiff . . . shepherd and teacher of all Christians, that he directs and governs the Church of God', but ends 'without prejudice to the privileges and rights' of the other patriarchs. The patriarchal 'privileges and rights', then, for them were a sort of limitation of the Roman primacy that they were accepting.

The kind of limitation they had in mind is suggested by the two restrictions that they had tried to impose on the papal privileges, restrictions that the Pope refused to accept. Those were that appeals to Rome against a patriarch should be tried on the spot and not in Rome, and that a pope should at least consult the other patriarchs before summoning a general council. A further indication of their mind can be found in their continued reluctance to approve of the addition of the *Filioque* to the Creed. As late as 10 June, the most advanced unionists among the Greeks admonished the Roman Church 'not to do such a thing again'. Their objection to the addition of the *Filioque* was not a mere isolated prejudice; it was the expression of the Greek belief that what affected the whole Church and its faith needed the action of the whole Church, and that no part of the Church, however august, should act alone.

Other pointers to the way in which the Greeks were thinking can be found in the few contacts between them and the Pope after the promulgation of the union. Eugenius wanted the election of the new patriarch to take place immediately and in Florence and hinted that he would consecrate him; the Greek prelates to whom he was talking resisted the papal pressure, 'because we have a custom that he should be elected in Constantinople by all our eparchy and consecrated in our cathedral church' (*A.G.*, p. 471). The Pope questioned the Greek discipline about divorce; he received the answer that it was allowed only for good reasons. In these cases and in others, such as the conferring of the sacrament of Confirmation by priests, the Greeks were on the defensive to allow no infringement of what they held to be their rights and customs.

When, therefore, they accepted the papal primacy 'without prejudice to all the privileges and rights' of the patriarchs of the East, they probably had in mind the retention not so much of the *status quo* as it had been, or as they vaguely imagined that it had been, in the past as the *status quo* as it was then (which they probably identified with the other), apart from the general right of appeal to Rome which they admitted, while they hoped that it would be used moderately. The concord reached by the Churches on the question that in Greek eyes was vastly more important, of the Procession of the Holy Spirit, was not dissimilar. It consisted in a mutual recognition of the orthodoxy of both the traditional Greek and Latin faiths that were expressed respectively by 'through' and 'from' but were substantially the same. Nevertheless, in the same breath as they agreed to unite with the Latins in respect of the Procession, the Greeks stipulated that they should not introduce the *Filioque* into their Creed nor change any of their customs (*A.G.*, pp. 432, 434)). Their idea was probably the same also as regards the primacy. They admitted the right of appeal and, apart from that, were set on making no other change in their traditional ways and customs, which were conveniently summarised as 'the privileges and rights of the patriarchs'.

The Latins may have had more precise ideas of what they meant by the phrase 'without prejudice to their privileges and rights'. In his speech to the Latin synod of 27 June 1439, Cardinal Cesarini referred to the Greek request 'that we should make some deliberation about the patriarchal Sees . . . as had been determined in the constitutions of the councils and, in the Lateran Council when Alexander [read: Innocent] III presided, he renewed the privileges of the patriarchal Sees'. It is noteworthy that the privileges are connected by Cesarini with the Council of the Lateran, and therefore it is not surprising that, when a few years later John of Torquemada wrote his commentary on the decree of union, he should have explained 'privileges' by reference to that council.

The patriarchs that the council of the Lateran had in view were Latin. The Patriarch of Constantinople was present in the council, having been appointed on the spot by the Pope who had quashed the elections of two other candidates come to vindicate their claims. The Patriarch of Jerusalem was also there in person and the Patriarch of Antioch by proxy. The Patriarch of Alexandria, though invited, did not come. In the eyes of Innocent III these Latins were the genuine holders of those ancient Sees and titles, in the line of succession from their Greek predecessors.

With reference to them, the relevant *capitulum* reads: 'Renewing the ancient privileges of the patriarchal Sees . . . we enact that after the Roman Church . . . the Constantinopolitan should hold the first place, the Alexandrine the second, the Antiochene the third, that of Jerusalem the fourth, to each its proper dignity being preserved; so that, after their prelates have received from the Roman Pontiff the pallium, which is the sign of the fulness of the pontifical office, and taken to him an oath of fidelity and obedience, they may lawfully bestow the pallium on their suffragans, receiving from them for themselves the canonical profession and for the Roman Church the promise of obedience. They may have the standard of the Lord's cross carried before them everywhere, except in the city of Rome and wherever the Supreme Pontiff or his legate with the insignia of his apostolic dignity is present. There shall be right of appeal to them in need in all the provinces subject to their jurisdiction, without prejudice to appeals made to the Holy See, which are always to have the preference'.[21]

The order of the patriarchs thus enumerated in the Council of the Lateran referred to the Latin patriarchs, understood as legitimate successors in the oriental Sees, and implicitly denied the legitimacy of any claims to possess those Sees made by Greeks. The repetition of the order, on the contrary, in the Council of Florence was a formal recognition of the Greek incumbents as legitimate patriarchs, even though there were Latins with the same titles and presumably the old pretensions. Nevertheless, it may be doubted whether the Fathers of Florence realised that they were doing anything more than merely repeating an old piece of legislation, and it can be taken as certain that they did not mean to make any change, although among the signatories of the definition of Florence there are to be read:' I, Blasio, Patriarch of Jerusalem signed', and 'I, Dorotheus, humble Metropolitan of Monembasia and procurator of the apostolic See of the most holy Patriarch of Jerusalem, my lord Joachim, agreed and signed'.

---

[21] MANSI, 22, 989–992.

They clearly had not considered the implications when they repeated the *capitulum* of the Lateran Council.

Cesarini and the Latins probably had this same *capitulum* of the Lateran Council in mind when they included 'without prejudice to their privileges and rights' in the first draft of the decree of union. What else they thought of, especially when by chance the word 'all' was added and finally accepted by a reluctant Pope, there is no knowing, and the meaning they attached to the word 'rights' of the patriarchs mentioned in the decree (the Lateran spoke only of 'privileges') is equally mysterious. Torquemada in his commentary repeated the Lateran to explain 'privileges'. About 'rights' he wrote only ' "For let the Apostolic See so retain its own strength, that it does not lessen the rights it had granted others", says St. Gregory in c. *quanto* dist. lxiii; and in c. *de ecclesiasticis* xxv q. ii: 'Just as we defend our rights, so do we preserve to all the individual churches their rights" '.[22]

Torquemada might have referred also to the Profession of Faith made by Michael VIII Palaeologus in the Council of Lyons (1274) and repeated by him several times afterwards, for it contains a statement on patriarchal Churches. Cesarini certainly and the Latins were familiar with it, for they had drawn their *cedula* about Purgatory from it, and so probably had it in mind also when they debated about the relations between the Churches.

'Also the same Roman Church holds the supreme and full primacy and principality over the universal Catholic Church. . . . To which anyone can appeal who has suffered oppression in what belongs to the ecclesiastical forum and can have recourse to its judgement in all causes that regard ecclesiastical tribunals; and to the same all Churches are subject: to it their prelates give obedience and reverence. The fullness of power however, belongs to it in such a way that it admits to part of the care [of the Churches: cf. 2 Cor. xi, 28] the other Churches, many of which and especially the patriarchal ones the same Roman Church has honoured with diverse privileges, [The Greek translation has: 'in such a way that the same Roman Church has honoured with diverse privileges the other Churches, especially the patriarchal ones,'] on condition, however, that her venerated prerogative whether in general councils or in other matters be always inviolate.'[23]

[22] *Ioannes de Torquemada, O.P. Apparatus super decretum Florentinum Unionis Graecorum*, ed. E. CANDAL (Romae, 1942), p. 114.
[23] MANSI, 24, 72E–73A.

286

What Michael VIII accepted when he made his Profession of Faith Eugenius asserted even more clearly in the Bull, *Non mediocri dolore*, written to settle the question of precedence between cardinals and metropolitans. There he wrote: 'The Roman Church founded all patriarchal, archiepiscopal, episcopal and cathedral dignities and, as was lawful to it, it gave power generously to one, more generously to another and most generously to still another as it judged fit',[24] in the same way as branches spring from the trunk of a tree or streams of water from a source, some bigger, some smaller. For the Latin mind, therefore, the 'rights' of the patriarchs originated in a grant from Rome and depended for their continued existence and their degree on the will of the Pope. Eugenius agreed to retain those rights, whatever they were, but in any case of doubt it would naturally be the Holy See that would settle what those rights were and what was their extension.

[24] *Bullarum, diplomatum et privilegiorum sanctorum Romanorum Pontificum Taurinensis editio* (*Magnum Bullarium Romanum*) vol. V (Turin, 1860), p. 36. Cf. W. ULLMANN, *Eugenius IV, Cardinal Kemp, and Archbishop Chichele*, in *Medieval Studies Presented to Aubrey Gwynn, S.J.*, edd. J. A. WATT, J. B. MORRALL, F. X. MARTIN, O.S.A. (Dublin, 1961), pp. 349–58.

XVIII

A PROFESSION OF FAITH OF MICHAEL BALSAMON, THE GREAT CHARTOPHYLAX

In the Cod. Marc. gr. III 5 (coll. 1077), *olim* Marcianus 229, there are two short items dealing with the Council of Florence, the second of which, a Profession of Faith of Michael Balsamon, the Great Chartophylax, is printed here.[1] Not much is known about Michael Balsamon, apart from what Syropoulus recounts of him in his *Memoirs*.[2] There he is depicted as a man of parts, regularly associated with the Great Ecclesiarches in his opposition to union. Several times he was nominated to committees – to deal with envoys from Basel in Constantinople (SYR. pp. 26, 34, 49), to arrange with the Latins (SYR. pp. 115, 148, 243), with two or three others to carry decisions to the Pope (SYR. pp. 229, 248, 291) or the Emperor (SYR. p. 189). He was associated with Syropoulus in the several distributions of the procuratorships of the oriental patriarchs (SYR. pp. 45, 66, 106) and was a member both of the group of ten Greeks who negotiated in May 1438 with the Latins on preliminary, private discussions (SYR. p. 115) and of the more select Greek committee that decided to discuss in Ferrara the *Filioque* as an addition rather than as a doctrine (SYR. p. 159). Later he was elected one of the six Greek orators for the public sessions (SYR. p. 161), though like three of the others he never spoke in them as far as is known.

Balsamon, therefore, was regarded by the Emperor, the Patriarch

---

[1] Professor Elpidio Mioni very kindly drew my attention to these two items and sent me photographs of them. I am most grateful to him. He describes the codex thus: saec. XVI, chart., mm. 315 x 215, ff. 438, a f. 235 binis columnis, italo-graecus, diversis manibus exaratus. Collectio canonum et litterarum canonicarum.

Balsamon's Profession is on ff. 316v–317v; the preceding item, on 315r–316v.

[2] Published under the title: *Vera historia unionis non verae*, by Robert CREYGHTON (The Hague, 1660).

and his fellows as capable and responsible, otherwise he would not have been entrusted with so many public offices. What is of greater interest in the context of this article is his attitude towards western theology and the union. The evidence we have shows that his later Profession of Faith (published here), repudiating the Council of Florence, is consistent with his previous behaviour. He opposed the ambiguous statement produced by Scholarius in May 1439, first in committee and again in the general Greek synod, about which Syropoulus recounts that he himself and Michael were relieved of the duty of carrying the statement to the Pope because of their disapproval of its tenor (SYR. p. 243). The Greek Acts also refer to this incident and mention the opposition of Balsamon and the Protekdikos, but say nothing of Syropoulus.[3] When the declaration of union became more probable, Balsamon went with Syropoulus and George Cappadox (the Protekdikos) to beseech the Emperor not to make them either sign the decree or attend the ceremony in liturgical vestments (SYR. pp. 287 seq.). The Emperor insisted. Balsamon, according to Syropoulus (p. 290), was ready to compromise by signing but not by wearing vestments. Syropoulus proposed the reverse. In the end all three yielded to pressure both to sign and to wear vestments. Back in Constantinople Balsamon and Syropoulus (the Protekdikos died on the journey home) functioned in the church of St. Sophia till Metrophanes was elected patriarch, but their services were boycotted (SYR. p. 331). Then they offered their resignations from office which, after vain persuasions from the Patriarch and the Emperor to get them to change their minds, were finally accepted (SYR. p. 341).

The Profession of Faith of the Marcian codex is dated 5 October 1440, which would correspond roughly with the time of Balsamon's resignation from office, as recounted by Syropoulus. It refers to his "enormous misdeed" committed in Italy and declares his repentance. It can safely be taken as a genuine document, though the text presented here is from a later copy.

A recantation of acceptance of the union of Florence by Balsamon

---

[3] *Quae supersunt actorum graecorum Concilii Florentini*, ed. J. GILL (Rome, 1953) pp. 416–7: "What we did was indeed a great step, but contrary to the votes of three of our patriarchal procurators; for Heraclea, Ephesus, Monembasia and also Anchialos did not vote for the statement of faith that was sent, and from the clerics, the Great Chartophylax and the Protekdikos."

(undoubtedly the Profession printed here) is referred to in the other document about the Council of Florence contained in the codex Marcianus gr. III 5. This document is a peculiar one. After a curious date (In the year 6947 [=1438], indiction 1, 2 June, action and document of the so-called eighth synod, in Florence)[4], it starts off impartially: (after a brief introduction)

"They convened... to effect the union of the holy churches of God and to bridge the big gap between the two parts... They decreed thus in their definition, that the Greeks should abide in their customs without disturbance as they had received them from of old from the seven holy general and ecumenical councils and in the Creed; also the Latins in their customs, and that the two parts should agree both to hold the holy gifts in the liturgy, whether in leavened or unleavened bread, the one and the other, holy; and at his desire each to celebrate in the churches of both without hindrance, but with his own antiminsion, and to receive and honour the sacrament of the other, they in their own way and we in ours, with no disagreement intervening" (f. 315r).[5]

The rest of the document is increasingly partial in tone. It continues:

"nevertheless, with all the enactments, customs and ceremonies of the Church of the Greeks preserved unbroken and

---

[4] Τῷ ͵ϚϠμζ' ἔτει, ἰνδ. α', μηνὶ ἰουνίῳ β': πρᾶξις καὶ τόμος τῆς λεγομένης ὀγδόης συνόδου τῆς ἐν Φλορεντίᾳ.

[5] Ἠθροίσθησαν... τοῦ ποιῆσαι τὴν ἕνωσιν τῶν ἁγίων τοῦ Θεοῦ ἐκκλησιῶν καὶ τὴν μακρὰν διάστασιν τὴν ἀπ' ἀλλήλων τῶν μελλῶν (leg. μελῶν) εἰς ἓν συνάψαι... Ὥρισαν ἐν τῷ τόμῳ οὕτως· ὅτι οἱ γραικοὶ μένειν ἐν τοῖς ἔθεσιν αὐτῶν ἀπαρασαλεύτως ὡς καὶ ἀρχῆθεν καθὼς παρέλαβον παρὰ τῶν ἁγίων ἑπτὰ καθολικῶν συνόδων καὶ οἰκουμενικῶν καὶ ἐν τῷ συμβόλῳ τῆς πίστεως· ἔτι δὲ καὶ οἱ λατῖνοι ἐν τοῖς αὐτῶν ἔθεσιν· καὶ λογίζοιντο καὶ φρονεῖν ἑκάτερα τὰ μέρη τὰ προσφερόμενα ἅγια δῶρα, εἴτε παρὰ ἐνζύμου ἢ ἀζύμου, τὸ ἓν καὶ τὸ ἕτερον, ἅγιον καὶ λειτουργεῖν ἐν ταῖς ἀμφοτέρων ἐκκλησίαις ὁ βουλόμενος ἀκωλύτως, μόνον μετὰ τοῦ ἀντιμινσίου αὐτοῦ καὶ τὰ ἐκείνων δέχεσθαι καὶ τιμᾶν· ἐκείνους δὲ κατὰ ταὐτῶν, [ἡμᾶς κατὰ] τὰ ἡμῶν, μηδεμιᾶς ἐγγινομένης διαφορᾶς (f. 315 r).

unchanged"[6] a principle that is thereupon applied to all the sacraments mentioned separately and to the Creed. The chief orators of the council are next named, beginning with Mark Eugenicus and ending with him and his arguments, reinforced by St. Cyril's κατ'οὐδένα τρόπον σαλεύεσθαι, on account of the rehabilitation of the Patriarch Photius and references to Chrysostom and Basil. "For this reason, because of the words of the addition, some of those who had signed, and among them the Great Chartophylax of the great church of Constantinople, Michael Balsamon, rejected such a synod, which they also anathematised" (316r).[7]

Of Balsamon's life after his resignation little is known. He was probably involved in most of the anti-unionist activities of the period before the capture of Constantinople in 1453 as a member of the "synaxis," of which Scholarius-Gennadius was the master mind. Balsamon's signature appears with fourteen others on the report presented in November 1452 by the "synaxis" to the Emperor Constantine, giving the reasons why they could not accept the union of Florence; Gennadius's name is not there, but that of Syropoulus is.[8] Balsamon, however, is not included among the seven who shortly before had signed the letter sent to the Hussites in Prague, though both Syropoulus and Gennadius are.[9]

Balsamon wrote at least one treatise of self-justification, entitled by Allatius: *Anaphora cleri constantinopolitani*, (the Greek title is not noted,) which seems to have been composed before the death of Mark of Ephesus, 1444/5.[10] Allatius gives three quotations from it. The

---

[6] σωζομένων ὅμως ἐν ἅπασιν ἀπαραθραύστως καὶ ἀμεταποιήτως ἐν τοῖς γραικοῖς πασῶν τῶν διατάξεων, τῶν ἐθίμων καὶ ἀκολουθιῶν τῆς ἐκκλησίας γραικῶν.

[7] "Ενεκεν τούτου, διὰ τὴν φωνὴν τῆς προσθήκης καί τινες τῶν ὑπογραψάντων ὧν εἷς ἐστι καὶ ὁ μέγας χαρτοφύλαξ τῆς μεγάλης ἐκκλησίας Κωνσταντινουπόλεως, κύριος Μιχαὴλ ὁ Βαλσαμών, ἀπεβάλοντο τὴν τοιαύτην σύνοδον· ἣν καὶ ἀναθεμάτισαν.

[8] *Oeuvres complètes de Gennade Scholarios*, ed. PETIT, SIDERIDES, JUGIE; III (Paris, 1930) p. 193.

[9] L. ALLATIUS, *De ecclesiae occidentalis atque orientalis perpetua consensione* (Cologne, 1748) 949.

[10] ALLATIUS, op. cit. 918.

first constitutes a kind of profession of faith (which, incidentally, contains the unusual word ἀπαρεγχείρητον, found also in the profession printed here) (Allatius, 918). The third quotation gives reasons why the anti-unionists were unwilling to discuss the dogma of the Trinity with the unionists: 1. because they had no doubt about it; 2. because their prelates, and especially Ephesus, and the monks were not at hand; and 3. because there was no independent arbitrator (Allatius, 924). The second quotation enlarges on the hardships undergone in Italy and is worth giving in full, even though it is rather long.

"In the first place, we declare that in no other way was it possible for us to return to our common fatherland. For the threat proclaimed by the Pope against us was a choice announced almost in so many words – either agree with him and, laden with numerous gifts, favours and honours, see the fatherland again, or first that we be reduced to starvation by hunger and thirst, then despatched by an obscure death. We, therefore, held ourselves in readiness to yield up our lives for the certain dogmas of our ancestors, but it did not seem to be to the best interests of our country that all the men of worth should be left behind there and miserably perish and leave our land empty of learning, a disgrace to the race, full only of ruins, though she had been the mother and source of scholarship. Made of flesh as we are and with a body, it terrified us, as no other form of violent death. For the truth shall be told, rather than the poetic phrase about Locrian Ajax: 'Ajax perished from drinking salt-water.' There befell us, too, terrified by the threats, what is expressed by the common saying: 'The bishop was being hanged, and so signed.' And that is, indeed, that."[11]

---

[11] Καὶ πρῶτον μὲν ἀναφέρομεν, ὅτι οὐχ οἶον τε ἡμῖν ἄλλως εἰς τὴν κοινὴν ἐπανιέναι πατρίδα. Ἡ γὰρ καθ᾽ ἡμῶν τοῦ πάπα διακηρυκευομένη ἀπειλὴ αἵρεσις ἦν μονονουχὶ διαρρήδην βοῶσα, ἢ ταὐτὰ φρονῆσαι αὐτῷ καὶ μεθ᾽ ὅτι πλείστων δωρεῶν, χαρίτων τε καὶ ἀξιωμάτων ὄψεσθαι τὴν πατρίδα, ἢ πενίᾳ [πείνῃ?] καὶ δίψῃ πρότερον ταριχευθέντας, ὕστερον ἀφανεῖ θανάτῳ παραπεμφθῆναι ἡμᾶς. Ἡμεῖς μὲν οὖν ἑτοίμως εἴχομεν ὑπὲρ τῶν πατρικῶν ἀσφαλῶν δογμάτων προέσθαι τὰς ψυχάς. Ἀλλ᾽ οὐ συνοίσειν τῇ πατρίδι ἐδόκει τοὺς λόγου ἀξίους σύμπαντας καταληφθῆναι τῇ Φλωρεντίᾳ κἀκεῖσε διαφθαρῆναι κακῶς, ταύτην δὲ καταληφθῆναι λόγων κενήν, εἰς αἰσχύνην τοῦ γένους, μεστὴν δὲ ἐρει-

This is a phantastic statement, as appears by comparing it even with Syropoulus, who does not minimise the hardships in Florence. According to Syropoulus it was the Emperor who insisted "at the risk of their incurring his displeasure" on their signing the decree and assisting at its promulgation clad in their sacred vestments. Balsamon makes the Pope responsible; otherwise nothing less than "starvation and an obscure death." This is worthy of the most impossibly thrilling spy-novel; yet some people will have believed it. It serves to show how 'history' is fabricated to suit a purpose.

PROFESSION OF FAITH OF MICHAEL BALSAMON, THE GREAT CHARTOPHYLAX

Ὁμολογία τοῦ μεγάλου χαρτοφύλακος τῆς μεγάλης ἐκκλησίας Κωνσταντινουπόλεως, κυρίου Μιχαὴλ τοῦ Βαλσαμῶνος, ἣν ἐποίησεν ἀπὸ τῆς Ἰταλίας καὶ τῆς λεγομένης ὀγδόης συνόδου ἐπανελθὼν εἰς Κωνσταντινούπολιν ἣν ὀφείλει πᾶς χριστιανὸς ἔχειν καὶ ὁμολογεῖν.

Πρῶτον στέργω καὶ ὁμολογῶ τὸ ἅγιον σύμβολον μέχρι τέλους καθὼς αὐτὸ παρέδοσαν αἱ ἑπτὰ σύνοδοι· πρὸς τούτοις δὲ λέγω, στέργω καὶ ἀποδέχομαι τὰς ἁγίας καὶ οἰκουμενικὰς ἑπτὰ συνόδους αἵτινες ἐπὶ συστάσει τῶν ὀρθῶν δογμάτων συνηθροίσθησαν, καὶ πάντας τοὺς ὑπ' αὐτῶν διωρισμένους κανόνας στέργω καὶ φυλάττω ἀπαρεγχειρήτους καὶ τὰς ἁγίας διατάξεις ὅσαι τοῖς ἱεροῖς ἡμῶν πατρᾶσι κατὰ διαφόρους καιροὺς καὶ χρόνους διετυπώθησαν· ἔτι δὲ καὶ τὰς λοιπὰς ἱερὰς καὶ συνοδικὰς πράξεις καὶ ἀποφάσεις, τὰς γενομένας κατὰ καιροὺς παρὰ τῆς καθολικῆς ἐκκλησίας ἡμῶν τῆς Κωνσταντινουπόλεως, κατά τε δήλωσιν τοῦ Ἀκινδύνου καὶ τῶν αὐτοῦ ὁμοφρόνων καὶ κατὰ τῶν λοιπῶν τῶν καθ' οἱονδήτινα τρόπον βλασφημησάντων εἰς τὰ θεῖα δόγματα καὶ εἰς τὰς λοιπὰς διατάξεις καὶ διατυπώσεις, ἐγγράφως τε καὶ ἀγράφως, τῆς εἰρημένης ταύτης καθολικῆς ἐκκλησίας μου τῆς Κωνσταντινουπόλεως.

Πάντας οὓς ἀποδέχεται αὐτή, καὶ αὐτὸς συναποδεχόμενος· καὶ οὓς

πίων καὶ μόνων τὴν τῶν λόγων μητέρα τε καὶ πηγήν. Ἐδέδιττε καὶ ἡμᾶς, ὡς σάρκα περικειμένους καὶ σῶμα, οὐκ ἄλλος τις βίαιος θάνατος. Εἰρήσεται γὰρ τ' ἀληθές, ἢ τὸ τῆς ποιήσεως ἐπὶ τῷ λοκρῷ Αἴαντι ἔπος· Αἴας δ' ἐξαπόλωλεν ἐπεὶ πίεν ἅλμυρον ὕδωρ. Συνέβη καὶ παθεῖν ἡμᾶς τὰς ἀπειλὰς πεφρικότες, ὅπερ ὁ κοινός φησι μῦθος· ἐπίσκοπος κρεμώμενος ὑπέγραψεν. Καὶ ταῦτα μὲν δὴ ταῦτα. (Allatius, 922–3)

ἀποβάλλεται συναποβαλλόμενος, ἄνευ τῆς ἐν Φλωρεντίᾳ γενομένης συνόδου· ταύτην γάρ, καὶ τὰ ἐν τῷ ὅρῳ αὐτῆς γεγραμμένα, πάντα ἀναθεματίζω καὶ ἀποβάλλομαι.

Ἔτι πρὸς τούτοις, ὅλῃ ψυχῇ καὶ καρδίᾳ καὶ νοῒ καὶ προαιρέσει καὶ διαθέσει, ὁμολογῶ καὶ φρονῶ καὶ πιστεύω καὶ ἓν αἴτιον καὶ μίαν ἀρχὴν ἐπὶ τῶν θεαρχικῶν ὑποστάσεων, τὸν Πατέρα καὶ μόνον, κατὰ τὴν τοῦ Κυρίου θεολογίαν καὶ τὴν τοῦ θείου συμβόλου τῆς πίστεως ἡμῶν ἀμεταποίητον ἔκθεσιν καὶ παράδοσιν, καὶ τὴν σφραγῖδα καὶ ἐπικύρωσιν τὴν εἰς τοῦτο τῶν ἁγίων ἑπτὰ καὶ οἰκουμενικῶν συνόδων, ἔτι δὲ καὶ τὰς θείας γνωμικὰς ἀποφάσεις τῶν ἁγίων ἡμῶν διδασκάλων καὶ θεολόγων τῶν ἐν ταύταις διαπρεψάντων δίκην ἡλίου.

Τὸν δὲ Υἱὸν οὔτε αἴτιον δοξάζω οὔτε ἀρχήν· μόνος γὰρ ὁ Πατὴρ αἴτιος καὶ ἀρχή, ὥσπερ τοῦ Υἱοῦ κατὰ τὴν ἄρρητον γέννησιν, οὕτω καὶ τοῦ Ἁγίου Πνεύματος κατὰ τὴν ἄφραστον αὐτοῦ ἐκπόρευσιν. Οὔτε οὖν ἐκ τοῦ Υἱοῦ, οὔτε διὰ τοῦ Υἱοῦ ὁμολογῶ τὸ Πνεῦμα τὸ Ἅγιον τὸ ὑπάρχειν ἔχειν ἐκ τοῦ Υἱοῦ· ἄπαγε τῆς βλασφημίας.

Οὕτως οὖν φρονῶ, οὕτω δοξάζω, οὕτω πιστεύω, οὕτως ὁμολογῶ, ὅλῃ ψυχῇ καὶ καρδίᾳ καὶ φρενὶ καὶ νοῒ καὶ διαθέσει καὶ προαιρέσει· καὶ ἐπὶ ταύτης τῆς πίστεως καὶ ἐβαπτίσθην καὶ ἀνετράφην καὶ ἱερώθην· μεθ' ἧς καὶ ζῶ καὶ μετ' αὐτῆς εὔχομαι καὶ τῷ φοβερῷ βήματι τοῦ Χριστοῦ παραστῆναι.

Εἰ δὲ συνέβη μοι τῷ ἀθλίῳ, παρασυρέντι μοι ὑπὸ καιρικῆς τινος ἀνάγκης πρὸ καιροῦ καὶ φόβου διεπηρτημένου καὶ σωματικοῦ κινδύνου, καταπατῆσαι τὴν ἡμετέραν συνείδησιν καὶ τὸν τοῦ Θεοῦ φόβον καὶ ὑπογράψαι ἐν τοῖς ὅροις τοῖς γενομένοις περὶ τῆς ἑνώσεως τῶν λατίνων καὶ συμφορέσαι τοῖς λατίνοις, φεῦ.

Ἀλλ' οὖν μεταμελλόμενος νῦν καὶ ἐξομολογούμενος ἐνώπιον τοῦ Θεοῦ, λέγω ὅτι ἀκουσίως πεποίηκα· καὶ ἡ μὲν χεὶρ ὑπέγραψεν ἐκεῖνα; οὐ μὴν δὲ ἡ ψυχὴ ἡ ἐμὴ οὐδὲ ἡ γνώμη· ἀλλὰ τοὐναντίον ἁπλῶς· οὐδὲ ἓν γὰρ πιστεύω ὅτι ἐστὶν ὀρθὸν τῶν γεγραμμένων ἐκεῖσε.

Διὸ ἀναθέματι καθυποβάλλω τὸν ὅρον ἐκεῖνον καὶ τὸν στέργοντα αὐτόν· καὶ δέομαι τοῦ Θεοῦ συμπαθείας τυχεῖν ἐπὶ τῷ μεγίστῳ μου τούτῳ σφάλματι· ἔδει με γὰρ ὑπὲρ τῆς εὐσεβείας μου μέχρι αἵματος ἀγωνίσασθαι.

Ἀλλ' ὅμως πάλιν μετανοῶ, καὶ ἐξομολογούμενος καταφεύγω εἰς τὴν ἄφραστον τοῦ Θεοῦ φιλανθρωπίαν, ἵνα τύχω ἐλέους ἐν τῇ ἡμέρᾳ τῆς κρίσεως· ᾧ ἡ δόξα εἰς τοὺς αἰῶνας ἀμήν·

Μηνὶ ὀκτωβρίῳ ε', ἰνδ. δ', τοῦ ‚ϛϡμθ' ἔτους.

Profession of the Great Chartophylax of the great church of Con-
stantinople, Kyr Michael Balsamon, which he made on his return to
Constantinople from Italy and the so-called eighth council and which
every Christian should hold and profess.

First, I accept and confess the holy Creed completely as the seven
councils have transmitted it. Also I affirm, accept and receive the
holy and ecumenical seven councils which were convened for the upholding of the right doctrines, and all the canons decreed by them I
hold and preserve inviolate, as well as all the holy enactments that
have been formulated by our holy Fathers on divers occasions and
times, as also the other holy and synodical actions and decisions
effected to meet some occasion by our catholic Church of Constantinople, both in the sense of the declaration in respect of Akindynus
and of those of like mind with him and against the rest of those who
in any way have blasphemed against the divine dogmas and the rest
of the enactments and formulations, both written and unwritten, of
this, my said catholic Church of Constantinople.

All whom She accepts, I also accept; and all whom She rejects, I
also reject, apart from the council that took place in Florence, for
this and what is written in its decree, all of it, I anathematise and
reject.

Further, with all my soul, heart, mind, will and disposition, I
confess, think and believe in one cause and one principle in the hypostases of the supreme deity, the Father only, according to the
doctrine of the Lord and the unchangeable exposition and tradition
of the divine symbol of our faith and the seal and ratification of this
by the seven holy, ecumenical councils and, too, the divine authoritative opinions of our holy doctors and theologians who have been as
conspicuous as the sun in these.

The Son I do not hold to be either source or principle, for only
the Father is source and principle; as he is of the Son according to
the ineffable generation, so is He also of the Holy Spirit according to
his unexpressible procession. Therefore I do not profess the Holy
Spirit to be from the Son or through the Son, or to have his existence
from the Son – avaunt the blasphemy.

Thus do I think, thus hold, thus believe, thus profess with all my
soul, heart, mind, intellect, disposition and will, and in this faith

was I baptised and educated and ordained. With it I both live and with it I wish to stand before the awful judgement-seat of Christ.

If it happened to me, poor wretch, swept away by a temporary need in face of the emergency and fear hanging over me and of bodily danger, to have trampled underfoot our conscience and the fear of God and to have set my signature to the decrees made in respect of the union with the Latins and to have worn my vestments with the Latins – alas.

Now, therefore, repentant and making my confession before God, I say that I did it against my will: my hand indeed signed those documents, but not my soul nor my mind – just the opposite, for I do not believe that even one of those things there written is right.

So I put under anathema that decree and whoso accepts it, and I beg of God that I may meet with compassion for this my very great misdeed, for I ought to have resisted even unto blood for my true faith.

However, again I repent and, making my confession, I put myself in the hands of the unspeakable loving-kindness of God, that I may receive pity in the day of judgement, to Whom be the glory for ever. Amen.

On the 5th day of the month of October, indiction 4, of the year 6949 [= 1440].

XIX

Eleven Emperors of Byzantium seek Union with the Church of Rome

ELEVEN EMPERORS OF BYZANTIUM seek union with the Church of Rome, that is to say, all the emperors from the capture of Constantinople by the Crusaders in 1204 till its capture in 1453 by Mehmet the Conqueror. Some of the negotiations were more serious and protracted, others less so. All of them were initiated by an emperor, but that should not be taken as implying that the Church was not involved in them. The Byzantine emperor had not only an influence, but also a position, in the Eastern Church that no western monarch ever had in the Latin Church. He was the 'God-crowned, divine emperor', elected through divine providence as the head of Christendom whose political aspect was the state and ecclesiastical aspect the Church. He was guardian of the Church, took part in its synods and embodied their decisions in his civil laws, designated patriarchs and bishops, and generally supervised the Church's activities. He was so much a necessary element of the Church's structure that as late as the last decade of the 14th century Patriarch Antony, writing to Prince Basil I of Moscow who had stopped commemoration of the Byzantine emperor in the Liturgy, remonstrated: 'It is not possible for Christians to have the Church and not to have the emperor, for Empire and Church are bound together in an indissoluble unity and affinity, and they cannot be reft asunder.'[1] About half a century later a group of determined anti-unionists after the Council of Florence refused to commemorate Emperor Constantine XI in the Liturgy on the grounds that he could not be emperor because he was belying the very title of emperor, since the word *basileus* was derived from *basis* (foundation), that is, the emperor of his nature was the foundation and support of orthodoxy, and Constantine by favouring the union of Florence showed that he was not such.[2] So, while the initiative in negotiations for union of the Eastern Church with the Western assuredly came from the emperor, he always had to persuade the Church to co-operate, which on each occasion it did with more or less of enthusiasm.

The chief motive of the emperors was always political. As long as the Latins held Constantinople, the aim was to evict them and to retake the city. When in 1261 Michael VIII did get it back, he used union to forestall Latin attempts at reconquest. In the 14th century, as the Turks encroached more and more on the Empire, the emperors desperately needed western

---

[1] F. Miklosich and J. Müller, *Acta et diplomata graeca medii aevi sacra et profana*, ii (Vienna 1862), p. 188.
[2] S. Lambros, *Palaiologeia kai Peloponnisiaka*, i (Athens 1912), pp. 124–5.

military help to stop their advance. The fact, however, that the occasions and the main motive of these contacts between East and West were political does not necessarily exclude also a genuinely religious purpose. The schism that divided the two Churches was sincerely deplored by both of them. Each wished it to be ended, but each was convinced that the other was to blame and that unity was to be achieved by the other repenting of its fault and abandoning its errors. And so they remained divided.

When the Latin crusaders captured Constantinople in 1204 two Greek kingdoms were set up, one centred on Nicaea in Bithynia (north-west Asia Minor), the other in the western area of mainland Greece, Epirus. On the death in 1206 of John X Camaterus who was the Patriarch of Con-stantinople at the time of the capture, Theodore I Lascaris, ruler in Nicaea, had a successor to him elected in Nicaea (1208), and by him he was crowned emperor of Constantinople. The kingdom of Nicaea grew steadily stronger and more stable, but so did the kingdom of Epirus which in 1218 began a campaign to take Thessalonica, the second city of the Byzantine Empire. The ruler of Epirus, Theodore Ducas, like Lascaris, was aiming at taking also the first city, Constantinople itself. The situation rather favoured the Epirote arms, for Ducas was at least on the same continent as Constantinople, whereas Lascaris was in Asia. So Lascaris tried other means. In 1219 Patriarch Manuel of Nicaea wrote to the leading prelate of Epirus announcing the convocation in Nicaea of a synod of the four Eastern Patriarchates to send envoys to 'the Pope of the Elder Rome with a view to eliminating scandals, to giving peace to the Churches and to bringing all Christians for the future to one mind'. The Church of Epirus, voicing the will of Ducas, deprecated with indignation such a parleying with the overbearing Latin Church, and the suggestion went no further.[3] A short time later, the approach to Constantinople via Rome having failed, Lascaris married the daughter of Yolande, Latin Queen Regent of Constantinople. In Greece Ducas's ambitions prospered. In 1224 he took Thessalonica, and shortly afterwards had himself crowned emperor of Constantinople.

Manuel was followed on the patriarchal throne in Nicaea by a man of stronger character, Germanus. He brought great pressure to bear on the Epirote hierarchy to make it acknowledge its dependence on himself, only to be told that, if he persisted, 'our powerful Emperor' Theodore Ducas might put the Epirote Church under the Pope of Rome.[4] The schism between the Churches of Epirus and Nicaea lasted only as long as Theodore Ducas was victorious. In 1230 he was defeated, captured and blinded by the Tsar of Bulgaria, John Asen, who in his turn became a

[3]V. G. Vasilevskii, 'Epirotica saeculi XIII', *Vizantiiskii vremennik*, iii (1896), *epp.* 14, 15. pp. 264–7.
[4]*Ibid., ep.* 26, pp. 288–93. date 1225/6.

contender for the throne of Constantinople and, hence, the rival of John Vatatzes, the ruler in Nicaea who had succeeded Theodore Lascaris. Vatatzes sought to compensate for his territorial disadvantage by adopting other means. He tried the way of church unity.

Patriarch Germanus, who in 1229 had written to the Greeks of Cyprus inveighing violently against the Latin Church, in 1232 transmitted to Pope Gregory IX and the cardinals by the hands of five Franciscan friars, who had passed through Nicaea on their way back from the Holy Land, letters suggesting conversations to restore harmony between the Churches. The Pope promptly summoned two Franciscans and two Dominicans, of whom one at least was very competent in Greek. They arrived in Nicaea on 15 January 1234. Discussions went on till 27 January, confined (in spite of the Latin preference for the Eucharist) entirely to the question of the *Filioque*. No agreement was reached. As the friars were about to depart the Emperor, seeing his hopes of union being frustrated, asked them how the Church of Greece could be reconciled with Rome. He was told – by believing what the Roman Church believes as it did before the schism; it would then be given a hearty welcome.

The four friars returned to Constantinople to await a report on the discussions that Patriarch Germanus had promised to send them. But instead of a report they received a most pressing invitation in letters from both Patriarch and Emperor to return and to take part in a synod of the Eastern Church. Everyone in Constantinople urged them to accept in order to win a year's truce for the city which was in the most dire straits. The synod opened on Easter Monday 1234. The friars insisted that this time they should treat of the Eucharist. The Orientals rejected outright the use of unleavened bread : that was heresy. The Latins freely allowed the use of leavened bread but denounced the Greek condemnation of their Western rite as heresy. The Greeks presented the Latins with a written statement of their condemnation. The Latins gave the Greeks a written profession of their belief in the *Filioque* and of their rejection of the Greek arguments against it. Tension mounted. The envoys left quickly to avoid possible violence, were stopped on their way and deprived of the Greek statement on the Eucharist (but they had made a Latin translation of it which was not found when their baggage was searched), and they were given instead a lengthy exposition of Greek teaching on the Blessed Trinity.[5]

So this attempt to ease the relations between the Churches and to win Constantinople by way of religion failed. Vatatzes then tried practical measures. He made an alliance with John Asen and together they launched two savage attacks on the city, but without success. Constantinople was

[5]The sources for these debates are G. Golubovich, 'Disputatio Latinorum et Graecorum', in *Archivum Franciscanum Historicum*, xii (1919), pp. 428–65; Nicephorus Blemmydes, *Curriculum vitae et carmina*, ed. A. Heisenberg (Leipzig 1896), pp. 63–80; P. Canard, 'Nicéphore Blemmyde et le mémoire aux envoyés de Grégoire XI (Nicée 1234)'; in *Orientalia Christiana Periodica*, xxv (1959), pp. 310–25.

too strongly fortified to be taken easily by force of arms. The way of religion was tried again. In 1248 Vatatzes asked Innocent IV to send the Minister General of the Franciscans, John of Parma, for theological discussions. He achieved nothing. A few years later (1253) Vatatzes sent to the Pope an imposing embassy empowered to offer union of the Churches in return for the restoration of Constantinople to the Greeks.

The proposal contained nine clauses: 'Complete acknowledgement [by the Greeks] of the primacy in the Catholic Church over the other Patriarchates [as belonging] to the Roman See and its Supreme Pontiff; canonical obedience to be given to the reigning pope and his successors canonically entering into office'; also free appeal and recourse to Rome of all Christians; obedience to the popes; first place in councils and acceptance of papal decisions, if not uncanonical. 'Besides this, the same envoys requested that the sovereignty of the city of Constantinople should be restored to the oft-mentioned Kalojan and the rights of the patriarchal sees, both there and elsewhere, to the [Greek] patriarchs, and that the Latin emperor and patriarchs should be removed from the same city and sees, the Patriarch of Antioch being left in his city for his life-time.'[6]

Innocent IV was delighted with this proposal, but he had to point out that it was not in his power to eject the Latin emperor with no cause shown and that to do so without legal process would be against justice: 'If the Latin emperor has not been cited, right given by law does not allow of anything being settled, because a settlement would seem to be voided unless it were a process against one who either had pleaded guilty or had been convicted.' All the same he would do everything in his power to 'bring about a mutually satisfactory agreement between Kalojan and the Emperor'. Innocent had also another reservation. In conversation the Greek prelates had insisted that they could not accept the addition of the *Filioque* to the Creed except in a general council which should define it as 'the witness of authentic Scripture or a divine utterance (*divinum oraculum*)'. This seemed to him to be illogical when they had expressed themselves as ready to follow the opinion of the Holy See on matters of faith in councils. But he hoped that these difficulties could be solved by discussion and, provided that the Greek Church concurred with the Latin in its faith, there could be no objection to its retaining its own form of the Creed.

Innocent gave plenipotentiary powers to the Bishop of Orvieto to represent him in Nicaea. Unfortunately, all three protagonists died in 1254, Patriarch Manuel in August, Emperor Vatatzes on 3 November and Pope Innocent on 3 December. So the commission to the Bishop of Orvieto lapsed.

It was not Innocent's successor, Alexander IV, but Emperor Theodore II

---

[6]This document is preserved in the registers of Innocent IV's successor, Alexander IV, *Acta Alexandri PP. IV (1254–1261)*, ed. T. T. Haluščynskyj and M. M. Wojnar (Rome 1966), doc. 28. It is found also in Raynaldus, *Annales ecclesiastici*, 1256, 48–53.

Lascaris who took the initiative in reopening negotiations. He wanted to know whether he would get Constantinople or not. The Pope immediately sent the Bishop of Orvieto with generous powers. But when Theodore learnt that those powers did not include the one thing he wanted, the cession of Byzantium, he lost interest. So ended a serious attempt at union. George Metochites, writing a few decades later, summed up his account of it: 'Whoso reflects on the full story of these negotiations will assuredly perceive that all that was then done in respect of the Church was the action of the whole body of the churchmen of that time and had their approval, and that there was no other obstacle [in the way of success] except what arose from the political element and controversy.'[7] In 1272 Emperor Michael VIII Palaeologus produced to the synod of bishops the document they had signed twenty years earlier for Emperor Vatatzes, approving the proposals put to Innocent IV.[8]

Constantinople returned to Greek hands again on 25 July 1261. The Greek Emperor at that time was Michael VIII who had gained the throne at the end of 1258 by thrusting aside Lascaris's eight-year-old son and heir, John, and ultimately blinding him. Having got the city of his desires back again, his chief concern thereafter was to retain it and to forestall attempts to retake it by the dispossessed Latin Emperor and his allies. For this end from the very beginning of his reign he carried on a lively correspondence with a series of popes about union of the Churches. Clement IV, to get from words to actions, in 1264 made plain what union with the Latin Church meant: it meant acceptance by Emperor and Church of Latin belief and of Roman primacy, which the pope expressed in a detailed profession of faith. Clement's successor, Pope Gregory X, on 31 March 1272 announced the convocation of a general Council to meet on 1 May 1274. One of its purposes was union of the Churches, and he invited the Greek Emperor and the Greek Church to attend. The Clementine profession of faith would still have to be accepted, but Gregory made the conditions of its acceptance less rigorous. Michael VIII set about persuading his Greek bishops to co-operate, but he came up against a great deal of stubborn resistance. Patriarch Joseph I refused to approve of the project of union but agreed to abdicate if union should be achieved. The Emperor urged persuasively that union was really innocuous. It implied, so he said, only recognition of the primacy of the pope, acceptance of the right of all to appeal to Rome, and commemoration of the pope in the Holy Liturgy: none of these points was doctrinal and none was likely to impinge much on Greek practice. This version of union of the Churches the synod was persuaded to accept, which it did on 24 December 1273. A vague kind of profession of faith, which certainly was not the Clementine profession of faith, was drawn up by the bishops and signed. staunchly unionistic bishops were appointed to represent the Church,

[7]G. Metochites, *Historia dogmatum*, ed. A. Mai, *Patrum nova bibliotheca*, viii (Roma 1871), p. 28.
[8]George Pachymeres, *De Michaele Palaeologo*, ed. I. Bekker (Bonn 1835 = CSHByz), p. 374–5.

and on 11 March 1274 the Greek embassy departed for Lyons, the city where the council was to meet.

It arrived there on 24 June, after three sessions had already been held. A few days later, on the Feast of St Peter and St Paul, the Greek bishops, who at the pontifical Mass were in the sanctuary near the Pope, spontaneously sang the *Filioque* clause three times when they were chanting in Greek their liturgical Creed. In the fourth session the Emperor's full profession of the Clementine faith, the document sent by the Church and a short communication from the co-Emperor, Andronicus, associating himself with his father's profession of faith, were read out. Again the Greek bishops joyfully chanted the *Filioque* not once but twice in their Greek Creed, and everyone rejoiced at the union of the Churches. In the sixth and last session on 17 July the doctrine of the Procession of the Holy Spirit, as the Latins and the Greeks in Lyons believed it, was defined. This definition probably was meant more to allay the misgivings of hesitant theologians of the Greek Church than to browbeat them into submission, for it met their chief objection against Latin belief by asserting that. the *Filioque* does not imply two principles in the Procession or two spirations, as they feared, but only one.[9]

The Greek envoys returned to Constantinople. On 16 January 1275 a solemn Liturgy was celebrated in the church of the Blachernae palace, when the Pope was commemorated, and in this way the union was promulgated. Then Michael had to win over the Greek Church and the Greek people to accept it. He failed. There was opposition from all ranks of society, chiefly from the innumerable monks. The synod honoured its agreement of 24 December 1273 with the Emperor, and in February 1276 it decreed excommunication for all who resisted the union. Suspects close at hand were called before the synod, interrogated and sentenced. Against anti-unionists in the provinces (and in particular, the Despot of Epirus and the ruler of Thessaly, who were making their courts refuges for those who fled from Constantinople), a solemn form of excommunication was enacted 'against those who do not accept that the Roman Church is mother and head of all the other Churches, the teacher of orthodox belief, and that its Supreme Pontiff is the first and the shepherd of all Christians'.[10]

But many of the bishops, too, were unhappy about it. Religious controversy led to political dissension. The Latin ex-emperor and his ally, the king of Sicily, convinced that the union on the Greek side was no more than a wily means of keeping them inactive, urged the Holy See to lift the restraints stopping them from recovering by military action the lost Latin Empire. Consequently the popes pressed Palaeologus to produce more tangible proofs of a virile union. That Michael could not do, though he resorted to brutalities and violence to force his subjects to acquiesce.

---

[9] A. Franchi, *Il Concilio di Lione (1274) secondo la Ordinatio Concilii Generalis Lugdunensis* (Rome 1965).

[10] J. Gill, 'The Church Union of the Council of Lyons (1274) portrayed in Greek Documents', in *Orientalia Christiana Periodica*, xl (1974), pp. 5–45, esp. doc. V, pp. 22–28.

Tensions mounted till in 1281 Pope Martin IV excommunicated Emperor Michael as a 'fomenter of heresy'. In 1282 a revolt in Sicily destroyed the Angevin fleet as it was about to sail against Constantinople. On 11 December 1282 Emperor Michael VIII Palaeologus died, excommunicated in his lifetime by the Latin Church of his adoption and after his death deprived of customary religious services by the Church of his birth. Yet Michael, arch-diplomat though he was, in my opinion was sincere in his unionism.

Michael's heir was Andronicus, the co-Emperor, who, whenever his father had made a profession of the Latin faith, had signified in writing and on oath his complete agreement, that 'he would inviolably observe and never abandon, deviate or differ from the faith that the sacrosanct Roman Church holds truthfully and faithfully teaches and preaches'.[11] Whether in these professions Andronicus was sincere[12] or was only yielding to pressure from his dominating father cannot be decided. Certainly at his father's death such was the state of public opinion that, if he wanted to keep the throne, he had to renounce the union. He did it very quickly and spent much of the next quarter of a century in pacifying the Church. Only towards the end of his reign did Andronicus make overtures again to the Western Church, but the negotiations were interrupted by a rebellion in Byzantium.[13]

On 28 May 1328 Andronicus II lost his throne to his grandson Andronicus III in the last of three civil wars that occasioned great devastation of the countryside and much popular discontent. The eyes of many were turned to the West in a quest for stability, since the papacy had been organizing 'Leagues' of maritime nations to put piracy down in the Aegean; also men hoped for help from the West to stem the advance in Asia Minor of the Turks, who had taken Nicaea in 1331. Hostility to the idea of union of the Churches diminished.[14] Indeed, there is reason to believe that the Emperor Andronicus III himself even joined the Latin Church. His wife Anna was a princess of Savoy and of Latin stock. At the court in Constantinople there were many Latin courtiers, attendants and clerics. According to a Franciscan chronicle, one of these last, Fra Garcia Arnoldi, 'In the year of the Lord 1332 . . . brought the Emperor of the Greeks and converted him to the true faith and the unity of the Church'. Incredible as it may seem, it may be true; but it would

---

[11]*Acta Romanorum Pontificum ab Innocentio V ad Benedictum XI (1276–1304)*, ed. F. M. Delorme and A. L. Tautu (Città del Vaticano 1954), doc. 19, p. 46, date 16 July 1277.

[12]*Ibid.*, doc. 17 of April 1277; doc. 46, of Sept. 1279. In 1277 he had been away campaigning 'against the Turks' when his father had renewed his profession of faith, so he sent a long letter of explanation to the Pope assuring him of his unflagging enthusiasm for the cause of union: *Ibid.*, doc. 16, date April 1277.

[13]Raynaldus, *Annales*, 1326, 26. A. Laiou, *Constantinople and the Latins. The Foreign Policy of Andronicus II 1282–1328* (Cambridge, Mass. 1972), pp. 308–29, is convinced that the Emperor was serious in his overtures for union.

[14]There are many witnesses for this; for instance. Marino Sanudo in his letter of 13 October 1334 to the king of France, in F. Kunstmann, 'Studien über Marino Sanudo der Alteren', in *Abh. der hist. Cl. der kgl. bayer. Akad. der Wiss.* vii (1855), *ep.* VI; Raynaldus *Annales*, 1333, 17–19.

have been done in secret and kept secret. At the least it offers a rational explanation of some cryptic phrases in a letter sent by Pope John XXII to King Philip VI of France, dated 18 July 1334: 'Wherefore he besought you in the Lord and asked that he might return to the bosom and unity of the said Church', where the context of negotiations about a League suggests that the 'he' referred to was Andronicus.[15]

Five years later in 1339 the Calabrian monk, Barlaam, sent to Avignon by Andronicus to ask for help against the Turks, told the Pope and the Consistory of cardinals that it was not so much difference of dogma as hatred caused by long years of Greek suffering at Latin hands that kept the Churches divided – words that since then have been quoted times innumerable as fairly depicting the relations between East and West in the mid-14th century. In view, however, of what has been briefly indicated above (and, one may add, of events yet to come), one may perhaps think that the Calabrian monk, to impress the Curia, was indulging in a little rhetorical exaggeration.

Andronicus III died young on 15 June 1341, leaving as heir to the throne his son John, not yet ten years old. Even though his mother had adopted the Greek rite at her marriage, John in his earliest years must have imbibed a certain sympathy for the Western Church from her, her entourage and even from his unfanatical father.[16] The latter's death practically coincided with the start of the Hesychast Controversy, which was one of the most important influences in the internal policies of the Empire for the next century and the start of a very bitter division among Greek churchmen. John in his teens would not have been involved in it, and even in his later life he seems to have stood apart from it.

The boy John was hurriedly crowned emperor in Constantinople on 19 November 1341, because his late father's friend and confidant, John Cantacuzenus, disappointed at not automatically becoming regent for the orphaned heir and so, if not emperor in name, emperor at least in practice, had donned the imperial purple to lay claim to be emperor as of right. There followed six years of civil war in which Cantacuzenus nearly lost but finally won by means of the hordes of his Turkish allies. On 21 May 1347 John VI Cantacuzenus was again crowned emperor in Constantinople and John V Palaeologus became co-emperor. No sooner was Cantacuzenus established on the throne than he got in touch with the Holy See. He assured Clement VI that, with the assent of the co-emperor, he had already subscribed a formal chrysobull giving the Pope his title and recognizing the primacy and universality of the Roman Church. He was ready to obey the Pope as did the King of France. For questions of faith there should be a general council. His four envoys reached Avignon on

[15]G. Golubovich, *Biblioteca bio-bibliografica della Terra Santa e dell'Oriente franciscano*, iii (Quaracchi 1919), p. 294. U. V. Bosch in *Andronicus III Palaeologos* (Amsterdam 1965), pp. 121–8. 194, is inclined to credit this testimony. For John XXII's letter, see Raynaldus, *Annales*, 1334, 6.
[16]Andronicus had enthusiastically adopted a number of knightly exercises and pastimes introduced by his wife's Savoyard household.

5 March 1348. Clement acknowledged their arrival. Cantacuzenus in his *History* claims that the Pope answered immediately, eager for a council. The truth is that two years passed before Clement sent an embassy and the only extant Latin documents concerning it are the letters of credence issued to its members. Clement's successor, Innocent VI, was more enthusiastic, but a new civil war in Byzantium, when John V had decided to vindicate his claims to be sole emperor, put an end to communications with the West. John V took possession of Constantinople towards the end of November 1354, and John VI Cantacuzenus retired to a monastery as a monk with the name of Joasaph.

By 1354 the Turks were in possession of the whole of Asia Minor, except for the city of Philadelphia which somehow managed to resist, and for the port Smyrna captured by one of the papal-sponsored Leagues and still in Latin hands. Indeed, they had also gained their first permanent foothold in Europe by occupying Gallipoli in 1354 and refusing all persuasions and money-offers to relinquish it. In the previous few decades Thrace and Thessaly had suffered appallingly from the Turks, who came sometimes as allies of one or other of the contending Greek parties, sometimes purely as raiders; but whether they came as 'friends' or foes they departed laden with booty of enslaved Greeks, of herds and of chattels. Between 1327 and 1359 the Turkish troops of Cantacuzenus' son-in-law Orchan raided European territory no less than sixteen times. Gallipoli in their hands was an open door into the Empire, whose plight became ever more desperate. Help could be looked for only from the West. So overtures to the popes and suggestions of church union became more urgent and more frequent.

John V did not wait long after his bloodless victory over Cantacuzenus before approaching Innocent with a project. The document dated 15 December 1355 assured the Pope of John's submission and obedience, and in return for fifteen ships with 500 cavalry and 4,000 infantry he promised the obedience of the Greek Church within six months, which he thought feasible. He would surrender his second son, Manuel, as a kind of hostage, accept a papal legate, and set up in Constantinople institutions to teach Latin to the sons of the nobility, but he himself should be commander of all the troops.[17] This project was at once fantastic and practical, but more fantastic than practical. There was no likelihood at all of bringing the Greeks quickly into the Latin Church, but the suggestion of bridging the gulf of ideas that lay between East and West by education was sound, though it would have taken many years to be of any effect. In fact the project was never tried out. Pope Innocent did not delay in answering. When his nuncio arrived in Constantinople John renewed on oath his promise 'from this time forward to preserve faith and fidelity to my Lord the Sovereign Pontiff as other princes of the

[17]*Acta Innocentii PP. VI (1352–1362)*, ed. A. L. Tautu (Roma 1961), doc. 84; Raynaldus, *Annales*, 1355, 33–37.

Roman Church preserve it', and he received the Eucharist from the papal nuncio's hands.[18] But all that Innocent could do in the way of immediate military aid was to divert the fleet of the Naval League, resuscitated in 1357, into Constantinopolitan waters where it took Lampsacus on the eastern side of the Dardanelles (1359).

Pope Innocent's successor, Urban V, was very active in trying to promote crusades, not only to liberate the Holy Land and to find a theatre of war outside Europe for the various marauding bands of mercenary soldiers who in the peaceful intervals of the Hundred Years' War between France and England were devastating the French countryside, but also to bring relief to John V and the Byzantine Empire. His many exhortations in the first three years of his reign to England and France, to Venice and Genoa, to the Roman Emperor Charles IV and Louis I of Hungary, produced only an expedition that was wasted on taking Alexandria and holding it for only six days. John was kept *au fait* with all these endeavours and, when they proved abortive, in the winter of 1365–6, he set off himself with two of his sons and a very small entourage to visit Louis in Buda, to persuade him to fight the Turk. The first contacts were most promising. Louis asked Venice to hire ships to him since he wanted to help Constantinople. Then he and John sent a combined embassy to the Pope to ask what conditions the Greek Emperor should fulfil to enter the Latin Church. Urban appointed the profession of faith as issued by Pope Clement, but before he did that, doubtful about the purity of John's motives in wishing to join the Latin Church, he gave Louis permission to defer for a year any undertaking he had entered into. At the same time in more than a dozen letters to princes, nobles and prelates he promulgated the crusade that Louis was to lead. But Louis, who so far had used his armies in the east only against Christian Bulgarians, now turned his attention to policies in the west and there was no crusade. John on his return from Buda, where he had to leave one of his sons as hostage, was held up by the Bulgarian Zupan Sišman and was released only when his cousin, the Count of Savoy, came to his help. John passed much of the latter part of that winter in the company of his cousin Amadeo and of the Latin Patriarch of Constantinople, Paul, and with them he entered into an engagement to visit the Pope either in his own person or in the person of his eldest son, Andronicus. Conversations in Constantinople brought the bright hope of a council with the Western Church and, when Amadeo returned to Italy in June 1367, he was accompanied by Patriarch Paul and a number of Greeks representing Church, state and city, intent on arranging the details of the council with the Pope. They found Urban in Viterbo and they went with him to Rome. Nothing is known of their negotiations with the Pope, but after they returned to Byzantium Urban addressed at least twenty-three letters, all dated 6 November 1367, to various personages or groups in the east, and in not one of them was the word 'council' ever

[18] *The Life of Saint Peter Thomas by Philippe de Mézières*, ed. J. Smet (Rome 1954), pp. 76–79, 75.

mentioned. There was no council. But John fulfilled his promise. On 17 October 1369 in Rome he made his profession of faith and on Sunday 21 October, on the steps before the Church of St Peter, he paid homage to the Pope and was embraced by him. His conversion was a purely personal act. In no way did it involve the Greek Church or the Greek state, but it must have created an anomalous situation in Byzantium when the 'God-crowned' emperor was not a member of the Greek Church. These persistent efforts of the eastern emperor to move the west to succour his almost beleaguered capital did not avail it much. Before ever he got back from his journey in the west the Turks had crushed the Serbs in a battle near the Marica River (26 September 1371), and within another couple of years John himself was a tributary of the Turks, bound to pay the equivalent of 15,000 Venetian ducats annually to his masters and to assist them in person with an army of 12,000 soldiers, if they demanded his help in any military action. All the same, one has the impression that, despite all the disappointments of his hopes in the Latins, John's adherence to the Latin Church was sincere; in fact, that at heart he had always been a Latin Christian. He died on 16 February 1391.

In the last two decades of his reign John V had to face four rebellions, three from his eldest son Andronicus and one from his grandson John VII. His faithful helper in all his adversities was always his second son Manuel, but even Manuel almost rebelled when at the *fiat* of their Turkish overlords he was deprived by his father of his right of succession to the throne in favour of Andronicus who by rebellion had forfeited it. Without reference to his father he took himself off to his appanage, Thessalonica, and there defied both Constantinople and the Turks. The Turks took up the challenge and Thessalonica was closely besieged from 1383 till its submission in 1387. Towards the end of the siege, when Manuel was in desperate need of men and money, he sent an embassy to seek aid from the Pope. A papal legate visited Constantinople (where he was very ill received) and Thessalonica where union was accepted and help promised. The flight, however, of Manuel from the city marked the end of whatever union there was and its capture made help superfluous.[19]

It is not likely that Manuel was anything but an opportunist in the negotiations for ecclesiastical union. Certainly, some fifteen years later when as Emperor of Constantinople he was in Paris seeking men and money for the defence of his Empire, to answer a theological critic he wrote a book of fifty-two chapters to refute the Latin doctrine of the *Filioque*. His Empire was, indeed, saved but not because of the help he received from the west. Timurlane, the Mongol Khan, defeated and captured the Turkish Sultan Bayezid (1402), and in the confusion that resulted among the Sultan's heirs Byzantium breathed freely again for a score of

---

[19]Nearly all the information that is available about this episode comes from letters of Demetrius Cydones, minutely analysed by G. T. Dennis, *The Reign of Manuel II Palaeologus in Thessalonica 1382-1387* (*Orientalia Christiana Analecta* 159: Roma 1960), pp. 132-50.

years. During this time Manuel sent his representatives to the Latin Council of Constance (1414–18) and exchanged frequent embassies with Pope Martin V. He died, however, on 21 July 1425 and it fell to his son, John VIII, to follow up the negotiations with Rome whose final result was that John VIII, Patriarch Joseph II with some 20 metropolitans, and about 700 Greeks met with Pope Eugenius and Latin bishops in Ferrara. On 9 April 1438 there was inaugurated what was, as regards fulness of representation from East and West, the most ecumenical of all ecumenical councils in the history of the Church.

Discussions about Purgatory in June and July 1438 were inconclusive. From 8 October to 13 December thirteen sessions were held dealing with the legitimacy of the addition to the Creed of the *Filioque* clause by the Latins. Was it or was it not contrary to the decree of the Council of Ephesus (A.D. 431) that forbade 'another faith'? The Greeks asserted that Ephesus prohibited all, even literal, changes – even of a syllable. The Latins argued that it referred only to the content, the meaning. The sessions ceased with no agreement reached. The Greeks were disheartened and wanted to return home. However, in January 1439 they went to Florence to which city the council was transferred. Eight sessions there were devoted to the doctrine of the *Filioque* and ended still with no accord. Weeks of expedients and parleys and tension followed. The solution came at the end of May. It was manifest that saints of the Latin Church believed that the Holy Spirit proceeds from the Father and the Son, and saints of the Greek Church that he proceeds from the Father or from the Father through the Son. This fact became the basis of an argument that convinced the Greeks when it was seen in the light of an axiom which all Greek theologians in Italy accepted without hesitation – that saints, just because they are saints and are, therefore, imbued with the Holy Spirit, cannot disagree in the faith for that would imply self-contradiction in the Spirit; if their expressions of the faith differ, their meaning must be the same. Union, therefore, of the Churches was not only possible but necessary, for to prolong schism without cause was unthinkable. The union of the Greek and the Latin Churches was proclaimed in the cathedral church of Florence on 6 July 1439 and the document was signed by both Churches. For the Oriental Church first the Emperor wrote in big, sprawly letters, 'John, in Christ God, faithful Emperor and Autocrat of the Romans, Palaeologus', and after him came the signatures of 4 procurators of the other Eastern patriarchs, 18 metropolitans (counting over again the bishop-procurators), a Russian bishop, 3 procurators of bishops, 5 *Stavrophoroi* deacons of the Great Church of St Sophia, Gregory the Protosyncellus (also a procurator), and 7 heads or representatives of monasteries.

The union freely concluded in Florence was ill-received in Constantinople, and soon the older prelates who had signed the decree in Italy recanted; but all the younger ones remained steadfast in their opinions, including the Metropolitan of Ephesus, the most outstanding opponent of the union. Unfortunately Pope Eugenius, meaning to honour the Oriental Church by creating two of its most capable prelates cardinals, thereby removed from the arena of controversy Bessarion of Nicaea at the same time as another of the foremost protagonists of union, Isidore, went to his See of Moscow in Russia. Mark Eugenicus had little opposition to his skilful propaganda against the union and he was followed by George Scholarius, a talented writer. So once more Constantinople was split over a union of the Churches achieved in the west.

Like Michael VIII, so also John VIII when he died on 31 October 1448 was refused the usual religious commemorations.[20] His brother constantine XI, who succeeded him on the throne, favoured the union, if only because he looked for help from the West. All his efforts to placate the obdurate core of anti-unionists gathered round the monk Gennadius (George Scholarius) failed; they even refused to commemorate him in the Liturgy. The situation changed when the new Sultan, Mehmet, built the fortress of Rumeli Hissar to dominate the Bosphorus and cut the route of Constantinople's grain from the Black Sea. He was setting the stage for his attack on the city. Constantine despatched an urgent embassy round Italy for troops and supplies of food and arms. The Pope sent as his legate Cardinal Isidore, Metropolitan of Kiev and All Russia, who arrived in Constantinople on 20 October 1452 with a troop of two hundred cross-bowmen that he had recruited at his own expense for the defence of the city. Rumeli Hissar was such a cogent argument for union that when on 12 December 1452 Isidore held a solemn Liturgy in which the Pope and the unionist Patriarch of Constantinople, Gregory, were commemorated, and the decree of union officially promulgated (it had not been promulgated before in Constantinople), the Church of St Sophia was thronged. On 8 April 1453 Mehmet laid siege to Byzantium. On 29 May he took it. Isidore fought in its defence, was wounded but escaped in disguise. Emperor Constantine fought in its defence and died. In the mosque of St Sophia Mehmet thanked Allah for his victory.[21]

[20]G. Scholarius, *Oeuvres complètes de Gennade-Scholarios*, ed. L. Petit, A. Sidéridès, M. Jugie, iii (Paris 1930), p. 100.
[21]J. Gill, *The Council of Florence* (Cambridge 1959), pp. 370–88.

XX

Pope Callistus III and Scanderbeg the Albanian

The capture of Constantinople by Mehmet II on 29 May 1453 took Europe by surprise. Immediately all the western powers began to say what should have been done and what should be done. But no one did anything worth while except Pope Nicholas V, and his endeavour was doomed to failure because it was isolated and late. A necessary condition for efficient action against the Turk was peace among the States of Italy. In autumn Nicholas invited them to negotiations in Rome. They came and went away again as divided as ever, and a crusade was no nearer. The two small fleets of five ships each which Nicholas sent after May 1453 were obviously too late to save Constantinople; they were also ineffective because they were hindered by the Venetians already in negotiation with the Sultan. Indeed, before the meeting in Rome was finished Venice, desirous at all costs to save its commerce, had already made a treaty with the Conqueror. Alfonso of Naples, who between 1448 and 1453, had received vast sums of money from Nicholas V to keep a fleet in the Aegean, had recalled it during the very siege of Constantinople to use it against Genoa, and later had the effrontery to blame the Pope for the lack of western aid to the beleaguered city (¹). Frederick III, the Roman Emperor, proposed a meeting of the princes at Ratisbon, but he

(¹) C. MARINESCU, Le pape Nicolas V (1447-1455) et son attitude envers l'Empire byzantin, in Actes du IV Congrès international des Etudes byzantines, Sofia 1935, pp. 331-42. The same author has written another article, useful in this context, unfortunately not at the moment available to me: Le Pape Callixte III (1447-1958), Alphonse V d'Aragon, Roi de Naples, et l'offensive contre les Turcs, in Académie Roumaine, Bulletin de la section hist. XIX (1935), pp. 77-97.

did not go himself, and neither there nor in several subsequent Diets was there any sign of viable combined action.

Pope Nicholas died on 24 March 1455 and was succeeded by Callistus III, aged 77.

Callistus was animated by one idea, to retake Constantinople and to drive the Turk out of Europe. He had not realised that "The idealistic enthusiasm of the Christian West for noble enterprises in the east had given place to a policy òf cold calculation and selfish indifference » (¹). He announced his purpose in the very conclave that had elected him (²) and within a month had issued a Bull to rouse the West, fixing the date for the crusade as 1 March 1456 (³). Legates were appointed to promulgate it in all countries, and preachers and collectors to rouse enthusiasm and to encourage donations to the cause (⁴). His aim was to provide both a fleet and an army. The fleet was the easier, for it depended less on others. Already in September 1455 he could send galleys to protect the islands of the Aegean, but Cardinal Urrea, Archbishop of Tarragona, his legate and commander of the fleet, used them against Genoa in favour of Alfonso of Naples. Since Venice was chary of offending the Sultan, and Alfonso of Naples, who had promised fifteen galleys, produced nothing but fine words, Callistus set up a shipyard on the Tiber that by the end of May 1456 had built sixteen galleys (⁵).

Cardinal Trevisan, who had been appointed to replace the treacherous Urrea, had no desire to leave Italy, but Callistus drove him on, just as he exhorted, cajoled and admonished by frequent letters his legates and preachers elsewhere to push the crusade. They failed, because there was not one of the big powers, apart from Hungary, that was interested or that realised that Turkish

(¹) L. PASTOR, Storia dei Papi, 2nd edit. (Roma 1925) p. 623.

(²) RAYNALDUS, Annales ecclesiastici, 1455, XVIII.

(³) Ibid. 1455, XIX

(⁴) Ibid. 1455, XXV seq.

(⁵) PLATYNA records of Alfonso after a serious earthquake in 1456: " Then Alfonso for the third time repeated the vow he had made against the Turk and declared that he would strictly fulfil what he vowed. But not even so could he be forced into the holy crusade, to such a degree was he ensnared by the attractions of the kingdom of Naples "; Liber de vita Christi ac omnium pontificum (= L. A. MURATORI, Raccolta degli Storici Italiani, III, 1, edd. G. CARDUCCI & V. FIORINI, Città di Castello 1913).

XX

ambitions extended as far as their victorious arms could take them. Hungary was interested because it was clearly the next big objective of the Conqueror. In 1456 Mehmed attacked Belgrade in force. He was opposed by John Hunyadi with a small and ill-equipped army, by Giovanni of Capistrano, a saintly and eloquent Franciscan preacher of the Holy War, and by a crusade of prayer organised by Callistus. But the Christian powers of Europe — even the king of Hungary, Ladislas — had not helped: some had run away at the first sign of real danger. " It would have been the end of that most cruel race, if the Christian powers had desisted from their intestine wars and rivalries and had followed up so great a victory by land and sea as Callistus begged and exhorted them " (¹). They did not. Callistus, therefore, concentrated on helping those who were making an effective resistance to the Turk — the frontier countries of Hungary, Bosnia and Albania.

The spirit of the Hungarian resistance was John Hunyadi. As a young man he had been in the service of Sigismund, King of Hungary, and had accompanied him to the Council of Constance (1414) and on his journey to Rome to be crowned Roman Emperor (1433). He fought against the Hussites and the Turks, and successfully, thus encouraging those who had begun to think that the Turk was invincible. A brilliant campaign against them in 1443 was, however, followed by the crushing defeat at Varna in 1444. Hunyadi, however, never gave up. He was defeated again at Kossovo in 1448, but still persevered. His most brilliant exploit was the saving of Belgrade against all the might of the Conqueror of Constantinople, but he died a few months later on 11 August 1456.

Hungary was a Catholic country. Bosnia was "the only medieval European state in which a heretical Church was pre-eminent and of long duration " (²). That was the Church of the Patarenes or Bogomils or, as they were known in western Europe, the Cathari or Albigenses, which offered the rulers of Hungary in the fourteenth century occasions for trying to impose their authority over Bosnia on the pretext of combating heresy. To keep

(¹) PLATYNA, Op. cit., p. 342.
(²) M. DINIČ, in *The Cambridge Medieval History* IV, pt 1 (Cambridge 1966) p. 547.

out the Hungarians, the rulers called in the Turks. Afterwards, to keep out the Turks, later Bosnian kings appealed to Hungary and the papacy, which meant condoning the banishment of the Bogomils. But the Bosnian nobility was always opposed. Eugenius IV legitimised King Stephen Thomas "a Catholic prince"[1], who (so records a letter of Eugenius recommending him to the nobility of Hungary) "after many and diverse, protracted negotiations with our venerable brother, the Bishop of Hvar, whom we have maintained for seven years as Apostolic Legate with him in his kingdom, at last became a Catholic" [2]. He was, however, opposed by the Bogomils with Turkish help [3] and even perhaps by renegade Catholics against whom Pope Nicholas V advocated strong ecclesiastical measures [4]. That the king and many of his nobles were sincere Catholics and staunch opponents of the Turks is demonstrated by many letters of Pope Callistus. When the reigning family of Serbia was exstinct, Stephen tried to occupy the throne by an invasion and a marriage alliance of his son, paying also tribute to the Turk for peaceful possession (February, 1458). Bosnia was occupied by Mehmet II in 1463 when Stephen Thomas's son was defeated and captured [5].

The story of Albania's defiance of Turkish arms is the story of one man, George Castriota, surnamed Scanderbeg (= Alexander-beg). Taken hostage in his youth, he learnt the art of war from the Turks themselves, with whom he gained a high reputation for skill and valour and earned promotion. But he remained at heart a Christian (he had adopted Islamism) and a patriot, and when Hunyadi's feats of 1443 pointed the way, he abandoned the Sultan in the confusion, adroitly acquired the city of Croja on the Albanian coast and started a national movement of resistance, which elected him ' Captain General of Albania ' at a meeting of nobles in Alessio, which was then in Venetian hands. He was encouraged by the West, chiefly the popes from Eugenius IV onwards, but also by Alfonso of Naples and, when it suited them,

[1] RAYNALDUS, 1445, XXIII.
[2] Ibid. 1445, XXIV.
[3] Ibid. 1450, XIII.
[4] Ibid. 1449, IX.
[5] For a letter from the Doge of Venice on the subject cf. V. MAKUSCEV, *Monumenta historica Slavorum meridionalium*, I (Warsaw, 1874) pp. 532-3.

the Venetians. There were, however, too many rivalries and quarrels among the Albanian nobles for the pact of Alessio to last long, and Scanderbeg was usually alone with never more then 20.000 men and frequently less. By utilising the mountainous terrain of Albania, by speed of movement, when necessary by Fabian tactics and always by immense personal valour, he defeated four Turkish armies between 1443 and 1448 and acquired wide territories at their expense. In 1450 the Sultan Murad II came in person to dispose of him. He besieged Kroja for five months but could not take it either by arms or by bribes. He retired and the western world exulted at this Christian success, for Hunyadi, the other hero, had been defeated shortly before at Kossovo. Murad died on 3 February 1451, and his successor, Mehmet II, at first showed himself pacific and accomodating. But not for long. He took Constantinople in 1453; the Serbian gold and silver mines of Novo Brdo with south-west Serbia fell to him in 1455; he accepted tribute from Moldavia in the same year and attacked Belgrade in 1456. During this last campaign a Turkish army invaded Albania to occupy Scanderbeg. Next year an expedition in force drove him back as far as Alessio, but on 2 September by a surprise attack he inflicted his most telling defeat on the Turks at Tomoritza, killing at least 15.000 and capturing the camp and its treasures. Pope Callistus gave him what help he could, as will be seen in greater detail later. Mehmet recognised the Albanian's conquests in May 1461, but Scanderbeg to support the crusade project of Pope Pius II opened hostilities again two years later. The Sultan retaliated in 1466 by laying siege to Croja and, though Scanderbeg with western help defeated the Turks in various engagements, he could not force them to abandon the siege, which was still going on when he died on 17 January 1468.

Callistus's vehemence against the Turk and his burning determination appear from very many of his letters. He wrote to Ragusa on 26 April 1457: " Many and indeed patent indications have witnessed to you the most burning zeal of Our mind for the destruction of that reprobate sect and people of the Turks and of other infidels, which keeps Our senses aflame with a fire inextinguishable. We have no other purpose or aim for Our endeavours than to avenge the shame brought on the orthodox faith and, by suppressing the savagery of the barbarians, to restore tranquillity and peace to holy religion" (¹). "For We desire more than anyone can possibly imagine to go against the most wicked Turk and to build and increase Our fleet in every possible manner "(²).

His endeavour was limited by the means at his disposal and often he had to excuse himself that he could give little practical assistance because his resources were exhausted. To two staunch warriors of Albania he had to reply: "Would that We had in hand means in proportion to Our intention and will to defend and propagate the orthodox faith. But since for some time We have spent large sums on sending and maintaining the fleet already despatched to the Turkish frontiers and We are now undertaking even larger expenses for the final preparation and arming of another fleet which We are building as fast as possible, to be sent for the protection of the faithful and the destruction of the infidels, and besides We have sent large sums of money to Hungary and promised to send even more, We are at a loss where to turn, to whom to address Our request, whence to seek help, from whom to receive aid, to be able to send some to you in the present contingency"(³). He remained, however, always optimistic of the ultimate issue, especially after the ' miracle ' of Belgrade (⁴). His trust in Providence helped him to exhort and encourage honestly those who,

---

(¹) Cf. Appendix doc. 7. The documents in the appendix are as yet, I believe, unpublished. They will be part of a vast collection connected with Scanderbeg, to be published under the auspices of the Centro Internazionale di Studi Albanesi presso l'Università di Palermo by Father G. Valentini, S.J., to whom I owe my thanks for help in writing this article. Cf. also docs. 5, 9, 17: RAYNALDUS, 1456, XLIV; 1458, XIV-XV.

(²) L. WADDING, Annales Minorum, Vol. XIII, (Quaracchi, 1932) p. 10, n. XV.

(³) RAYNALDUS, 1456, XLIV. Cf. also docs. 5, 11, 17; RAYNALDUS, 1457, XXI-XXII, 1458, XIV-XV.

(⁴) Nec te terreant ulle mine, nec numerosas copias formides: nam Deus non deseret plebem suam, qui vel solo nutu suis propugnatoribus victoriam contra innumerabiles exercitus dare potest. Quis enim superiore anno magnitudine impendentis periculi prostratus non erat cum impius Turcorum tirannus in faucibus Hungarie cum inaudita potentia ad eam occupandam obstinatissimo animo immineret? Atque Deus omnipotens dominus exercituum divinam infudit virtutem cordibus Christifidelium et in eorum brachiis potentiam fecit. Qui non modo non cessere furialibus ausis turchi, sed eum qui terrore suo mundum bene complerat exutum castris, amissisque infinitis bellici apparatus instrumentis, in fugam turpissimam cum maxima strage compulerunt. Sed quamvis hec magna fue-

in their dire straits, appealed to him, even when he could not help them immediately ([1]).

Callistus put great reliance on the Franciscans whom he used freely as preachers, collectors and reformers. The story of St John Capistrano and the part he played in the defence of Belgrade is well known. Besides him there were dozens of others who worked loyally to support the crusade. For instance Callistus wrote to the King of Bosnia on 23 April 1457: " Our beloved son, Fra Nicoló da Sibinico O.M. whom We sent last year to those parts for certain commissions has returned and has delivered to Us your letter from which and from his more detailed verbal report We have understood clearly your holy, pious and devoted purpose " ([2]). For this they were empowered to found monasteries and to draw on other monasteries of their Order ([3]) for suitable personnel. Fra Eugenio of Albania, for example, was encouraged to find other Albanian friars to assist him ([4]). They were to work in conjunction with the legates that the Pope had appointed. These, besides promulgating the crusade, were to present the crusader's cross to those deemed worthy to receive it ([5]), and had also to try to keep the peace between rival nobles. Nicholas V instructed his legate in Hungary to put an end to the hostilities between the King of Bosnia and George the Prince of Rascia, Vuković Branković ([6]). A few years later (1452) his Apostolic Nuncio, the Bishop of Drivost, was to reconcile Scanderbeg with two Albanian nobles ([7]). These allied themselves with the Turks, and therefore incurred excommunication. Later, reconciled with Scanderbeg and penitent for their treachery and the harm they had done to

---

runt, maiora adhuc restant, que Deus pro victoria populi sui peraget ». RAYNALDUS, 1457, XXI. Cf. also Ibid. XXIII-XXIV, A. THEINER, *Vetera monumenta historica Hungariam sacram illustrantia*, vol. II, 1352-1526, (Romae 1860) doc. LXXII, pp. 303-4.

([1]) Cf. Doc. 8. Also RAYNALDUS 1456, XLIV; 1457, XXI-XXII; THEINER, *Doc. Hung.* CCCCLXVI pp. 297-8; ibid. LXXII pp. 303-4.

([2]) THEINER, *Docs. hung.* CCCCLVII p. 291. Cf. also doc. 7; THEINER, op. cit., CCCCLXIV pp. 296-7; CCCCLXVII pp. 298.

([3]) E.g. WADDING, XII, p. 124 et passim.

([4]) WADDING, XIII, p. 14.

([5]) Cfr. THEINER, *Doc. hung.*, CCCCLVII, p. 292; CCCCLXIV pp. 296-7.

([6]) Doc. 1.

([7]) Doc. 3.

the Christian cause, they asked for and received absolution from the Holy See ([1]).

Ragusa was too near the Turk and the Patarenes of Bosnia to want to identify itself too closely with the papal crusade. A certain Bogomil noble Stephen attacked Ragusa with the aid of Christian mercenaries. Pope Nicholas forbade Christians to enrol under him " ne dictus patarenus cum christianis opprimat christianos " ([2]). The incident, however, had a happy ending: Duke Stephen became a Catholic ([3]). Later as Turkish arms prevailed more and more, Ragusa, which had paid tribute to the Sultan from the days of Murad II, hastened to confirm its good relations with Mehmet both at his accession and when he had all but absorbed Serbia ([4]). Pope Callistus had to write several letters threatening censures to make the city release the money that had been deposited there, the proceeds of the tenth imposed in favour of the crusade ([5]). And those censures were in fact imposed ([6]).

Callistus gave help in money and by the protection of a fleet. But the fleet needed to be constructed, and that needed money. Hence his repeated appeals all over the western world for generosity to the cause ([7]). To Scanderbeg he promised that, notwith-

---

([1]) A. THEINER, *Vetera monumenta Slavorum Medionalium historiam illustrantia*, Tom. I, 1198-1549, (Romae 1863) doc. DLXXXVIII, pp. 413-4,. dated 22 Aug. 1454.

([2]) THEINER, *Doc. slav.*, DLXXXII, p. 408 dated 9 June 1451.

([3]) Doc. 2.

([4]) F. BABINGER, *Mehmed der Eroberer und seine Zeit*, (München 1953) pp. 70, 165.

([5]) Doc. 9, 12, 13: THEINER, *Doc. slav.* DCXIII p. 432.

([6]) Doc. 14.

([7]) Letter to his Legate in Hungary: " Our fleet, which We have constantly at heart to increase and strengthen, already is harassing the seaboard of the Turks, and has taken several islands of considerable size; and our transports with some other ships and vessels have already set sail to the fleet with victuals, money, corn and other necessaries. We are striving to send other galleys which We are having constructed here and finished as quickly as possible. From here, from Sicily and from Our States and those of the holy Roman Church and also from the March of Ancona there is never an end of our sending, so that the faithless Turk may be greatly harassed and Constantinople may be retaken, the thought of whose recapture is for ever, as it were, a sword in our heart. There will arrive also with his strong and numerous fleet Our dearest son in Christ the illustrious King of Portugal, since We have been informed that

542

standing the cost of the fleet already in action, " all the same We will send with all possible speed one galley completely fitted out and armed in aid of Your Nobility and your people and thereafter We will procure some more to be sent as quickly as possible " (¹). Three months later (Sept. 1457) he promised to instruct his legate to employ the fleet in his assistance (²).

What money Callistus had over after fitting out the fleet, he distributed among the valiant defenders of Christianity on the Turkish frontiers and it grieved him sadly that he had not more to give. He wanted to use the proceeds of the tenth from Ragusa and Dalmatia to repay money he had borrowed for the crusade, the rest to be divided between the Kings of Hungary and Bosnia and Scanderbeg (³). To this purpose he appointed a special envoy, John Navarr. (⁴). Ragusa was unco-operative and apparently excused its reluctance to free the money on the grounds that Hungary claimed it all. Callistus replied: " Seeing that We have after prudent and mature consideration decided what We want done with that money, you and the King of Hungary ought to

---

he has ordered his fleet to set sail towards Us on the first of this month of April. When his fleet is united with Ours, the force will be more powerful to extend the strength of the enemy who, harassed simultaneously at many points, will necessarily have to spread his army out. From France We expect at least thirty galleys as can be plainly concluded from the agreement between Us and the King of France about raising a tenth each year. About England you will hear shortly and about Burgundy and the King of Aragon. If We were to describe each and every one, there would not be enough paper. Also from Castile, for even if Our most dear son in Christ the illustrious King of Castile and León attacks Granada, in a certain way he helps Us. Would that the Venetians, who are so cold, would listen to Our warnings and would be with Us "; THEINER, *Doc. hung.* CCCCL, p. 287, dated 10 April 1456. Alas for Pope Callistus. Not one of all the ships promised ever arrived, unless Aragon in the end sent some — but that is very doubtful. Cf. also doc. 7, 17; THEINER, op. cit., CCCCLXVII p. 298.

(¹) RAYNALDUS, 1457, XXII.
(²) THEINER, *Doc. hung.*, LXXII p. 303-4.
(³) Doc. 7, 9, 11; THEINER, *Doc. hung.* CCCCLXXII, CCCCLXXIII.
(⁴) THEINER, *Doc. slav.* DCIV pp. 246-7: " Tu vero adhibita pro magnitudine rei et periculi celeritate, receptis dictis pecuniis factaque equa divisione, quam primum cures, ut portio dicto Scanderbech destinata solvatur, ut earum subsidio periculum, in quod adductus dicitur, propulsare valeat »; Cf. also Doc. 10.

be satisfied with Our disposition of it " ([1]). But it seems that before his death he had not had his way with it, for to meet the urgent needs of Scanderbeg, who could not wait, he sent him 5.000 florins from Rome ([2]).

Hungary, Bosnia and Albania were the centre of the Pope's greatest concern, whose princes " prope soli oppositi sunt furori barbarorum et Turchorum, prohibent aditu, ne scelerato impetu in Christianitate irruant » ([3]). Towards Stephen-Thomas, King of Bosnia, and Scanderbeg he showed the greatest admiration, affection and gratitude for their continued resistance to Turkish pressure. Stephen-Thomas was a Latin Catholic ([4]) who had abandoned the Bogomil sect, a man after Callistus's own heart, who asked to be given the crusader's cross and banner ([5]). After the Christian victory of Belgrade he refused to continue paying tribute to the Sultan ([6]), and was (so the Collector Fra Mariano da Siena reported to the Pope) "continuously involved in war against the treacherous Turkish foes of Christ and ready to start a campaign in the beginning of September [1457] " ([7]). To encourage him Callistus told him of the money being sent to him and ended: " Do not wait till September" to lead out your army. But by May 1458 he was again paying tribute to the Turk.

On Scanderbeg, even more than on the King of Bosnia, Callistus lavished the greatest praise. He was his hero *par excellence*. Scanderbeg and the family of the Castriota were lords of a Latin Catholic territory in the dioceses of Albanese (suffragan of Antivari) and of Croja (suffragan of the Latin archdiocese of Durazzo). The Archbishop of Durazzo could speak of the year 1462 as being

---

([1]) Doc. 9, 12; THEINER, *Doc. slav.* DCXIII p. 432.

([2]) Doc. 14, 15; RAYNALDUS, 1458 XIV-XV.

([3]) THEINER, *Doc. slav.* DCIV p. 427.

([4]) Doc. 2; « spretis atque abiectis manichaeorum erroribus quibus irretitus fuerat, primus inter Reges Bosnie sanctam fidem catholicam acceptaverat, ipsamque publice confessus est, ipsum et regnum et heredes ... " We receive under Our protection; THEINER, *Doc. hung.* CCCXCV p. 237. Pastor, however, on the testimony of Aeneas Sylvius Piccolomini says that Stephen-Thomas was baptised only in 1457 by Card. Carvajal (Op. cit. p. 668).

([5]) THEINER, *Doc. hung.* CCCCLVI pp. 291-2; CCCCLVII p. 292; CCCCLXIV pp. 296-7.

([6]) THEINER, *Doc. hung.* CCCCLXIV.

([7]) THEINER, *Doc. hung.* CCCCLXVIII pp. 298-9.

a time " qua sub Illustri domino Scanderbehg, Albanie domino, ecclesiastica dignitas libertate tuituque plurimum gaudet " (¹).

Scanderbeg was always under Turkish attack, and time and again the Pope wrote to console him " since with intense grief " he had been informed " about the incursion of the Turks into your territories, about the devastation of that province and the injury to your subjects and lastly about the siege by which you say that you are shut in " (²). The history of some of those attacks is furnished by the archives of various Italian cities. A letter from Naples, dated 22 May 1455, records that Alfonso of Naples had sent a certain Palermo to Scanderbeg to report back on the situation, and then had decided to send help to the extent of 1200 infantry and 500 ' casalli '. Arrived there, they were surprised by a sudden attack of 40.000 Turkish cavalry. Between 5.000 and 6.000 Christians were killed including Scanderbeg's brother-in-law, and of the Neapolitan contingent only some 200 survived (³). In consequence Scanderbeg feared that the important city of Croja might surrender to the enemy for "the people of that country [Albania] are very well disposed to the Turk who gives them a good and humane governance " (⁴). In summer 1456 Scanderbeg wrote to the papal legate, Cardinal Carvajal, that the Turks were moving in force and that " we, for fear, have not dared await in our castle called Zendon the coming of the Emperor of the Turks, but we have for the time being retired to the region of Beche "; he asked for help "so that we can oppose the said Emperor and defend Christianity " (⁵). A year later a report, dated 31 July 1457, informed the Doge of Venice that Albania had been devastated by the Turks up to a mile from the (Venetian) town of Alessio, " that the greater part of the country has gone with the Turk;

(¹) N. IORGA, Notes et extraits pour servir à l'histoire des Croisades au XVᵉ siècle, IV (Bucharest, 1915) p. 195.

(²) RAYNALDUS, 1457 XXIII.

(³) Letter of Johannes Petrus Missalia to Ep.o Novara et comiti, in V. MACUSCEV, Monuments historiques des Slaves Méridionaux et de leurs voisins, II (Belgrade 1882) p. 227: letters of Orators of Duke of Milan in Naples, Ibid., pp. 148 (dated 14 Aug. 1455: ' casalli = cavalli '?) and 150 of date 8 Aug. 1455.

(⁴) Report of Treasurer of Sicily to King of Two Sicilies, of date 8 Dec. 1455, Ibid. p. 152.

(⁵) From a copy sent to the Duke of Milan from Buda 10 July 1456, Ibid. pp. 110-111.

the Magnifico Signor Scanderbeg has taken refuge in the mountains hiding [fuzendo] his head, for he has been abandoned by all his lieutenants, who are gone with the Turk " (¹). But Scanderbeg did not give in and in 1461 Mehmet recognised his rights to his territories.

. Pope Callistus was well informed of events either by means of letters or more often by word of mouth of messengers sent by Scanderbeg. In September 1457, for example, the Pope told his Commissario, John Navarr, to visit Scanderbeg quickly with money because he had been informed of " the incursion into Albania made by the Turk and the disaster which has befallen the Christians there, so that even Scanderbeg is besieged and surrounded by a Turkish army" (²). Callistus often praised Scanderbeg, and sincerely. To Navarr he wrote: " We are most concerned about the situation in Albania and of that valiant soldier and athlete of God, Scanderbeg, and what you have arranged with him " (³). To Scanderbeg himself he wrote: " We have weighed ... the marvellous greatness and courage of your soul, which, as befits a Catholic prince, is the chief weapon you employ against them [the Turk] to check their fury, and the continuous labours that you sustain in consequence. We thank God, who has set you like a bulwark and a most strong wall to resist in those areas through which, as through a door, there could be easy entry for that perfidious and most savage enemy to fall upon Christianity, and who afflicts with many a disaster that same enemy against whom you must often be locked in combat, to your very great praise and renown. Would that We had many of the Christian princes of a mind like yours; then We should not be so anxious and worried for the defence of the faith. Persevere, most dear son, in your devotion and your holy and wholesome intent ... " (⁴). Writing to Alfonso of Naples two days later, he repeated his words of praise for " that most firm wall " and added: " Though We are overburdened by intolerable expenses in every direction for the upkeep of Our fleet and of other operations which We have

---

(¹) From the Bailie and Capitan of Durazzo, Ibid., p. 113-4.
(²) Letter to Navarr dated 12 Sept. 1457, THEINER, Doc. slav. DCIV p. 427. Cf. RAYNALDUS, 1457, XXI; XXIII-XXV; 1458, XIV-XV; Doc. 11.
(³) Doc. 13, dated 3 Dec. 1457.
(⁴) RAYNALDUS, 1458, XIV, dated 6 February 1458

546

continuously in hand for the furtherance of this task, still, to encourage Scanderbeg to oppose the infidel, We are giving him a subsidy of 5.000 ducats and will give him an even more generous one when Our means allow it (¹).

Pope Callistus died on 30 July 1458 after three years of pontificate dedicated to the defence of Christianity and the defeat of the Turk, which then was the same thing. After his death there was found among his effects a copy of the vow he had made on his election to the throne of Peter: " I, Callistus III, Pope, promise and vow to the most Sacred Trinity, Father, Son and Holy Ghost...
... if necessary with the shedding of my blood ... to use all my energy for the recovery of Constantinople ... for the liberation of Christian captives, the exaltation of the orthodox faith and the extermination of the diabolical sect of the reprobate and perfidious Mohamet in the eastern world, where the light of the faith is well-nigh spent " (²). Scanderbeg passed nearly three decades in almost continuous warfare " to oppose the said Emperor and to defend Christianity", as he wrote to the cardinal legate. His name will be ever coupled with that of Pope Callistus for single-minded devotion in the crusade to restrain the advance of the Crescent at the expense of the Cross. The year 1968 marks the fifth centenary of the death of this Christian and national Albanian hero.

APPENDIX OF DOCUMENTS

I.

1449 III 1   Reg. Vat. t. 390, f. 290 v - 291 v

Petrus de Noxeto]
Littera de Curia directa Card.li Strigoniensi]

Nicolaus etc. Dilecto filio Dyonisio titulo sancti Ciriaci in Termis presbitero Cardinali Salutem etc. Inter cetera nostra solicitudinis studia hoc nouimus fore precipuum ut inter discordes quos idem christiani nominis titulus et eiusdem fidei professio consortes essent pacis

(¹) Doc. 15.
(⁷) RAYNALDUS, 1455, XVIII; PASTOR, Op. cit. p. 603

et bone voluntatis consilia cogitemus. Scimus (f. 291^r) etenim quod sine pace Dei et proximi dilectio non habetur neque pacis actor neque iustitia congrue colitur et dominia recte nequeunt gubernari. Sane cum ad nostram noticiam et plurimorum fidedignorum insinuatione prouenerit quod inter carissimum in Christo filium nostrum Bosne Regem Illustrem et dilectum filium Georgium Despotum Rassie vigent inimicitie satis graues ex quibus fidelium strages dietim secuta fuit et, nisi paterne prouisionis eis remediis occurratur, etiam maior ac magna personarum suarum dispendia et vtinam non animarum pericula tranquillique ipsorum status ac Terrarum commotiones et scandala erunt verisimiliter prouentura, Nos huiusmodi scandalis et periculis salubribus remediis quibus possumus obuiare volentes circumspectioni tue, de cuius probitate et industria in ceteris tibi creditis ministeriis laudabiliter comprobata confidimus, huiusmodi discordias ac inimiciciarum et iurgiorum obstacula quantumcumque durissima destruendi, tollendi et sedandi ac inter ipsos discordes et inimicos secundum a Deo tibi datam prudentiam omnia que sunt pacis vel concordie disponendi et ordinandi, contradictores quoslibet oportunis de quibus expedire cognoueris remediis compescendi, mulctandi et detinendi ceteraque alia precipiendi (¹) que in premissorum executione vtilia fuerint, plenam et liberam concedimus auctoritate apostolica facultatem, mandantes vniuersis et singulis Communitatibus, Ciuitatum et Vniuersitatibus opidorum et aliorum ipsarum partium locorum eorumque Rectoribus et Gubernatoribus, quos in tui fauorem duxeris requirendos, vt tibi oportunis fauoribus assistant et plene pareant in premissis. Nos enim quecumque circa predicta rite fereris ac penas, quas inter non obseruantes [*verso*] pacem vel concordiam statueris, rata habebimus et faciemus auctore domino usque ad satisfactionem condignam inuiolabiliter obseruari. Datum Rome apud Sanctum Petrum Anno etc. Millesimoquadringentesimoquadragesimonono Kal. Marcii pontificatus nostri Anno Tercio.

Gratis pro persona Cardinalis

Jacobus de Steccatis

2.

1452 VII 1   Reg. Vat. 421, f. Cxxxviij v

Petrus de Noxeto:

Nicolaus etc Venerabili fratri Thome Episcopo Farensi in Bosne et Croacie regnis ac in prouintia Ragusina illorumque Comitatibus et Diocesibus nostro et apostolice sedis legato misso Salutem etc. Dum eximie fidelitatis, deuotionis et reuerentie ceterasque a Domino tibi traditas virtutes ac fructuosa et laudabilia necnon Deo plurimum grata

---

(¹) precipiendi] percipiendi *Ms.*

et accepta opera, que alias in Bosne et Croatie regnis noster et dicte
sedis legatus missus existens etiam ad ipsorum regnorum fidelium
animarum salute[m] hactenus impendisti, ex quibus in prefatis regnis
laudabiles fructus hactenus prouenerunt ac, ut speramus, prouenient
in futurum attendimus et debita meditatione pensamus, ex hiis profecto certa experientia nobis nota non immerito confidimus et pro
certo tenemus quod in fidelitate deuotionis, prudentie et virtuosorum
operum huiusmodi laudabili continuatione persistens ea que etiam (?)
tibi de nouo duxerimus committenda curabis feliciter solicite et pru-
denter adimplere. Dudum siquidem felicis recordationis Eugenius
papa iiij. predecessor noster te in prefatis regnis legatum missum suum
et dicte sedis fecit, constituit et (Cxxxviiij) deputauit et deinde,
prefato predecessore sicut domino placuit sublato de medio, diuina
fauente clementia ad apicem summi apostolatus assumpti constitu-
tionem et deputationem predictas approbauimus et confirmauimus
ac nonnulla alia tunc expressa fecimus, prout in diuersis predicti pre-
decessoris ac nostris inde confectis litteris quarum tenores de verbo
ad verbum presentibus haberi volumus pro insertis plenius continetur.
Cum autem nuper Nobilis vir Stephanus Dux Sancti Sabbe et Comes
Dinnensis, postquam per nos accepto quod ipse cum copioso peditum
et equitum exercitu, nullo per eum indicto bello, [. . . . . . ?] Ciui-
tatem Ragusin. seu illius territorium inuaserat et innumeras clades et
maxima detrimenda illi intulerat, nonnulla quoque grauia et contra
fidem catholicam moliendo (?), et in (?) antedicta scelera tunc expressa
etiam in maximam christiani nominis ignominiam et fidei catholice
opproprium commiserat, per uenerabilem fratrem nostrum Paganinum
Episcopum Dulcinensem ut ab inuasionibus huiusmodi penitus desi-
steret moneri feceramus, quosdem ad nos destinaverit oratores seu
nuntios ex quorum relationibus, non solum inter prefatum Ducem et
dilectos filios Rectorem et Consilium dicte ciuitatis concordiam et
pacem subsequi, sed etiam eiusdem ducis mortifere heresis huiusmodi
per eum depositis erroribus ad viam ueritatis fidei reductionem sicque
totalem dicte heresis de prefato Regno eliminationem (1) et extirpationem subsequi posse speremus, si te, cuius olim dum in dictis
regnis legatus missus ut prefertur existeres opera et industria median-
tibus sicut experientie probatione didicimus carissimus in Christo
filius noster Thomasstephanus Rex Bosne Illustris ac eius vxor et
eciam quam plures Barones nobiles, milites et alie utriusque sexus
persone diuina illustrati gratia quoscumque Patarenorum (2) heresis
deponentes errores ac ueritatis lumen recognoscentes, quod mater
omnium et magistra sancta Romana Ecclesia tenet et profitetur, pro-
fessi fuerunt, profitentur et tenent quique in prefato regno Bosne
quamplura alia ad Dei laudem nostrumque et prefate sedis honorem
necnon animarum salutem concernentia operatus fuisti, Nos consti-

---

(1) eliminationem] elimationem *Ms.*
(2) Patarenorum] Paterenorum *Ms.*

tutionem, deputationem, concessionem et confirmationem et omnia alia et singula tam in nostris quam in predecessorum [*verso*] litteris predictis contenta horum serie approbantes et iuribus subsistere decernentes illosque ad provintiam Ragusin. ac ciuitates et dioceses predictas et ipsarum quamlibet extendentes, te legatum missum in illis cum potestate legati de latere usque ad nostrum et dicte sedis beneplacitum auctoritate apostolica facimus, constituimus et etiam deputamus, [ut](¹) inibi omnia et singula geras, ordines et disponas que ad illarum partium necnon ducis, Rectoris et Consilii (²) predictorum pacem et concordiam expedire cognoueris et sicut ibi dominus ministrabit. Et insuper cum summopere desideremus Ducem, Rectorem et Consilium(³) predictos, si fieri poterit, ad pacem et concordiam reduci, alioquin absque iudiciorum strepitu in premissis iusticiam habenti ministrari fidelitati tue partes ipsas ad pacem et concordiam reducendi, seu auditis hinc inde per utramque partium predictarum propositis etiam summarie similiter et de plano sine strepitu et figura iudicii, sola facti ueritate inspecta, quod iustum fuerit, appellatione remota, decernendi et que decreueris per censuram ecclesiasticam et alia iuris remedia, prout oportunum fuerit, obseruari faciendi necnon super huiusmodi ac uniuersis et singulis aliis negotiis heresis extirpationem et alia (⁴) fidei negotia, pacem quoque et concordiam ac tranquillitatem, tam dicti ducis et aliorum incolarum prefati regni quam Rectoris et Consilii ciuitatis et diocesis predictorum illorum statum concernentibus, prout tibi expediens uidebitur agendi, disponendi, statuendi, ordinandi et precipiendi, contradictores quoque et rebelles quoslibet cuiuscumque status, gradus, ordinis uel conditionis existant per censuram eandem, appellatione postposita, compescendi plenam et liberam auctoritate apostolica tenore presentium concedimus facultatem, non obstantibus quibuscumque constitutionibus ac priuilegiis et indulgentiis apostolicis generalibus uel specialibus quorumcumque tenorum et quibusuis personis, locis et ordinibus concessis, per que presentibus non expressa uel totaliter non inserta huiusmodi tue legationis et potestatis officium posset quomodolibet impediri aut etiam retardari, seu si aliquibus comuniter uel divisim a sede apostolica sit indultum quod interdici, suspendi uel excommunicari aut extra uel ultra certa loca ad iudicium euocari non possint per litteras apostolicas non facientes plenam et expressam ac de uerbo ad uerbum de indulto huiusmodi (Cxl) mentionem. Datum Rome apud Sanctum Petrum Anno etc. Millesimoquadringentesimoquinquagesimosecundo Kalendis Julii pontificatus nostri Anno Sexto.

L. Bussa: —

(¹) ut] *om. Ms.*
(²) Consilii] Concilii *Ms.*
(³) Consilium] Concilium *Ms.*
(⁴) alia] alias *Ms.*

550

3.

1452 VII 20   Reg. Vat. t. 421, F. CCXJ.

Marcellus]

Nicolaus etc. Venerabili fratri Paulo (¹) episcopo Driuastensi apostolice sedis nuncio et oratori nostro Salutem etc. Intelleximus grauia odia suscitata esse et in dies acerbiora fieri inter dilectum filium nobilem virum Georgium Castriot Scanderbech ac Paulum et Nicolaum Ducaginos in Albania dominos, que res magna molestia nos afficit et dolemus maxime ut inter christianos principes [bella] (²) et dissensiones vigeant, hoc presertim tempore in quo nedum deberent uires eorum vnitas habere ut potentie Teucrorum facilius resistere valerent. Verum etiam instante bello aliorum ascitis et conuocatis auxiliis, omni studio ac diligentia intinnibendum (sic) est ne christiani nominis hostes habeant occasionem nacti eos inualidos et ad alia molienda (³) intentos subita excursione adorsi magna detrimenta non solum ipsis sed finitimis populis inferrent, quod ne eueniat continuo Deum suppliciter oramus. Et quoniam non possumus malis istis per nosmet mederi, deputamus te, quem ad huiusmodi sanctum opus exequendum propter loci oportunitatem et tuam integritatem ac prudentiam optimum mediatorem pacis et concordie existimamus, mandantes tue fraternitati ac in virtute sancte obedientie precipientes ut, omnibus priuatis respectibus reiectis, Dei honorem mediatorem (sic) et christianitatis commodum pre oculis habens ad memoratos dominos te conferas et, adhibitis his suasionibus que ad concordiam et reconciliationem pertinere cognoueris prout tibi videbitur et expediens fuerit, ea tractes ac pratices quod, depositis animi indignationibus, in mutuam caritatem reducantur et seipsos inuicem diligant ac connexi et confederati circa oppugnandos Teucros sint. Et ut facilius omnia iuxta nostrum desiderium ad effectum deduci (sic) possis, tibi facultatem per presentes concedimus ut eos principes ac ipsorum adherentes et sequaces, quos inueneris excommunicationis sententia innodatos esse, ad cautelam durante tractatu huiusmodi absoluere possis, ita tamen ut, si post tuam extremam operam concordes non remanserint, illico in easdem censuras et penas relabantur. Tu igitur hoc onus tibi impositum tanta integritate et solercia perficere (⁴) studeas ut sperati fructus proueniant ac apud nos sis summopere commendandus. Datum Rome apud Sanctum Petrum Anno etc.

(¹) Paulus Angelus Dussius, later Archbishop of Craia or Craina, near Scutari.

(²) bella] om. Ms.

(³) molienda] corr. in Ms. ab molenda.

(⁴) perficere] preficere Ms.

Millesimoquadringentesimoquinquagesimosecundo. Terciodecimo Kal.
Augusti pontificatus nostri Anno Sexto.,

[decima

F. de Bonitate

4.

1453 X 24   Reg. Vat. t. 427, f. CXVIJt., CXVIIJr.t.

Petrus Lanen.]

Nicolaus etc. Vniuersis et singulis christifidelibus Salutem etc.
Decet Romanum pontificem ex debito sui pastorali officii eos qui christiane fidei oppugnatores impugnant fauoribus prosequi ac ipsorum
statui salubriter prouidere, dilectum itaque filium no- (f.CXVIIJ)
bilem virum Georgium Illustrem regni Rasie Dispotum ac Alben.
Rane (¹) totiusque vsonie (²) dominum paterna caritate, licet absen-
tem, intuentes et quam animose constanter ac uiriliter quantoue desi-
derio flagret et incensus sit contra perfidissimos Teucros et infideles
cum omni suo potentatu congredi, et pro uerissima ac indubitata
Christi fide ad illigandam (³) eneruandamque eorum prauam et ini-
quam intentionem in christicolas se obicere digna consideratione pen-
santes, atque ideo huiusmodi laudabile propositum suum confirmare,
nedum uolentes in Domino sed augere, vt cum Dei omnipotentis auxilio
quietius et tutius adimpleri posset et ex tam pio ac bono opere meritum consequatur, auctoritate apostolica et presentium tenore stricte
precipiendo, mandamus omnibus et singulis principibus, Ducibus, Mar-
chionibus, Comitibus, Baronibus, Comunitatibus necnon universitati-
bus et personis quibuslibet, tam ecclesiasticis quam secularibus, cuius-
uis status, dignitatis, gradus et proeminentie extiterint, quatenus prefatum Despotum, filios, familiam, subditos et vaxallos suos ac homines
sub exercitu suo militantes, quando et quotienscumque cum predictis
gentibus et hominibus suis ad bellum contra dictos Teucros et infideles se preparare eumque ac filios suos pugnare contigerit, nulla-
tenus in dominio suo uel terris, castris, uillis et locis quibuscumque
sibi subiectis, ac omnibus rebus et bonis suis ubicumque et in quibuscumque locis consistentibus, inquetare, turbare, molestare, uexare,
inuadere, damnificare, ledere et molestiam uel offensionem ullam eis
inferre per se uel alium seu alios, aliquo quesito colore, pretestu, oc-
casione uel causa, palam uel occulte, aut alio quouis modo presumant
sub pena excommunicationis late sentente, anathematis et perdi-
ctionis eterne. Quinymo ob reuerentiam Dei in exterminium et confu-
sionem dictorum Teucrorum ac infidelium suis assistant consiliis et

(¹) Rama?
(²) (t)ribunie = Trebinje?
(³) illigandam] eligendam *Ms*.

552

fauoribus opportuniter. Insuper, quia ad aures nostras peruenit nonnullos fuisse et esse inuasores, [verso] vastatores, uiolatores et offensores, ymaginum, ac picturarum ecclesiarum et piorum locorum eorundem deturpatores, ad euitationem deterioris scandali quod inde posset obuenire, et ut predictus Dispotus ac sui contra prenominatos christiani nominis inimicos feruentius animentur, eadem auctoritate et harum serie antedictis, inuasoribus, vastatoribus, violatoribus, offensoribus, deturpatoribus, omnibusque aliis et singulis quicumque fuerint et sint, damus etiam sub dicta pena in mandatis ne pictures ipsas ac ymagines de cetero inuadere, vastare, uiolare ac deturpare audeant. Ceterum (?), cum (?) Dispotus ipse cum suis amplectatur et teneat formam fidei que in sacro ycumenico concilio Florentino ab occidentali et orientali ecclesia que ibi conuenit deffinita est, uolumus et apostolica auctoritate mandamus, ne quicumque cuiuscumque conditionis existat ipsum aut suos perturbare, irritare uel compellere possit aut debeat, ut alios ritus seu cerimonias sequatur aut teneat quam huc usque tenuerit, ritum grecorum sequendo, sicut etiam prefatum concilium ordinauit ac statuit. Datum Rome apud S. Petrum Anno etc. Millesimoquadringentesimoquinquagesimotertio Nono Kal. Nouembris pontificatus nostri Anno Septimo.

[De curia
[duplicata

Johannes de Cremonensibus
Johannes de Ciechinis

5.

1456 XII 15

F. 56.

Liber Brevium Calisti III pg. 56 (53)
(Arch. Vat. Arm. XXXIX, 7)

Calistus etc.

Dilecte fili Salutem etc. Accepimus literas tuas, et eas libenter legimus, et intelleximus libentius que in eis continebantur de gestis in Albania per dilectos filios nobiles viros Simonem et Alfonsum dominos de Astrouileri; et que ipsi egerant et que restabant agenda, recte intelleximus. Commendamus in primis diligentiam et prudentiam tuam in his scribendis. Quod autem a nobis impresentiarum petant subsidium personarum, respondemus eis quatenus impensis exhauste sunt facultates nostre, et in quibus speremus eisdem auxilium afferri officium tuum erit, pro tua erga nos fide, deuotione et affectione, considerata hac necessitate in qua nunc pro expedicione alicuius classis proximo vere mittenda, valde laboramus, principibus istarum partium pro tua solita prudentia taliter persuadere, ut incepta constanti et forti animo perseuerent; narrare eis prouisiones quas in dies facimus tum in paranda classe tum in colligendis decimis tum in cohortandis et sustentandi[s] mundi principibus ut in hac tanta necessitate nobis succurrant; et eos usque ad ver futurum bonis exhortationibus, sua-vissimis suasionibus tuis, manutenere in opere incepto perficiendo, quod audaces sint pro fide Christi pugnare qui nullum fidum (¹) atle-tem suum irremuneratum abire sinit, qui coronam brauii perseveran-tibus donat eternum, qui ut ipsum sequeremur tanta pro nobis tor-menta subire voluit. Te autem pro laboribus tuis tali prosequamur honore ut te bene laborasse cognoscas. Datum die xv decembris. MCCCCLvi° Pontificatus etc. — Fratri Ludovico Constano,

6.

1457 I 30   Liber Brevium Calisti III pg. 67 (64) rv
                          (Arch. Vat. Arm. XXXIX, 7)

F. 67

Calistus etc. Dilecti fili Salutem etc. Supplicatum fuit nobis pro parte vestra quod pro salute anime vestre, vos a falso [verso] testi-monio inscienter prestito absolvere de benignitate apostolica dignare-mur, cum parati sitis tribuere ad expeditionem sancte Cruciate. xij. ducatos auri: vestris igitur precibus inclinati a dicto testimonio vos et quemlibet vestrum auctoritate apostolica absoluimus, satisfacto tamen prius per vos proximo aut leso.

Datum XXX Januarii Anno Secundo

Mariano Canonico Antibarensi et Vitto Rectori ecclesie santi Elie Antibarensis.

7.

1457 IV 26   Liber Brevium Calisti III pg. 89 (86) v
                          (Arch. Vat. Arm. XXXIX, 7)

F. 89v.

Calistus etc. Dilecti filii Salutem etc. Pluribus et quidem eviden-tibus signis uidistis vehementissimum ardorem mentis nostre ad destructionem perdite secte et gentis Turcorum aliorumque infidelium, que cura inextinguibili flamma urit sensus nostros, nec in alio intenti sumus nec alio properat conatus noster, nisi ut illatam fidei ortodoxe ignominiam ulciscamur et, barbarorum rabie perdomita, religioni sancte quietem pacemque restituamus. Quod divinum propositum nostrum cum ceteris christifidelibus notum fecerimus, tum etiam uobis maxime patuit. Vidistis enim qua festinantia classem parauerimus et legatum miserimus, et quot impensas subierimus ut labanti fidei subueniremus. In quo proposito non solum persistimus, sed in horas magis magisque accendimur, et augende et corroborande classis iam emisse continue rationem habemus (²); et nouam properantissime

(¹) fidum] fidem Ms.
(²) habemus] habuerunt Ms.

554

facimus fabricari; nuncque unam galeatiam nostram insignem cum
nonnullis aliis nauigiis grano, armis, pannis, victualibus et pecuniis
aliisque rebus necessariis onustis (¹) in maxima copia, uix nobis ad
uictum necessaria remanendo, in orientem ad legatum nostrum reli-
quamque classem iam citissime misimus. Et quia ob istos apparatus
inestimabilibus grauamur sumptibus, quibus sustinendis ipse facultates
non sufficiunt, necesse est ut christifidelium (²) potentatus sotia nobis
suppeditent auxilia et defensione[m] rei publice christiane ipsique pro
uirili suscipiant. Quam primum visis presentibus quascumque sancte
Cruciate pecunias penes vos et vestros existentes, et per dilectum filium
Marianum de Senis Ordinis Minorum de Senis (sic) nuntium nostrum
et collectorem ad hec specialiter deputatum depositas, et que in futurum deponi contigerit, dilecto filio Martino Clarini mercatori fiorentino
Ragusii commoranti ac recipienti nomine dilectorum filiorum Petri
et Jacobi de Paziis et sotiorum de Romana Curia, qui circa premissa
nobis et camere apostolice subuenerunt et in dies se offerunt necessitatibus subuenire, realiter et cum effectu consignatis per vos pecuniis,
tria publica similia eiusdem tenoris quetantiarum instrumenta reci-
piatis, quorum unum penes vos pro uestra, alium ipse Marianus penes
se pro sui cautela retineatis, tertium uero ad nos et apostolicam came-
ram quantotius destinare curetis. Datum xxvij Aprilis 1457 Anno Ter-
tio. Prioribus, Communi et Consilio Ciuitatis Ragusii

8.

1457 VI 9 (?) Liber Brevium Calisti III pg. 102 (99)
(Arch. Vat. Arm. XXXIX, 7)

F. 102

Calistus etc. Dilecte fili, Salutem etc. Ex his que de tuis virtutibus
et singulari bonitate nobis retulit dilectus filius Hieronimus Bellaui-
sta (³) frater tuus, magnam cepimus in corde nostro consolationem.
Explicavit enim nobis idem Hieronimus quantus sit zelus et deuotio
tua erga nos et statum sancte sedis apostolice et quantum cupias sancte
religionis fidei christiane exaltationem. Pro quibus meritis tuis tuam
nobilitatem plurimum in Domino commendamus hortamurque ut in
tuo laudando et sancto proposito de bono in melius perseveres, habi-
turum operum tuorum recognitorem Deum qui nullum bonum inremu-
neratum relinquit. De nobis autem volumus ita tibi persuadeas: nos
paratissimos semper futuros ad omnia que honorem, statum et exaltationem tuam concernere videbuntur. Tu igitur perge ut cepisti, et
quandoquidem tempus acceptabile in quo Christifideles erga fidem
ortodoxam devotionem ostendere possunt collige, et animum ad eas

(¹) onustis] onustas Ms.
(²) christifidelium] christi fidelibus Ms.
(³) = Blevishti.

cogitationes converte que apud homines gloriam et honorem tibi afferant et apud Deum celestis premii coronam pariant.

Datum

Nobili viro Progono Maxichi (¹).

9.

1457 IX 18   Liber Brevium Calisti III pg. 124 (122) rv
                                 (Arch. Vat. Arm. XXXIX, 7)
F. 124.

Calistus etc. Dilecti filii salutem etc. — Scripsimus nuper deuotionibus uestris ex animo et voluntate nostra ut pecunias illas istuc pro sancta Cruciata collectas, et per dilectum filium fratrem Marianum de Senis collectorem nostrum et sedis apostolice nuntium apud uos seu vestros depositas, et quas in futurum deponi contingeret, dilecto filio Martino Clarini mercatori florentino Ragusii commoranti cum effectu consignaretis: recipienti nomine dilecti filii Petri et Jacobi de Pazis et sotiorum de Romana Curia, qui pro ipsa Cruciata in magnis nostris necessitatibus de pluribus pecuniarum quantitatibus nobis subuenerunt et subuenturos, si opus sit, sese pollicentur. Quodquidem minime adhuc a uobis factum esse audimus, et de ea re non paruam admirationem capimus. Credebamus enim vos promptiores futuros in exequenda voluntate nostra in re tam iusta et bonum totius fidei christiane concernenti, quod toti orbi patet cum quicquid habuimus, habemus et habere possumus soli nos in negotio fidei et prosecutione negotii sanctissime Cruciate contra perfidissimos Turchos christiani nominis hostes teterrimos exposuerimus et exponamus exponereque usque ad sanguinis effusionem deuouerimus et deliberamus. Quare ne vlterius in hac re supersedeatur et creditum apud mercatores qui in his fidei necessitatibus non paruo nobis sunt adiumento conseruationis, omnino volumus dictis sotiis mercatoribus de Pazis satisfiat; proptereaque mittimus istuc et ad alias partes dilectum filium Joannem Nauarr, scutiferum nostrum presentium exhibitorem, cui commisimus vt omnes et singulas eas pecunias istic et alibi per totam Dalmatiam collectas nomine nostro recipiat, et, satisfacto dictis mercatoribus et sotiis de Paziis vsque ad summam decemmilium [verso] (²) ducatorum, residuum ipsarum pecuniarum inter equas partes diuidet, et carissimis in Christo filiis (³) nostris Hungariae et Bosnie Regibus Illustribus duas, tertiam uero dilecto filio Georgio Scandarbech Albanie domino persoluat, vt earum adiumento virilius in Turchos depugnare possint, prout in bulla commissionis huiusmodi dicti Johannis Nauarr plene continetur et latius ab ipso audietis, cui fidem dabitis. Horta-

(¹) = Mazi?
(²) *Post* decemmilium *scribitur iterum* milium *in Ms.*
(³) filiis] filii *Ms.*

556

mur itaque vos et in uirtute sancte obedientie ac sub excomunicationis pena mandamus, vt sine ulteriori mora et difficultate aliqua mandata nostra circa pecunias collectas et colligendas tanquam filii boni obedientie exequamini et exequi faciatis eisque omnino pareatis et obediatis, quemadmodum confidimus et speramus, ne oporteat nos contra vos si contrarium attemptaueritis quoquomodo censuris ecclesiasticis et aliis oportunis remediis procedere, tanquam sacrilegos et bonorum ecclesiasticorum occupatores. Alienum enim esse debet cuilibet christiano que ex Cruciata colliguntur usurpare aut quoquomodo retinere seu differre et tam iussibus nostris apostolicis contraire. Datum xviij Septembris 1457 Anno iij°.

Prioribus, Consilio et Communi Ragusii.

10.

1457 IX 19   Liber Brevium Calisti III pg. 125 (123)
                              (Arch. Vat. Arm. XXXIX, 7)

F. 125.

Calistus etc. Dilecte fili Salutem etc. Et si per nostras literas sub bulla plumbea tibi commisimus, vt omnes et singulas pecunias collectas et colligendas pro sancta Cruciata per totam Dalmatiam recipias easque, exceptis xᵐ. ducatorum de camera quos factoribus banchi de Pazis et sotiorum mercatorum Romane Curie et in partibus illis moram trahentibus assignari volumus, inter equas partes diuisas carissimis in Christo filiis nostris Hungarie et Bosne Regibus Illustribus necnon dilecto filio nobili viro Georgio Scandarbech Albanie domino distribuas, prout in ipsis nostris literis latius continetur. Tamen quia intelleximus bone memorie episcopum Craiensem (¹) qui in partibus illis apostolice sedis nuntius et collector erat, ab hac luce migrasse et nonnullas pecunias reliquisse, quas pro eadem Cruciata collegerat (²), volumus et tenore presentium tibi committimus et mandamus vt, postquam in Albaniam vt tibi committimus [te] (³) contuleris, ilico pecunias huiusmodi a dicto episcopo relictas et alias quascumque ratione decime et Cruciate in terris prefati Scandarbech et Albania collectas et colligendas [a] (⁴) quibusuis collectoribus, subcollectoribus et depositariis aut aliis in quorum manibus esse continget, recipias, petas et exigas, easque integre prefato Georgio Scandarbech aut eius procuratori siue negotiorum gestori nomine nostro, vltra alias pecunias quas eidem ex prefatis dari mandamus, trades et assignes vt ampliori subsidio et celeriori (⁵) ipsi Scandarbech ut cupimus succurratur.

(¹) Craiensem] Croiensem *Ms.* (Paulum Angelum Dussium, nuncium pontificium pro Cruciata; cfr. FARLATI, *Illyricum Sacrum*, V. VII).

(²) Collegerat *bis scribitur.*

(³) te] *om. Ms.*

(⁴) a] *om. Ms.*

(⁵) celeriori] sceleriori *Ms.*

Mandantes dictis depositariis, collectoribus, subcollectoribus et aliis prefatis vt sub pena excommunicationis late sentencie pecunias predictas tibi sine mora aut dilatione integre consignent, in contrarium facientibus non obstantibus quibuscumque. Datum etc. die xviiij Septembris M.cccLvij°. Anno iij°.

Johanni Nauarr familiari et Scutifero nostro:

II.

1457 IX 20   Liber Brevium Calisti III pg. 125 (123) v

                         (Arch. Vat. Arm. XXXIX, 7)

F. 125v.

Calistus etc. Dilecte fili Salutem etc. Cum, pro defensione fidei orthodoxe et ad excidium nefande nationis Turchorum et infidelium, dies ac noctes animus noster sine vlla anxietatis requie, non solum quicquid per nos fieri potest ac comparari ad hoc diuinum opus conficiendum terra marique efficimus, in quo iam orbi palam est quam incredibili celeritate (¹) classem in magnis rerum difficultatibus fabricari simul et emitti fecerimus quantaque mole impensarum pro ea augenda et sustentanda opprimamur, sed et non desiuimus omnibus modis christifideles principes ad hanc necessariam amprisiam excitare et excitatos oportunis subuentionibus et subsidiis quantum possumus (²) adiuvare. Mittimusque impresentiarum dilectum filium Johannem . Nauarr, scutiferum nostrum presentium exhibitorem, Ragusium et ad alias Dalmatie partes vt, nostro et sedis apostolice nomine, pecunias in ipsis partibus quomodocumque collectas accipiat et iuxta commissionem per nos sibi factam inter carissimos in Christo filios nostros Hungarie et Bosne Reges Illustres necnon dilectum filium nobilem virum Georgium Scandarbech Albanie dominum equis portionibus distribuat, vt earum subsidio, alteri ad expugnationem Turcorum uirilius animentur, alter, scilicet Scandarbec, intra cuius fines exercitus seuissimi hostis grassatur, facilius impetum eius sustentare possit. Quare superfluum existimamus pluribus super his cum tua nobilitate agere. Ipsa enim res loquitur que, cum necessaria et honestissima sit, decet nobilitatem tuam pro eius uotiua executione nobis non modo morem gerere, sed fauorabiliter et pro uiribus assistere vt debito effectui (³) res ipsa quamprimum demandetur. Hortamur itaque et stricte requirimus ipsam nobilitatem tuam, vt dicto Johanni Nauarr pecunias huiusmodi sine ulla contradictione accipere permittat et acceptas secundum laudabilem ordinationem nostram distribuere, exhibendo ei fauores oportunos in omnibus que tua nobilitas neces-

---

(¹) incredibili celeritate] *Ms.* incredibile celeritatem
(²) possumus] *melius leg.* possunt
(³) effectui] effectus *Ms.*

558

saria cognoscet aut eandem dictus Iohannes duxerit requirendam. Datum etc. die xx Septembris 1457 Anno iij⁰.

Francisco Foscari Duci Venetiarum

12.

1457 X 22

Liber Brevium Calisti III pg. 129 (127) rv
(Arch. Vat. Arm. XXXIX, 7)

F. 129.

Calistus etc. Dilecti fili salutem etc. Recepimus literas vestras per quas intelleximus quid scribitis super facto pecuniarum Cruciate istic collectarum. Et quia quid de ipsis pecuniis fieri velimus dudum mature et oportune disposuimus, ita vt de huiusmodi dispositione nostra et Rex Hungarie et vos ipsi merito contentari debeatis, misimus superioribus diebus unum familiarem et scutiferum nostrum plene super huiusmodi dispositione nostra informatum, qui si nondum istuc applicuit, prope diem tamen speramus affuturum, a quo plenissime intelligetis oportunam dispositionem et ordinationem quam de ipsis pecuniis fecimus. Hortamur igitur deuotiones vestras ut quemadmodum per eundem scutiferum nostrum scripsimus et ex eo intelligetis, ita velitis ea que scribimus executioni mandare, et quantum vobis referet idem scutifer nomine nostro adimplere. Excusationes vestras friuolas reputantes, nisi parueritis tam iustis mandatis nostris, sencietis quid est mandatis apostolicis contraire. Non enim ad [verso] Regem sed ad nos et ad sedem apostolicam disponere pertinet de omnibus et singulis ex Cruciata peruenientibus, vosque cum effectu faciendo quod mandamus indemnes vos tuebimini, vt benignitas sedis apostolice deuotis suis consueuit. Datum xxij octobris 1457 Anno iij⁰.

Rectori et Consilio Regiminis Ciuitatis Ragusii

13.

1457 XII 3

Liber Brevium Calisti III pg. 137 (135)
(Arch. Vat. Arm. XXXIX, 7)

F. 137

Calistus etc. Dilecte fili Salutem etc. Accepimus literas tuas quibus nobis significasti diligentiam et studium quod fecisti apud Ragusinos vt pecunias, res et bona apud eos collecta iuxta (¹) commissionem per nos tibi factam haberes tergiuersationesque et subterfugia quibus iidem (²) Ragusini vtuntur in consignandis eiusmodi pecuniis. Fuit nobis satis molestum Ragusinos eosdem nostram et sedis apostolice reuerentiam tam paruifacere et existimare in hac re presertim fidei et sanctissime Cruciate. Quare subterfugia eorum egre ferentes nec vltra ea ferre volentes, scribimus eis sub magnis penis quos volumus ipso

(¹) iuxta] iusta *Ms.*
(²) iidem] idem *Ms.*

facto incurrant vt tibi dictas pecunias, res et bona, quemadmodum alias eis scripsimus et tibi commisimus, tibi tradant et consignent prout in literis quarum copiam hic iussimus introcludi plenius poteris videre. Itaque fili dilecte te hortamur ut omni cura, studio, diligentia, mente denique tota, enitaris vt dicte pecunie, res et bona ratione Cruciate collecta, quemadmodum mandauimus, tibi consignentur et, solutis x^m ducatorum societati de Pazis cui obligati sumus, reliquum volumus vt, non obstante quacumque alia commissione per nos tibi facta de ipsis per te distribuendis personis notatis in commissione, quarum distributionem iustis et rationabilibus causis animum nostrum mouentibus nolumus fieri nullo modo ad presens, sed omnes illas pecunias prefate societati de Pazi (?) similiter consignari, quod cum feceris nos confestim auisare, procures vt tibi super ipsis precipere valeamus prout res exegerit ad gloriam Dei, sic igitur te habeas in omnibus vt laudem et retributionem a nobis merearis et de te confidimus et operamus. Affectamus scire valde de statu Albanie et illius strenui militis et Dei athlete Scandarbech, et quid cum eo peregisti. Nos enim conuocationem facimus imperatoris, Regum et potentum christianorum ad nos per oratores suos cum quibus hac hieme taliter effectiue operabimur ad exaltationem fidei ortodoxe, ad perditionem perfidi Turchi et damnate secte machometice quod in estate ipse Scandarbech et alii catholici, Christo dante, vt victores contra inimicos fidei quiescent et triumphabunt vndique. Datum vt supra proxime.

Johanni Nauarr scutifero et Commissario nostro.

14.

1458 II 6   Liber Brevium Calisti III pg. 141 (139) v
                              (Arch. Vat. Arm. XXXIX, 7)
F. 141v.

Calistus etc. Dilecte fili Salutem etc. Scripsimus tibi nouissime ut, non obstantibus quibusuis aliis commissionibus per nos tibi factis quas iustis causis exequi nolebamus, efficeres quod omnes pecunie, res et bona ratione Cruciate Ragusii et in tota Dalmatia collecta et colligenda consignarentur cum effectu Martino Clarini mercatori florentino pro societate (¹) de Pazis Ragusii existenti, et vt ita fieret sub excommunicationis late et interdicti et aliis grauioribus penis Ragusinis mandauimus. Credimus ita fuisse factum. Et si forsan non esset, iterato sub eisdem penis et aliis cum rigore ipsis scribimus vt omnino efficiant que mandamus, circa cuius rei executionem nonnulla etiam ordinauimus. Itaque cum ob alia nostra negocia te hic optemus habere. Volumus et presentium tenore tibi mandamus quatenus, visis presentibus, posthabitis quibuscumque, te ad nos conferas. Venias tamen de omnibus rebus quas ad nos scire pertineat ita informatus vt ex te ea que ex istis partibus scire optamus intelligere valeamus.

(¹) societate] societati *Ms*.

560

Dilecto autem filio Georgio Castrioth Scandarbech subuentionem oportunam fecimus, quam per oratores suos quos ad nos misit prope diem
habebit. Datum etc. die Sexta februarii Mcccclviij. Anno 3°
Johanni Nauarr Scutifero et Commissario nostro

15.

1458 II 8 Liber Brevium Calisti III pg. 142 (140) v-143(141)
(Arch. Vat. Arm. XXXIX, 7)
F. 142v.

Calistus etc. (¹) Carissime in Christo fili Salutem etc. Fuit apud
nos dilectus filius Iohannes Nevport (²), miles Anglicus, presentium
exhibitor, ex quo et ex literis tuis quas nobis attulit, intelleximus
quanta affectione dilectum filium nobilem virum Scandarbech Albanie
dominum nobis commendaris; quod nobis fuit iocundissimum tam et
si nostrapte voluntate illum pro suis virtutibus et ingentibus factis,
quibus (143) non solum de nobis sed de universa christianitate optime
meritum arctiori quam dici possit caritate complectamur. Videmus
enim eum prope solum furori seuissimorum turchorum quasi murum (³)
quendam firmissimum esse oppositum, qui ipsorum aditum precludit
ne in christianitatem irrumpant; nec nos latet quot cladibus ipse cum
suis subditis affectus fuerit. Quasobres licet undique intollerabilibus
expensis fatigamur propter sustentationem classis nostre aliosque
apparatus quos ad prosecutionem huius operis continue facimus,
tamen vt idem Scandarbech ad resistendum infidelibus animetur,
facimusque ei subuentionem de .Vᵐ. ducatorum, facturi ampliorem
subuentionem quantum nostre subpeditare poterunt facultates, hor-
tantesque Serenitatem tuam ut eidem Scandarbech vti etiam consueui-
sti oportunis subsidiis subuenire eumque tot angustiis circumseptum
adiuuare velis. Super quibus eidem Iohanni nonnulla commisimus
Celsitudini tue referenda, commendantes eidem ipsum Johannem qui,
ut decet christianum et catholicum, viriliter magnoque animo in hoc
sancto negocio operatur, cui in referendo super his nostro nomine
fidem adhibeas Serenitas tua et ipsum contemplatione nostri commen-
datum habeat. Datum etc. 8 februarii 1458
Regi Aragonum.,

16.

1458 VI 3 Liber Brevium Calisti III pg. 176 (174)
(Arch. Vat. Arm. XXXIX, 7)
F. 176.

Callistus etc. Dilecte fili Salutem etc. Fuit hic apud nos dilectus
filius Michael Tarba quem ad nos misisti, ex quo et ex literis tuis

(¹) Dilecte deletum in Ms.
(²) Nevport] nlvport Ms. i.e. Newport
(³) murum] mirum Ms.

quas nobis diligenter reddidit intelleximus seruitium tuum bonum et causam ob quam a classe nostra recesseris et ad Scandarbechum ueneris, ob quod te de deuotione tua erga nos et sedem apostolicam ac obediencia plurimum in Domino commendamus, teque hortamur vt perseuerare et continuare velis quemadmodum in te confidimus et speramus. Aduentus tuus ad Scandarbechum constitutus erat in necessitatem maximam; placuit nobis multum quod oportuno tempore a nobis per te succursum habuerit, cum feceris id quod maxime ei opus fuit. Volumus reuertaris ad eamdem classem nostram, ad quam per viam Ancone misimus sex naues onustas grano et aliis victualibus per Iohannem Nauarr, qui etiam pro eadem classe pecuniam numeratam in bona summa portat. Sunt iam multi (¹) dies quibus recessit ex Ancona et vt arbitramur ad dictam classem debuit applicuisse. Facimus fieri et aliam prouisionem grani et rerum aliarum quam per totum mensem Augusti indubie ad classem eandem mittemus. Michaeli uero tuo prefato dedimus hic CCCCᵗᵒˢ ducatos de camera pro subuentione tue galee. Itaque pro tua erga nos deuotione grato et libenti animo studeas continuare in seruicio classis nostre quam illiusque legatum confortabis et animabis ad perseuerandum ad faciendum que decent classem apostolicam, nam nos pro illius sustentatione et fortificatione continue laboramus et in breui per scribam rationis (²) dicte classis mittemus quattuor galeas quas hic iam paratas et in ordine habemus. Contractamusque cum oratoribus christianorum principum quorum multi hic apud nos iam sunt de prosecutione decenti (?) huiusmodi amprisie. Itaque speramus quod mari terraque talis potencia fiet quod de perfidissimo Turcho et secta eius nephanda victoriam reportabimus, Deo cuius causa agitur auxiliante, gloriosam. Datum etc. iij Junii 1458

Michaeli de Borga

17.

1458 VI 8   Liber Brevium Calisti III pg. 175 (173)v
                              (Arch. Vat. Arm. XXXIX, 7)

F. 175v.

Fuerunt expedita tria sub hac forma]

Calistus etc. Dilecti fili Salutem etc. Cum prosecutionem sanctissime Cruciate contra perfidum Turchum hactenus humeris nostris sustinuerinus et sustinere etiam quamdiu vixerimus vsque ad sanguinis effusionem proponamus, oportet nos subsidia undique conquerere. Itaque deuotiones vestras hortamur vt pecunias per dilectum

(¹) *Post* multi, *verba* qui etiam pro eadem Classe *scripta sunt in Ms. et deleta.*

(²) scribam rationis, i.e., Berengario (Belanguer) Vila, scriba rationis or Paymaster General of the pontifical fleet.

562

filium Marianum [de] (¹) Fregeno nuntium nostrum in partibus ipsis collectas et apud vos depositas consignetis illico et sine aliqua difficultate dilectis filiis Conrado Pangrotiner et sociis de Norinberg, quoniam de eis sumus bene securi, in quo ita diligenter vos habeatis vt de prompta obediencia et deuotione valeatis a nobis commendari. Nam necessitates nostre ob amprisiam huiusmodi sunt maxime. Tenemus enim in partibus orientalibus classem satis magnam. Subuenimus Scandarbecho et aliis terris et locis ne a perfidis Turchis damnis afficiantur. Circa aliudque nostre cogitationes non magis versantur quam ut perfidum Turchum exterminare et perdere possimus, ob quod habemus iam apud nos plurimos principum christianorum oratores cum quibus de huiusmodi prosecutione tractamus. Speramus quod talis mari terraque parabitur potentia quod, Deo auxiliante, de nefanda secta Turcorum victoriam reportabimus gloriosam. De pecuniis huiusmodi per vos assignandis dictis mercatoribus mittatis ad nos quetantiam
  Datum viij Junii etc.

(¹) de] *om. Ms.*

INDEX